Beta Sigma Phi International

presents

The Dining Room

A Cookbook Featuring
Breakfast, Brunch, Lunch and Dinner Menus.

© Favorite Recipes®Press/Nashville EMS MCMLXXIX
P. O. Box 77, Nashville, Tennessee 37202
Library of Congress Cataloging in Publication Data
Main entry under title:
Beta Sigma Phi International presents The dining room.
   Includes index.
   1. Cookery 2. Menus.   I. Beta Sigma Phi.
II. Title: The Dining room.
TX715.B4858   641.5   79-18899
ISBN 0-87197-127-5

Beta Sigma Phi

Dear Friends,

Faced with the practical challenge of creating meals and menus for growing children and hungry husbands, you probably know more than you realize about the ageless art of cooking. Library shelves are filled with all the things you know, practices that have taken thousands of years to perfect. Think of it this way—it is homemakers and cooks like yourself who have created the art of cooking.

Yet, there are times when you feel completely uninspired—just when it seems to matter the most! A special occasion is drawing near, and you want to invite friends over for brunch, or to prepare an impressive dinner for business associates. Or, you may just feel the need to add a little artistry to family meals. But, you still wonder what to prepare, which foods would complement one another in a new way, and what colors and textures would be more appealing. It can be exasperating at times!

Here is a cookbook that is designed to help! The recipes are organized into an appetizing selection of menus for Breakfast, Brunch, Lunch and Dinner. Feel free to use these menus with confidence, but don't feel locked in! If a menu serves only to inspire you to bigger and better things, then it has done its job.

Remember, **The Dining Room** is wherever a meal is served, but it takes an inspired cook to create a truly delicious meal. You can depend on these Beta Sigma Phi recipes to inspire the success you wish to achieve everyday or for special occasions!

Sincerely,

Marge Thomas
International Cookbook Chairman
Beta Sigma Phi

Contents

Creative Dining.................................... 7
Menus With a Flair............................... 12
Appetizers....................................... 19
Salads... 43
Eggs and Cheese................................. 57
Vegetables....................................... 77
Meats.. 91
Seafood.. 115
Poultry.. 127
Breads... 143
Desserts... 157
Color Photo Recipes............................. 185
Equivalent Chart................................ 189
Substitution Chart.............................. 190
Metric Conversion Chart........................ 190
Index.. 192

Our sincere appreciation to all who submitted the hundreds of recipes for inclusion in this cookbook. We regret we were unable to incorporate all of the recipes due to similarity and lack of space.

Creative Dining

Mealtime! Throughout the ages it has been an important focus of man's attention—if not the most important. In fact, there are historians who claim that although history may be quite certainly shaped by men and events, it has been made by food. There is no doubt that man must eat to live, and could never have accomplished anything of importance without eating—and eating properly.

But, that need for food does not account for what mealtime has become today. For thousands of years, "mealtime" was no more than a daily hand-to-mouth struggle for survival. Like the animals, man ate without even the "luxuries" of fish hooks, hunting weapons, cooking utensils or even fire—and certainly without any thought of pleasure, artistry, or good manners.

Now, mealtime has become the pleasurable art of dining. Cookbooks outsell all other books, and the dining room, be it large or small, plain or fancy, has become one of the most popular rooms in the house. And, around dining, manners have emerged—and "rules" designed to make dining both comfortable and memorable. Commonly called "etiquette," this set of rules unfortunately conjures up the idea of so many senseless regulations that do more to make people uncomfortable than comfortable. But, etiquette is actually the reflection of a sensitivity to the rights of others, and a desire for basic social order of living together harmoniously.

Even the rough-and-tumble cowboys of the American West had their own set of rules for good manners, making mealtime more pleasant for everyone on the hot, dusty trail. Because they served themselves from tin pots at the chuck wagon fire, it was a cardinal rule to keep sand and dirt off of the lids when they were removed from the cooking pots. If he arrived early for "grub," a cowboy never ate until he was called along with the others, regardless of how hungry he might be. Then, each cowboy would be very careful to sit or stand downwind of the others to keep from kicking dust into another man's dinner. Careless cowboys were likely to end up with a six gun for dessert.

Proper table manners changed and developed over the years, as seen in the history of the fork. Because forks are a somewhat recent addition to the table, a late 15th Century book first warns the diner not to place his hand in the serving platter (usually shared by two) until the other person had removed his hand. Secondly, the diner wasn't to leave his hand in the platter "too long." Luckily, it was also considered the

utmost in courtesy to wash one's hands in plain view of all prior to the meal, even if they were already clean. And, there were many more rules about keeping hands clean during dinner, as well.

Catherine de' Medici of Italy introduced the fork to France early in the 1500's, but it apparently did not catch on for over 100 years. When the fork finally became acceptable, a proper gentleman carried his own fork with him, as many households did not own sets of tableware. Many more years passed before the fork was accepted throughout Europe. Even as late as the turn of this century, the use of eating utensils was still discouraged in the English military ranks because it was considered undisciplined!

At this same time—the late Victorian Era—English civilians had brought the rules of etiquette to a zenith, and were dining regularly in a fashion more opulent than people ever had before, or probably ever will again. Even modest households owned one or two sets of silverware—a piece for every imaginable dish. Dinner for a few friends might last 3 or more hours, the guests being served 10, 12 and sometimes 18 courses, with a glass of wine accompanying each course. Rules for the proper centerpiece were very exacting, down to the very spacing of the flowers and candles. All in all, each hostess would do her best to outdo the last dinner, and even a small dinner party was beyond formal—it was an event, a pageant, and quite expensive.

One very delightful point of etiquette perfected during the Victorian Era was the art of napkin folding. Fanciful designs included lillies, slippers, roses, stars, hats, and fans. See the color photograph on page 33 of The Dining Room for a sample of the popular fan-folded napkin. To make a fan-fold napkin, fold a large well-starched and ironed dinner napkin in half. Accordian-pleat each side into ⅝-inch folds. Iron (and spray starch, if needed) each pleat as it is made. Reverse the last fold on one side and tuck the other side into it. Pin the napkin in place at the center until it is well set. Remove the pin just before dinner. Very impressive!

Today's rule of mealtime manners doesn't carry the life and death importance of those on the cowboy trail, or the opulence and expense of the Victorian Era. But, their goal is just the same—to assure that dining is enjoyable and relaxed, whether it's an everyday family meal, a festive holiday picnic, or an

elegant seated dinner for 12. Today, the success of a hostess is measured by her hospitality, as well as the food she serves.

Breakfast

The Breakfast Menu has gone from one extreme to another over the years, for a while being very sumptuous, then changing to a light meal eaten only to "break the night's fast."

Early Romans, who ate only 2 meals per day, usually began the day with only bread and wine, sometimes accompanied by honey or olives. For early Egyptians, breakfast consisted only of bread, meat and beer.

The English are probably most famous for their hearty breakfasts, and beginning in the late 1300's, breakfast was the main meal of the day, with a menu full of meats, fish, sauces, stews and so forth. This habit seemed to lose favor by the end of the 16th Century, although author Samuel Pepys recorded a very large breakfast for several guests on New Year's Day, 1661. Apparently, breakfast was unimportant by the end of the 1600's, and continued so all during the 18th Century. But, by the early to mid-1800's, during the elegant Victorian Era, large breakfasts were back in style—especially before the hunt at large country manors.

In Colonial New England, families rose at dawn or before, consumed a hearty breakfast to prepare for the day of hard work ahead. Plantation life in the South was different, however. The master rose very early to survey his fields and attend to business, then returned to the house to enjoy a reasonably filling breakfast at 10 or 11 a.m.

The Industrial Age has regulated mealtimes as never before to meet work schedules, so, most families eat breakfast about 7:00 a.m. Because modern man must be more conscious of his weight than his more active ancestors, today's typical breakfast is light and uncomplicated. But, weekend breakfasts are usually more elaborate, consisting of English muffins and marmalade, waffles and blueberry syrup, biscuits and homemade preserves, as well as omelets, sausage and apples, even broiled steak and potatoes.

Brunch

The Brunch Menu combines the best of breakfast with the best of a good luncheon, and it is not as modern as many might think. Breakfast and lunch

(hence, brunch) had exchanged places of importance as the day's main meal for many years—before industrialization and more regulated dining hours became typical. Originally called "company breakfasts," brunches were favored in literary and artistic circles and featured dressed-up variations on the egg, bacon and toast theme, as well as favorite main dish entrees.

Today's brunches are very much the same, yet influenced by the casual life-style most modern families prefer. The food is often served buffet-style—some kept piping hot in chafing dishes, while others such as fresh fruits are kept frosty cold on ice. Typical biscuits are dressed up with a touch of cheese or herbs, and eggs and bacon or ham appear as zesty quiches. Popular entrees include poultry, seafood and vegetable casseroles. Dessert depends on the menu; fruit and cheese balance with coffee cake or sweet breads served prior to dessert, while rich cookie bars or a trifle balances a less filling menu.

Brunches are great for special weekends with out-of-town friends or sports events, but shouldn't be limited to that. What deserving family wouldn't feel truly special when treated to a Sunday Brunch, just for the fun of it!

Lunch

The Lunch Menu was once the main menu of the day, carried over today in the tradition of the Sunday dinner, or luncheons held on special occasions. It seems that Victorian England was first responsible for moving the main meal of the day to the evening. The midday meal became luncheon; but in those days of 12-course dinners even lunch was a 5 or 7-course repast.

Again, it was the advent of the Industrial age that has shaped the modern lunch menu. Workers and school children are no longer able to gather at home for a large noon meal, so they carry their lunches or dine at a cafeteria.

Lunch pail menus call to mind sandwiches, or soup, fresh fruit and cookies, but that is only the beginning. Creative variations include raisin, pumpernickle, whole wheat breads, and leftover meats and poultry dressed up with various relishes, seasonings and spreads. Muffins, cheese, bean salads, a variety of pickles, plus cookie bars and wedges of pie are also good for a change of pace.

Dieters can take lunch feasts in a brown bag, too. An assortment of sliced, fresh vegetables with a tangy dip are refreshing, as are fruit salads, cold cuts and cheese. Hard-working, hungry men enjoy Dagwood sandwiches, or roast beef slices on a hard roll with au jus in a vacuum jug for dunking, accompanied by slaw or potato salad, and a filling dessert.

Dinner

The dinner meal, as defined by a Victorian author, is that meal whenever it may be served, that is the main meal of the day, and the one in which meat is the most important food. The need to define "dinner" was there, because mealtimes and menus were in chaos. The main meal of the day had almost always been served at midday or just after, but suddenly even Queen Victoria was eating dinner as late as 8:00 p.m. Who could possibly know what to do?

Today, dinner means the evening meal, and it can range from a simple Chef's salad, cheese and crackers, or soup and sandwich fare to a classic five-course repast for elegant entertaining. Busy families, off to baseball, bridge, ballet and bowling after a full day of work and school, no longer want a heavy meal. So, soups and sandwiches, and salads for calorie counters are perfect suppertime foods.

Even though hearty dinners of meat, potatoes, several vegetables, bread and a dessert are not as common as they once were, even the busiest of today's families value a relaxed, "sit-down" family meal. It is the perfect time to talk and share the day's experiences and to enjoy mom's most delicious array of homemade foods. The backyard barbecue is another of the most popular dinners, not only because it is casual, but because the whole family can work together to create something delicious—including mouth-watering grilled meats as well as seafood and poultry, plus fresh vegetables just barely cooked to absorb the outdoor flavor then topped off with hand-turned ice cream for dessert.

The Dining Room has come a long way. In man's early history, it may have been a large rock in a dark cave, in the Renaissance, it was a large, drafty hall that was the gathering place for gallant noblemen and conquering kings. For Beta Sigma Phi members, however, The Dining Room is wherever a good meal is served, be it Breakfast, Brunch, Lunch or Dinner.

Menus With A Flair

After-the-Theater Breakfast
Fruits Glaces, page 169
Do-Ahead Breakfast, page 60
Pecan Coffee Cake, page 154

* * *

Family-at-Home Breakfast
Easy Eggs Benedict, page 62
Caramel-Nut Biscuit Rounds, page 151
Citrus Starter, page 41

* * *

Derby Day Brunch
Kentucky Governor's Egg Casserole, page 66
Barbecued Smoky Sausage, page 28
Kentucky Corn Bread, page 144
Bourbon Slush, page 41

* * *

Patio Brunch
Fruited Shrimp Kabobs, page 119
Artichoke Cheese Squares, page 31
Molded Waldorf Salad, page 47
Sour Cream Coffee Cake, page 155

* * *

Christmas Morning Brunch
Frosty Fruit Soup, page 168
Make-Ahead Brunch Casserole, page 60
Cranberry Coffee Cake, page 155

* * *

Sunday Brunch
Cheese Custard Tartlets, page 73
Oriental Spinach Salad, page 51
Butter Dips, page 144
Rum Cream Pie, page 180
Mock Pink Champagne, page 40

* * *

Ladies-Day-Out Luncheon
Betty's Chicken Divan, page 141
Champagne Fruit Cocktail, page 44
Candy's Millionaire Pie, page 178

* * *

Kid's Treat
Deep-Dish Pizza, page 22
Homemade Chocolate Ice Cream, page 172
M and M Party Cookies, page 163
Fruit Punch, page 40

* * *

Patio Tennis Luncheon
Lobster a la Newburg, page 119
Frozen Cranberry Salad, page 45
Delicious Crispies, page 149

* * *

Seafood Spree
Clam Chowder, page 39
Stuffed Red Fish, page 123
Cauliflower with Shrimp Sauce, page 81
Raspberry Dessert, page 169

* * *

Lunch-in-a Bag
Chicken-Corn Chowder, page 39
Pickled Pineapple Chunks, page 40
Mother Holston's Energy Drops, page 163

* * *

Camper's Special
Chicken Salad Supreme, page 54
Deviled Ham Snacking Loaf, page 25
Bean Salad, page 48
Brooks Three Ice Cream, page 171
Peanut Butter Squares, page 164

* * *

Indian Summer Supper
Brown-Baked Pork Chops, page 113
Herbed Squash Casserole, page 87
Scalloped Corn, page 82
Blueberry Cheesecake Pie, page 176

* * *

Meatless Tuesday
Spinach Quiche, page 73
Garden Vegetable Salad, page 53
Chocolate-Glazed Eclairs, page 159

* * *

Pancake Supper
French Pancakes with Orange Sauce, page 152
Apple Pie Pancakes, page 153
Rice-Buttermilk Waffles, page 153
Yolanda's Sausage Balls, page 27

* * *

Wedding Shower Supper for HIM
Cheesy Potato Bake, page 84
Delicious Grilled Flank
Steak, page 98
Green Beans Supreme, page 78
Bread Made Easy, page 146
Devil's Food Cake, page 183

* * *

Shamrock Supper
The Luck of the Irish, page 98
Lime Perfection, page 54
Broccoli Special, page 80
Mint Crunch Dessert, page 172

* * *

Santa's Helpers Supper
Special Baked Chicken, page 130
Winter Holiday Salad, page 188
Santa's Chocolate Pie, page 171
Hot Buttered Rum, page 41

* * *

"Out-of-This-World" Dinner
Heavenly Pot Roast, page 97
Heavenly Carrots, page 81
Heavenly Biscuits, page 144
Chocolate Angel Pie, page 159

* * *

Dinner for Two
Cornish Game Hens with Wild Rice Dressing, page 128
Fresh Mushroom Salad, page 49
Butterfly Rolls, page 148
Sicilian Dessert Crepes, page 158

* * *

Bon Appetit

Carolyn's French Onion Soup, page 40
Corden Bleu au Poulet, page 134
Julienne Vegetables, page 184
Cheese Petit Fours, page 20
Chocolate Mousse, page 171

* * *

Mexican Fiesta

Betty's Guacamole Dip, page 38
Mexican Cheese Dip, page 38
Gringo Chili, page 107
Chilies Rellenos, page 107
Chicken Tortillas Casserole, page 132
Border Buttermilk, page 40

* * *

Bon Voyage Buffet

Antipasto, page 28
Coq au Vin, page 133
Guatemala Squash, page 87
Hawaiian Rice with Shrimp, page 75
Pita Bread, page 147
English Trifle, page 166

* * *

Oriental Cocktail Buffet

Hawaiian Potluck Meatballs, page 108
Chinese Roll-Ups with Mustard Sauce, page 23
Sweet and Sour Sausage Bites, page 28
Mandarin Chicken, page 138
Oriental Rice, page 75
Chinese Vegetable Salad, page 53
Orange Blossom Tea Cakes, page 184

Appetizers

The term hors d'oeuveres means "outside the chef's main work," and as the preface to a meal, appetizers are as important as the meal itself. Yet, these little easy-to-handle foods should only pique the appetite, not satisfy it. And, the foods you feature in your appetizer selection should complement rather than compete with the foods on the main menu.

If there were a problem with appetizers, it would be in trying to categorize them—so don't try! Instead, just let your imagination lead the way in creating a kaleidoscope of tasty, colorful foods that are sure to please every palate. Fillings and spreads may range from sweet to savory, utilizing jams, citrus flavorings, anchovies, hot chilies, onion, cream cheese, and so forth. Plan some for uniform appearance, others with a touch of individuality. Use garnishes galore—decorative citrus slices, pimento twists, fresh parsley sprigs, as well as dustings of confectioners' sugar, spices and herbs. Apply soft cheeses with a pastry tube for an added touch of artistry. Finally, use your prettiest trays to serve your appetizers, brightly decorated with flowers, colorful napkins and paper doilies.

A lively way to serve appetizers is to let your guests "do-it-yourself," which is especially good for brunch or patio party buffets. Plan to serve mini-kabobs that the diners can grill over hibachis. Ingredients for the kabobs might include cubed ham or lamb, fresh pineapple tidbits, maraschino cherries, pearl onions and button mushrooms.

First things first! The Beta Sigma Phi flair for great beginnings shines through in every appetizer recipe that follows, so use them with confidence.

Braunschweiger Ball

1 8-oz. package cream cheese, softened
1 lb. braunschweiger, at room temperature
¼ c. mayonnaise
¼ tsp. garlic salt
2 tbsp. dill pickle juice
½ to ¾ c. chopped dill pickle
¼ c. (or more) chopped onion
3 drops of Tabasco sauce
1 tbsp. Worcestershire sauce
½ c. chopped salted peanuts

Combine half the cream cheese with the remaining ingredients except peanuts; mix well. Spread in a mold. Chill for several hours. Unmold. Frost with remaining cream cheese. Garnish with chopped peanuts.

Donna Pierson, Pres.
Preceptor Epsilon XP327
Spencer, Iowa

Cheese Wafers

¼ lb. butter
¼ lb. grated sharp Cheddar cheese
2 c. flour
½ tsp. salt
Dash of cayenne pepper

Cream butter and cheese together. Add flour, salt and pepper; mix well. Form into 1-inch roll. Chill well. Cut into thin slices. Bake at 350 degrees about 8 minutes or until light brown.

Valborg Skorpen, Pres.
Xi Pi X3257
Valley City, North Dakota

Marilyn's Cream Cheese Spread

2 8-oz. packages cream cheese, softened
¼ c. soft butter
1 tsp. anchovy paste
½ tsp. chopped capers
2 tsp. prepared mustard
1 tsp. crushed caraway seeds
½ tsp. salt
Dash of pepper
2 tbsp. paprika
4 tsbp. chopped chives
Party pumpernickel bread

Blend cream cheese and butter until smooth. Add next 6 ingredients; mix well. Add 1 tablespoon paprika; mix well. Shape mixture into a cone or ball with a spatula. Mix chives with 1 tablespoon paprika. Pat mixture around cone with fingers. Cover carefully with plastic wrap, using toothpicks to keep wrap from mixture. Refrigerate at least 24 hours before serving. Serve with party pumpernickel bread slices.

Marilyn R. Aase
Preceptor Beta XP141
Bismarck, North Dakota

Cheese Dainties

2 loaves whole white bread, sliced lengthwise
1 lb. cream cheese, softened
2 eggs yolks
Sugar
½ lb. sweet butter
Cinnamon

Cut crust from bread slices. Roll slices of bread flat. Combine cream cheese, egg yolks and ½ cup sugar until creamy. Spread on bread slices. Roll lengthwise. Melt butter. Add additional sugar and cinnamon to taste. Brush mixture on bread logs. Refrigerate until firm. Remove; slice into 1-inch pieces. Brush each piece again with butter mixture. Place pieces on cookie sheet. Bake in 350 degree-oven for 20 minutes or until lightly browned. Yield: 80-100 servings.

Randi Cohen
Zeta Nu No. 9060
Goldsboro, North Carolina

Cheese Petit Fours

1 lb. margarine, softened
2 lb. package Old English cheese, softened
2 loaves sandwich-sliced bread

Freeze bread. Combine margarine and cheese with mixer to spreading consistency. Cut bread slices into fourths. Spread cheese mixture between 3 frozen bread slices; spread around sides. Place on cookie sheet. Continue until all ingredients are used. Bake in 350 degree-oven for 15 minutes. Yield: 30-40 servings.

Shirley Ryan, Pres.
Xi Beta Upsilon X3409
Edmond, Oklahoma

Cheesy Cheese Ball

3 3-oz. packages cream cheese, softened
4 oz. bleu cheese, softened
8 oz. Cheddar cheese spread, softened
1 medium onion, grated
1 tsp. Worcestershire sauce
1 c. chopped pecans
1 c. chopped parsley

Combine cheeses, onion and Worcestershire sauce; blend thoroughly with pastry blender. Chill for 2 hours or more. Shape into ball. Combine pecans and parsley. Roll cheese ball in nut mixture to coat. Chill. Remove from refrigerator 30 minutes before serving. Garnish with 3 cherries and sprigs of parsley, if desired. May be refrigerated for 1 week. Freezes well. Yield: 25-30 servings.

Florence Meyers, Rec. Sec.
Pi Lambda No. 9259
Pompano Beach, Florida

Two-Tone Pickle-Cheese Spread

2 8-oz packages cream cheese, softened
½ c. chopped sweet gherkins
3 tbsp. catsup
2 tsp. imitation bacon bits
½ c. cream-style cottage cheese
1 tbsp. sweet pickle liquid
¼ tsp. dillweed
Dash of onion powder
Dash of Tabasco sauce
Pickles
Radishes

Beat 1 package cream cheese in small bowl until smooth; add ¼ cup gherkins. Add catsup and bacon bits; mix well. Spread evenly in lightly oiled 3-cup mold. Beat remaining cream cheese. Add cottage cheese, remaining ¼ cup gherkins, pickle liquid and seasonings. Spread over layer in mold. Chill, covered, for several hours. Dip mold in warm water; loosen and unmold onto plate. Garnish with pickles and radishes. Serve with assorted crackers. Yield: 3 cups.

Photograph for this recipe on page 21.

French Cheese Balls

2 c. grated Swiss cheese
1½ to 2 tbsp. flour
½ tsp. salt
¼ tsp. cayenne pepper
4 egg whites, beaten stiff
Bread crumbs
Oil

Mix cheese, flour, salt and pepper into beaten egg whites. Shape into small balls, shaping until ball is firm. Roll in bread crumbs. Refrigerate for at least 1 hour, or until ready to use. Fry in deep hot oil, until golden brown.

Marilyn K. Welsch, Sec.
Xi Gamma Zeta X1267
Massillon, Ohio

Life does not give you joy unless you will it; God gives you time and space, but you must fill it. Sharon Evander

Pineapple-Nut Ball

2 8-oz. packages cream cheese, softened
2 c. chopped pecans
1 8-oz. can crushed pineapple, drained
¼ c. chopped green pepper
1 tbsp. (or more) grated onion
1 tsp. salt
1 tsp. celery salt (opt.)

Combine cream cheese, 1 cup pecans, pineapple, green pepper, onion, and celery salt; mix well. Refrigerate for 1 hour. Divide in half, shape into balls. Roll in remaining pecans. Chill. Remove from refrigerator 30 minutes before serving. Serve with assorted crackers.

Mary Lou Burns, City Coun. Pres.
Preceptor Sigma X1072
Rockford, Illinois

Party Cheese Pineapple

4 3-oz. packages cream cheese, softened
¼ lb. Roquefort or blue cheese
½ jar snappy cheese spread
1 Tbsp. Worcestershire sauce
½ tsp. paprika
1 sm. clove of garlic, grated
1 sm. onion, grated
1 c. finely chopped parsley
1 c. finely chopped pecans
Olive slices (opt.)

Combine first 7 ingredients with ½ cup parsley. Add ½ cup pecans. Shape into a pineapple shape. Roll in remaining parsley and nuts. Place on waxed paper. Refrigerate for at least 12 hours. Place a pineapple top on top of the cheese mold. Press olive slices for pineapple eyes. Chill.

Helen Ruth Scarano, V. P.
Preceptor Epsilon Phi XP1233
San Lorenzo, California

Chicken and Chestnut Spread

1½ c. cooked cubed chicken breasts
8 chestnuts, boiled and diced
3 tbsp. finely chopped celery
4 tbsp. mayonnaise
Dash of salt and pepper

Combine chicken, chestnuts and celery with mayonnaise. Season with salt and pepper to taste. Chill, covered, for 4 to 5 hours. Serve with assorted crackers. Yield: 2½ cups.

Janice Ford, Ext. Off.
Alpha No. 7395
Hartford, Connecticut

Chicken Liver Pate

4 oz. butter
1 onion, chopped fine
1 clove of garlic, chopped fine
1 bay leaf
1 sprig dried thyme
¼ tsp. dried parsley
8 oz. chicken livers
1 or 2 tbsp. Brandy
Clarified butter

Melt 1 ounce butter in 2-quart saucepan. Saute onion and garlic over medium heat until onion is soft but not browned. Add herbs. Add chicken livers. Saute lightly for about 4 to 5 minutes. Allow to cool. Whip remaining butter in mixing bowl. Blend liver mixture in blender until creamed. Push through fine sieve. Blend liver cream, Brandy and whipped butter well. Place on attractive dish. Cover with clarified butter. Refrigerate. Serve with fingers of thin whole wheat toast. Yield: 4-8 servings.

Nancy Rollinson
Beta Sigma
Guelph, Ontario, Canada

Chicken Livers in Wine Sauce

2 tbsp. butter or margarine
1 lb. chicken livers, cut into bite-sized pieces
¼ c. dry Sherry
2 tbsp. parsley
1 tbsp. lemon juice
¼ tsp. salt
⅛ tsp. pepper

Melt butter in an 8-inch skillet or chafing dish. Stir in chicken livers. Cook and stir, uncovered, over medium heat for 4 to 5 minutes. Add Sherry, parsley, lemon juice, salt and pepper; heat through. Serve livers on appetizer rounds or in chafing dish with picks. Yield: 6 servings.

Mary Ann Clark, Courtesy Chm.
Preceptor Nu XP1498
Frederick, Maryland

Crisp Roll Cups

4 long crisp rolls
1 c. minced cooked chicken
6 tbsp. India relish
4 drops of Worcestershire sauce
2 tbsp. salad dressing
½ tsp. grated onion
¼ tsp. salt
8 stuffed olives, sliced

Cut a 2-inch thick slice from each end of each roll. Remove centers from each slice. Combine remaining

Through the eyes of love you discover a new wondrous world. Nancy Gillis

ingredients except olives; mix well. Fill each hollow bread cup with chicken mixture. Place olive slices in overlapping pattern on each cup. Garnish with sieved egg yolks. Yield: 8 servings.

Jessie Smith, Treas.
Preceptor Beta Theta No. 1676
Iola, Kansas

Sweet-Sour Chicken

1 lb. boned chicken breast
1 tbsp. oil
1 tsp. chopped garlic
1 green pepper, chopped
1 med. carrot, chopped
½ c. chicken broth
4 tbsp. sugar
4 tbsp. wine vinegar
1 tsp. soy sauce
1 tbsp. cornstarch

Cook chicken breast; remove skin. Cut into 1 inch cubes. Place in fondue pot. Pour oil in a 9 or 10-inch skillet. Heat to smoking. Add garlic, green pepper and carrot. Stir-fry for 2 to 3 minutes; do not burn. Pour in chicken broth, sugar, vinegar and soy sauce; bring to a boil. Combine cornstarch with 2 tablespoons cold water. Add to boiling mixture. Cook 1 to 2 minutes longer, stirring constantly to thicken. Pour over chicken in fondue pot. Combine and serve. Yield: 4 servings.

Marilyn Griffiths
Xi Alpha Eta X5076
Cheshire, Connecticut

Deep-Dish Pizza

1 lb. hamburger
¼ c. onion
¼ c. green pepper
1 16-oz. can whole tomatoes
1 15¾-oz. package cheese pizza mix
1 16-oz. package mozzarella cheese

Brown hamburger. Add onion and green pepper; cook until tender. Add tomatoes, spices and sauce from pizza mix. Simmer for 15 minutes. Prepare pizza dough according to package directions. Spread dough on greased 13 × 9-inch pan. Place layer of cheese over dough. Alternate layers of meat mixture and cheese until all ingredients are used. Top with Parmesan cheese. Bake at 425 degrees for 20 to 25 minutes. Yield: 8 servings.

Carol D. Collier, Treas.
Xi Delta Mu X3533
Connersville, Indiana

Chinese Roll-Ups with Hot Mustard Sauce

1 lb. ground beef
1 can water chestnuts, chopped
2 tbsp. chopped onion
1 pkg. onion and mushroom soup mix
1 tbsp. beef bouillon
1 can bean sprouts drained
3 pkgs crescent rolls
¼ c. prepared mustard
¼ c. mayonnaise
1 clove of garlic, chopped
¼ tsp. hot sauce
2 tsp. horseradish

Brown ground beef. Add next 5 ingredients. Simmer for 5 minutes. Remove from heat. Cut crescent triangles in half. Place 1 tablespoon meat mixture in center of each ½ crescent triangle. Pull corners over meat mixture; pinch together to seal. Place on baking sheet. Bake at 350 degrees for 15 minutes or until browned. Combine remaining ingredients; mix well. Refrigerate until serving time. Serve hot mustard sauce over roll-ups while still warm. May be frozen: Yield: 20 servings.

Lucille E. Thompson, Prog. Chm.
Xi Gamma Beta X2785
Littleton, Colorado

The Dallas Monster

1 lb. ground beef
1 onion, chopped
Salt and pepper to taste
Tabasco sauce to taste
1 1-lb can refried beans
1 4-oz. can chopped green chili peppers
2 to 3 c. shredded Monterey Jack cheese
1 8-oz. bottle of taco sauce
1 avocado, mashed
Lemon juice
1 c. sour cream
¼ c. chopped green onions (opt.)
1 c. chopped black olives

Brown ground beef; drain. Saute onion, salt, pepper and Tabasco with beef until tender. Layer refried beans, meat, chili peppers, cheese and taco sauce on ovenproof platter. Bake in 350-degree oven for 15 to 20 minutes. Combine avocado and lemon juice; season to taste. Garnish with avocado mixture and ring of sour cream. Sprinkle with green onions and olives. Serve with chips. May be frozen. Yield: 6-8 servings.

Pam McBroom
Epsilon
Mt. Juliet, Tennessee

Lord, help me to remember that nothing will happen to me today that you and I together can not handle. Barbara Slumsky

Mini Pizzas

1½ lb. hamburger
1 egg, beaten
1 pkg. onion soup mix
1 loaf cocktail rye bread
1 sm. jar Ragu spaghetti or pizza sauce
1 lb. mozzarella cheese

Combine hamburger, egg and soup mix: mix well. Spread on slice of bread. Top with 1 tablespoon sauce and 1 slice cheese. Place on cookie sheets. Freeze for about 20 minutes. Store in a bag in freezer. Bake for 15 to 20 minutes at 350 degrees when ready to serve. Yield: 30 servings.

Jackie Lynn Kiley, Hist.
Alpha Mu No. 1493
Two Rivers, Wisconsin

Party Meatballs with Sauce

1 lb. ground beef
½ c. corn flake crumbs
½ c. evaporated milk
¼ c. chopped onions
2 dashes of chili powder
Dash of onion salt
Dash of garlic salt
Dash of chef seasoning (opt.)
¼ c. catsup
1 tbsp. Worcestershire sauce
1 tsp. salt
1 tsp. pepper
Party Meatball Sauce

Combine all ingredients; mix well. Shape into heaping-teaspoon sized meatballs, using wet hands. Place in preheated 400-degree oven for 12 to 15 minutes or until brown. Serve warm with sauce. Yield: 36 servings.

Party Meatball Sauce:
1 8-oz. can tomato sauce
½ c. catsup
2 tbsp. Worcestershire sauce
2 tbsp. brown sugar
2 tbsp. chopped onions
1 tbsp. vinegar
Dash of pepper
2 tbsp. pickle relish, drained
2 dashes of chili powder

Combine all ingredients and 2 tablespoons water in a saucepan; mix well. Simmer for 15 minutes. Serve hot over meatballs.

Nancy Haines, Corr. Sec.
Iota Zeta No. 7464
Lafayette, Indiana

Party Ryes Deluxe

1½ to 2 lb. ground chuck
1 lb. hot pork sausage
2 lb. Velveeta cheese, cubed
2 tsp. oregano
3 loaves party rye bread
1 10-oz. package mozzarella cheese, shredded

Brown ground chuck; drain. Brown sausage; drain. Add Velveeta to meats. Add oregano. Cook until cheese melts. Spread ¼ inch thick on party rye bread. Sprinkle with mozzarella cheese. Bake at 400 degrees for 10 minutes. May be frozen. Yield: 90 to 100 servings.

Nancy L. Manning, Pres.
Xi Zeta Lambda X4704
Meadville, Pennsylvania

Elegant Canapes

1 lb. spicy hot sausage
1 lb. ground beef
1 tsp. oregano
½ tsp. garlic salt
½ tsp. Worcestershire sauce
1 lb. Velvetta cheese, thinly sliced
2 loaves cocktail rye bread

Cook sausage; drain fat. Add ground beef. Cook just until done but not dry or brown. Add spices and cheese slices. Cook on low heat until cheese melts. Spread quickly on cocktail rye bread. Freeze on cookie sheets; store in plastic bags in freezer. Bake in 450-degree oven for 8 minutes. Serve hot. Great to have on hand to serve. Yield: 75 servings.

Katherine Bell
Xi Gamma Theta X2998
Red Oak, Iowa

Tamale Balls

1 lb. ground beef
1 lb. pork sausage
1½ c. cornmeal
¾ c. tomato juice
¼ c. flour
3 cloves of garlic, crushed
2 tbsp. chili powder
4 tsp. salt
3 No. 2 cans tomatoes

Combine first 6 ingredients with 1 tablespoon chili powder and 2 teaspoons salt; mix well. Shape into small balls. Combine remaining ingredients in saucepan. Bring to a boil. Drop meatballs into simmering

The door to happiness opens outward. Mrs. J. A. Cox

sauce. Simmer for 2 hours. Serve hot in a chafing dish with toothpicks. Yield: 100-150 servings.

Nelda I. Urban, Pres.
Xi Tau Phi No. 5157
Canyon Lake, Texas

Deviled Ham Snackin' Loaf

2 4½-oz. cans deviled ham
¼ c. chopped onion
3 tbsp. chopped sweet pickles
6 slices process cheese, cut in half diagonally
1 loaf French Bread

Combine deviled ham, onion and pickles in a bowl. Spread mixture on one side of cheese slice. Cut bread diagonally every inch to within ¼-inch bottom. Fill each slit with a cheese slice. Wrap loaf in foil. Bake in preheated 325-degree oven for 15 to 20 minutes or until bread is heated and cheese is melted. Slice loaf between cheese slices to serve. Yield: 12 snacks.

Elizabeth Karry, Pres.
Gamma No. 653
Scarborough, Ontario, Canada

Ham and Cheese Mousse

2 env. unflavored gelatin
1¼ c. milk
2 c. diced cooked ham
¾ c. cubed Swiss cheese
1 tbsp. prepared horseradish
2 tsp. dry mustard
1 c. heavy cream, whipped

Sprinkle gelatin in 1 cup cold water in saucepan. Let stand until gelatin is moistened. Place over low heat, stirring constantly for 5 minutes or until gelatin is dissolved. Remove from heat; stir in milk, ham, cheese, horseradish and mustard. Place half the gelatin mixture in 5-cup blender container. Blend, on Low for 15 seconds or until ham and cheese are shredded. Pour mixture into large bowl; repeat process with remaining gelatin mixture. Chill, stirring occasionally, until slightly congealed. Fold in whipped cream. Pour into 6-cup mold. Chill until firm. Yield: 8 servings.

Photograph for this recipe on page 25.

The love we give away is the only love we keep.   Sue A. Jedlicka

Ham Balls Deluxe

1¼ lb. ham
1¼ lb. ground beef
2 c. bread crumbs
2 eggs
1 c. milk
1 c. (packed) brown sugar
1 tsp. prepared mustard
¼ c. vinegar

Combine first 5 ingredients in order listed. Shape into walnut-sized balls. Place in 9 × 13-inch baking dish. Combine remaining ingredients in order listed, ending with ¾ cup water. Pour over meatballs. Bake at 325 degrees for 30 minutes. Turn meatballs; bake for 30 minutes longer. Yield: 30 servings.

Mary Taylor, Hist.
Preceptor Alpha Omega
Coffeyville, Kansas

Peanut-Deviled Ham Ball

1 8-oz. package cream cheese, softened
1 4½-oz. can deviled ham
2 tbsp. grated onion
1 tsp. horseradish
¼ tsp. liquid hot pepper seasoning
¼ tsp. dry mustard
¼ c. chopped salted peanuts
1 tbsp. dried parsley

Beat first 6 ingredients until smooth and well blended. Chill. Shape into a ball. Roll in peanuts and parsley to coat. Chill for 30 minutes before serving. Serve with party rye bread or assorted crackers.

Phyllis Brinegar, Pres.
Xi Epsilon Epsilon X4260
Newburgh, Indiana

Fancy Dogs

1 6-oz. jar mustard
1 6-oz. jar currant jelly
1 lb. wieners, cut diagonally

Combine mustard and jelly in fondue pot; mix well. Heat to boiling point. Add wieners. Heat until warm. Place over fondue flame, stirring occasionally. Recipe can be doubled or tripled. Yield: 12 servings.

Beth Ann Maglott, Treas.
Epsilon Tau No. 2618
Mansfield, Ohio

Hot Dogs L'Bourbon

2 tbsp. finely chopped onion
1 tbsp. butter
½ c. catsup
⅓ c. (packed) brown sugar
¾ c. Bourbon
1 lb. package or 10 hot dogs

Cook onion in butter in 1½-quart saucepan over medium low heat until tender. Add remaining ingredients, except hot dogs; blend thoroughly. Slice each hot dog on bias into 4 pieces. Add hot dogs to sauce. Simmer over low heat for 25 minutes, or until sauce glazes, stirring occasionally. Add a small amount of bourbon if sauce becomes too thick. This recipe can be frozen up to two months. To reheat frozen hors d'oeuvres, place in lightly buttered overproof dish; cover. Heat in preheated 350-degree oven until sauce bubbles. Place dish on hot tray to keep warm while serving.

Dayle Nelson, Life Member
Preceptor Laureate Beta PL190
Cheyenne, Wyoming

Spicy Wieners

5 lb. wieners, cut into ¾ in. chunks
2 tbsp. salt
6 tbsp. sugar
4 to 6 peppercorns or 1 tsp. pepper
1 sm. jar pepper sauce
1 qt. white vinegar
2 onions, diced

Combine all ingredients, except onions in saucepan. Bring to a boil. Remove from heat. Add onions. Place in crockpot on low heat. Serve hot. Yield: 50 servings.

Barbara Alford, Rec. Sec.
Lambda Iota No. 3644
Lubbock, Texas

Peanut Butter Pips

¼ c. peanut butter
2 tbsp. mayonnaise
2 slices crisp cooked bacon, crumbled
1 tsp. minced green pepper or onion

Blend peanut butter and mayonnaise together until smooth. Stir in bacon and green pepper. Spread on crackers. Place on cookie sheet. Broil 3 inches below heat until bubbly; do not brown. Serve hot. Yield: 8 servings.

Martha Cogdill, Prog. Chm.
Preceptor Iota XP1557
Greenville, South Carolina

Much can be accomplished if you do not worry who receives the credit. Marjorie K. E. Lessman

Pineapple-Bacon Roll-Ups

1 small pineapple
½ lb. bacon

Cut off crown and stem end of pineapple. Stand pineapple upright; cut off rind in lengthwise strips. Remove eyes with pointed knife. Cut into lengthwise quarters, cut away core. Cut pineapple into large chunks. Cut bacon slices in half. Wrap bacon slice around each pineapple chunk; fasten with wooden pick. Place on broiler rack set 5 inches from source of heat. Broil for 5 to 8 minutes or until browned. Turn and broil for 2 to 3 minutes until browned and crisp. Yield: 32 servings.

Photograph for this recipe on page 18.

Pineapple Kabobs

1 sm. pineapple
½ c. salad oil
¼ c. lemon juice
½ tsp. dry mustard
1 tsp. dried leaf rosemary
½ tsp. salt
Cherry tomatoes, halved
Ham cubes
Cheese cubes

Cut off crown and stem end of pineapple. Stand pineapple upright; cut off rind in lengthwise strips. Remove eyes with pointed knife. Cut into lengthwise quarters, cut away core. Cut pineapple into large chunks; place in bowl. Combine oil, lemon juice, dry mustard, rosemary and salt mix well. Pour over pineapple. Refrigerate for several hours or overnight. Drain; place on skewers, alternating with tomatoes, ham and cheese. Yield: 10-12 servings.

Photograph for this recipe on page 18.

Sausage-Cheese Puffs

10 oz. coon cheese
12 oz. pork sausage
3 c. Bisquick

Melt cheese in top of double boiler or in microwave oven. Place sausage and Bisquick in large bowl. Pour melted cheese over top. Mix all ingredients together with hands; mix well. Refrigerate mixture for 30 minutes. Roll into balls. Place 1 inch apart on cookie sheet. Bake at 375 degrees for 20 minutes. Serve hot. Yield: 10-11 dozen.

Penny B. Read, Coun. Rep.
Alpha Epsilon No. 5829
Presque Isle, Maine

Shirley's Sausage Balls

1 lb. hot sausage, at room temperature
10 oz. extra sharp cracker barrel cheese, grated
3 c. Bisquick

Mix Bisquick and grated cheese; add sausage. Blend well. Shape into small balls. Freeze on cookie sheet. Store in a plastic bag in the freezer. Place frozen on cookie sheet. Bake at 300 degrees for 35 to 45 minutes. Serve hot. Yield: 4 dozen.

Shirley Mae Lock, Prog. Comm.
Laureate Nu PL393
Carrollton, Missouri

Yolanda's Sausage Balls

1 lb. bulk sausage, at room temperature
1 lb. sharp cheese, grated, at room temperature
3 c. Bisquick

Mix all ingredients together well. Form into small walnut-sized balls. Place 1 inch apart on ungreased cookie sheet. Bake at 325 degrees for 20 to 30 minutes or until lightly browned. Serve warm. May be frozen and reheated. Yield: 55 servings.

Yolanda M. Flory, Treas.
Xi Beta Epsilon X2027
Swartz Creek, Michigan

Party Rye Pizzas

1 lb. mild pork sausage
1 lb. hot pork sausage
1 onion, finely diced
1 bell pepper, finely diced
2 lb. Velveeta cheese, cubed
½ bottle of aniseed
2 tsp. oregano
4 sm. loafs party rye bread

Fry sausage with onion and bell pepper until lightly brown. Pour off excess fat. Add cheese gradually to sausage, stirring until melted. Add oregano and aniseed. Simmer for 10 to 15 minutes. Place party rye on cookie sheets. Spoon sausage mixture onto rye slices. Mixture should be thick enough to stack one on top of another. Place in freezer until needed. Bake in preheated 375-degree oven for 12 to 15 minutes or until lightly browned. Serve hot. Yield: 150 servings.

Marci Wilcox
Beta Epsilon No. 5436
Greenville, Mississippi

The true test of intelligence is not how much we know, but how we behave when we do not know what to do. Helen Hetrick

Sweet-Sour Sausage Bites

1 c. (packed) brown sugar
3 tbsp. all-purpose flour
2 tsp. dry mustard
1 c. unsweetened pineapple juice
½ c. vinegar
2 tsp. soy sauce
1 lb. smoked sausage links or cocktail franks, cooked

Blend brown sugar, flour and mustard in saucepan. Stir in pineapple juice, vinegar and soy sauce. Cook, stirring constantly, over medium heat until thick and bubbly. Serve hot over warmed sausage bits or cocktail franks. Yield: 2 cups sauce.

Betty Ann Oros
Xi Alpha Psi X586
Joliet, Illinois

Barbecued Smoky Sausages

1 can tomato soup
1½ c. (packed) brown sugar
3 tbsp. vinegar
1 tsp. prepared mustard
1 tsp. celery seed
3 tbsp. barbecue sauce
½ tsp. salt
½ tsp. liquid smoke
1½ lb. Smoky sausage links

Combine first 8 ingredients; mix well. Pour over sausage links in a saucepan. Heat through. Serve hot as hors d'ouevres. Use remaining sauce for barbecuing meats. Yield: 8-10 servings.

Virginia Fast, City Coun. Rep.
Preceptor Mu XP753
Knoxville, Iowa

Antipasto

2 cans solid tuna, flaked fine
1 med. jar stuffed green olives, chopped fine
1 can button mushrooms, chopped fine
1 jar sweet mixed pickles, chopped fine
6 to 8 dill pickles, chopped fine
1 lg. bottle of catsup
2 sm. bottles of chili sauce
Juice of a ½ lemon
1 tsp. Worcestershire sauce
1 tsp. horseradish

Combine tuna, olives, mushrooms and pickles. Add remaining ingredients; mix well. Serve with assorted crackers. Antipasto may be frozen up to 6 months.

Delicious standby for those unexpected entertaining occasions. Yield: 50 servings.

Gwen Sharp, City Coun. Pres.
Xi Iota X2580
Winnipeg, Manitoba, Canada

Tosetti's Antipasto

1 sm. can boneless sardines
1 6¼-oz. can tuna
1 sm. jar cocktail onions, drained
1 sm. jar stuffed olives, drained
1 sm. can mushrooms, drained
2 sm. dill pickles, diced
1 c. catsup
1 tbsp. olive oil
1 tbsp. vinegar
Dash of salt and pepper

Place all ingredients in a large bowl; mix well. Refrigerate, covered, for several hours for flavors to blend. Serve with assorted crackers and hard bread. Yield: 4-6 servings.

Mrs. Nancy A. Tosetti
Omicron Delta No. 6941
Nokomis, Illinois

Creamy Shrimp Mold

1 tbsp. unflavored gelatin
1 can cream of celery soup
1 8-oz. can shrimp
1 8-oz. package cream cheese
1 onion, chopped
1 c. celery
1 c. mayonnaise

Dissolve gelatin in 3 tablespoons water. Heat celery soup until smooth; add gelatin. Combine remaining ingredients; pour in soup. Pour into mold. Chill until set. Serve with assorted crackers.

Ann-Marie Grzinich
Xi Iota X335
Hyde Park, New York

Double Shrimp Mold

1 can cream of shrimp soup
1 env. unflavored gelatin
2 8-oz. packages cream cheese, softened
1 c. mayonnaise
1½ tbsp. green onion, chopped
¾ c. celery, chopped fine
2 6-oz. cans small deveined shrimp
Salt and pepper to taste

A cheerful look makes a dish a feast. Rose E. King

Heat undiluted soup to boiling point. Add gelatin to ½ cup cold water. Add to soup; mix well. Add cream cheese; blend well. Cool slightly. Add remaining ingredients; mix well. Spoon into mold or molds. Refrigerate for several hours. Unmold and serve with assorted crackers. May be frozen. Yield: 20-25 servings.

Linda Riegel, Pres.
Preceptor Xi XP395
Denver, Colorado

Easy Fresh Shrimp

¼ c. sliced onion
2 stalks and leaves celery
1 clove of garlic
1 bay leaf
1½ tsp. salt
⅛ tsp. cayenne pepper
2 lb. fresh shrimp
½ lemon, sliced

Combine 8 cups water with onion, celery and seasonings. Simmer for 15 minutes. Add shrimp and lemon. Simmer for additional 15 minutes. Cool in water. Shell and devein. Chill. Serve with favorite cocktail sauce.

Janis Hampton
Xi Gamma Iota X1193
Mt. Vernon, Illinois

Party-Pleasing Marinated Shrimp

1 tbsp. Wesson oil
2 tbsp. lemon juice
1 tbsp. vinegar
1 tbsp. prepared mustard
1 stalk celery, diced
2 green onions, sliced
1 can shrimp

Combine all ingredients; mix well. Marinate for 6 hours or overnight. Serve with Waverly wafers. Double, triple or quadruple the recipe according to party size. Yield: 4 servings.

Dee Sarver, V. P.
Epsilon Rho No. 9831
Magnolia, Arkansas

Shrimp Cocktail Brasilienne Supreme

3 c. mayonnaise
¾ c. honey
½ tsp. salt
3 tbsp. ground ginger
¼ c. cider vinegar
1 tbsp. white pepper

¼ c. orange juice
Pineapple tidbits
Alaskan baby shrimp

Combine first 7 ingredients. Blend until smooth and flavors are well blended. Place pineapple tidbits in each cocktail cup to cover bottom. Top with shrimp to cover. Pour ginger dressing over all. Garnish with toasted almonds and a cherry.

Rosanna Fahl, Corr. Sec.
Xi Gamma Xi X1194
Oroville, California

Crab Meat Appetizers

1 24-oz. loaf fresh white bread, thinly sliced
Butter or margarine, softened
1 10-oz bottle Durkee Famous Sauce
1 7-oz. can or 6-oz. package frozen crab meat
1 tbsp. grated onion
½ tsp. Worcestershire sauce
2 3-oz. packages cream cheese, softened
Olives (opt.)

Trim crusts from bread slices. Spread one side bread slice with butter; the second side with Durkees. Mix crab meat with grated onion, Worcestershire sauce and cream cheese to sandwich-spread consistency. Spread 2 to 3 teaspoons crab meat mixture over Durkees. Roll each slice up; secure with a toothpick. Cover. Refrigerate or freeze until needed. Place sandwich rolls on broiling pan. Broil until brown on each side. Placed olive on end of toothpick before serving. Serve immediately. Yield: 24 servings.

Carla Scranton, City Coun. Pres.
Xi Pi X448
Lamar, Colorado

Crab Spread

12 oz. cream cheese, softened
2 tsp. Worcestershire sauce
½ lg. onion, minced
Garlic salt to taste
1 tbsp. lemon juice
2 tbsp. mayonnaise
9 oz. chili sauce
2 12-oz. cans crab meat, drained
Parsley flakes

Blend first 6 ingredients well. Spread on 12-inch serving dish. Pour chili sauce over top. Place crab meat over chili sauce. Sprinkle with parsley flakes. Serve with Sociable crackers. Yield: 8-10 servings.

Shirley Craig, Corr. Sec.
Delta Rho No. 7192
La Place, Louisiana

Feel in your heart that every day is the loveliest day of your life.   Rose Ann Hopkins

Crab Meat Puffs

1 stick butter or margarine, softened
1 sm. jar Old English cheese spread
1 pkg. frozen crab meat
½ tsp. seasoned salt
Dash of garlic salt
1½ tbsp. mayonnaise
9 English muffins, toasted and quartered

Combine butter and cheese spread until smooth and creamy. Add next 4 ingredients; mix well. Spread on English muffin quarters. Bake at 350 degrees for 15 minutes. These can be frozen. Yield: 72 hors d'oeuvres.

Patty Gilnack, Rec. Sec.
Xi Alpha Beta X3976
East Hartford, Connecticut

Crab Loaf

1 10-oz. can cream of mushroom soup
1 env. unflavored gelatin
1 6-oz. package cream cheese
1 c. chopped celery
1 green onion, chopped
1 c. mayonnaise
1 sm. can crab meat

Heat soup. Dissolve gelatin in 3 tablespoons hot water. Add dissolved gelatin to warm soup. Combine cream cheese, celery, green onion, mayonnaise and crab meat in bowl. Mix with soup. Place in loaf or fish mold. Chill overnight. Serve with crisp Ritz crackers. Yield: 12 servings.

Dink Rife
Theta Lambda No. 3145
Portola, California

Salmon Spread

1 8-oz. package cream cheese, softened
2 tsp. lemon juice
2 tsp. grated onion
¼ tsp. liquid smoke
Salt to taste
2 or 3 dashes of Worcestershire sauce
Dash of hot sauce
2 tsp. horseradish
Dash of cayenne pepper
1 15½-oz. can salmon
Chopped pecans
Chopped fresh parsley

Blend cream cheese until smooth. Add remaining ingredients except salmon; mix well. Drain and debone salmon. Add salmon to creamed mixture; mix well. Shape into a ball on waxed paper. Sprinkle with pecans and parsley. Place on serving plate on a bed of lettuce.

Mrs. Judy Taylor
Beta Theta
Laurel, Mississippi

Shrimp-Olive Appeteasers

1 lb. sirloin steak, 1-inch thick
1 lb. cooked shrimp
1 c. canned pitted ripe olives
⅓ c. salad oil
2 tbsp. wine vinegar
⅛ tsp. garlic powder
1 tsp. Worcestershire sauce
½ tsp. coarsely ground black pepper
½ tsp. salt

Broil steak to rare; cut into bite-sized pieces. Combine with all remaining ingredients. Marinate several hours. Alternate olives, steak and shrimp on skewers. Heat over small hibachi. Yield: 24 servings.

Photograph for this recipe on page 31.

Asparagus Rolls

24 thin slices white bread
8 slices bacon, cooked and crumbled or ¾ c. Baco's
12 oz. cream cheese, softened
24 asparagus spears, canned or cooked fresh
Melted butter

Trim crusts from bread; roll thin. Mix bacon and cream cheese. Spread on bread slices. Place cold asparagus spear on each bread slice; roll up. Place on baking sheet, seam side down. Brush with melted butter. Broil until lightly browned. May slice into ¼ or ½-inch rounds then broil each side until crisp brown. Yield: 24 servings.

Kathy Norwood, Corr. Sec.
Beta Gamma No. 4176
Clanton, Alabama

Bacon-Wrapped Water Chestnuts

1 8-oz. can water chestnuts, drained
¼ c. soy sauce
¼ c. sugar
1 lb. bacon

Marinate water chestnuts in soy sauce for 30 minutes. Roll in sugar. Cut bacon strips in half. Wrap each

---

Hearts speak to hearts not in words but by gestures. Rose Ann Hopkins

water chestnut in a bacon strip. Spear with toothpick. Bake at 400 degrees for 20 minutes. Drain. Heat 5 minutes at 350 degrees, or under the broiler for 2 to 3 minutes. Yield: 10 servings.

Kaye Dunham, Pres.
Iota Alpha No. 9113
Oklahoma City, Oklahoma

Artichoke-Cheese Squares

4 jars marinated artichokes
8 eggs, well beaten
1 lb. medium Cheddar cheese, grated
20 saltine crackers, crushed
Salt and pepper to taste
Cayenne pepper to taste

Drain artichokes; chop well. Combine artichokes with next 3 ingredients; mix well. Season with salt, pepper ad cayenne pepper to taste. Press into a well-greased 9 × 12-inch pan. Bake at 350 degrees for 30 minutes. Serve hot. This recipe can also be halved for smaller groups. Yield: 14 servings.

Dixie Cook
Beta Nu No. 5136
Shreveport, Louisiana

Artichoke Nibbles

2 6-oz. jars marinated artichoke hearts
1 sm. onion, chopped fine
1 clove of garlic, minced
4 eggs, well beaten
¼ c. bread crumbs
½ tsp. salt
⅛ tsp. pepper
⅛ tsp. oregano
⅛ tsp. Tabasco sauce
½ lb. sharp Cheddar cheese, grated
2 tbsp. minced fresh parsley

Drain artichokes, reserving 1 jar oil. Chop finely; set aside. Saute onion and garlic in small frying pan in reserved oil. Combine eggs, crumbs and seasonings in medium bowl. Stir in cheese, parsley, artichokes and onion-garlic mixture; mix well. Spread in 7 × 11-inch baking pan. Bake at 325 degrees for 30 minutes. Cut into 1-inch squares. May be served hot or cold.

Carol Bockmon, Hist.
Xi Tau Pi X5001
Stockton, California

Add a little sugar and spice to your life and soon you will have a recipe everyone will love. Nadine Powell

Flaky Artichoke Appetizers

1 6-oz. jar marinated artichoke hearts
1 2-oz. can mushroom stems and pieces, drained
½ c. sour cream
1 8-oz. can refrigerator crescent rolls
2 tbsp. crushed seasoned croutons.

Drain artichokes; cut into ½-inch pieces. Combine mushrooms, sour cream and artichoke pieces. Separate crescent dough into 4 rectangles. Place 2 rectangles in ungreased 8 or 9-inch square pan. Press over bottom to form crust, sealing perforations. Spread artichoke mixture over crust. Place remaining rectangles over artichoke mixture. Stretch gently to cover. Sprinkle with croutons. Bake in preheated 350-degree oven for 30 to 35 minutes or until golden brown. Cool 15 minutes before cutting. Cut into small squares. Prepared recipe can be kept in refrigerator up to 2 hours before baking. Yield: 12-15 servings.

Mary K. Brown, Rec. Sec.
Preceptor Theta XP248
Houston, Texas

Jackie's Artichoke Squares

2 jars marinated artichoke hearts
1 med. onion, chopped
1 clove of garlic, chopped
1½ lb. Cheddar cheese, grated
4 eggs, well beaten
½ tsp. salt
Pepper to taste
½ tsp. oregano
Dash of Tabasco sauce
¼ c. bread crumbs

Drain artichoke, reserving oil from 1 jar. Chop artichoke into small pieces. Saute artichoke, onion and garlic in reserved oil until tender. Combine eggs, cheese, seasonings and artichoke mixture. Pour into 9 × 13-inch baking dish. Top with bread crumbs. Bake at 350 degrees about 30 minutes or until knife inserted in center comes out clean. Cut into 1-inch squares; insert toothpicks. Arrange on serving tray. Serve hot.

Barbara Arnold, Pres.
Xi Beta Upsilon X2213
Sedalia, Missouri

Mushroom Cups

12 slices thin white bread
4 tbsp. butter or margarine, softened
½ lb. mushrooms
2 green onions, coarsely chopped
2 tbsp. flour
½ tsp. salt
Dash of pepper
1 tbsp. chopped parsley
1 tsp. lemon juice
1 c. light cream, heated
2 tbsp. grated Parmesan cheese

Trim crusts from bread. Grease the inside of twelve 3-inch muffin cups with 2 tablespoons soft butter. Press bread slice into each cup; mold to fit with fingertips. Bake at 400 degrees for 10 minutes. Remove from oven; cool. Wash and trim mushrooms; cut in half if large. Place mushrooms, a small amount at a time, into blender container; blend on low speed for 2 seconds. Empty into medium saucepan; repeat until all mushrooms are chopped. Place onions, flour, salt, pepper, parsley, lemon juice, remaining butter and heated cream into blender container. Blend on high speed for 3 seconds. Combine in saucepan with mushrooms. Cook over moderate heat for about 3 minutes, stirring constantly. Cool; chill thoroughly. Fill each cup with mushroom mixture at serving time. Sprinkle each with Parmesan cheese. Bake at 350 degrees for 10 minutes. Serve hot. Yield: 6 servings.

Flora R. Stephens, Serv. Comm. Chm.
Epsilon Nu No. 8262
Centreville, Virginia

Sausage-Stuffed Mushroom Squares

2 cups Bisquick
½ lb. bulk pork sausage
¼ c. chopped green onion
½ c. mayonnaise or salad dressing
2 c. fresh large mushrooms
2 c. shredded Cheddar cheese
Paprika

Combine Bisquick and ½ cup cold water; mix well. Beat until fluffy. Press into greased 9 × 13-inch pan. Brown pork sausage; drain. Combine with onion and mayonnaise. Cut off and chop mushroom stems. Add to sausage mixture. Stuff each mushroom cap with sausage mixture. Place stuffed mushrooms in rows on top of Bisquick crust. Cover with shredded cheese; sprinkle with paprika. Cover pan with aluminum foil. Bake at 350 degrees for 20 minutes. Remove foil; bake for 10 minutes longer. Remove from oven. Let stand for 10 minutes before cutting into squares. Yield: 35-40 appetizers.

Nan Rutkowski, Rec. Sec.
Alpha Epsilon No. 1409
Maple Grove, Minnesota

A day of worry is more exhausting than a week of work.   Irene Linvill

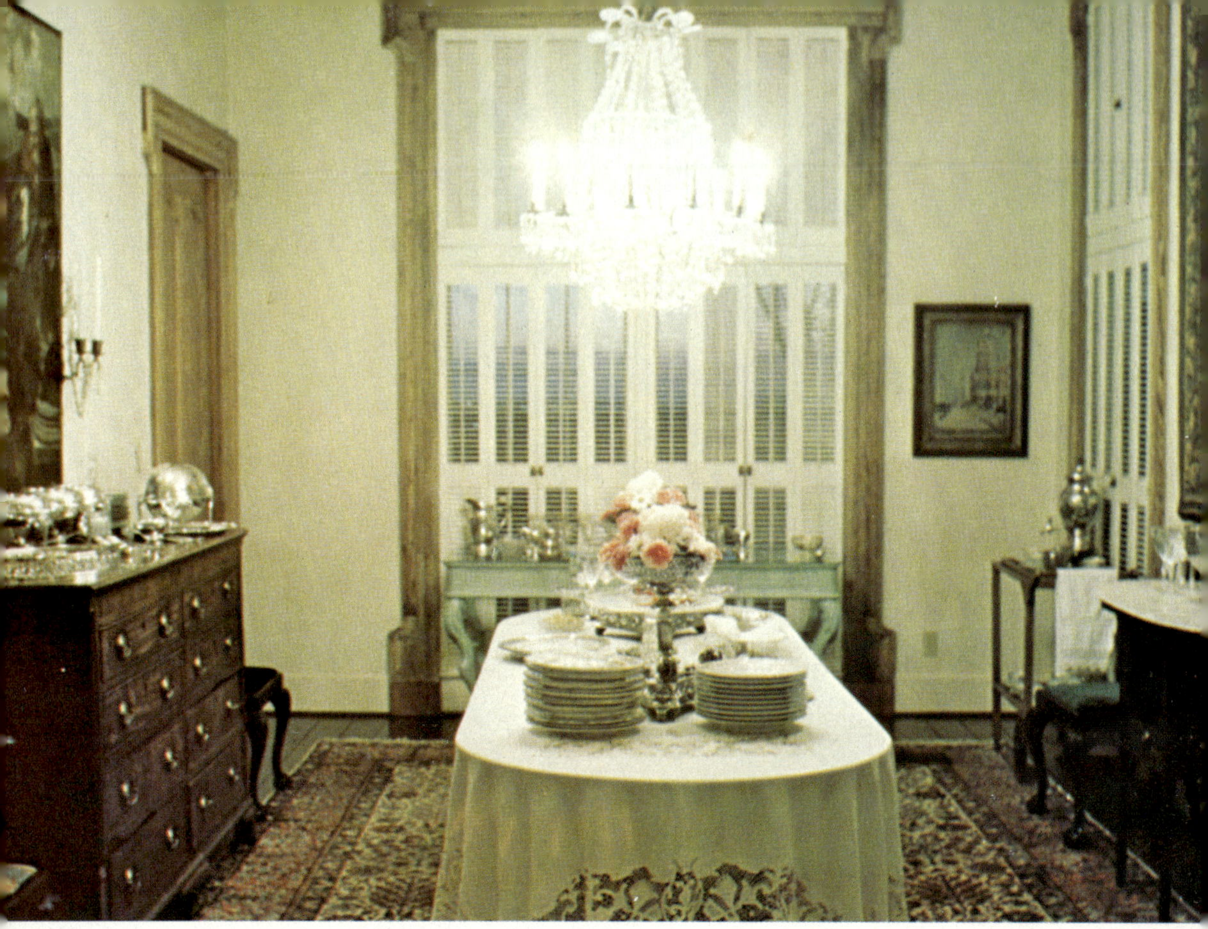

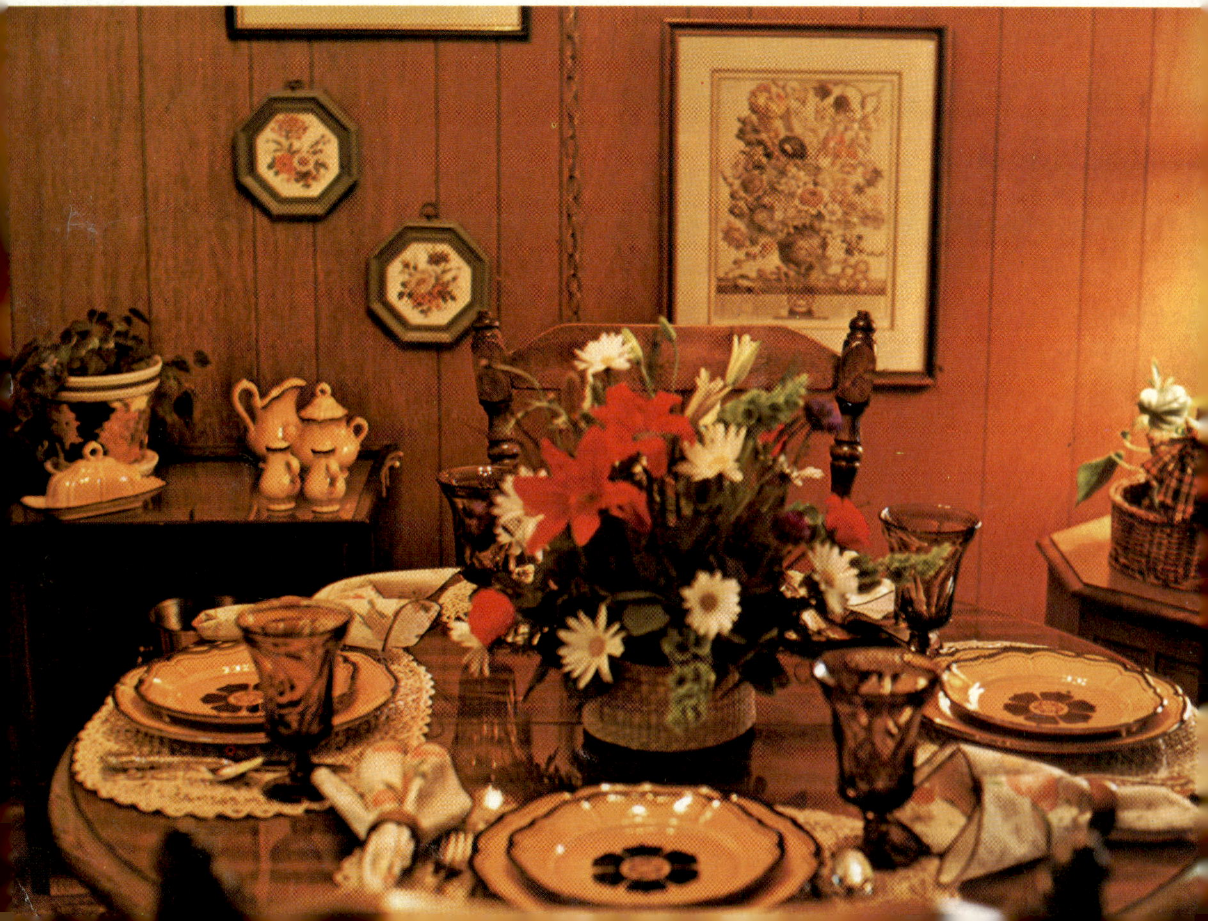

Stuffed-Mushroom Appetizers

1 7½-oz. can crab meat
5 scallions, thinly sliced
Grated Parmesan cheese
Pinch each of rosemary, thyme, oregano, savory, salt
    and pepper
½ c. mayonnaise or salad dressing
12 jumbo mushrooms caps or 24 med. caps
½ c. butter or margarine

Drain crab meat; remove cartilage. Press to remove excess liquid; flake. Combine crab meat, scallions, ¼ cup Parmesan cheese, seasonings and mayonnaise; mix well. Remove stems and scrape gills from mushrooms with spoon to make deep cups. Cook mushrooms, cap-side down, in butter for about 10 minutes, basting frequently. Remove caps; drain and cool. Stuff caps generously with crab mixture. Place in ungreased shallow baking dish. Bake in preheated 325-degree oven for 5 minutes. Sprinkle caps lightly with additional Parmesan cheese. Increase temperature to broil. Broil appetizers until golden brown, about 5 minutes. Yield: 12 servings.

Margaret Nelson, Corr. Sec., Girl of the Year, 1977-78
Xi Gamma Chi X1468
Baytown, Texas

Onion Snack Squares

2 frozen pie shells
2 cans French-fried onion rings
1 c. shredded Cheddar cheese
3 eggs, beaten
1½ c. milk
1 tsp. salt
1 tsp. Seasoned Salt
½ tsp. pepper

Stretch thawed pie shells to cover bottom and up sides of a 9 × 13-inch baking pan, pressing with fingers to make slight edge; seal well; Crush onion with rolling pin. Sprinkle over shell, reserving a little for top. Sprinkle cheese over onions, reserving a little for top. Beat eggs, milk, salts and pepper together well. Pour over onions and cheese. Sprinkle with reserved onion and cheese. Bake in 425-degree oven for 15 minutes. May be baked in 350-degree oven for 25 minutes. Remove from oven. Cut into squares to serve. Yield: 36-40 servings.

Mrs. Cissie Carpenter
Xi Psi X2967
Albert Lea, Minnesota

Sauerkraut Balls

4 tbsp. margarine
1 med. onion, chopped
1⅓ c. chopped cooked ham
½ clove of garlic, minced
All-purpose flour
½ c. sauerkraut liquid
3 c. sauerkraut, drained and chopped
1 egg, beaten
1½ c. milk
Bread crumbs

Melt margarine in skillet. Add onion; brown slightly. Add ham and garlic; brown slightly. Stir in 4 tablespoons flour; cook thoroughly. Add sauerkraut liquid, sauerkraut and parsley. Cook, stirring constantly, for a few minutes longer. This forms a stiff paste. Chill. Form into balls about 1 inch in diameter. Beat 1 egg, and milk together. Dip balls in additional flour, then egg mixture. Roll in fine bread crumbs. Fry in deep fat at 375 degrees until golden brown. Serve hot. Yield: 50 balls.

Beverly Martin, Soc. Com.
Delta Omega No. 4546
Merritt Island, Florida

Zucchini Appetizers

3 c. thinly sliced unpared zucchini
1 c. Bisquick
½ c. finely chopped onions
½ c. grated Parmesan cheese
2 tbsp. snipped parsley
½ tsp. seasoned salt
½ tsp. salt
½ tsp. dried marjoram or oregano leaves
Dash of pepper
1 clove of garlic, finely chopped
½ c. vegetable oil
4 eggs, slightly beaten

Combine all ingredients; mix well. Spread in greased 9 × 13-inch baking pan. Bake in preheated 350-degree oven for about 25 minutes. Cut into 2 inch squares to serve. This is very good with ½ pound hamburger added, decreasing vegetable oil to ¼ cup or less. Yield: 48 squares.

Margaret E. Niemeyer, Pres.
Preceptor Xi XP1900
Aberdeen, South Dakota

Anchovy Dip

1 c. mayonnaise
½ c. chopped lettuce
1 2-oz. can anchovies, chopped
1 clove of garlic, minced
1 tsp. grated lemon rind (opt.)
2 tbsp. lemon juice

Combine all ingredients. Chill. Serve as dip for assorted fresh vegetables. Guaranteed to please anchovy-haters.

Margaret Hogan, Pres.
Xi Beta Beta X2343
Hanmer, Ontario, Canada

Progress is the activity of today and the assurance of tomorrow. Wanda Gaeken

Chipped Beef Dip

2 c. sour cream
2 8-oz. packages cream cheese, softened
3 pkg. chipped beef, cut up
3 bunches green onion and tops minced
1 lg. green pepper, minced

Combine all ingredients; mix well. Place in 1-quart baking dish. Bake in 325-degree oven for 30 minutes. Serve this dip warm with fresh vegetables or crackers.

Nancy Burden, City Coun. Pres., W. and M. Chm.
Xi Alpha Beta X674
LaPorte, Indiana

Hot Beef Dip

1 c. dried beef
¼ c. chopped green onion
1 tbsp. margarine
1 c. milk
1 8-oz. package cream cheese, cubed
1 3-oz. can sliced mushrooms, drained
¼ c. grated Parmasan cheese
2 tbsp. chopped parsley

Rinse dried beef in hot water; drain and chop. Cook onion in margarine until tender. Stir in milk and cream cheese, mixing until well blended. Add dried beef and remaining ingredients. Serve hot. Keep warm in fondue pot. Serve with toasted bread triangles or wheat thins. Yield: 2 cups.

Sandra K. Gilmore
Kappa Tau No. 9849
Louisburg, Kansas

Capers Dip

1 8-oz. package cream cheese, softened
1 stick butter, softened
Dash of garlic salt
1 3-oz. bottle of capers, well drained

Combine cream cheese and butter; mix well. Add garlic salt to taste; mix well. Add capers, folding in gently. Serve with assorted chips and crackers.

Betty Hale Johnston, Rec. Sec.
Preceptor Alpha Eta XP956
Shawnee Mission, Kansas

Chili Con Queso Dip

¼ c. green pepper, diced
1 sm. clove of garlic, crushed
1 sm. onion, diced
1 tbsp. butter
2 med. tomatoes, diced
1 sm. can chopped green chilies or hot peppers
1 lb. process cheese, grated

Saute green pepper, garlic and onion in butter. Add tomatoes and green chilies; mix well. Melt grated cheese in top of double boiler. Add all ingredients to the cheese; blend well. Serve at once in a chafing dish with chips.

V. Jerry Everett, Rec. Sec.
Preceptor Alpha Xi XP1254
Rushville, Missouri

Hot Clam Dip

2 cans minced clams
1 stick butter or margarine
1 sm. onion, chopped
2 c. crushed Ritz crackers

Drain clams, reserving liquid from 1 can. Melt butter in small saucepan. Saute onion until just tender. Add crushed crackers, clams and reserved liquid; mix well. Pour into casserole or crock. Bake, covered, at 350 degrees for 30 minutes. Serve hot with Ritz crackers.

Elen Desjardin, Pres.
Preceptor XP1113
Auburn, Maine

Tomato-Clam Dip

1 3-oz package cream cheese, softened
2 tbsp. finely diced tomatoes
2 tbsp. minced clams
1 tbsp. clam juice
1½ tbsp. minced parsley
¾ tsp. salt
⅛ tsp. ground pepper
1/16 tsp. minced garlic

Combine all ingredients; beat until fluffy. May be used as dip for celery sticks. Yield: 1 cup.

Photograph for this recipe on page 37.

Hot Crab Dip

1 8-oz. package cream cheese, softened
1 or 2 tbsp. milk
1 6½-oz. can crab meat
2 tbsp. chopped onion
½ tsp. cream-style horseradish
¼ tsp. each salt and pepper
⅓ c. slivered almonds (opt.)

Combine cream cheese and milk, Add remaining ingredients, except almonds. Place in 2-quart greased casserole. Top with slivered almonds. Bake at 375 degrees for 15 minutes. Serve with rounds of Melba toast. May be kept warm in chafing dish.

Patricia Lee Rock, Pres.
Beta Psi XP1795
Fredericktown, Missouri

He that is of a merry heart hath a continual feast. Mary Kotter

Cucumber Dip

2 cucumbers sliced
1 med. onion, sliced
½ c. vinegar
¼ to ½ c. sugar
4 oz. cream cheese, softened
2 pt. sour cream
Salt and pepper to taste

Soak cucumbers and onion overnight in vinegar and enough water to cover. Drain well and chop fine. Drain well again. Blend cream cheese with sour cream. Add cucumbers and onions; mix well. Chill for several hours. Serve with assorted chips and crackers.

Ann M. Seabury, Rec. Sec.
Xi Theta X4006
Hudson, New Hampshire

Daffodil Dip

½ c. mayonnaise
1 8-oz. package cream cheese, softened
½ c. parsley, chopped
1 hard-cooked egg, chopped fine

2 tbsp. chopped onion
1 clove of garlic, minced
Dash of salt and pepper

Combine all ingredients. Mix until well blended. Serve with assorted fresh vegetables.

Sheryl C. Bates, Pres.
Kappa Psi No. 9317
Mt. Vernon, Indiana

Guacamole

1 lg. ripe avocado
4 tsp. lemon juice
½ c. finely chopped tomato
¾ tsp. salt
¾ tsp. finely chopped onion
Dash of minced garlic
Dash of cayenne pepper

Cut avocado in half lengthwise, remove seed. Peel and dice into bowl with lemon juice to prevent discoloration. Mash until smooth. Add remaining ingredients. Chill. Serve as a dip for celery hearts. Yield: 1 cup.

Photograph for this recipe on page 37.

Lord, watch over me and thee while we are absent one from another.   Gayle E. Swanson

Dillweed Vegetable Dip

1 c. sour cream
1 c. mayonnaise
1 tbsp. dried onions or 4½ tbsp. minced onions
1 to 2½ tbsp. parsley flakes
1 to 2½ tsp. dillweed
½ to 3 tsp. seasoned salt
½ tsp. monsodium glutomate (opt.)
2 dashes of garlic powder (opt.)

Combine all ingredients; mix well. Refrigerate at least 2 hours before serving. Serve with cauliflower, carrot sticks, celery sticks, radishes, cucumber slices and sweet green pepper strips. Also makes an excellent topping for baked potatoes.

Jean Timmons, Pres.
Preceptor Laureate Iota PL312
Columbus, Ohio

Betty's Guacamole Dip

4 med. avocados, mashed
½ c. diced, canned green chiles
¼ c. minced onion
1 tbsp. salt
¼ c. lemon juice
Diced tomatoes

Combine all ingredients in order listed, adding tomatoes last; cover. Chill for several hours. Keeps for days in refrigerator in airtight container. Serve with taco chips or crackers. Yield: 8 cups.

Betty Lash, Pres.
Delta Theta No. 8738
Tempe, Arizona

Mexican Cheese Dip

½ stick margarine
2¾ tbsp. flour
2 c. milk
1 whole pod jalapeno pepper, chopped
½ tsp. garlic powder
½ to 1 lb. Velveeta cheese
1 tsp. paprika
¼ tsp. dry mustard
1 tsp. chili powder
¾ tsp. camino powder
1 tbsp. catsup
1 tsp. hot pepper sauce

Melt margarine in saucepan. Stir in flour. Add milk gradually. Cook for 1 minute. Add remaining ingredients. Cook over low heat until cheese melts and flavors blend. Serve hot with tortilla chips.

Sharon D. Sullivan
Psi No. 2194
Little Rock, Arkansas

Pineapple-Cheese Dip

1 8-oz. carton whipped cream cheese
2 8-oz. cups shredded Cheddar cheese
¼ c. milk
3 tbsp. Port wine
1 tsp. Worcestershire sauce
½ tsp. salt
½ tsp. dry mustard
1 fresh pineapple

Combine cheeses, milk, wine, Worcestershire sauce, salt and dry mustard in bowl; beat well. Cut pineapple in half crosswise. Scoop pulp from bottom half of pineapple to make shell. Cut pulp into cubes. Fill shell with cheese mixture. Refrigerate. Cut crown off top half of pineapple. Cut off rind, cut into quarters. Cut away core; cut pulp into chunks. Refrigerate. Let cheese-stuffed pineapple stand at room temperature for 15 minutes to soften before serving. Place on serving plate; surround with pineapple chunks. Spear pineapple chunks with cocktail picks; dip into cheese mixture. Yield: 2½ cups cheese mixture.

Photograph for this recipe on page 18.

Onion-Cheese Dip

1 3-oz. package cream cheese, softened
3 tbsp. sour cream
1½ tsp. finely chopped onion
Dash of finely chopped garlic
⅛ tsp. salt
Dash of ground white pepper
Fresh parsley

Combine first 6 ingredients; mix until smooth. Sprinkle with parsley. Serve as dip for celery sticks. Yield: ⅔ cup.

Photograph for this recipe on page 37.

Onion-Cottage Cheese Dip

½ c. creamy cottage cheese
½ c. sour cream
2 tbsp. finely chopped onion
Dash of finely chopped garlic
1 tbsp. chopped parsley
⅛ tsp. salt

Combine all ingredients; mix well. Serve in bowl surrounded by celery hearts. Yield: 1 cup.

Photograph for this recipe on page 37.

Shrimp Dip

1 sm. can shrimp
1 3-oz. bottle of chili sauce

Love is not yours until you share it or give it away.   Ina Constance Best

1 8-oz. package cream cheese, softened
½ sm. onion, grated
¼ tsp. Worcestershire sauce
¼ c. mayonnaise
Lemon juice to taste
Salt, pepper and paprika to taste

Blend half the shrimp with chili sauce in blender or mixer to form a paste; set aside. Blend softened cream cheese and remaining ingredients, except remaining shrimp. Add paste-like mixture; blend. Chop remaining shrimp into small pieces. Fold into entire mixture. Refrigerate in small bowl until set. Serve with assorted crackers.

Lois L. Gardiner, Pres.
Xi Gamma Eta No. 3247
Bothell, Washington

Spinach Dip

1 10-oz. package frozen spinach, thawed
½ bunch green onions, chopped
1 tsp. garlic salt
½ tsp. lemon juice
½ tsp. Worcestershire sauce
2 c. mayonnaise
Salt to taste

Squeeze moisture from spinach; shape into a small ball. Combine with remaining ingredients. Mix well. Serve with assorted chips and crackers. So simple and delicious they never know it's spinach! Yield: 3 cups.

Helen Axline
Iota Beta No. 8228
Medicine Lodge, Kansas

Curried Tuna Dip

¼ c. butter or margarine
2 tbsp. chopped onion
1 tsp. curry powder
½ c. sour cream
1 7-oz. can flaked tuna, drained

Melt butter in saucepan. Stir in onion and curry powder. Cook until onion is tender. Stir in sour cream and tuna. Serve hot in chafing dish with favorite snack crackers. Yield: 1½ cups.

Carolyn Sue Michlik, Pres.
Xi Delta Beta X2871
State College, Pennsylvania

Tabouli

1 1-lb. package cracked wheat
8 oz. salad oil
8 oz. lemon juice
1 lg. onion, chopped
1 green pepper, chopped

½ bunch parsley, chopped
1 cucumber, chopped
1½ lbs. fresh tomatoes, chopped
Salt and pepper to taste
Tabasco sauce to taste (opt.)
Garlic powder to taste (opt.)

Rinse wheat several times in cool water. Combine salad oil, lemon juice and wheat. Let set in refrigerator overnight. Add remaining ingredients, seasoning to taste. Let stand for several hours to improve in flavor. Serve with chips and crackers.

Florence Brady, Prog. Chm.
Preceptor Epsilon XP330
Spearfish, South Dakota

Chicken-Corn Chowder

5 slices bacon
¾ c. diced celery
¾ c. chopped onions
2 cans cream of chicken soup
1 17-oz. can cream-style corn
1 8¾-oz. can kernel corn
1 c. diced cooked potato (opt.)
3 c. milk
1 sm. can mushrooms and liquid
½ tsp. basil
1 tsp. salt
Dash of pepper

Fry bacon until crisp; drain and crumble. Saute celery and onions in a portion of bacon fat until tender, not brown. Add remaining ingredients. Heat, stirring occasionally, until chowder is hot, but not boiling. Serve with oyster crackers. Yield: 6-8 servings.

Jeanette Johnson, Pres.
Preceptor Iota XP1110
Wausau, Wisconsin

Clam Chowder

1½ c. chopped clams
¼ c. chopped onions
¼ lb. butter
1½ c. diced potatoes
1 pt. cream
1 tsp. salt
1 tsp. pepper
½ tsp. sugar

Drain clams, reserving liquid. Saute onions and clams in small amount of butter on low heat for 1 or 2 minutes. Add potatoes, clam liquid and enough water to cover. Bring to a boil. Cook potatoes until just tender. Add cream, remaining butter, salt, pepper and sugar. Reheat slowly until hot. Thicken with flour and water mixture, if desired. Yield: 4 servings.

Charlene Swan, Pres.
Xi Mu Mu X2947
Cypress, California

Nothing great was ever achieved without enthusiasm. Judith Neher

Carolyn's French Onion Soup

4 onions, thinly sliced
Butter
2 tbsp. flour
Salt to taste
Freshly ground pepper to taste
1 clove of garlic
1 tsp. sugar
Parsley and thyme to taste
1 qt. chicken stock or consomme
1 c. dry wine
1 tbsp. Cognac
French bread slices
Parmesan cheese or Cheddar cheese, freshly grated

Saute onions in 3 tablespoons butter until tender. Add flour, salt, freshly ground pepper, garlic and sugar. Cook over medium heat until mixture is golden brown. Add small amount of parsley and thyme, chicken stock and wine. Simmer for 45 minutes. Add Cognac. Toast French bread; butter each slice. Place in overproof onion soup bowls. Sprinkle generously with Parmesan cheese. Pour soup in bowls. Add additional grated cheese. Place under broiler until cheese is melted and soup bubbles. Serve with dry red wine. Bon Appetit! Yield: 6 servings.

Carolyn Laskey, W. and M. Chm.
Delta Pi No. 6005
Burlington, Ontario, Canada

Pickled Pineapple Chunks

2 c. pineapple chunks
1¼ c. sugar
6 or 8 whole cloves
¾ c. vinegar
Dash of salt
14 pieces stick cinnamon

Drain pineapple, reserving juice. Heat juice in saucepan. Combine with remaining ingredients except pineapple chunks. Cook for 10 minutes. Add pineapple chunks. Bring to a boil. Refrigerate for at least 2 days.

Donna Darnold, Pres.
Delta Omicron No. 4347
Derby, Kansas

Bread and Butter Pickles

16 c. thinly sliced cucumbers
½ c. coarse salt
8 c. sliced onions
5 c. sugar
4 c. white vinegar
1 tbsp. celery seed
2 tbsp. mustard seed

1½ tsp. turmeric
½ tsp. white pepper

Combine cucumbers, salt and onions in a crock. Cover with ice. Let stand 2 or 3 hours until crisp. Bring remaining ingredients to a boil. Continue boiling for 10 minutes. Drain cucumbers and onions. Add to boiling liquid. Bring to boiling point. Pack at once in sterilized jars. Seal immediately. Store in a cool place for at least 1 month before using.

Pauline Campbell
Zeta Rho No. 8069
Niagara Falls, Ontario, Canada

Border Buttermilk

1 sm. can frozen pink lemonade
Tequila

Place pink lemonade with 1 lemonade can Tequila in standard blender. Fill blender container with ice; blend until creamy. Pour into 4 ounce serving glasses. The treat of your life from down on the Mexican border. Yield: 5 servings.

Jane Pratt, Pres.
Xi Omicron Lambda
Del Rio, Texas

Fruit Punch

1 12-oz. can frozen pink lemonade
1 12-oz. can frozen Hawaiian punch
1 6-oz. can frozen orange juice
1 46-oz. can pineapple juice
1 bottle of ginger ale,
Lemon or orange sherbet.

Combine all ingredients; mix well. Chill well. Ladle into punch cups. Garnish with scoop of sherbet. Serve immediately. Yield: 20-30 servings.

Patti Abell, Rec. Sec.
Gamma Theta No. 6679
Lunenburg, Massachusetts

Mock Pink Champagne

½ c. sugar
1 6-oz. can frozen orange juice
1 6-oz. can frozen grapefruit juice
28 oz. chilled ginger ale
⅓ c. grenadine

Combine sugar and 1 cup water in saucepan. Boil for 5 minutes; cool. Add frozen juices. Refrigerate. Add ginger ale and grenadine at serving time; stir lightly. Serve in wine or Champagne glasses.

Linda Boyle
Beta Theta No. 7510
Columbia, Maryland

Ability is a great thing, but its value is greatly enhanced by dependability. Carolyn Zoza

Hot Buttered Rum

1 lb. butter, softened
1 qt. French vanilla ice cream
1 lb. confectioners' sugar
1 lb. (packed) brown sugar
2 tsp. cinnamon
2 tsp. nutmeg
Rum to taste

Add butter to soft ice cream, sugars and spices; mix thoroughly. Place in freezer container with tight lid. Freeze until serving time. Scoop into serving cups to serve. Add rum to taste and enough hot water to fill cup. Yield:12 servings.

Frances P. Wills
Xi Alpha Omega X2649
Arlington, Virginia

Hot Cinnamon Mocha

½ c. semisweet chocolate chips
½ c. strong coffee
1 tsp. cinnamon
Dash of salt
3 c. milk
1 tbsp. sugar
¼ tsp. vanilla extract
Whipped cream

Place chocolate chips, coffee, cinnamon and salt in a saucepan. Heat and stir with wooden spoon over medium-low heat until chocolate is melted and mixture is smooth. Stir in milk; heat thoroughly. Stir in sugar and vanilla. Beat with rotary beater until foamy. Pour into mugs. Add dollop of whipped cream to each mug. Yield: 4 servings.

Donna Aven
Lambda Eta No. 9109
Pittsburgh, Pennsylvania

Hot Cranberry Punch

2 c. pineapple juice
2 c. cranberry juice
½ c. sugar
½ tsp. ground cloves
Pinch of salt
2-inch cinnamon sticks or pinch of ground cinnamon

Combine 1¾ cups water with all ingredients except sticks of cinnamon. Place in a percolator without the basket. Heat for 10 minutes. Pour into serving cups. Add 1 cinnamon stick to each cup. Yield: 10 servings.

Lois P. Johnson, Pres.
Xi Beta Omega X4643
Lawrenceburg, Tennessee

Bourbon Slush

2 tea bags
¼ to ½ c. sugar
1 6-oz. can frozen orange juice
1 6-oz. can frozen lemonade
½ to 1 cup. Bourbon

Boil 1 cup water. Add tea bags; steep for a few minutes. Combine 3½ cups water with remaining ingredients; mix well. Freeze. Remove from freezer a short while before serving for mixture to become slushy. Serve immediately.

Nancy House, Yearbook Com.
Preceptor Alpha Tau XP765
Austin, Texas

Champagne Punch

½ gal. Sauterne, chilled
8 oz. Brandy, chilled
1 qt. 7-Up, chilled
2 fifths Champagne, chilled

Pour first 3 ingredients over ice into 2-gallon punch bowl. Add chilled Champagne just before serving. Yield: 34 servings.

Norma Geirk, Hist.
Preceptor Theta Delta XP1720
Vista, California

Candlelight Punch

1 46-oz. can apricot nectar
12 7-oz. bottles of 7-Up
2 6-oz. cans frozen orange juice concentrate, thawed
2 12-oz. packages frozen peaches
1 pt. vanilla ice cream

Combine all ingredients; mix well. Chill thoroughly. Serve chilled from punch bowl. Yield: 35 servings.

Connie Mueller
Xi Nu Tau No. 3155
San Jose, California

Citrus Starter

2 c. sugar
2 1-lb. cans grapefruit and/or oranges
Juice of 1 lemon

Boil sugar and 4 cups water for 10 minutes in a saucepan. Cool. Add fruit and lemon juice. Pour into loaf pan. Freeze. Remove from freezer at least 20 minutes before serving. Ladle into serving cups. Yield: 12 servings.

Theo Clark, Pres.
Alpha Alpha No 7253
Rockford, Illinois

Remember—the members of your family are mirrors reflecting the quality of your life in your home. Barbara Lapp

Salads

Salads are the menu planner's best friend! Full of nutrition, eye-appeal, color and flavor, salads can be prepared to blend in almost anytime with almost any food, and to suit virtually every taste. Moreover, they can appear on the table before, along with, or following the main entree. Then, frozen and fresh fruit salads can be a refreshing dessert!

The tossed green salad is probably the classic salad. Often tastiest at its simplest, this salad incorporates only hand-torn pieces of crisp greens tossed lightly with an oil and vinegar dressing in a garlic-rubbed bowl. But, most salad-makers don't consider the salad "worth its salt" until an array of other ingredients also find their way into the bowl—herb-flavored croutons, hearts of palm, fresh mushroom slices, chopped nuts, olives, artichoke hearts, cherry tomatoes—all pretty as a picture! But the key is freshness!

Gelatin salads are favorites for brunches, luncheons and dinners. To a plain lemon or fruit-flavored base can be added almost any fruit, or vegetable, or both, for a dramatic and delicious dish. Learn to "engrave" aspics for an impressive decorative salad. Popular stand-bys such as chicken, seafood and potato salads blossom delightfully with unique additions—curried mayonnaise, chives, ripe olives, capers, anchovies, sour cream, and even raisins, pineapple, cherries or shredded coconut.

Fruit salads are menu makers for breakfast, brunch, lunch or dinner because they are easy and always appetizing. They never fail to complement the flavors of so many favorite meats, seafood, poultry, and vegetable dishes.

Just think! There is a salad combination for every menu, every taste! Let the following collection of Beta Sigma Phi salad recipes prove it to you in your Dining Room, again and again!

Champagne Fruit Cocktail

4 med. bananas, sliced
4 med. apples, peeled and diced
4 med. oranges, sectioned
½ bottle of maraschino cherries, halved
1 16-oz. can pears, sliced
1 16-oz. can peaches, sliced
1 16-oz. can fruit cocktail
2 26-oz. bottles of pink Champagne, chilled
2 c. chilled orange juice

Mix fresh fruits together in large fruit or punch bowl. Add cherries and canned fruit. Chill thoroughly. Add champagne and orange juice to fruit; mix well. Chill. Serve individual portions of the fruit cocktail mixture in a champagne glass and enjoy. This will add a sparkling opening act to any brunch gathering. Yield: 12-15 servings.

Nancy Prout, Leity Coun. Rep.
Zeta Theta No. 7760
Oshawa, Ontario, Canada

Citrus Cup with Lime Dressing

5 med. oranges, peeled and sliced
3 white grapefruit, peeled and sliced
1 lg. can pineapple chunks in own juice
1 c. sugar
Juice of 2 limes
1 tsp. grated lime rind

Combine fruit slices with pineapple chunks. Chill. Combine sugar and ¼ cup water. Bring to a boil. Remove from heat. Stir in juice and rind. Chill. Serve fruit in a cup with 2 tablespoons Lime Dressing on top. Yield: 6-8 servings.

Linda Ling, Prog. Chm.
Xi Beta Chi X4349
Memphis, Tennessee

Frog Eye Salad

1 c. sugar
3 tbsp. flour
2½ tsp. salt
1 ¾ c. pineapple juice
2 eggs, beaten
1 tbsp. lemon juice
1 tbsp. cooking oil
1 16-oz. package Acini de Pepe macaroni
3 sm. cans mandarin oranges
2 c. crushed pineapple
1 lg. carton Cool Whip
1 c. miniature marshmallows
1 c. shredded coconut

Combine sugar, flour and salt in small saucepan. Stir in pineapple juice and eggs. Cook over medium heat

until thickened. Add lemon juice; mix well. Cool. Bring 3 quarts water to a boil. Add oil and Acini de Pepe. Cook until done. Drain and rinse. Add to sauce mixture in 3-quart. dish; cover. Refrigerate overnight. Add remaining ingredients; mix well. Refrigerate in airtight container. Keeps in refrigerator 2 weeks or may be frozen. Yield: 15-20 servings.

Roberta Hradecky, City Coun. Sec.
Xi Alpha Zeta X1074
Sterling, Colorado

Orange and Onion Salad

½ tsp. dry mustard
¼ c. wine vinegar
½ c. salad oil
½ tsp. salt
½ tsp. pepper
½ tsp. sugar
1 c. Spanish onion
4 oranges, peeled and sliced

Mix mustard and vinegar in medium bowl. Beat in oil; add salt, pepper and sugar. Peel and chop onions, reserving a few inside rings for garnish. Add onion to bowl; chill for 1 hour. Arrange orange slices on plate. Top with chopped onion dressing. Garnish with reserved onion rings. Yield: 4 servings.

Photograph for this recipe on page 44.

A dilligent cook makes a happy man. Mrs. E. W. Booth

Pistachio Salad

1 20-oz. can crushed pineapple in own juice
1 c. miniature marshmallows
½ c. chopped nuts
½ c. maraschino cherries
1 9-oz. carton Cool Whip
1 3¾-oz. package instant pistachio pudding mix

Place all ingredients in a 3-quart bowl in order listed; mix well. Chill overnight. Yield: 20 servings.

Ima M. Green, Treas.
Xi Delta Omicron X4905
Wynnewood, Oklahoma

Frozen Cranberry Salad

12 oz. cream cheese, softened
4 tbsp. mayonnaise
4 tbsp. sugar
1 can cranberry sauce
1 can whole cranberry sauce
2 15-oz. cans crushed pineapple
1½ c. chopped pecans
2 c. whipped cream or Cool Whip

Blend cream cheese, mayonnaise and sugar until smooth. Add fruit and pecans. Fold in whipped cream. Pour into mold. Freeze overnight. Let stand at room temperature for 15 minutes to serve. Cut into squares. Yield: 30 servings.

Frankie Wooster, Pres.
Xi Delta Zeta X1500
Wichita Falls, Texas

Catherine's Frozen Salad

2 c. Cool Whip
1 8-oz. package cream cheese
Pinch of salt
¾ c. salad dressing
1 lg. can apricots, drained
1 lg. can pineapple chunks, drained
1 c. strawberries
1 c. blueberries
½ c. raspberries

Combine Cool Whip, cream cheese, salt and salad dressing, beating until smooth. Fold fruit into dressing mixture. Pour into fruit cans. Freeze at least 4 hours. Remove from cans; slice. Yield: 10-12 servings.

Catherine Goff, Pres.
Beta Nu XP1399
Chester, Illinois

Jewel's Fruit Salad

2 1-lb. 4-oz. cans crushed pineapple
1 1-lb. can sliced peaches
1 c. white seedless grapes, halved
¼ lb. marshmallows, quartered
1 tsp. crystallized ginger, finely chopped
½ env. unflavored gelatin
½ c. orange juice
2 tbsp. lemon juice
1¼ c. sugar
¼ tsp. salt
1 c. chopped pecans
1 pt. heavy cream, whipped
1½ c. mayonnaise
3 pkg. dessert topping mix
1½ c. maraschino cherries or strawberries

Drain fruit, reserving 1½ cups pineapple juice. Cut peaches in ½-inch cubes. Combine fruit, marshmallows and ginger. Soften gelatin in ⅛ cup cold water. Bring pineapple juice to a boil. Add gelatin; stir to dissolve. Add orange and lemon juice, sugar and salt; stir to dissolve. Chill until partially set. Add fruit mixture and pecans. Fold in whipped cream and mayonnaise. Spoon into 1-quart cylindar cartons or cupcake paper cups. Cover; freeze. Remove from freezer; thaw enough to slip out of carton. Cut into 1 inch slices. Prepare dessert topping mix according to package directions. Spread over salad. Yield: 36 servings.

Jewel Hancock, Pres.
Xi Beta Omega X2284
Muncie, Indiana

Apricot Salad

1 20-oz. can apricot halves
1 sm. can crushed pineapple
1 6-oz. package apricot Jello-O
½ c. sugar
3 tbsp. flour
1 egg, well beaten
2 tbsp. butter
1 sm. carton Cool Whip
Grated cheese to taste

Drain apricot halves and pineapple, reserving juice. Prepare Jell-O according to package directions. Add apricot halves and pineapple. Chill until set. Combine sugar and flour. Blend in egg. Stir in 1 cup reserved juice. Cook until thick. Remove from heat. Add butter; mix well. Cool to room temperature. Fold in Cool Chip. Spread topping over Jell-O. Sprinkle with grated cheese. Chill. Yield: 10-12 servings.

Jeanne Fradiska, Treas.
Xi Beta X551
La Vale, Maryland

Isn't it nice come what may—love is here to stay. Dorothy Williamson

Linda's Frozen Salad

Red food coloring
¾ lb. cream cheese, softened
¾ c. sugar
1 No. 2 can sliced peaches, drained
1 med. jar red cherries, halved
1 med. jar green cherries, halved
1 No. 2 can crushed pineapple
1 pt. Cool Whip

Add red food coloring to cream cheese. Add sugar and fruit to cream cheese; stir well. Fold in Cool Whip. Freeze. Cut into squares to serve. Yield: 12 servings.

Linda Sankpill
Pi Chi No. 4615
Harlingen, Texas

Creamy Cranberry Salad

1 lg. package raspberry Jell-O
1 can cranberry sauce or whole cranberries
Chopped English walnuts
½ c. Burgundy
1 sm. can crushed pineapple, drained
1 8-oz. package cream cheese
2 tsp. sugar
1 lg. carton Cool Whip

Mix Jell-O and cranberry sauce in 2 cups boiling water. Add ⅓ cup walnuts, Burgundy and pineapple; stir to mix. Pour into 8 x 8-inch pan. Chill until set. Mix cream cheese and sugar. Fold into Cool Whip. Spread over Jell-O mixture. Sprinkle with ½ cup walnuts. This salad should be made the day before to blend flavors. Yield: 12 servings.

Marjorie J. Strohl, Pres.
Xi Theta Gamma X3670
Shelbyville, Illinois

Grandma's Cranberry Salad

1 qt. raw cranberries
Rind of 1 orange
2 c. sugar
2 3-oz. packages red gelatin
1 c. chopped celery
2 apples, chopped fine
2 oranges, cut fine
½ c. chopped nuts

Grind cranberries and orange rind together. Add sugar. Let stand for 2 hours. Dissolve gelatin in 2 cups hot water. Add cranberries, celery, apples, oranges and nuts to gelatin. Stir well. Pour into 1 large or 2 medium-sized bowls. Chill until set. Yield: 20-24 servings.

Caryl Barnaby, Pres.
Kappa Alpha No. 9360
Humboldt, Kansas

Nancy's Cranberry Salad

1 8-oz. can crushed pineapple
1 3-oz. package raspberry Jell-O
1 16-oz. can whole cranberry sauce
1 tsp. grated orange peel
1 11-oz. can mandarin oranges, drained
1 c. whipping cream, whipped

Drain pineapple, reserving juice; add enough water to measure 1 cup. Dissolve Jell-O in heated juice mixture. Add cranberry sauce and grated orange peel; mix well. Chill until partially set. Add pineapple and oranges. Fold in whipped cream. Chill until set. Yield: 8-10 servings.

Nancy Allen, V. P.
Xi Beta Psi No. 2856
Colfax, Washington

Grapefruit and Cucumber Mold

2 env. unflavored gelatin
3 tbsp. sugar
3 tbsp. tarragon vinegar
¾ tsp. salt
2¼ c. grapefruit juice
3 c. grapefruit sections
1 c. diced pared cucumber
2 tbsp. minced onion
3 tbsp. chopped parsley

Sprinkle gelatin over ½ cup water in saucepan. Stir over low heat until dissolved, about 3 minutes. Add sugar, vinegar, salt and grapefruit juice. Chill, stirring occasionally, until consistency of unbeaten egg white. Fold in grapefruit sections, cucumbers, onion and parsley. Pour into 6-cup mold. Chill until set. Unmold and garnish with salad greens. Yield: 6-8 servings.

Photograph for this recipe on page 44.

Mandarin Sherbet Salad

1 11-oz. can mandarin oranges
2 sm. packages orange Jell-O
1 pt. orange sherbet
1 pkg. Dream Whip

Drain oranges, reserving juice. Add enough water to reserved juice to measure 1 cup. Pour into saucepan. Bring to a boil. Add to Jell-O in mixing bowl; stir until dissolved. Add sherbet; mix well. Chill until mixture begins to thicken. Prepare Dream Whip according to package directions. Fold into sherbet. Add oranges. Chill for 2 hours before serving. Yield: 6 servings.

Theresa Wollin
Nu Omega No. 6859
St Peter, Illinois

A friend may well be reckoned the masterpiece of nature. Cyndy Scantlan

Lemon-Fruit Salad

1 sm. can crushed pineapple
1 sm. package lemon Jell-O
2 med. bananas, sliced
½ c. miniature marshmallows
½ c. chopped walnuts (opt.)
½ c. sugar
2 tbsp. cornstarch
1 egg, well beaten
2 tbsp. butter or margarine
1 c. whipping cream, whipped
2 c. grated mild cheddar cheese

Drain pineapple, reserving juice. Prepare Jell-O according to package directions. Chill until partially set. Add pineapple, bananas, marshmallows and walnuts; stir well. Pour into 8 or 9-inch square pan. Chill until set. Add enough water to reserved pineapple juice to measure 1 cup. Pour into heavy saucepan. Add sugar, cornstarch, egg and butter. Cook over medium-high heat. Cook until thick. Cool completely. Add whipped cream. Pour mixture over Jell-O. Sprinkle enough cheese on top to cover. Yield: 6-8 servings.

Sue Musser, Sec.
Tau No. 2802
Caldwell, Idaho

Molded Waldorf Salad

1 3-oz. package lemon gelatin
½ c. mayonnaise
2 c. unpeeled diced apples
1 c. diced celery
½ c. chopped walnuts
½ c. whipping cream, whipped

Dissolve gelatin in 1 cup boiling water in mixing bowl. Chill until partially set. Blend gelatin and mayonnaise until smooth with electric mixer. Fold in apples, celery and walnuts. Fold in whipped cream. Pour into 1½-quart mold. Chill until firm. Yield: 8 servings.

Jackie Powers
Preceptor Laureate Alpha PL111
Oakland, Oregon

Seven-Up Salad

1 No. 2 can crushed pineapple
1 3-oz. packages lemon Jell-O
1 12-oz. bottle of cold 7-Up
3 med. bananas, sliced
1½ c. miniature marshmallows
1 tbsp. cornstarch
1 8-oz. package cream cheese, softened
1 pkg. prepared topping mix
4 to 6 oz. Cheddar cheese

Drain pineapple reserving juice. Mix Jell-O and 2 cups hot water. Let cool. Add 7-Up. Let the mixture begin to thicken. Fold pineapple, bananas and marshmallows into Jell-O. Pour into a 9 x 13-inch dish. Chill until set. Add enough water to reserved pineapple juice to make 1 cup. Combine pineapple juice with cornstarch; cool until thick. Add cream cheese; stir until smooth. Prepared the topping mix according to package directions. Add to cream cheese mixture. Spread over Jell-O. Grate cheese over top of salad. Yield: 15-18 servings.

Betty J. Wilson
Sigma Sigma No. 10789
Holts Summit, Missouri

Sweetheart Salad

1 sm. can crushed pineapple
2 pkg. lemon Jell-O
1 3-oz. package cream cheese, at room temperature
1 c. chopped celery
½ c. chopped pecans
½ can pimentos, chopped fine
1 pt. whipping cream, whipped and sweetened

Drain pineapple reserving juice. Dissolve Jell-O in 1 cup boiling water. Allow to cool. Mix cream cheese and reserved pineapple juice in separate bowl. Add celery, pecans, pimentos and pineapple to cream cheese mixture. Fold into Jell-O. Fold in whipped cream. Pour into chilled mold. Chill until set. Yield: 10-12 servings.

Roberta L. Ramsay, Pres.
Xi Epsilon Beta X3722
Tyrone, Pennsylvania

Yummy Holiday Salad

1 14-oz. can crushed pineapple
1 sm. package Hawaiian-flavored Jell-O
2 c. miniature marshmallows
1 8-oz. package cream cheese, softened
1 c. cashews

Drain pineapple, reserving juice. Add enough water to prepare Jell-O according to package directions with juice mixture as cold liquid. Allow to partially set. Combine marshmallows and cream cheese in glass bowl. Microwave on Low for 3 to 4 minutes. Add pineapple; mix well. Combine 2 mixtures in blender container; blend until smooth. Stir in cashews. Pour into 4-cup mold. Refrigerate until set. Yield: 4 servings.

Heather Miyauchi
Xi Alpha Alpha X5146
Brooks, Alberta, Canada

A rumor is like a check—never endorse it until you know it is genuine. Linda Boyle

Special Fruit Salad Dressing

2 eggs
⅓ c. sugar
2 tsp. lemon juice
3 tbsp. orange juice
3 tbsp. pineapple juice
1 8-oz. package cream cheese, softened
Fresh fruit

Beat together eggs, sugar, lemon juice, orange juice and pineapple juice. Cook in double boiler until thick. Add juice mixture slowly to cream cheese; mix thoroughly. Toss with any combination of fresh fruit. Yield: 8 servings.

Myra Loring, Hon Mem.
Preceptor Mu.
Grenlock, New Jersey

Marion's Salad Dressing

½ lb. butter
1 c. sugar
⅛ tsp. cayenne pepper
1 tbsp. mustard
1 tbsp. tumeric
1 tsp. celery seed
1 tbsp. flour
4 eggs, beaten
1 c. vinegar

Mix first 7 ingredients well. Combine eggs and ½ cup water in small bowl. Add to first mixture. Cook slowly until thickened. Add vinegar. Pour over any combination of fruit or vegetables. Yield: 1 cup.

Marion M. Graham, Hon Int. Mem.
Saskatoon City Coun.
Saskatoon, Saskatchewan, Canada

Bean Salad

1 16-oz. can green beans, drained
1 16-oz. can wax beans, drained
1 16-oz. can kidney beans, drained
½ c. diced celery
½ c. diced green pepper
⅓ c. chopped onion
½ c. sugar
½ c. cider vinegar
1 tbsp. salad oil
1 tsp. salt
1 tsp. white pepper

Combine all ingredients; toss lightly. Refrigerate, tightly covered, for 12 hours. Drain excess liquid before serving. Yield: 12 servings.

Wanda Arnold, Coun. Rep.
Xi Alpha Delta X2460
Knoxville, Tennessee

Cauliflower-Broccoli Salad

1 sm. cauliflower
1 sm. broccoli
1 pkg. frozen peas, thawed
½ c. sour cream
½ c. mayonnaise or salad dressing
1 tbsp. horseradish
1 sm. onion chopped

Break cauliflower and broccoli into flowerets; combine with remaining ingredients. Refrigerate overnight. Yield: 8-10 servings.

Patricia Till, Treas.
Xi Alpha Chi X3827
Slidell, Louisiana

Cauliflower Salad Bowl

4 c. thinly sliced cauliflower
1 c. coarsly chopped olives
⅔ c. coarsely chopped green pepper
½ c. chopped onion
½ c. salad oil
3 tbsp. lemon juice
3 tbsp. vinegar
2 tsp. salt
½ tsp. sugar
¼ tsp. pepper

Combine vegetables in salad bowl. Combine remaining ingredients; blend with rotary beater. Pour dressing over vegetables. Refrigerate, covered, overnight. Yield: 8 servings

Judy Ott, Corr. Sec.
Theta Nu No. 7744
Fort Atkinson, Iowa

Chinese Salad

1 16-oz. can LaChoy mixed Chinese vegetables
1 8-oz. can sliced water chestnuts
1 16-oz. can mixed vegetables
1 sm. jar chopped pimento
1 c. chopped celery
1 c. chopped green onions
1 c. sugar
¾ c. white vinegar
½ c. Wesson oil.

Drain canned vegetables. Add celery and onions. Combine sugar, vinegar and oil in saucepan. Heat until sugar dissolves; cool. Pour over salad ingredients. Refrigerate overnight. Yield: 4-6 servings.

Carmelene Sandidge
Alpha Mu Chi No. 9478
Madisonville, Texas

Your life on earth is a mortgage from God—you are expected to pay off your loan before you are repossessed. Sheri Colwell

Fresh Mushroom Salad

1 lb. large mushrooms, thinly sliced
6 tbsp. lemon juice
1 tbsp. snipped chivps
1 tbsp. chopped parsley
1 tsp. dried tarragon leaves
½ c. Italian dressing
¼ c. finely chopped pimento
3 stalks celery, sliced diagonally
½ tsp. salt
⅛ tsp. pepper
1½ tsp. sugar
2 tsp. prepared mustard
Watercress

Place mushrooms in large bowl. Sprinkle with lemon juice, chives, parsley and tarragon; stir gently. Refrigerate, covered, 1 hour. Combine Italian dressing, pimento, celery, salt, pepper, sugar and mustard; stir to mix well. Refrigerate, covered, for 1 hour. Pour dressing mixture over mushrooms; toss. Arrange on bed of watercress.

Linda Darlene Zittle
Alpha Theta No. 722
Harlingen, Texas

Hot Vegetable Salad With Herbed Walnuts

1 tbsp. butter
1 c. walnut halves and pieces
¼ tsp. dried dill, rosemary or oregano
2 c. hot cooked carrots
2 c. hot cooked wax or green beans
2 c. hot cooked cauliflowerets
Small crisp lettuce leaves
1 tsp. seasoned salt
1 bottle French or Italian dressing, heated

Melt butter in skillet. Add walnuts; sprinkle with dried dill. Cook over moderate heat, stirring, for 5 minutes or until walnuts are lightly toasted. Arrange hot cooked vegetables and walnuts on lettuce on serving platter. Sprinkle with seasoned salt. Serve with heated salad dressing.

Photograph for this recipe on page 49.

Pea and Peanut Salad

2 sm. packages frozen peas, thawed
½ c. sour cream
½ c. Hellmann's mayonnaise
¾ tbsp. curry powder
1 c. Spanish peanuts
½ tbsp. Lawry's salt
Chopped onion to taste

Combine all ingredients; mix well.

Christine Mitchell, Sec.
Exemplar Preceptor Alpha Tau XP1756
Bloomington, Indiana

Be lazy—do it right the first time. Cynthia Hanselman

Hot German Potato Salad

6 med. potatoes
6 slices bacon
½ c. chopped onion
2 tbsp. flour
3 tsp. sugar
1 ½ tsp. salt
½ tsp. celery seed
Dash of pepper
½ c. vinegar

Boil potatoes; cool and dice. Fry bacon; crumble. Combine onion, flour, sugar, salt, celery seed and pepper in saucepan. Cook over low heat until smooth and bubbly, stirring, constantly. Remove from heat; stir in vinegar and ½ cup water. Bring to a boil, stirring constantly. Stir in potatoes and bacon. Yield: 6-8 servings.

Bonnie J. Riddle, Corr. Sec.
Xi Gamma Lambda
Burlington, Iowa

Marge's Hot German Potato Salad

12 slices bacon
6 lg. potatoes
3 med. onions, chopped
1 c. plus 2 tbsp. white vinegar
2½ tbsp. sugar
1½ tsp. salt
¼ tsp. pepper
¾ tsp. Accent
2 tbsp. dried parsley flakes
½ tsp. celery seed

Fry bacon; cool and dice. Boil potatoes in jackets; cool and slice. Pour 6 tablespoons bacon drippings in skillet. Add onions; saute until tender. Stir in vinegar, sugar, salt, pepper, Accent, parsley flakes and celery seed. Bring to a boil; add bacon. Pour mixture over potatoes; toss lightly. Serve hot. Yield: 6 servings.

Marge Jensen, Pres
Xi Delta Tau X1475
Antioch, California

Mardi Gras Potato Salad

⅓ c. creamy French dressing
⅓ c. mayonnaise
3 c. diced cooked potatoes
4 hard-cooked eggs, chopped
3 c. cottage cheese
⅓ c. diced pimento
⅓ c. diced green pepper
2 tbsp. minced onion
1½ tbsp. dried parsley
2 tsp. salt

Combine French dressing and mayonnaise. Add potatoes and eggs; let stand. Combine remaining ingredients, add to dressing mixture. Pack potato mixture tightly into 1½-quart lightly greased ring mold. Chill thoroughly. Yield: 8 servings.

Betty Mayer, Pres.
Beta Zeta No. 1308
Benton, Illinois

Sour Cream Potato Salad

5 med. potatoes
⅓ c. Italian dressing
1 c. celery, diced
4 eggs, hard-boiled and diced
1 lg. onion, chopped
1 c. mayonnaise
1½ tsp. prepared mustard
½ c. sour cream

Boil potatoes until tender; drain and dice. Add dressing; place in refrigerator for 2 hours. Add celery, eggs, onion, mayonnaise and mustard; mix well. Add sour cream; chill for 2 hours. Yield: 6-8 servings.

S. Kay Symons, City Coun. Pres.
Alpha Chi
Findlay, Ohio

Frances' Slaw

3 to 4 lb. cabbage
2 med. onions
1 to 2 green peppers
1 c. oil
1 c. vinegar
1 tsp. salt
Sugar
¾ tsp. celery seed

Chop cabbage, onions and green peppers separately in blender container. Place equal amounts of cabbage, onions and green peppers in blender container; cover with water. Blend well; drain. Repeat process. Place cabbage mixture in large bowl. Pour 2 cups sugar over cabbage mixture; let stand for 1 hour. Combine oil, vinegar, salt, 2 tablespoons sugar and celery seed in saucepan; bring to a boil. Cool 3 minutes. Pour over cabbage mixture. Refrigerate overnight. Yield: 20-25 servings.

Frances E. Osthoff, Pres.
Xi Iota Gamma X4572
Fort Lauderdale, Florida

Jo Ann's Coleslaw

1 head cabbage, shredded
½ green pepper, shredded

1 carrot, grated
½ onion, shredded
½ c. mayonnaise
1 tbsp. salt
1 tbsp. vinegar
2 tbsp. sugar
Juice of lemon

Combine cabbage, green pepper, carrot and onion in salad bowl. Combine remaining ingredients. Pour over vegetables; mix well. Yield: 8 servings.

JoAnn Breeding, Rec. Sec.
Xi Beta Gamma X2822
Duncan, Oklahoma

Peanut Crunch Slaw

4 c. shredded cabbage
1 c. finely diced celery
½ c. sour cream
½ c. mayonnaise
1 tsp. salt
¼ c. chopped green onion
¼ c. chopped green pepper
¼ c. chopped cucumber
1 tbsp. butter
½ c. salted peanuts, chopped
2 tbsp. Parmesan cheese

Toss cabbage and celery; chill. Combine sour cream, mayonnaise, salt, onion, green pepper and cucumber; chill. Melt butter in small skillet. Add peanuts; cook until lightly browned. Stir in cheese. Toss chilled vegetables with mayonnaise mixture. Sprinkle with peanuts. Yield: 8 servings.

Margaret E. Boatright, V.P.
Xi Gamma Lambda No. 4946
Savannah, Georgia

Fresh Spinach Salad

½ c. salad oil
2 tbsp. vinegar
1 sm. onion minced
¼ c. sugar
1 tsp. Worcestershire sauce
1 tsp. salt
2 tbsp. catsup
¼ lb. bacon, fried and crumbled
4 oz. bean sprouts
1 sm. can water chestnuts
2 hard-boiled eggs, sliced
1 lg. package fresh spinach, rinsed

Combine, oil, vinegar, onion, sugar, Worcestershire sauce, salt and catsup; stir. Set aside. Combine bacon, bean sprouts, water chestnuts and eggs. Toss with spinach in salad bowl. Add desired amount of dressing; toss lightly. Yield: 6 servings.

Betty Cookendorfer
Xi Eta Iota X3512
Harrison, Ohio

Naomi's Spinach Salad

8 slices bacon,
1 pkg. fresh spinach
1 can bean sprouts, drained
3 hard-boiled eggs, chopped
½ c. salad oil
¾ c. sugar
1 med. onion, minced
½ c. catsup
¼ c. vinegar
1 tbsp. Worcestershire sauce

Fry bacon; cool and crumble. Combine bacon, spinach, bean sprouts and eggs. Toss well. Combine remaining ingredients. Toss with salad. Yield: 8 servings.

Naomi Golden, Pres.
Beta Rho XP1604
Van Buren, Ohio

Oriental Spinach Salad

1 lb. fresh spinach
½ lb. bacon,
1 No. 2 can bean sprouts, drained
¼ lb. fresh mushrooms, sliced
3 hard-boiled eggs, grated
1 c. salad oil
⅔ c. sugar
⅓ c. catsup
1 tbsp. Worcestershire sauce
¼ c. wine vinegar
½ tsp. salt
1 med. onion, grated

Rinse, dry and chill spinach. Fry bacon until crisp; crumble. Sprinkle bean sprouts, mushrooms, eggs and bacon over spinach in large salad bowl. Place remaining ingredients in blender container; blend thoroughly until thick and creamy. Refrigerate several hours. Toss with salad just before serving. Dressing keeps well for several months if placed in tightly sealed jar in refrigerator. Yield: 6-8 servings.

Jacqueline A. Elrick, Treas.
Xi Iota X3584
Claymont, Delaware

Shadows fall behind when we walk towards the light.   Gloria Brooks

Kitty's Spinach Salad

1 lb. spinach, torn into small pieces
6 slices bacon, fried and crumbled
6 green onions, sliced
1 egg
1 clove of garlic, minced
½ c. oil
½ c. Parmesan cheese
½ tsp. salt
5 tsp. white vinegar
⅛ tsp. red pepper (opt.)

Place spinach, bacon and onions in salad bowl. Blend remaining ingredients in blender. Toss well with spinach. Top with sliced hard-boiled egg, if desired. Yield: 6–8 servings.

Kitty Lawson, Pres.
Xi Omega X660
Washington, Indiana

Eight-Layer Lettuce Salad

1 lg. head lettuce
1½ c. diced celery
6 to 8 hard-boiled eggs, diced
1 10-oz. package frozen peas, cooked and chilled
1 lg. onion, chopped
10 to 12 slices bacon, fried and crumbled
2½ tbsp. sugar
2½ c. Miracle Whip salad dressing
1½ c. shredded Cheddar cheese

Cut lettuce into small pieces. Place enough lettuce in large rectangular dish until half filled. Layer with celery, eggs, peas, onion and bacon in order listed. Combine sugar and salad dressing; spread over salad sealing to sides of dish. Sprinkle with cheese. Refrigerate, covered with plastic wrap, for 8 to 12 hours. Yield: 12 servings.

Marjorie M. Rinker, Pres.
Xi Delta Mu X2689
Titusville, Florida

Nine-Layer Green Salad

Lettuce, shredded
Celery, chopped
1 lg. green pepper, diced
2 pkg. frozen peas, partially cooked and cooled
Spanish onion, chopped fine
2 c. Hellmann's mayonnaise
3 tbsp. sugar
Parmesan cheese, grated
Bacon bits

Layer 2-quart salad bowl with lettuce, celery, green pepper, peas, onion, sugar, cheese and bacon bits in order listed. Refrigerate, covered, overnight. Yield: 10 servings.

Doreen Kray, V.P.
Preceptor Sigma XP952
Summerland, British Columbia, Canada

Patti's Peanut-Layered Salad

Peanuts, unsalted dry-roasted
Lettuce, torn into bite-sized pieces
Spinach, torn into bite-sized pieces
1 can bean sprouts, drained
1 can alfafa sprouts drained
1 pkg. frozen peas
Celery, chopped
Green onions, chopped
Tomatoes, sliced
Carrots, sliced
Mushrooms, sliced
Radishes, sliced
Water chestnuts, sliced
1 tsp. salt
1 tsp. garlic salt
1 tsp. pepper
1 tsp. sugar
Mayonnaise

Layer first 13 ingredients in order listed in large salad bowl. Combine salt, garlic salt, pepper and sugar; sprinkle over salad. Cover with mayonnaise. Refrigerate for 24 hours. Garnish with Cheddar cheese, ham, hard-boiled eggs, shrimp or tomatoes. Yield: 8-10 servings.

Mrs. William T. Milne, W. and M. Chm.
Xi Beta Eta X2421
Klamath Falls, Oregon

Marinated Vegetable Salad

1 c. sliced carrots
1 c. sliced red onion
1 c. halved cherry tomatoes
1½ c. cauliflowerets
2 c. broccoli flowerets chopped stems
2 c. sliced yellow squash
4 c. sliced zucchini
2 c. vegetable oil
½ c. white wine
1 c. white vinegar
½ c. lemon juice
1 tbsp. salt
1 tsp. oregano
1 tsp. dry mustard
1 tsp. instant onion
1 tsp. garlic powder
½ tsp. aniseed

Sorrow knocked at the door, faith answered, and found no one there.   Eileen Shuttleworth

Combine vegetables in large bowl. Combine remaining ingredients; mix well. Pour 2 cups dressing over vegetables. Refrigerate several hours, stirring occasionally. Refrigerate remaining dressing for later use. Yield: 12-14 servings.

Kay Burkett, Rec. Sec.
Xi Psi X385
West Liberty, Ohio

Chinese Vegetable Salad

½ c. salad oil
2 tbsp. vinegar
½ tsp. dry mustard
¼ tsp. paprika
1 tbsp. sugar
1 tsp. salt
Pepper, freshly ground
1 clove of garlic, crushed
3 c. finely sliced Chinese celery cabbage
½ c. thinly sliced carrot
½ c. sliced green onions
1 c. bean sprouts, rinsed
½ c. sliced water chestnuts

Combine oil, vinegar, seasonings and garlic; mix well. Chill for 1 hour. Combine remaining ingredients in salad bowl. Pour salad dressing over vegetables; toss lightly until vegetables are coated with dressing. Yield: 6 servings.

Doris Gerkowski
Xi Alpha Chi X1657
Ludington, Michigan

Deloris' Salad

½ head lettuce, chopped
½ head cauliflower, chopped
½ sm. onion, chopped
4 oz. sharp Cheddar cheese, shredded
⅛ c. shredded Parmesan cheese
½ lb. bacon, fried and crumbled
1 tbsp. sugar
1 c. salad dressing

Combine lettuce, cauliflower and onion; add cheese. Sprinkle bacon over mixture. Combine sugar and salad dressing. Pour over vegetable mixture; mix well. Yield: 6-8 servings.

Joanne H. Greene, Soc. Chm.
Xi Beta Tau No. 4303
Washington, West Virginia

Garden Medley Salad

1 24-oz. package frozen mixed vegetables
1 15-oz. can red kidney beans, drained
½ med. onion, diced
1 green pepper, diced
1 c. diced celery

½ cider vinegar
2 tbsp. prepared mustard
1 c. sugar
2 tbsp. flour

Prepare mixed vegetables according to package directions; drain and cool. Combine mixed vegetables, beans, onion, green pepper and celery in 8-cup refrigerator bowl. Combine remaining ingredients with ½ cup water in small saucepan. Cook, stirring constantly, until thickened; cool. Mix with vegetables, mixing well. Refrigerate, covered, overnight. Stir before serving. Yield: 8-10 servings.

Beverly J. Boughner, Corr. Sec.
Preceptor Phi XP955
Goshen, Indiana

Garden Vegetable Salad

1 cauliflower
1 pkg. frozen chopped broccoli
1 c. chopped onion
1 c. chopped celery
1 c. chopped green pepper
1 c. chopped cucumber
1 c. sliced radishes
2 c. prepared original-flavored Hidden Valley Ranch Dressing

Break cauliflower into small flowerets. Place vegetables in large salad bowl. Pour in dressing; toss. Refrigerate covered, for several hours. Toss lightly before serving. Yield: 12 servings.

Karen Malan, Pres.
Xi Beta Mu X1955
Butler, Missouri

Michelle's Award-Winning Salad

Bibb lettuce
Head lettuce
Fresh spinach
Escarole
Endive
Boston lettuce
3 oz. blue cheese crumbled
8 oz. bacon, fried and diced
1 c. corn oil
6 tbsp. sugar
1 tsp. dry mustard
1 med. onion, chopped
½ c. apple cider vinegar
1 tsp. celery seed

Rinse greens; drain well. Layer greens, cheese and bacon in large salad bowl. Place remaining ingredients in blender; blend well. Pour dressing over salad; toss lightly. Yield: 12 servings.

Millie M. Vickery, W. and M. Chm.
Exemplar Xi Eta Lambda No. 3333
Lena, Illinois

A stranger is the friend you have not met yet. Mary Taylor

Vegetable Salad Supreme

3 to 4 carrots
2 zucchini
1 head cauliflower
1 bunch of broccoli
2 to 3 stalks celery
1 turnip
1 basket of cherry tomatoes
1 bottle of Italian dressing

Rinse carrots, zucchini, cauliflower, broccoli, celery and turnip; cut into bite-size pieces. Add tomatoes and dressing. Place in sealed plastic container. Refrigerate 24 hours, stirring frequently. Drain before serving; retain excess liquid for later use. Yield: 8-12 servings.

Wendy Mitchell
Iota No. 2304
Edmonton, Alberta, Canada

Carrot Salad

1 3-oz. package orange or orange-pineapple Jell-O
1 5-oz. jar pimento cheese, at room temperature
½ c. salad dressing
1 16-oz. can crushed pineapple
1 c. grated carrots

Dissolve Jell-O in 1 cup hot water; cool slightly. Add pimento cheese and salad dressing; beat. Set aside until slightly thickened. Add pineapple and carrots. Place in mold or salad bowl. Chill until firm. Yield: 6-8 servings.

Jo Tarp, Pres.
Kappa Xi
Lexington, Oklahoma

Lime Perfection

1 sm. package lime Jell-O
2 tsp. vinegar
1 c. mayonnaise
½ c. grated carrot
¾ c. grated cabbage
1½ tsp. grated onion
½ c. whipping cream

Dissolve Jell-O in 1 cup boiling water; stir in vinegar. Chill until slightly thickened. Add mayonnaise; beat until blended. Fold in carrot, cabbage and onion. Whip cream until stiff; fold into mixture. Pour into mold. Chill for 12 hours or until firm. Yield: 8 servings.

Sandra Aiken, Pres.
Xi Kappa Exemplar No. 2654
Prince Albert, Saskatchewan, Canada

Windsor Salad

2 tbsp. gelatin
2 10-oz. cans tomato soup
1 8-oz. package cream cheese
1 c. chopped green pepper
1 c. chopped celery
½ c. chopped onion
1 4½-oz. can chopped ripe olives
1 c. mayonnaise

Dissolve gelatin in ½ cup cold water. Heat soup and cream cheese until cream cheese is melted. Beat with egg beater until smooth. Add gelatin; cool. Add remaining ingredients; beat well. Chill until firm. Yield: 12 servings.

Isobel Saville, Soc. Spon.
Laureate Delta
Saskatoon, Saskatchewan, Canada

Sukiyaki Beef Salad

2 tbsp. brown sugar
½ tsp. ginger
½ c. mayonnaise
¼ c. soy sauce
1 tbsp. vinegar
1 tbsp. snipped parsley
4 c. julienne strips cooked beef
2 c. pieces spinach
1 16-oz. can bean sprouts, drained
1 8-oz. can water chestnuts, drained and sliced
½ c. sliced green onion
Buttered croutons (opt.)

Combine brown sugar and ginger. Stir in mayonnaise, soy sauce and vinegar until completely blended. Stir in parsley. Fold half the dressing into beef strips. Chill for 1 hour or more. Add spinach, bean sprouts, water chestnuts and green onion. Add buttered croutons. Toss lightly until well mixed. Serve with remaining dressing. Yield: 6 servings.

Photograph for this recipe on page 42.

Chicken Salad Supreme

2½ c. cold cooked chicken, diced
1 c. finely chopped celery
1 c. sliced white grapes
½ c. slivered toasted almonds
1 to 2 tbsp. minced parsley
¾ to 1 tsp. salt
½ c. whipped cream (opt.)
1 c. mayonnaise or salad dressing
Lettuce
Olives

Mothers are those wonderful people who get up in the morning before the bacon is frying. Suzanne Andersen

Combine first 8 ingredients. Serve on lettuce leaves. Garnish with olives. Yield: 8 servings

Kathryn Weber
Xi Upsilon X3677
Casper, Wyoming

Chicken Salad With Yeast-Riz Cheese Crust

6 tbsp. sugar
¾ tsp. salt
1 pkg. dry yeast
1 egg, slightly beaten
2¾ c. sifted flour
1 c. grated Cheddar cheese
2 c. diced cooked chicken
1 c. finely chopped celery
2 tsp. minced onion
2 tbsp. lemon juice
¾ c. mayonnaise
½ c. chopped nuts
1 c. crushed potato chips

Combine ⅓ cup hot water, sugar and ¼ teaspoon salt; cool to lukewarm. Dissolve yeast in ¼ cup warm water; add to sugar water, stirring well. Beat in egg and 1½ cups flour, beating until smooth. Add cheese and 1¼ cups flour. Knead on floured surface until smooth. Place in greased bowl, turning once to grease surface; cover. Let rise 1 hour and 15 minutes in a warm place, free of draft, or until doubled in bulk. Punch down; divide into 3 pieces. Store 2 pieces for later use. Roll remaining piece into 10-inch circle. Press firmly into 9-inch pie pan. Press edge with tines of fork. Brush with egg white. Let rise for 20 minutes or until doubled in bulk; prick with fork. Bake at 300 degrees for 8 minutes; do not brown. Combine chicken, celery, ½ teaspoon salt, onion, lemon juice, mayonnaise and nuts. Pat into pie shell. Sprinkle with potato chips. Bake at 350 degrees for 15 to 20 minutes. Serve hot. Yield: 6 servings.

Ila F. McCallum, Treas.
Xi Delta Alpha X5193
Woodburn, Oregon

Hot Chicken Salad

½ c. mayonnaise
1 c. cream of mushroom soup
1 tsp. salt
½ tsp. pepper
2 c. cooked diced chicken
2 c. cooked rice
¼ c. chopped onion
2 hard-boiled eggs, chopped
1 c. crushed potato chips

Mix mayonnaise with mushroom soup. Add salt and pepper. Add mayonnaise mixture to chicken, rice, onion, and hard-boiled eggs in a large bowl. Place in 9 x 13-inch casserole. Sprinkle with crushed potato chips. Bake at 325 degrees for 45 minutes.

Mrs. Dale Daniel
Lambda Eta No. 7752
Lamar, Missouri

Hot Ham Salad

1 c. diced ham
1 sm. jar diced pimento
1 can cream of mushroom soup
2 tsp. chopped green onions
1 c. cooked instant rice
½ tsp. salt
¾ c. mayonnaise
½ c. toasted sliced almonds or ½ c. sliced water chestnuts
3 tsp. lemon juice
1 c. diced celery
3 hard-boiled eggs, chopped
Corn flakes

Mix all ingredients except corn flakes in a greased 2-quart baking dish. Cover with rolled corn flakes. Bake at 350 degrees for 30 minutes. Yield: 6-8 servings.

Dr. Elta Pfister Smith, Hon. Mem.
Burbank, California

Sweet Cherry-Chicken Salad

1 16-oz. can pitted Bing cherries
2½ c. cooked chicken or turkey
1 c. sliced celery
½ c. green pepper strips (opt.)
1 5-oz. can water chestnuts, sliced thin
1 c. mayonnaise
2 tsp. lemon juice
1 tsp. sugar
2 tsp. soy sauce
1 to 2 tsp. curry powder
½ c. slivered almonds, toasted

Drain cherries well. Combine with chicken, celery, green pepper, and water chestnuts. Mix mayonnaise, lemon juice, sugar, soy sauce and curry powder in small bowl. Add to chicken; toss lightly. Chill thoroughly. Top with almonds. Yield: 6-8 servings.

Gloria Smethers
Theta Preceptor XP819
Beatrice, Nebraska

It often shows a fine command of language to say nothing. Jane Mielke

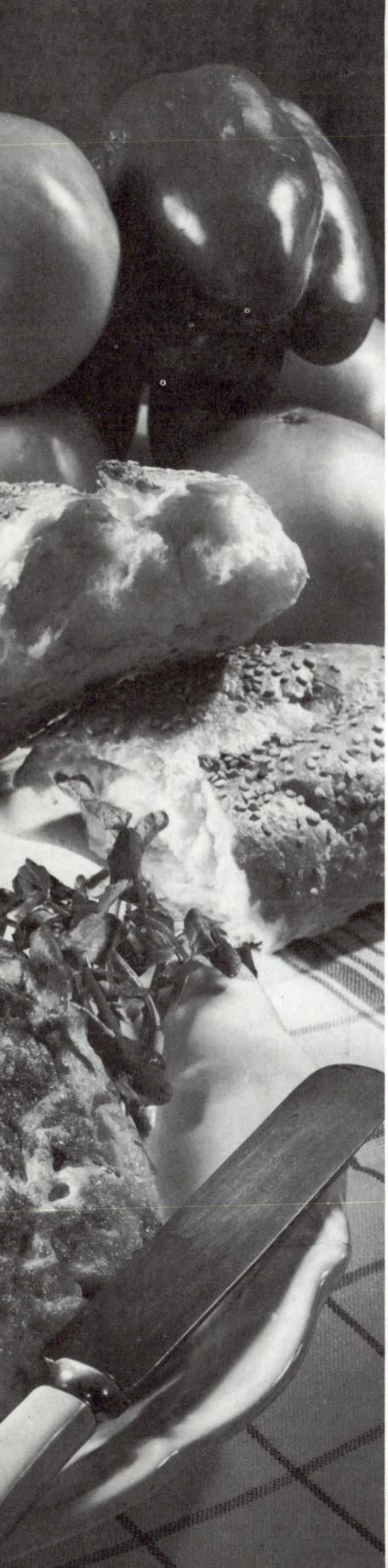

Eggs & Cheese

The joy of egg and cheese cookery is in the tasting because the results include light and airy souffles, savory quiches, mouth-watering fondues, delectable omelets, as well as rich puddings, custards and sauces. So, not only can eggs and cheese stand alone or together in a delicious dish, but they are also a "hidden" ingredient in many favorite dishes, lending the right texture and just a touch of taste.

Eggs have been called the original packaged food, full of nutrition, flavor and uses galore. Indispensable in garnishing, perfect both in salads and as a salad, eggs are the cook's best friend when they appear as an omelet. When unexpected guests arrive and stay for mealtime, or if the family wants something easy and different, it's a snap to prepare a fancy omelet with most any ingredients on hand. One New York restaurant lists 553 variations on the omelet, and the owner says these are just a few of his favorites. The varieties of the souffle are, without a doubt, equally numerous, the perfect showcase for vegetables and fruits, cheeses, seafood, chocolate and other dessert foods.

It has been said that the true cheese connoisseur enjoys just reading about cheese and its near 350 known varieties. But, for most of us, English gourmet Ernest Oldsmeadow said it best—"the only way to learn about cheese is to eat it."

One of the best ways to enjoy cheese is in a quiche, which is a French peasants answer to Italy's pizza. An excellent brunch or luncheon dish, this superb peasants pie is appropriate served at a dinner for four, or hors d'oeuvres at a casual party for 40. A cheesy quiche is also a perfect presentation for zucchini, tomatoes, and other vegetables as well as seafood, sausage and onions.

An unbeatable pair! These Beta Sigma Phi recipes featuring eggs and cheese will leave no doubt that there are innumerable ways to prepare these two amazing foods.

A.M. Leftovers

¼ c. chopped green pepper
¼ c. chopped onion
6 slices ring bologna, quartered or chopped leftover
 meat
1 tbsp. vegetable oil
2 leftover baked potatoes, chopped
4 eggs, beaten
½ to 1 c. milk
Dash of salt
Dash of pepper
Dash of baking powder

Saute green pepper, onion and meat in oil. Add potatoes. Combine eggs, milk, salt, pepper and baking powder in bowl. Set aside. Heat through. Add egg mixutre; cook until eggs begin to set. Turn mixture as for an omelet. Yield: 4 servings.

Karen L. McAndrew, Corr. Sec., Pres. City Coun.
Beta Omega No. 9805
Allentown, Pennsylvania

Baked Sandwich

12 slices bread
Butter or margarine
6 slices Cheddar cheese
Ground ham or tuna
Cheddar cheese, grated
4 eggs, beaten
Milk
1 tsp. salt
⅛ tsp. pepper
¼ tsp. dry mustard
½ can mushroom soup

Trim crusts from bread. Butter one side. Place 6 slices bread in 9 × 13-inch baking dish, buttered side up. Cover with sliced Cheddar cheese and ham. Cover with grated Cheddar cheese. Top with remaining bread. Combine eggs, 3 cups milk, salt, pepper and dry mustard; pour over bread. Refrigerate, covered, overnight. Bake at 300 degrees for 1 hour. Dilute soup with ½ soup can milk. Pour over baked sandwiches. Bake at 300 degrees for 30 minutes. Cut in squares. Yield: 8 servings.

Dolores I. Salyer
Preceptor Beta Beta No. 1593
Canon City, Colorado

Beta Brunch Souffle

12 slices bread, crusts removed
2 pkg. frozen chopped broccoli
2 c. diced ham
1 lb. Cheddar cheese, grated
1 tsp. grated onion
6 eggs, beaten
3 c. milk
1 tsp. salt

Line 9 × 13-inch casserole with trimmed bread slices, reserving some slices for top. Cook broccoli slightly; drain. Spread on bread. Add ham, ¾ of the cheese, and onion. Top with remaining slices of bread. Combine eggs, milk and salt; mix well. Pour over casserole, saturating top layer. Sprinkle remaining cheese on top. Refrigerate overnight. Bake at 350 degrees for 50 minutes. Let stand for 10 minutes before serving. Yield: 8 serving.

Carol Voss, Corr. Sec.
Gamma Kappa No. 8112
Fairmont, Minnesota

Breakfast Before

1 lb. spicy pork sausage
6 eggs, beaten
2 c. milk
1 tsp. salt
1 tsp. dry mustard
2 slices bread, cubed
1 c. grated Cheddar cheese

Saute sausage; drain. Combine eggs, milk, salt and dry mustard. Layer bread, sausage and cheese in 9 × 13-inch casserole. Pour egg mixture over top. Refrigerate overnight. Bake at 350 degrees for 45 minutes. Yield: 6-8 servings.

Nina Sue Crowell, Pres.
Xi Alpha Gamma XP806
Kissimmee, Florida

Breakfast Brunch

2 c. croutons
2 c. grated sharp Cheddar cheese
2 lb. sausage, browned
4 eggs, beaten
½ c. milk
Dash of salt
1 can cream of mushroom soup

Layer buttered 9 × 12-inch casserole with croutons, cheese and sausage. Combine eggs, ¼ cup milk and salt; pour over casserole. Combine soup and ¼ cup milk; pour over casserole. Bake at 300 degrees for 1 hour. Yield: 15 servings.

Connie E. Benson, Pres.
Xi Phi X3359
Hot Springs, South Dakota

The secret of happy living is not to do what you like but to like what you do. Marilyn C. MacLeod

Breakfast Buffet Brunch

2 slices bread, cubed
1 lb. mild sausage, browned
8 oz. medium Cheddar cheese, grated
6 eggs, beaten
1 c. milk
1 tsp. dry mustard
1 tsp. salt
12 oz. frozen hashed brown potatoes, thawed

Line glass 13 × 9-inch baking dish with bread. Layer sausage and cheese over bread. Combine eggs, milk and seasonings. Pour over mixture. Sprinkle potatoes on top; cover with foil. Refrigerate for 24 hours. Bake, covered, at 350 degrees for 35 minutes. Bake, uncovered, for 10 minutes. Slice into 8 squares. Yield: 8 servings.

Rosemary Buchanan, Pres.
Xi Iota Alpha X4541
Belle Glade, Florida

Breakfast Casserole

6 slices bread, crusts removed
1 lb. pork sausage
1 6-oz. package shredded Cheddar cheese
5 eggs, beaten
1 pt. half and half
1 tsp. mustard

Line 9 × 13-inch buttered casserole with bread. Brown sausage; drain. Sprinkle over bread. Sprinkle cheese over sausage. Combine eggs, half and half and mustard; pour over casserole. Refrigerate overnight. Bake, covered, at 350 degrees for 25 minutes. Bake, uncovered, for 5 minutes. Yield: 6-8 servings.

Eloise Sellars
Xi Zeta Sigma X3107
Herrin, Illinois

Breakfast Dish Supreme

Butter
12 slices bread
2 c. grated Cheddar cheese
2 lb. link sausage, browned and cut into pieces
8 eggs, beaten
4 c. milk
Salt and pepper to taste
1½ c. crushed corn flakes

Butter bread; cube. Line greased 9 × 13-inch baking dish with half the bread. Layer with cheese, sausage and remaining bread. Combine eggs, milk and seasonings; pour over casserole. Refrigerate over-

night. Top with corn flakes. Bake at 350 degrees for 45 to 60 minutes. Yield: 8 servings.

Barbara Turner, Pres.
Psi Xi No. 5685
Sattley, California

Breakfast In One

1 12-oz. package hashed brown potatoes
1½ c. ham or sausage, chopped
½ c. onion, chopped
½ c. chopped green peppers
1 4-oz. can mushrooms, drained
8 eggs, beaten
Salt and pepper to taste
American cheese slices

Saute potatoes until soft. Press into pie pan to make one 9-inch pie shell. Saute ham, onion, peppers and mushrooms; drain. Combine eggs, salt and pepper. Add ham mixture to eggs. Pour into shell. Arrange cheese slices on top. Bake at 350 degrees for 10 minutes. Bake at 400 degrees for 10 minutes longer or until potatoes are brown. Yield: 6-8 servings.

Rose Marie Guthrie, V. P. City Coun.
Alpha Delta Preceptor XP647
Xenia, Ohio

Brunch Pizza

1½ c. flour
½ tsp. salt
⅛ tsp. pepper
½ c. shortening
8 thin slices boiled ham
½ lb. sliced Swiss cheese
1 lb. bacon, cooked and crumbled
4 eggs, beaten
1¼ c. milk

Combine flour, ¼ teaspoon salt and pepper. Cut in shortening with fork until mixture is coarse and crumbly. Sprinkle 5 to 6 tablespoons cool water over mixture to make dough. Pat out rectangle ½ inch thick to fit into 10 × 15-inch jelly roll pan, extending slightly on sides. Layer with ham, cheese and bacon. Combine eggs, milk and ¼ teaspoon salt. Pour egg mixture over top. Bake at 425 degrees for 25 minutes. Bake 5 minutes longer if refrigerated. Yield: 6-8 servings.

Sandra Freeman, Treas.
Xi Gamma X399
Manchester, Connecticut

Well done is better than well said. Jacqueline L. Salisbury

Breakfast Puff

9 eggs
3 c. milk
1 tsp. salt
½ loaf bread, cubed
1 lb. sausage
1 can sliced mushrooms
1 c. grated cheese

Beats eggs, milk and salt; let stand. Combine remaining ingredients; add to egg mixture. Pour into 9 × 12-inch casserole. Refrigerate overnight. Bake at 350 degrees for 2 hours. Yield: 8 servings.

Lil Gray, W. and M. Chm.
Delta Eta No. 2726
Glenwood, Iowa

Breakfast Dressing

8 slices bread, cubed
2 c. grated American cheese
1½ lb. cooked link sausage, cut in thirds
4 eggs, beaten
Milk
¾ tsp. dry mustard
1 can cream of mushroom soup

Line greased 9 × 13-inch casserole with bread. Sprinkle with cheese and sausage. Combine eggs, 2¼ cups milk and dry mustard; pour over mixture. Refrigerate overnight. Dilute soup with ½ soup can additional milk; pour over casserole. Bake at 300 degrees for 1 hour and 30 minutes. Let stand 20 minutes. Yield: 12-14 servings.

Diana A. Burge, Pres.
Xi Beta Alpha X1876
Niles, Michigan

Denver Sandwich Ring

1½ c. Bisquick
Salad oil
1¾ c. milk
1 egg, beaten
1½ c. cooked ham, cubed
⅓ c. finely chopped onion
⅓ c. finely chopped green pepper
3 tbsp. four
½ tsp. salt
1½ c. shredded Cheddar cheese

Combine Bisquick, ⅓ cup oil, ¼ cup milk and egg in large bowl; mix by hand. Stir in ham, onion and green pepper. Drop by spoonfuls in a ring on ungreased cookie sheet. Bake at 400 degrees for 25 to 30 minutes. Blend flour, salt and 3 tablespoons oil in medium saucepan. Add remaining milk gradually. Cook until thickened, stirring for 1 minute. Remove from heat.

Add cheese; stir until melted. Pour cheese sauce over ring. Yield: 6-8 servings.

Claudia Vann, Pres.
Xi Alpha Delta X523
Atwater, California

Do-Ahead Breakfast

½ lb. ground sausage
6 eggs, well beaten
1½ c. milk
1 tsp. dry mustard
¾ tsp. salt
2 slices bread, cubed
1 c. shredded Cheddar cheese

Brown sausage; drain. Combine eggs, milk, dry mustard and salt. Add bread and sausage to egg mixture. Pour into 8 × 8-inch casserole. Sprinkle with cheese. Refrigerate, covered, overnight. Bake, uncovered, at 325 degrees for 45 to 50 minutes. Yield: 4-6 servings.

Jacquelynn L. Salisbury, Rec. Sec.
Omicron Omega No. 7470
East Moline, Illinois

Easy One-Dish Pancake

1 c. all-purpose flour
2 tbsp. sugar
1 tbsp. baking powder
½ tsp. salt
1 egg, beaten
¾ c. milk
1 c. shredded sharp American cheese
3 tbsp. bacon drippings
6 slices bacon, crumbled

Combine flour, sugar, baking powder and salt. Combine egg, milk and bacon drippings. Pour into dry mixture; beat until smooth. Stir in bacon. Pour into greased and floured 10 × 15-inch baking pan; spread evenly. Bake at 425 degrees for 15 minutes. Remove from oven; sprinkle with cheese. Bake for 2 to 3 minutes or until cheese melts. Cut into squares. Yield: 4-6 servings.

Gail E. Frics
Xi Eta X574
Omaha, Nebraska

Make-ahead Brunch Casserole

1 lb. bulk sausage
6 eggs, beaten
2 slices bread, cubed
2 c. milk
1 c. Cheddar cheese, grated

Of all the things you wear your expression is the most important. Theodora P. Stymack

1 tsp. dry mustard
Salt to taste

Brown sausage; drain. Cool; add remaining ingredients. Pour into greased 9 × 9-inch casserole. Bake at 350 degrees for 1 hour. Let stand for 5 minutes before slicing. Yield: 6-8 servings.

Georgianna Maier, Soc. Chm.
Xi Gamma Sigma X3119
Mason, Michigan

Pinwheels

1 8-oz. package cream cheese, softened
½ c. grated carrot
12 slices whole wheat bread, crusts trimmed
Watercress sprigs or canned asparagus spears

Blend cream cheese and carrot. Flatten bread slices with rolling pin. Spread cheese mixture lightly over bread. Place watercress sprig at one end of each slice. Roll up. Wrap in plastic wrap; chill. Slice roll-ups ½ inch thick.

Photograph for this recipe on page 61.

Ribbon Tea Sandwiches

½ c. grated milk Cheddar cheese
2 oz. cream cheese, softened
1 canned pimento, chopped
¼ tsp. Worcestershire sauce
12 slices white bread, crusts trimmed
½ c. butter or margarine, softened
¼ c. chopped parsley
6 slices whole wheat bread, crusts trimmed

Combine Cheddar cheese, cream cheese, pimento and Worcestershire sauce; mix well. Spread on 6 slices white bread. Combine softened butter with chopped parsley. Spread on slices of whole wheat bread. Place over cheese layer. Top with remaining 6 slices of white bread. Cut each sandwich into 7 narrow slices. Yield: 42 servings.

Photograph for this recipe on page 61.

Sandwich Supreme

12 slices bread
Butter
6 thin slices American cheese
6 slices ham
4 eggs, beaten
2½ c. milk

Trim crusts from bread and reserve for crumbs. Butter bread. Place 1 slice cheese and 1 slice ham between 2 slices bread. Arrange 6 sandwiches in 9 × 13-inch pan.

Mix eggs and milk well; pour over sandwiches. Dot with additional butter. Refrigerate at least 12 hours. Top with crumbs. Bake at 350 degrees for 1 hour and 15 minutes. Let stand 15 minutes before serving. Yield: 6 servings.

Iva Jane Mingus, Parlimentarian
Xi Gamma Nu X3153
Waverly, Iowa

Sunny Morn

1¼ c. coarsely grated sharp Cheddar cheese
8 eggs
½ c. milk
2 tbsp. butter or margarine
2 tsp. prepared mustard
½ tsp. salt
4 drops of Tabasco sauce
6 slices bread

Combine cheese, 2 eggs, milk, butter, mustard, salt and Tabasco in top of double boiler. Cook, stirring frequently, until cheese is melted and sauce is smooth. Remove from heat. Poach 6 eggs; toast bread. Spoon about 2 tablespoons sauce on each slice toast; top with poached egg. Spoon remaining sauce over eggs. Garnish with parsley, if desired. Yield: 6 servings.

Theodora P. Stymack
Alpha Delta No. 2246
Brookfield, Georgia

The most difficult thing to give away is happiness—it always returns. Nina Sue Crowell

The Temptress

1 8-oz. package cream cheese, softened
½ c. grated Cheddar cheese
8 slices multi-grained bread
1 tomato, thinly sliced
8 fresh mushrooms, thinly sliced
⅛ to ¼ c. sliced almonds
⅛ to ¼ c. sliced black olives
Butter

Combine cream cheese and Cheddar cheese; spread evenly on each slice of bread. Arrange tomato slices, mushroom slices, almonds and olives evenly over cheese mixture on 4 slices bread. Place bread slices together to form 4 sandwiches. Lightly butter top and bottom of each slice of bread. Grill in skillet or in oven until cheese melts and bread is slightly browned. Yield: 4 servings.

Jeanie Lombardi, Pres.
Xi Nu Iota X3096
Santa Rosa, California

Creamy Scrambled Eggs

6 tbsp. minced onions
1 tbsp. butter
18 eggs, beaten
1 c. sour cream
⅜ tsp. thyme
2¼ tsp. salt
Dash of Tabasco (opt.)
3 tbsp. chopped parsley

Saute onions in butter until soft. Combine eggs, sour cream and seasonings; mix well. Add to onions. Cook over low heat, stirring occasionally. Garnish with parsley. Yield: 12 servings.

Norma M. Findlay, Pres.
Preceptor Alpha XP396
Halifax, Nova Scotia, Canada

Baked Eggs

¼ lb. butter
24 eggs
2 tbsp. cream cheese
2 c. milk
Salt and pepper to taste

Melt butter in 9 × 13-inch casserole. Blend 12 eggs with cream cheese for 30 seconds in blender. Beat remaining 12 eggs with mixer; add blended egg and cheese mixture. Add milk, salt and pepper; mix well. Pour into buttered casserole. Bake at 350 degrees for 30 minutes, stirring at 10-minute intervals.

Ayleen Nelson, Serv. Chm.
Preceptor Laureate Beta PL149
Racine, Wisconsin

Easy Eggs Benedict

1 10-oz. can mushroom soup, undiluted
⅓ c. mayonnaise
1 tbsp. lemon juice
4 English muffins, halved
8 slices ham
8 eggs, poached

Heat first 3 ingredients; do not boil. Warm muffin in slow oven. Place 1 slice ham on each muffin half. Place poached egg on top of ham; top with sauce. Garnish with tomato slice or parsley. Yield: 8 servings.

Teresa Smart, Pres.
Preceptor Alpha Iota XP1076
Guelph, Ontario, Canada

Eggs Benedict

2 egg yolks
¼ tsp. salt
¼ tsp. Tabasco
½ c. melted butter
1 tbsp. fresh lemon juice
6 whole eggs
6 slices cooked ham
3 English muffins, halved and toasted

Beat egg yolks, salt and Tabasco with electric beater until thick and lemon colored. Add ¼ cup melted butter, 1 teaspoon at a time, beating constantly. Combine remaining butter with lemon juice. Add slowly, beating constantly. Cover; set aside. Butter skillet. Add enough water to cover eggs 1 inch. Bring to a boil. Reduce heat to simmering. Break eggs, one at a time into cup; gently let egg slide out of cup into water. Cover skillet. Cook eggs until whites are solid, about 3 to 5 minutes. Heat ham through. Toast English muffins. Remove poached eggs gently from skillet with slotted spoon. Place ham on muffins; top with poached egg. Spoon Hollandaise sauce over all. Garnish with parsley, if desired. Yield: 6 servings.

Photograph for this recipe on page 63.

Egg Brunch

1 can cream of chicken soup
10 eggs
1 lb. bacon, fried and crumbled
½ lb. fresh mushrooms, sliced
1 tbsp. parsley
Garlic
1 tsp. butter
½ lb. grated Cheddar cheese

Pour soup into 9 × 13-inch casserole. Beat eggs with 10 teaspoons water; pour over soup. Sprinkle bacon over egg mixture. Saute mushrooms, parsley and garlic in butter, pour over bacon. Cover with cheese. Refrigerate overnight. Bake at 350 degrees for 30 minutes. Yield: 10 servings.

Cheryl Hogle, Pres.
Delta Pi No. 5283
Marysville, Washington

Baked Eggs with Chili Peppers

½ c. butter or margarine
10 eggs
½ c. unsifted flour
1 tsp. baking powder
½ tsp. salt
12 oz. Monterey Jack cheese, grated
2 c. cottage cheese
2 3-oz. cans diced green chilies

Melt butter in 9 × 13-inch casserole. Beat eggs with electric mixer until fluffy. Combine flour, baking powder and salt; stir into eggs. Stir in Monterey Jack cheese, cottage cheese and chilies. Pour into casserole. Bake at 350 degrees for 35 minutes. Crisp bacon may be sprinkled on top. Yield: 12 servings.

Margie Slacum, Rec. Sec.
North Whidbey Island Coun. XP1635
Oak Harbor, Washington

Baked Eggs with Bacon

6 eggs
6 strips bacon, diced
1 pkg. croutons
1 c. grated Cheddar cheese

Break eggs into buttered 6 × 8-inch baking dish, taking care not to break egg yolks. Cover with bacon. Sprinkle croutons around outer edge of baking dish. Top with cheese. Bake at 350 degrees for 12 to 15 minutes or until eggs are set. Yield: 4-5 servings.

Darlene A. Liesmann, Area Coun. Pres.
Preceptor Beta Nu XP1821
Port Orchard, Washington

Eggs with Shrimp Sauce

2 tbsp. butter
2 tbsp. flour
1 10-oz. can cream of shrimp soup
1 soup can milk
½ c. shredded Cheddar cheese

Melt butter in saucepan; stir in flour. Add soup and milk; cook stirring until thickened. Add cheese; stir. Pour over scrambled eggs, if desired. Yield: 6 servings.

Jan MacDonald
Preceptor Alpha Sigma
Waterloo, Ontario, Canada

The person who never makes a mistake is the person who never does anything. Sandra Freeman

Egg-Cheese Baked Delight

6 slices bread, crusts removed and cubed
1 lb. American cheese, grated
8 eggs, beaten
4 c. milk
1 tsp. dry mustard
Salt and pepper to taste
1 c. shrimp, fried sausage or cubed ham

Line 9 × 12-inch casserole with bread. Sprinkle with cheese. Combine eggs, milk, dry mustard, salt and pepper; pour over cheese. Cover with shrimp. Refrigerate overnight. Let stand at room temperature for 1 hour before baking. Bake at 340 degrees for 50 to 60 minutes. Yield: 8 servings.

Naomi Vaughn, Treas.
Preceptor Beta XP234
Rapid City, South Dakota

Eggs Goldenrod

6 lg. eggs, boiled
2 tbsp. Wondra flour
2 tbsp. margarine
¼ tsp. salt
⅛ tsp. pepper
2 c. cold milk
6 slices bread, toasted or English muffins

Cut eggs in half; set egg yolks aside. Chop egg whites into small pieces. Combine flour, margarine, salt and pepper in saucepan. Add milk slowly, stirring constantly. Bring to a boil; cook for 1 minute. Add egg whites. Crumble eggs yolks. Spoon white sauce over bread; add egg yolks. Serve warm. Yield: 6-servings

Connie J. Rains, Past Pres.
Epsilon Chi No. 5612
Muskogee, Oklahoma

Overnight Eggs

6 eggs, beaten
3 c. milk
1 tsp. salt
10 slices bread, crusts removed, cubed
½ lb. shredded Cheddar cheese

Combine eggs, milk and salt. Alternate layers of bread and cheese, beginning with bread and ending with cheese in 1-quart casserole. Pour egg mixture over casserole. Refrigerate overnight. Bake at 350 degrees for 1 hour. Yield: 10-12 servings.

Peggy A. Holmes, Pres.
Xi Alpha Phi X2410
Grafton, Virginia

Capered Eggs

24 hard-boiled eggs, sliced
2 c. mayonnaise
1 c. whipping cream
1 bottle capers
Salt and pepper to taste
Dillweed to taste

Arrange egg slices in casserole. Combine mayonnaise, whipping cream and capers with juice. Sprinkle eggs with salt and pepper. Pour mixture over eggs; sprinkle with dillweed. Yield: 24 servings.

Phyllis Caudill, Pres.
Xi Eta Lambda No. 2231
Graham, Texas

Italian Egg Casserole

1 lb. Italian sausage
8 mushrooms, sliced
½ med. red onion, chopped
12 eggs, beaten
1 c. milk
2 med. tomatoes, peeled and chopped
8 oz. mozzarella cheese, shredded
½ tsp. seasoned salt
½ tsp. pepper

Fry sausage; drain. Add mushrooms and onion; cook until tender. Combine remaining ingredients. Add to sausage mixture. Pour into greased 9 × 13-inch casserole. Bake at 400 degrees for 30 to 40 minutes. Yield: 8-10 servings.

Suenel Caffroy, Corr. Sec.
Xi Tau Lambda X4878
Cherry Valley, California

Yvonne's Souffle

1 c. shredded process cheese
1 c. mushroom soup
6 eggs, separated

Combine cheese and soup. Add beaten egg yolks. Beat egg whites until stiff. Fold into cheese mixture. Pour into 2-quart casserole. Bake at 300 degrees for 1 hour. Yield: 6 servings.

Yvonne Hoveling
Preceptor Zeta XP182
Yakima, Washington

Donna's Brunch Egg Casserole

1 stick butter or margarine
24 lg. eggs, beaten
¼ c. cream or milk

The greatest of all arts is the art of losing ourselves in the service of others.   Delores I. Salyer

½ tsp. salt
1 10¾-oz. can cream of mushroom soup
1 lb. bacon or diced ham
1 8-oz. can sliced mushrooms, drained
½ lb. Cheddar cheese, grated
Paprika

Melt butter in large skillet over medium low heat. Combine eggs, cream and salt in large bowl; stir. Scramble egg mixture in butter until soft and moist; set aside. Heat soup in large saucepan until smooth. Fry bacon; drain. Break into small pieces. Add bacon and mushrooms to soup. Layer eggs, soup mixture and cheese in a 4-quart casserole. Repeat layers, ending with cheese. Sprinkle with paprika. Refrigerate overnight. Place casserole in unheated oven. Bake at 250 degrees for 1 hour. Yield: 8-10 servings.

Donna Outhier, Pres.
Delta Alpha Nu No. 6695
Yorba Linda, California

Connie's Egg Souffle

6 slices bread, crusts removed and quartered
½ lb. sliced Cheddar cheese
6 eggs, beaten
2 c. milk
¼ tsp. salt
¼ c. butter
1 tbsp. Sherry

Line buttered oblong casserole with bread. Cover bread with cheese slices. Combine eggs, milk and salt. Pour over bread and cheese. Refrigerate overnight Melt butter; add Sherry. Pour over casserole before baking. Bake at 300 degrees for 1 hour. Yield: 6-8 servings.

Connie Fisher, W. and M. Com.
Xi Iota Nu X4770
Bolingbrook, Illinois

Sandra's Brunch Egg Casserole

10 slices bread, crusts removed and cubed
½ lb. Cheddar cheese, grated
Butter
3 eggs, beaten
2 c. milk
½ tsp. salt
¼ tsp. pepper
1 tsp. dry mustard

Layer bread and cheese in buttered 9 × 13-inch casserole. Dot with butter between layers. Combine remaining ingredients; pour over bread mixture. Let stand 8 to 24 hours in refrigerator. Bake, covered, at

350 degrees for 45 minutes. Bake, uncovered, for 15 minutes. Yield: 10 servings.

Sandra Johnson, Ext. Off.
Xi Gamma X2565
Stanberry, Missouri

Paulette's Italian Eggs

½ lb. Italian sausage, crumbled
2 tbsp. olive oil
1 c. chopped green pepper
1 lg. potato, cubed
1 lg. onion, chopped
1 c. diced tomatoes
8 eggs, beaten
¼ c. cream
Salt and pepper to taste

Cook sausage in olive oil until browned lightly. Stir in green pepper. Add potato and onion, stirring until potatoes are brown. Add tomatoes; cook 1 minute. Combine eggs, cream, salt and pepper. Stir into vegetable mixture. Cook over medium heat until eggs are set. Yield: 4-5 servings.

Paulette Semmes, Member at Large
Fort Lauderdale, Florida

Baked Eggs Mornay

15 eggs, hard-boiled
Mayonnaise to taste
3 tsp. horseradish
Sweet pickle juice to taste
Butter
5 tbsp. flour
2½ c. milk
1¼ tsp. salt
Pepper to taste
½ c. heavy cream
4 tbsp. Parmesan cheese
4 tbsp. Swiss cheese
Buttered bread crumbs

Slice eggs in half lengthwise; scoop out yolks. Mash yolks. Add mayonnaise, horseradish and sweet pickle juice. Return yolk mixture to egg halves. Place deviled eggs in buttered 13 × 9-inch casserole. Melt 5 tablespoons butter in saucepan over low heat. Blend in flour; stir in milk slowly. Cook until thickened. Add cream, Parmesan cheese, Swiss cheese and 2½ tablespoons butter. Stir until cheese melts. Pour over deviled eggs. Sprinkle with buttered bread crumbs. Bake at 350 degrees for 20 to 30 minutes. Yield: 6-8 servings.

Rita Burke
Epsilon Eta No. 3703
Hawarden, Iowa

Happy times, Happy places, but most of all Happy faces. Donna Outhier

Egg Fondue

1 lb. sausage
6 slices bread, cut into ¼-inch cubes
¼ lb. American cheese, grated
2 c. milk
4 eggs, slightly beaten
1 tsp. salt
½ tsp. dry mustard

Brown sausage; drain. Layer bread, sausage and cheese in 2-quart casserole. Combine milk, eggs, salt and dry mustard; pour over sausage mixture. Bake at 350 degrees for 50 minutes. Yield: 6 servings.

Edith Jane Smith, Pres.
Xi Alpha Zeta X4230
Ellsworth APB, South Dakota

Eggs Eisenhower

Butter
4 tbsp. flour
1 tsp. salt
2 c. scalded milk
1 c. cracker crumbs, crushed
½ c. grated American cheese
4 hard-boiled eggs, chopped
1 7-oz. jar pimentos, chopped

Melt 4 tablespoons butter. Add flour and salt; stir. Add milk gradually; cook until thick and smooth. Line 1½-quart buttered casserole with half the cracker crumbs. Moisten well with half the white sauce. Layer cheese, eggs and pimentos. Repeat layers. Cover with remaining white sauce. Top with remaining cracker crumbs. Dot with additional butter. Bake at 350 degrees for 25 minutes. Yield: 6 servings.

Margaret A. Eby
Xi Alpha Delta X1530
Richmond, Virginia

Kentucky Governor's Egg Casserole

½ c. chopped onion
2 tbsp. butter
2 tbsp. flour
1¼ c. milk
1 c. shredded sharp cheese
6 hard-cooked eggs, sliced
1½ c. crushed potato chips
10 to 12 slices crisp bacon, chopped

Cook onion in butter until tender but not brown. Blend in flour. Add milk, stirring constantly until thick. Add cheese; stir until melted. Layer eggs, cheese sauce, potato chips and bacon in a 10×6×2-inch casserole.

Repeat layers. Bake at 350 degrees for 30 minutes. Yield: 8 servings.

Marjorie A. Fink, V. P.
Preceptor Zeta XP1086
Louisville, Kentucky

Marion's Egg and Cheese Casserole

¼ c. diced onion
3 tbsp. margarine
3 tbsp. flour
3 c. milk
2 c. grated American cheese
½ tsp. dry mustard
6 hard-boiled eggs, sliced
20 slices cooked bacon, crumbled
½ c. potato chips, crushed
½ tsp. salt
½ tsp. pepper

Saute onion in margarine; add flour gradually. Add milk, cheese, and mustard. Cook over low heat, stirring until cheese melts. Layer greased baking pan with eggs, cheese sauce, bacon and potato chips. Season with salt and pepper. Bake, uncovered, at 350 degrees for 30 minutes.

Marion C. Jinkens
Eta Theta No. 6380
Overland Park, Kansas

Spanish Vegetable Omelet

Olive oil
Butter or margarine
½ c. finely chopped onion
1 med. green pepper, chopped
2 sm. tomatoes, peeled, seeded and diced
¼ c. chopped pimento-stuffed olives
1 tbsp. chopped parlsey
½ tsp. salt
8 eggs, beaten

Heat 1 tablespoon olive oil and 1 tablespoon butter in 10-inch omelet pan. Add onion; cook until tender. Add a small amount of olive oil, if necessary. Add green pepper and tomatoes. Cook, stirring occasionally, until pepper is tender. Remove from pan with a slotted spoon; discard any liquid in pan. Stir vegetable mixture, chopped olives, parsley and salt into beaten eggs. Wipe pan dry with paper towels. Heat 1 tablespoon butter in pan. Add egg mixture. Cook over low heat, running a spatula around edges occasionally to allow uncooked egg to go to bottom. Loosen around edges and invert plate over top of pan when omelet is almost firm. Turn omelet out onto plate. Clean bits from pan. Add a small amount of butter. Discard all liquid from omelet. Slide omelet back into pan. Cook over low heat until light browned. Invert onto serving plate in same manner as before. Garnish with small olives and watercress. Yield: 4 servings.

Photograph for this recipe on page 56.

The beginning of wisdom is silence. Harriette M. Bilbro

Sandra's Egg Fondue

1 lb. sausage
6 slices bread, crusts removed and cubed
¼ lb. American cheese, grated
4 eggs, beaten
2 c. milk
1 tsp. salt
½ tsp. dry mustard

Brown sausage; drain. Layer bread, sausage and cheese in 2-quart casserole. Combine remaining ingredients; pour mixture over layers. Bake at 350 degrees for 50 minutes. Yield: 4-6 servings.

Sandra Purdue
Xi Beta X169
Las Vegas, Nevada

Letelle's Eggs Superb

18 eggs, beaten
1 c. sour cream
1 c. milk
Salt to taste
Pepper to taste
1 sm. onion, chopped
1 stick butter or margarine

Combine eggs, sour cream, milk, salt, pepper and onion in large bowl; stir. Pour half the mixture into blender. Blender will not hold all of mixture. Blend for 30 seconds. Repeat for remaining mixture. Melt butter in 9 × 13-inch casserole; pour mixture into casserole. Bake at 350 degrees for 30 to 35 minutes or until toothpick inserted in center comes out clean.

Letelle C. Stafford, W. and M. Chm.
Xi Beta Rho X2035
Sarasota, Florida

Egg-Sausage Casserole

6 eggs, beaten
2 c. milk
1 tsp. salt
1 tsp. dry mustard
2 slices bread, cubed
1 c. grated Cheddar cheese
1 lb. sausage, browned and drained

Combine eggs, milk, salt and dry mustard. Add bread; stir. Add cheese and sausage. Place in 8 × 12-inch baking dish. Refrigerate overnight. Bake at 350 degrees for 45 minutes. Let stand 5 minutes. Yield: 6 servings.

Jeanetta M. "Jickie" Simpson, Rec. Sec.
Preceptor Alpha Psi XP1550
Golden, Colorado

Eggs and Sausage Brunch

8 eggs, beaten
3 c. milk
1½ tsp. dry mustard
Salt and pepper to taste
9 slices bread, crusts removed and cubed
2 lb. sausage, browned and drained
10 oz. sharp Cheddar cheese, grated

Combine eggs, milk, dry mustard, salt and pepper. Layer 9 × 13-inch greased baking dish with bread, sausage and cheese. Pour egg mixture over casserole. Refrigerate overnight. Bake at 350 degrees for 1 hour. Yield: 12 servings.

Patricia Pettit, Pres.
Epsilon Gamma No. 9707
Fort Rucker, Alabama

Tuna and Eggs a la King

1 can tuna, drained and flaked
6 tbsp. butter or margarine, melted
6 tbsp. flour
1 tsp. salt
3 c. milk
4 tsp. chopped green pepper
4 tsp. chopped pimento
4 hard-boiled eggs, quartered

Melt butter in top of double boiler. Stir in flour and salt. Add milk gradually, stirring constantly, until mixture boils and thickens. Add tuna, green pepper, pimento and eggs. Serve hot on toast or biscuits. Yield: 6-8 servings.

Harriette M. Bilbro, Treas.
Xi Mu Tau X2984
Fair Oaks, California

Salmon-Scrambled Eggs

1 3¾-oz. can salmon
½ 10-oz. can cream of vegetable soup
3 eggs, beaten
Salt and pepper to taste
¼ tsp. grated nutmeg
2 tbsp. butter
2 English muffins, halved and toasted

Flake salmon with juice, mashing bones. Combine soup and eggs. Add salmon and seasonings. Melt butter in skillet. Add salmon, stirring frequently. Serve over English muffins. Yield: 2 servings.

Juanita D. Dymond, Pres.
Xi Gamma Psi X4018
Orleans, Ontario, Canada

There is only one thing more exasperating to a man than the wife who can cook and won't—that's the wife that can't cook and will. Phyllis Caudill.

Egg and Sausage Souffle

1 lb. bulk sausage
6 eggs, beaten
2 c. milk
1 tsp. salt
1 tsp. dry mustard
2 slices bread, cubed
1 c. Cheddar cheese, grated

Brown sausage; drain. Combine eggs, milk, salt, dry mustard and bread; mix well. Add cheese and sausage. Pour into 8 × 12-inch glass baking dish; refrigerate overnight. Bake at 350 degrees for 45 minutes. Let stand a few minutes; cut into squares. Yield: 8 servings.

Marilyn C. MacLeod, City Coun. Rep.
Xi Eta Upsilon X3497
Elgin, Illinois

Ham and Egg Brunch

9 slices bread, cubed
1 lb. smoked ham, cubed or 1 lb. fried bacon
½ lb. Old English cheese, cubed
3 eggs, beaten
2 c. milk
½ tsp. dry mustard
½ tsp. salt
¼ c. butter, melted

Combine 7 slices of bread and ham; place in greased 9 × 13-inch casserole. Cover with cheese. Combine eggs, milk, dry mustard and salt; pour over casserole. Crumble 2 slices of bread over casserole. Pour butter over top. Refrigerate overnight. Bake at 325 degrees for 1 hour. Yield: 12 servings.

Elender Barrett, Hon. Mem.
Eta Psi No. 5397
Albany, Missouri

Festive Eggs

10 slices bacon, fried
1 5-oz. jar dried beef, cut in strips
1 8-oz. can mushroom stems and pieces, drained
1½ stick margarine
½ c. flour
½ tsp. seasoned pepper
4 c. milk
16 eggs, beaten
1 c. evaporated milk
1 4-oz. can button mushrooms

Crumble half the bacon; cut remaining into pieces. Saute beef strips and mushroom stems and pieces in bacon drippings; set aside. Melt 1 stick margarine; add flour and pepper. Remove from heat. Add milk, stirring constantly. Replace on heat; cook until thickened. Add bacon, mushroom pieces and stems and beef to cream mixture; set aside. Combine eggs and evaporated milk; scramble lightly in ½ stick margarine. Alternate layers of cream sauce and eggs, ending with cream sauce. Top with, button mushrooms. Bake covered, at 275 degrees for 45 minutes. Bake, uncovered, 15 minutes. Yield: 12 servings.

Marie Kuper, V.P.
Preceptor Alpha Beta XP600
St. Joseph, Missouri

Chipped Beef Puff

4-oz. package dried beef, diced
Butter
3 tbsp. flour
2 c. milk
Dash of pepper
2 tbsp. diced pimento
1 3-oz. can mushrooms, drained
3 eggs, separated
¼ tsp. salt
½ c. cheese, shredded

Saute dried beef in butter until slightly crisp. Blend flour into ¼ cup butter. Add milk gradually, stirring until thickened; add pepper. Stir in pimento and mushrooms. Remove from heat. Beat egg whites with salt until stiff peaks form. Beat egg yolks until thick and yellow. Fold egg yolks into egg whites; fold into cheese. Pour over beef mixture. Bake at 375 degrees for 20 minutes. Yield: 4-5 servings.

Donna L. Aith
Xi Zeta Theta X4412
Waverly, Missouri

Sally's Egg-Ham Casserole

1 can celery soup
1 c. milk
2 c. grated sharp cheese
2 tsp. Worcestershire sauce
½ tsp. Tabasco sauce
2 c. diced ham
6 eggs, hard-boiled and sliced
1 can mushrooms, drained
¾ c. dried bread crumbs
Melted butter

Combine soup, milk and cheese in a saucepan over low heat; stir until cheese melts. Add Worcestershire sauce and Tabasco sauce. Layer ham, eggs and mushrooms in shallow casserole; pour sauce over top. Combine bread crumbs and melted butter. Sprinkle bread crumbs over casserole. Bake at 350 degrees for 25 minutes. Let stand a few minutes before serving. Yield: 6 servings.

Sally Bickford, Treas.
Xi Chi X730
Cedar Rapids, Iowa

Too old too soon—too smart too late. Dee Lemser

Viv's Company Strata

1 10-oz. package frozen chopped broccoli
12 slices day-old bread
12 slices Cheddar cheese
2 c. diced cooked ham
6 eggs, beaten
3½ c. milk
2 tbsp. instant minced onion
½ tsp. salt
¼ tsp. dry mustard

Cook broccoli according to package directions; drain. Cut 12 doughnuts from bread, using doughnut cutter. Line 3-quart rectangular baking dish with bread scraps. Layer with cheese, broccoli and ham. Top with doughnuts and doughnut holes. Combine eggs, milk, onion, salt and dry mustard. Pour over casserole. Refrigerate, covered, at least 6 hours. Bake at 325 degrees for 1 hour and 15 minutes. Let stand 10 minutes. Yield: 12 servings.

Viv Richards, Pres.
Xi Mu Xi X2964
Fair Oaks, California

Green Chili and Cheese Casserole

¼ c. butter or margarine
1 c. chopped onions
4 c. cooked rice
2 c. sour cream
1 c. cottage cheese
½ tsp. salt
⅛ tsp. pepper
1 tsp. bay leaves
3 4-oz. cans diced green chilies
3 c. grated cheese
Chopped parsley

Melt butter in large skillets. Saute onions. Remove from heat; stir in rice, sour cream, cottage cheese, salt, pepper and bay leaves. Alternate layers of rice mixture chilies and cheese in 12 × 8-inch casserole. Bake at 375 degrees for 25 minutes. Garnish with parsley. Yield: 6 servings.

Ida Wickizer, Pres.
Epsilon Epsilon
Tucson, Arizona

Cheese-Ham Bake

12 slices bread
2 c. ham, cubed or ground
1 10-oz. package chopped broccoli, thawed
4 c. Cheddar cheese
6 eggs, beaten
3½ c. milk
½ tsp. salt

1 tsp. dry mustard
2 tsp. chopped onion

Remove bread centers using biscuit cutter; set aside. Arrange bread scraps in buttered casserole. Layer ham, broccoli and 3 cups cheese over bread. Combine next 5 ingredients; pour over casserole. Cover; refrigerate overnight or 6 to 8 hours. Bake at 325 degrees for 55 minutes; remove. Place bread centers over casserole; top with remaining cheese. Return to oven; bake until cheese melts and bread centers are brown. Yield: 12 servings.

Rhoda Wilkinson, Rec. Sec.
Phi Alpha Xi
St. Joseph, Missouri

Karen's Strata

6 slices bread
2 lb. pork sausage
4 eggs, beaten
1½ c. milk
¾ c. half and half
1 tsp. mustard
1 tsp. Worcestershire sauce
6 oz. Swiss cheese, grated

Line 9 × 13-inch casserole with bread. Brown sausage; drain. Distribute evenly over bread slices. Combine eggs, milk, half and half, mustard and Worcestershire sauce; scramble lightly. Pour mixture evenly over casserole. Sprinkle cheese over top. Bake at 350 degrees for 30 to 45 minutes or until brown. Yield: 8-10 servings.

Karen Keskey, Pres.
Xi Alpha Alpha X774
Midland, Michigan

Welsh Rarebit with Oysters

1 tbsp. butter
½ pt. oysters, drained
1 lb. sharp Cheddar cheese, grated
¾ c. beer
1 tsp. dry mustard
½ tsp. Worcestershire sauce
Dash of cayenne pepper
1 egg, slightly beaten

Melt butter in top of double boiler. Add oysters, cheese and beer reserving 1 tablespoon beer. Cook over hot water until cheese melts. Combine dry mustard, Worcestershire sauce, cayenne pepper and 1 tablespoon beer. Stir into oyster mixture. Stir in egg. Serve immediately over toast or English muffin. Yield: 4 servings.

Mary Louise Simpson, Pres.
Preceptor Delta XP371
Alexandria, Virginia

To be closer to God, be closer to people.   Janet L. Buchholz

Shrimp-Cheese Pie

1 9-in. unbaked pastry shell
1 c. mild Cheddar cheese, shredded
1 c. cooked shrimp pieces
1 med. onion, finely diced
3 eggs, beaten
1 c. canned milk
½ tsp. salt
¼ tsp. dry mustard

Layer pastry shell with cheese, shrimp and onion. Combine remaining ingredients. Pour over cheese mixture. Bake at 325 degrees for 45 minutes. Let stand for 5 to 10 minutes. Yield: 6 servings.

Mary Jo Banks
Alpha Chi No. 3191
Fort Bragg, North Carolina

Cheese Souffle Casserole

10 slices bread, crusts removed and cubed
1½ lb. Cheddar cheese, grated
1 lb. cubed ham bacon or sausage
2½ c. half and half
1 tbsp. brown sugar
1 med. onion, chopped
¼ tsp. paprika
½ tsp. Worcestershire sauce
½ tsp. dry mustard
1 tsp. salt
Pinch of pepper
½ tsp. Beau Monde seasoning
6 eggs, beaten
2½ c. corn flakes, crushed
½ c. butter, melted
1 10½-oz. can mushroom soup
Milk

Alternate layers of bread, cheese, and ham in a greased 9 × 13-inch glass casserole. Combine half and half, brown sugar, onion, paprika, Worcestershire sauce, dry mustard, salt, pepper and seasoning. Add eggs to liquid mixture; pour over layers. Combine corn flakes and butter. Spread evenly over top. Let stand overnight. Place casserole uncovered, in pan of water. Place in cold oven. Bake at 350 degrees for 1 hour. Dilute soup with small amount of milk; heat. Serve over casserole. Yield: 12 servings.

Carole Maltrud, Pres.
Alpha Tau No. 2470
Detroit Lakes, Minnesota

Barbara's Cheese Fondue

1 sm. onion, diced
1 16-oz. can tomatoes, drained
1 tbsp. chopped chilies
1 2-lb box Velveeta cheese, room temperature
1 loaf French bread, toasted and cubed

Saute onion; add tomatoes and chilies. Cut cheese into small pieces; add to tomatoes and onion. Cook over medium heat until cheese melts. Pour into fondue pot. Spear bread on fondue fork; dip into cheese mixture. Yield: 8-10 servings.

Barbara Hanson, V.P.
Xi Theta Zeta X2107
Escondido, California

Julie's Cheese-Egg Fondue

8 slices bread, crusts removed and cubed
½ stick butter
½ lb. Cheddar cheese, grated
2 c. milk
4 eggs, beaten
Ham, cubed

Line 1½-quart casserole with bread. Melt butter and cheese over low heat. Add milk gradually, stirring constantly. Add cheese mixture to eggs; pour over bread cubes. Sprinkle with ham. Refrigerate overnight. Bake at 350 degrees for 1 hour and 15 minutes. Yield: 8 servings.

Julie S. Favorite
Beta No. 471
Rogers, Arkansas

Pauline's Cheese Strata

½ lb. butter
1 lb. Velveeta cheese, cubed
8 eggs, beaten
4 c. milk
¼ tsp. salt
⅛ tsp. pepper
20 slices bread, trimmed and cubed

Melt butter and cheese over low heat, stirring constantly. Combine eggs, milk, salt and pepper. Add cheese mixture to egg mixture. Place bread cubes in 9 × 13-inch casserole. Pour cheese and egg mixture slowly over bread. Cover; refrigerate overnight. Remove from refrigerator 1 hour before baking. Bake at 325 degrees for 1 hour. Let stand for 10 minutes; cut into squares. Yield: 12 servings.

Pauline Scharf, Corr. Sec.
Eta Kappa No. 3388
Oswego, Illinois

To enjoy someone else's company you must first enjoy yourself. Karen Borrelli

Cheese-Custard Tartlets

1 recipe 2-crust pie pastry
¼ lb. med. Cheddar cheese, cubed
3 eggs, beaten
¼ c. milk
Pinch of salt

Line tart pans with pastry. Place cheese in each shell. Combine eggs, milk and salt; mix well. Pour over cheese. Fill shells ¾ full. Bake at 400 degrees for 6 minutes; reduce heat to 350 degrees. Bake 20 minutes or until pastry is lightly browned and custard is firm.

Alice Lister, Rec. Sec.
Laureate Zeta PL1383
Richmond, British Columbia, Canada

Patricia's Quiche

1 c. half and half
1 c. shredded Swiss cheese
3 eggs, beaten
½ tsp. salt
¼ tsp. each pepper and nutmeg
1 c. diced green pepper
½ lb. fried bacon, crumbled
1 pie shell

Combine first 8 ingredients; pour into pie shell. Bake at 375 degrees for 45 to 60 minutes.

Patricia Seifert
Nu Xi No. 8677
O'Fallon, Missouri

Ina's Quiche Loraine

3 c. bread, toasted and cubed
3 c. cubed ham
½ lb. cheese, grated
1 tbsp. dry mustard
3 eggs, beaten
3 c. milk

Combine bread, ham, cheese and dry mustard; place in 8 × 14-inch baking dish. Combine eggs and milk; pour over casserole. Refrigerate overnight. Let stand at room temperature for 1 hour before baking. Bake at 350 degrees for 1 hour or until set.

Ina M. Waldrop
Preceptor Omicron X1398
Bethany, Oklahoma

Sandy's Ham Quiche

2 c. flour
1 tsp. salt
½ tsp. baking powder
1 tsp. sugar
¾ c. Crisco
2 tbsp. butter at room temperature
3 lg. eggs
1½ c. milk
½ c. diced ham

Combine flour, ½ teaspoon salt, baking powder and sugar. Cut in Crisco and butter until crumbly. Add 6 tablespoons water, mixing until dough forms. Divide dough in half. Fit into 9-inch pie pan. Store remaining dough for later use. Combine eggs, milk and ½ teaspoon salt in small bowl. Beat with egg beater until well mixed. Sprinkle ham in pie shell. Pour egg mixture over ham. Bake at 400 degrees for 30 to 35 minutes. Yield: 6 servings.

Sandy Hatala, Rec. Sec.
Xi Beta Eta X3227
Weirton, West Virginia

Darnell's Quiche

1 baked 10-inch pie crust
2 c. grated Swiss cheese
1 c. cooked shrimp ham, chicken or bacon
1 13-oz. can evaporated milk
4 eggs, beaten
1 tsp. salt
¼ tsp. pepper
⅛ tsp. nutmeg
1 tbsp. Sherry (opt.)
1 tbsp. parsley flakes
½ c. chopped onions

Sprinkle crust with cheese. Arrange shrimp over cheese. Blend milk, eggs, salt, pepper, nutmeg and Sherry Stir in parsley flakes and onions. Pour over cheese and shrimp. Bake at 425 degrees for 35 minutes or until slightly brown. Allow to set 5 minutes before cutting. Yield: 8-10 servings.

Darnell Russo
Xi Epislon X1909
Galveston, Texas

Spinach Quiche

2 10-oz. packages frozen chopped spinach
1 pie crust
1 lb. provolone cheese, shredded
3 eggs, beaten
½ c. sour cream

Cook spinach; drain. Cover pie crust with shredded cheese. Combine spinach, eggs and sour cream spoon onto cheese. Bake at 325 degrees for 45 minutes. Yield: 6 servings.

Rebecca Ann Blake, Soc. Chm.
Delta No. 263
Indianapolis, Indiana

Where there is room in the heart—there is always room in the house.   Joella D. Hultgren

Chili-Cheese Puff

1 stick margarine
10 eggs, beaten
½ c. flour
3 tsp. baking powder
1 tsp. salt
¼ tsp. pepper
2 c. cottage cheese
1 lb. Monterrey Jack cheese, grated
2 sm. cans chopped chilies

Melt butter in 8 × 13-inch baking dish. Combine eggs, flour, baking powder, salt and pepper. Fold cottage cheese, Monterey Jack cheese and chilies into egg mixture. Pour into casserole. Bake at 350 degrees for 30 minutes. Yield: 12 servings.

Betty Crowe, Pres.
Xi Zeta Zeta X1753
Castella, California

Virginia's Cheese Fondue

1 2 lb. package Velveeta cheese
1 4-oz. can Ortega chili strips
½ c. diced canned tomatoes
1 tsp. garlic powder
1 tsp. Worcestershire sauce
1 tbsp. oil
1 tbsp. prepared mustard
⅛ tsp. Accent
1 11-oz. Cheddar cheese soup
1 tsp. instant minced onion

Combine all ingredients in top of double boiler; heat through. Serve with bread, sticks or Melba toast.

Virginia Rice, Pres.
Preceptor Mu XP496
Brokings, Oregon

Sally's Ham and Cheese Strata

12 slices bread
2 c. diced ham
1 12-oz. jar Old English cheese
6 eggs, beaten
3½ c. milk
2 tbsp. instant onion
½ tsp. salt
1 tsp. dry mustard

Cut bread into 12 rounds; set aside. Cut up bread scraps; place in 9 × 13-inch greased casserole. Top with diced ham. Place bread rounds on ham. Combine remaining ingredients in a blender. Pour mixture over casserole. Refrigerate for several hours. Bake at 325 degrees for 1 hour and 30 minutes.

Sally J. Finch, Pres.
Xi Alpha Gamma X292
Galesburg, Illinois

Joan's Cheese Fluff

6 slices bread, crusts removed
1 c. grated American cheese
2 eggs, beaten
1½ c. milk
2 tbsp. melted butter
Salt and pepper to taste

Arrange 3 slices bread in buttered casserole to cover entire surface. Cover bread with ½ cup cheese. Repeat layers using remaining bread and cheese. Combine eggs, milk, melted butter, salt and pepper. Pour over bread and cheese to saturate. Bake at 350 degrees for 30 to 40 minutes until casserole is puffed and brown. Yield: 6 servings.

Joan Aronson, Rec. Sec.
Alpha Alpha Sigma No. 6699
Carrollton, Texas

Barbara's Swiss Brunch

1 c. onion, sliced
1 tbsp. margarine
8 hard-boiled eggs, sliced
2 c. grated Swiss cheese
1 can cream of mushroom soup
1 tsp. prepared mustard
¼ tsp. dillweed
¾ c. milk
½ tsp. salt
¼ tsp. pepper
6 slices bread, cut into triangles, buttered and
    toasted

Saute onion in margarine until onion is tender. Arrange onion slices in 11½ × 7½-inch casseole. Cover onion with egg slices; sprinkle with cheese. Combine next 6 ingredients. Pour over cheese. Place bread triangles on top, overlapping slightly, butter side up. Bake at 350 degrees for 30 to 35 minutes or until heated through. Yield: 6-8 servings.

Barbara J. Courtemanche
Gamma Phi No. 6042
Sterling, Virginia

Continental Cheese Bake

1 c. sliced onions
1 tbsp. butter or margarine
8 hard-cooked eggs, sliced
3 c. shredded Cheddar cheese
10½-oz. can condensed cream of mushroom soup
¾ c. milk
1 tsp. prepared mustard
½ tsp. seasoned salt
¼ tsp. dillweed

Bad habits are like soft beds—easy to get into but hard to get out of. Margie Slacum

¼ tsp. pepper
6 slices buttered whole wheat bread

Saute onion in butter until tender. Place onions in 11½ × 7½-inch casserole. Top with egg slices. Sprinkle with cheese. Combine next 6 ingredients. Mix well. Pour soup mixture over cheese. Cut bread slices into 4 triangles. Arrange triangles over casserole. Bake at 350 degrees for 30 to 35 minutes or until heated through. Place casserole under broiler; broil for 1 minute or until bread is toasted. Yield: 6 servings.

Shirley Williams, V. P.
Xi Beta Iota X2934
Elk City, Oklahoma

Butter-Baked Rice

2 tsp. salt
1 c. long grain rice
⅓ c. butter
1 tsp. garlic powder
1½ tsp. salt
1¾ c. chicken stock
Chopped parsley
Toasted slivered almonds
Paprika

Add salt to rice. Pour enough boiling water over rice to cover. Let stand 30 to 40 minutes. Strain rice; rinse with cold water thoroughly. Drain well. Melt butter in a skillet. Add rice; cook over medium heat, stirring frequently, until butter is absorbed. Place rice in casserole. Sprinkle with garlic powder and salt. Add chicken stock. Bake at 350 degrees, uncovered, for 50 to 60 minutes stirring occasionally until all stock is absorbed. Sprinkle with chopped parsley and toasted slivered almonds before serving garnish with paprika. Yield: 4-6 servings.

Susan K. Mackintosh, Pub Chm.
Alpha Phi No. 6124
Castlegar, British Columbia, Canada

Oriental Rice

2 1-lb. sausage rolls, 1 hot, 1 mild
1 c. finely chopped green pepper
¾ c. chopped onion
2½ c. coarsely chopped celery
¼ c. melted butter
1 can mushrooms
1 can water chestnuts
2 pkg. cream-style chicken flavor soup mix
½ tsp. salt

Slice sausage into patties. Brown patties in large skillet; drain. Drain fat from skillet. Saute green pepper, onion and celery in melted butter in same skillet. Add mushrooms and water chestnuts; saute until tender. Combine soup mix, 4½ cups boiling water and salt. In large saucepan. Mix until smooth. Add rice. Simmer, covered, for about 30 minutes until rice is tender and liquid absorbed. Crumble sausage patties in large mixing bowl. Add sauted vegetables and rice mixture. Mix well. Place in 9 × 13-inch glass baking dish. Bake at 350 degrees for 30 or 40 minutes or until heated through. Yield: 12 servings.

Beverly S. Lawler, Treas.
Xi Eta Pi X2258
Fort Worth, Texas

Hawaiian Rice with Shrimp

4 strips bacon, diced
½ lb. ground beef
1 c. chopped onion
3 c. cooked rice
1 4½-oz. can shrimp
⅓ c. minced celery leaves
½ tsp. salt
½ tsp. dry mustard
Dash of pepper
2 tbsp. soy sauce
1 can pineapple tibbits

Cook bacon until crisp. Add beef and onion. Stir until onion is tender. Add remaining ingredients except fruit; mix well. Heat through. Add pineapple; heat through. Yield: 6 servings.

Diane McAplin, Pres.
Preceptor Laureate Nu No. 284
Olympia, Washington

Wild Rice with Almonds

½ c. butter
1 8-oz. can mushroom pieces
1 garlic clove
2 tbsp. chopped green pepper
2 tbsp. chopped green onion
½ c. slivered almonds
1 c. wild rice
3 c. chicken broth
Salt and pepper to taste

Melt butter. Add mushrooms, garlic, green pepper, onion and almonds. Cook over low heat for 5 minutes. Add rinsed rice. Cook until rice begins to turn yellow. Add chicken broth, salt and pepper. Pour into 9-inch buttered casserole. Bake, covered, at 325 degrees for 1 hour. Yield: 6 servings.

Mildred S. Mahler
Preceptor Delta XP0759
Cookeville, Tennessee

Vegetables

The most appealing part of any good menu, plus color and sumptuous variety—that's vegetables! Moreover, they are all packed with an abundance of flavor and nutrition, all for very low cost and very few calories. A stunning brunch, a wholesome lunch, a memorable dinner—none are complete without vegetables.

Inventive cooks, who want every meal to be special, depend on the versatility of vegetables. They can be prepared in so many inviting ways, and respond beautifully to thoughtful additions of herbs, spices, sauces and garnishes. But, the key to vegetable success is in the cooking; resolve now to allow no more overcooked or mushy vegetable dishes on your table! Cook or steam vegetables only until they are tender-crisp, in as little liquid as possible. For a complete change of pace, prepare your vegetables by the ancient Oriental stir-fry method.

Make full use of the many ways you can present your vegetables for the most appetizing effect. Bright, whole kernels of corn become even more colorful with the addition of diced green pepper, pimento strips and a sprinkling of coarsely-ground black pepper. Sliced, fresh tomatoes on a platter becomes a work of art when sprinkled with dillweed and drizzled with a zesty Italian dressing. For a way to transform "ordinary" mashed potatoes into a special dish, pipe them back into their jackets or around a platter of meat and then broil until just golden. Or, pipe them into the shape of little cups, broil until golden, and then fill each cup with small green peas and mushroom slices. Consider plump blueberries as a uniquely delicious garnish for baked or stuffed squash.

There's no question! You can be inventive as you wish with today's vegetable cookery. And, with Beta Sigma Phi vegetable recipes, you will discover new ways to prepare old favorites, plus new vegetables to introduce to your meals, as well.

Artichokes and Cheese

2 8½-oz. cans water-packed artichokes
1 stick butter or margarine
¾ c. flour
Milk
½ tsp. Worcestershire sauce
¼ tsp. paprika
Dash of red and black pepper
½ lb. grated Cheddar cheese

Drain artichokes, reserving liquid. Place artichoke liquid in saucepan. Add melted butter. Add flour. Stir in enough milk to make a medium white sauce. Add Worcestershire sauce, paprika and peppers. Add half the grated cheese; cook until melted. Place artichokes in a 2-quart baking dish. Pour cheese mixture over artichokes. Sprinkle remaining grated cheese over artichokes. Bake at 325 degrees about 45 minutes. Yield: 6 servings.

Michele M. Fish
Xi Lambda Chi No. 3398
Hurst, Texas

Asparagus-Pea Casserole

4 c. canned asparagus, drained
2½ c. canned peas
1 can mushroom soup
½ c. milk
2 c. grated sharp Cheddar cheese
3 slices bread, cut into strips
1 stick margarine, melted

Place asparagus in a 9 x 13-inch casserole. Combine mushroom soup and milk. Layer soup mixture over asparagus. Cover with cheese. Saturate bread in margarine. Cover cheese with bread strips. Bake at 350 degrees for 30 minutes. Yield: 10-12 servings.

Marcia Nestler, Pres.
Kappa Gamma No. 9854
Davenport, Iowa

Elegant Baked Asparagus

2 cans green asparagus, drained
1 large can English peas, drained
1 can mushroom soup, undiluted
Salt and pepper to taste
1 can water chestnuts, diced
½ lb. grated sharp cheese
4 slices bread, trimmed and cut into 4 strips
1 stick of margarine

Arrange asparagus in lightly buttered 9 x 12-inch dish. Mix peas and soup. Spread over asparagus. Salt and pepper to taste. Cover with water chestnuts and cheese. Saturate bread strips in melted margarine. Cover cheese with bread strips. Bake, covered, 25 to 35 minutes at 350 degrees. Bake, uncovered, 5-10 minutes. Yield: 8-10 servings

Judy Schies
Xi Kappa Tau X3175
Dallas, Texas

Green Bean Supreme

1 pkg. French-cut green beans
1 sm. onion, chopped
2 tbsp. margarine
1 tbsp. flour
½ tsp. salt
Dash of pepper
½ c. sour cream
⅓ c. grated Cheddar cheese

Cook green beans according to package directions. Saute onion in margarine. Add flour, salt and pepper. Add sour cream; heat thoroughly. Drain beans. Stir in sour cream mixture. Place in shallow baking dish. Cover with cheese. Bake for 15 minutes at 350 degrees. Yield: 4 servings.

Helen P. Jarvis
Gamma Gamma No. 4426
Greensboro, North Carolina

Green Bean Casserole

2 cans cream of mushroom soup
1 tbsp. soy sauce
1 tsp. salt
¼ tsp. pepper
1 c. grated Cheddar cheese
1-2 oz. jar pimento slices, drained
1 sm. onion, grated
1 4½-oz. jar sliced mushrooms
1 can water chestnuts, drained
2 cans julienne-style green beans, drained
1 can French-fried onions, crumbled

Pour cream of mushroom soup in saucepan. Dilute with 1 soup can water. Blend soy sauce, salt, pepper and Cheddar cheese until thickened and smooth. Combine pimento, grated onion, mushrooms and water chestnuts with green beans. Pour sauce over green bean mixture. Place in 3-quart casserole. Top with crumbled onions. Bake at 350 degrees for 25 minutes. Yield: 8 servings.

Helen L. Palamand, Pres.
Eta Zeta No. 3324
Hanover Park, Illinois

Spanish-Style Beans

½ c. coarsely chopped onions
1 med. green pepper, diced

About the time you learn to make the most of life, most of it is gone. Barbara Gundy

1 clove of garlic, finely chopped
2 tbsp. butter
2 1-lb. 12-oz. cans baked beans
½ c. hot catsup
¼ c. honey
1 c. grated sharp cheese
½ c. dry bread crumbs
Salt to taste
Pepper to taste
Paprika to taste

Saute onions, green pepper and garlic in butter until tender. Remove from heat. Combine onion mixture with baked beans, hot catsup and honey. Pour into 2-quart casserole. Combine cheese, bread crumbs, salt, pepper, and paprika. Spoon over bean mixture. Bake, uncovered, at 350 degrees for 45 minutes. Yield: 8 servings.

Janel Blancher, Prog. Chm.
Preceptor Alpha XP140
Regina, Saskatchewan, Canada

Kay's Broccoli-Rice Casserole

1 c. rice
1 tsp. salt
2 10-oz. packages chopped broccoli, thawed
1 stick butter
1 onion, grated
1 can cream of chicken soup
1 8-oz. jar Cheez Whiz
1 can water chestnuts, sliced and drained
Cheese Nips

Cook rice in 2 cups cold water; add salt. Bring to a boil. Simmer, covered, for 15 minutes. Cook broccoli according to package directions. Drain broccoli; mash. Add butter and onion. Combine broccoli with rice. Add remaining ingredients, except Cheese Nips. Pour into a 9 x 13-inch casserole. Sprinkle with Cheese Nips. Bake at 350 degrees for 20 minutes. Yield: 8 servings.

Kay Bland
Epsilon Eta No. 9208
Paragould, Arkansas

Broccoli-Cauliflower Au Gratin

1½ lb. fresh broccoli
1 lg. head cauliflower
3 tbsp. butter
3 tbsp. flour
½ tsp. salt
Dash of pepper
1½ c. milk
1 to 1½ c. Cheddar cheese, grated
1 8 oz. can sliced water chestnuts

½ c. slivered almonds
1 c. croutons, crushed

Wash broccoli and cauliflower. Trim flowerets from stalks. Boil for 10 minutes or until tender; drain well. Melt butter in heavy saucepan. Add flour, salt and pepper; mix well. Add milk gradually; stir well. Bring to a boil. Reduce heat. Add cheese; stir until cheese melts. Mix broccoli, cauliflower, water chestnuts and slivered almonds in greased 11¾ x 7½-inch casserole. Cover with cheese sauce. Top with croutons. Bake at 325 degrees for 25 minutes. Yield: 10-12 servings.

Sherry Silsbee, Pres.
Gamma Psi No. 6217
Beaverton, Oregon

Sunshine Broccoli Casserole

2 10-oz. packages frozen cut broccoli
2 eggs, beaten
1 c. mayonnaise
1 can celery soup
1 c. sharp Swiss cheese, shredded
½ c. milk
Lemon juice to taste
Onion salt to taste
Worcestershire sauce to taste

Cook broccoli according to package directions, omitting salt. Drain thoroughly. Combine remaining ingredients. Blend mixture into broccoli. Pour into 2-quart casserole. Bake at 350 for 1 hour. Yield 8 servings.

Evelyn R. Alexander, Pres.
Preceptor Zeta XP436
Caldwell, Idaho

Janet's Broccoli-Rice Casserole

1 16-oz. frozen broccoli
¼ c. chopped onion
¼ c. chopped celery
4 tbsp. butter
1 can cream of chicken soup
1 can cream of mushroom soup
1 c. grated Cheddar cheese
1½ c. cooked rice

Cook broccoli according to package directions until tender. Saute onion and celery in butter. Combine soups and Cheddar cheese; add onion and celery. Mix with broccoli. Season to taste. Add rice; pour into a greased casserole. Bake at 350 degrees for 30 minutes. Yield: 4-6 servings.

Janet L. Buchholz
Gamma Pi No. 2364
Bridgeton, Missouri

The difference between the right word and almost the right word, is the difference between the lightening and the lightening bug.   Kitty Lint

Broccoli Special

2 10-oz. packages frozen chopped broccoli
½ lb.-Velveeta cheese, cubed
1 stick butter
¼ lb. Ritz crackers, crushed

Cook broccoli for 5 minutes in boiling salted water. Drain, reserving ½ cup liquid. Place broccoli in baking dish. Pour reserved liquid over broccoli. Add cheese and ½ stick butter to broccoli. Stir until melted. Melt ½ stick butter. Add cracker crumbs; mix well. Top broccoli with crumbs mixture. Bake at 350 degrees for 25 minutes. Yield: 8 servings.

Linda S. Jandernal, Pres.
Gamma Pi No. 7102
Dover, New Jersey

Marinated Brussels Sprouts

1½ lb. fresh Brussels sprouts
⅓ c. tarragon vinegar
½ c. salad oil
1 sm. clove of garlic, minced
1 tbsp. sugar
1 tsp. salt
2 tbsp. green onions, thinly sliced
Dash of hot sauce

Wash fresh Brussels sprouts. Cook in salted water 8 to 10 minutes. If using frozen Brussels sprouts, cook according to package directions. Drain. Combine remaining ingredients. Pour over Brussels sprouts; toss well. Chill for 8 hours. Drain; serve cold. Yield: 10 servings.

Edna Martin, 1st V.P.
Xi Nu Upsilon No. 3977
Nederland, Texas

Fried Cabbage with Noodles

1 lg. onion, chopped
Margarine
1 med. cabbage, shredded
1 8-oz. package noodles
Salt to taste

Saute onion in margarine until tender. Add cabbage. Cook for 20 to 30 minutes. Cook noodles according to package directions; drain. Add noodles; mix well. Add salt to taste. Yield: 6-8 servings.

Suzanne Holliday, Corr. Sec.
Xi Gamma X146
Canal Fulton, Ohio

Cabbage Bundles in Paprika Cream Sauce

1 3 to 3½ lb. cabbage
1 3-oz. package onion flavor meat extender
1 lb. ground chuck
2 eggs
1 c. cooked rice
4 tbsp. margarine
1 med. onion, chopped
2 carrots, sliced
1 tbsp. paprika
1 tsp. salt
1 can condensed beef broth
1 8-oz. can tomato sauce
1 c. sour cream at room temperature
1 tbsp. flour

Remove 12 to 16 outer leaves from cabbage. Cook in boiling water to cover for 2 minutes or until soft and pliable. Shred remaining cabbage. Combine meat extender and 1¼ cup warm water in large bowl. Add ground chuck, eggs and rice; mix well. Place ¼ cup of meat mixture on each leaf. Fold sides over meat mixture; roll up from thick end of cabbage leaf. Saute onion in margarine in a large saucepan. Stir in carrots and chopped cabbage; saute for 10 minutes, stirring frequently. Add paprika, salt, broth and tomato sauce. Arrange stuffed cabbage bundles seam side down over cabbage mixture. Cook over low heat 50 to 60 minutes; baste frequently. Remove cabbage bundles carefully; keep warm. Stir flour into sour cream; add to cabbage mixture. Bring to a boil; stir constantly. Boil for 1 minute. Layer cabbage mixture and cabbage bundles in serving dish. Yield: 6-8 servings.

Mary Ellen Grossman, Serv. Chm.
Xi Epsilon Sigma X4941
Lawrenceburg, Indiana

Carrot Ring

2 tbsp. butter
2 tbsp. flour
½ c. milk
4 eggs, separated
2 c. carrots, grated
1 tsp. salt
Dash of pepper
1 tbsp. sugar
Cracker crumbs

Cook butter, flour and milk until thickened. Beat egg yolks. Add to carrots, salt and pepper. Beat egg whites until foamy. Add sugar; beat until stiff. Fold carrot mixture into egg whites. Pour into greased ring mold. Sprinkle with cracker crumbs. Set in pan of water. Bake at 350 degrees for 25 to 30 minutes. Let stand; cool for 5 minutes. Yield: 12-16 servings.

Nan Howard, Soc. Chm.
Xi Iota
Loyall, Kentucky

Release me from craving to straighten out everyone's affairs. Debbie Meins

Sweet and Sour Carrots

6 c. thinly sliced carrots
1 med. onion, thinly sliced
1 c. sugar
½ c. oil
½ c. vinegar
1 tsp. dry mustard
1 tsp. salt
1 can tomato soup
1 green pepper, thinly sliced

Place carrots and onion in a 2-quart saucepan. Cover with water; cook until tender. Drain; set aside. Combine sugar, oil, vinegar, dry mustard, salt and tomato soup. Bring to a boil. Add green pepper; pour over carrots and onion. Cover; let stand at least 1 hour. Reheat over medium heat until bubbly. Yield: 8-10 servings.

Diane Baker, Rec. Sec.
Iota Theta No. 3348
Concord, California

Heavenly Carrots

4 c. cooked sliced carrots
1½ c. croutons
1 c. grated sharp Cheddar cheese
2 eggs, beaten
¼ c. light cream
¼ c. melted butter
1½ tsp. Worcestershire sauce
1 tsp. salt

Place carrots in a greased 1½-quart casserole. Stir in croutons and Cheddar cheese. Mix remaining ingredients. Pour over carrot mixture. Bake, uncovered, at 400 degrees for 20 minutes or until brown. Yield: 6 servings.

Pam W. Kettering, V.P.
Alpha Upsilon No. 5952
Yankton, South Dakota

Cauliflower Con Queso

1 cauliflower
2 tbsp. butter or margarine
¼ c. chopped onion
2 tbsp. flour
1 1-lb. can tomatoes
1 bay leaf
1 4-oz. can green chilies, drained, seeded and
    chopped
1 tsp. salt
¼ tsp. Tabasco pepper sauce
1 c. shredded Monterey Jack or mild Cheddar cheese

Wash cauliflower; remove leaves. Place in 1 inch boiling salted water in large saucepan. Cook for 5

minutes; cover. Cook 15 to 25 minutes or until crisp-tender. Melt butter in medium saucepan. Add onion; cook until tender, about 5 minutes. Blend in flour. Stir in tomatoes. Cook, stirring constantly, until mixture thickens and comes to a boil. Add bay leaf, green chilies, salt and Tabasco; cook for 5 minutes. Add cheese; stir until melted. Drain cauliflower; serve with sauce. Yield: 4 servings.

Photograph for this recipe on page 81.

Cauliflower with Shrimp Sauce

1 lg. head cauliflower
1 13-oz. can cream of shrimp soup
½ c. sour cream
½ tsp. salt
⅛ tsp. pepper
½ c. chopped slivered almonds

Break cauliflower into flowerets. Place in small amount of boiling salted water; cook for 10 minutes. Drain. Combine soup, sour cream, salt and pepper; heat thoroughly. Place cauliflower in casserole; cover with soup mixture. Cover with slivered almonds. Bake at 350 degrees for 30 minutes. Yield: 6-8 servings.

Jeanne R. Patterson, Rec. Sec.
Preceptor Beta Delta XP1777
Bloomsburg, Pennsylvania

Patience like any other good quality is a matter of habit. M. Louise Cahill

Xi Iota Pi's Corn Pie

1¼ c. saltine cracker crumbs
¼ c. melted butter
1¼ c. milk
2 c. whole kernel corn
½ tsp. salt
¼ tsp. white pepper
2 tbsp. instant minced onion
2 tbsp. all-purpose flour
2 eggs, beaten
Paprika
Chives or parsley

Combine cracker crumbs and butter; reserve ½ cup mixture. Press remaining crumbs into 9-inch pie pan to form a shell. Mix 1 cup milk, corn, salt, pepper and onion in saucepan. Bring to a boil; reduce heat. Simmer for 3 minutes. Blend flour and remaining ¼ cup milk; stir into hot mixture until thickened. Cool slightly. Slowly add eggs, stirring vigorously. Pour into crumb-lined pan; cover with reserved crumbs. Sprinkle with paprika. Bake at 400 degrees for 15 minutes. Sprinkle with chives. Let Stand 10 minutes before cutting. Cut into wedges; serve hot. Yield: 6-8 servings.

Catherine Matthews, Treas.
Xi Iota Pi X4930
Largo, Florida

Pennie's Corn Pudding

3 tbsp. cornstarch
1 13-oz. can evaporated milk
1 16-oz. can whole kernel corn, crushed
⅔ c. sugar
2 eggs, beaten
½ stick butter

Combine cornstarch, milk, corn, sugar and eggs. Pour into greased 1½-quart baking dish. Dot with butter. Bake at 350 degrees for 1 hour. Yield: 6 servings.

Hazel M. Moffett, Soc. Chm.
Xi Alpha Theta
Chestertown, Maryland

Scalloped Corn

2 c. cream-style corn
2 eggs, beaten
¼ tsp. salt
⅛ tsp. pepper
½ c. cracker crumbs
2 tbsp. butter
¾ c. milk

Mix corn, eggs, salt and pepper. Place ½ of the mixture into greased 1½-quart casserole. Cover with ¼ cup cracker crumbs. Add remaining corn mixture; top with remaining cracker crumbs. Dot with butter. Pour milk over all. Bake at 325 degrees for 30 minutes. Yield: 4 servings.

Vivien Davis
Preceptor Beta Epsilon XP1642
Topeka, Kansas

Chili Corn

2 16-oz. cans cream-style corn
2 eggs, well beaten
1 7½-oz. can chopped green chilies
¾ c. yellow cornmeal
½ tsp. baking powder
¾ tsp. garlic salt
½ c. vegetable oil
¾ c. Cheddar cheese, grated

Combine all ingredients. Pour into 9 x 13-inch baking dish. Bake at 350 degrees for 1 hour.

Dena Porter
Alpha Alpha Mu No. 6660
Ozona, Texas

Eggplant Casserole

1 lg. eggplant
1 c. cracker crumbs
½ green pepper, chopped
Sharp Cheddar cheese, shredded
1 med. tomato, chopped
1 can cream of mushroom soup
1 egg, beaten
1 c. milk
Salt and pepper to taste

Peel and cube eggplant. Place in salted water for 15 minutes. Drain; rinse. Parboil until tender; drain. Layer cracker crumbs, eggplant, green pepper, 1 cup cheese, tomato and mushroom soup in a greased 2-quart casserole. Season with salt and mix egg and milk; pour over casserole. Sprinkle with additional cheese. Bake, covered, at 350 degrees for 40 to 60 minutes. Yield: 6 servings.

Ernestine Nobles, Hon. Mem.
Alpha Alpha
Amarillo, Texas

Stuffed Eggplant

6 eggplant
½ c. diced celery
½ c. chopped onion
¼ c. chopped green pepper
1 4-oz. can mushroom pieces, drained
½ c. butter
1 lb. crab meat

Life is what you make it, so make it a good one. M. Louise Cahill

2½ lb. cooked shrimp
2 c. Italian-style bread crumbs
2 c. milk
1 11-oz. can Cheddar cheese soup
1 tsp. garlic salt
1 tsp. salt
½ tsp. pepper

Cut eggplant lengthwise and scoop out pulp to make shells. Boil pulp in a small amount of water until tender; drain. Parboil eggplant shells for 3 minutes. Drain; let cool. Saute celery, onion, green pepper and mushrooms in butter. Combine crab meat, shrimp, bread crumbs, milk, soup, garlic salt, pepper and salt in large saucepan; cook over low heat. Add sauteed vegetables, butter, and eggplant pulp. Place eggplant shells on cookie sheet; fill with stuffing. Bake at 325 degrees for 30 minutes. Yield: 12 servings.

Jane M. McGowen
Xi Phi X4275
Hattiesburg, Mississippi

Moussaka

4 med. eggplant
¾ c. oil
2 med. onions
Butter
¾ lb. ground beef
¼ tsp. garlic salt
Salt and pepper to taste
Thyme to taste
1 lg. can tomato sauce
½ c. sour cream
4 tbsp. flour
4 c. milk
Parmesan cheese
Bread crumbs

Peel eggplant. Cut into ½-inch slices. Sprinkle with salt. Let stand 30 minutes; pat dry. Saute eggplant slices in oil; drain. Saute onions in 2 tablespoons butter until yellow. Add ground beef, garlic salt, salt, pepper and thyme. Cook until brown; add tomato sauce. Simmer, uncovered, for 30 minutes. Melt 2 tablespoons butter in a saucepan. Remove from heat. Add sour cream and flour; cook until brown. Add milk gradually over medium heat until thickened. Cover bottom of large casserole with half the white sauce. Layer with 2 rows eggplant and ground beef mixture. Repeat layers. Cover with remaining white sauce. Top with cheese and bread crumbs. Bake, covered, at 350 degrees for 30 minutes. Bake, uncovered, for 30 minutes. Broil 2 minutes. Yield: 12 servings.

Moha Stino
Alpha Theta
Auburn, Alabama

Kay's Stuffed Mushrooms

2 doz. large mushrooms
2 tbsp. butter
6 slices bacon, chopped
1 med. onion, finely chopped
2 tbsp. dry Sherry
½ c. mozzarella cheese, shredded
4 tbsp. grated Parmesan cheese

Rinse mushrooms. Remove stems; finely chop. Melt butter in skillet. Turn mushroom caps in melted butter. Arrange, cup-side up, in a 9 x 13-inch baking pan. Fry bacon until crisp; drain. Reserve 2 tablespoons drippings. Add onion; cook until tender. Stir in mushroom stems, Sherry and bacon. Cook until liquid has evaporated; remove from heat. Stir in mozzarella and 2 tablespoons Parmesan cheese. Mound onion mixture on mushroom caps. Sprinkle with remaining Parmesan. Bake, uncovered, at 400 degrees for 10 minutes.

Kay Nation, Pres.
Delta Upsilon No. 9654
Angel Fire, New Mexico

Patricia's Stuffed Mushrooms

2 slices dry bread
1 lb. fresh mushrooms
1 sm. onion, chopped
¼ c. margarine
½ c. Parmesan cheese
Salt to taste

Place bread in blender container; blend to fine crumbs. Remove stems from mushrooms; chop finely. Saute onion in margarine until tender. Add mushroom stems; heat through. Mix cheese, bread crumbs and salt; add to onion mixture. Cook until heated through. Cool slightly. Place mushroom caps in baking dish. Fill with onion mixture. Bake at 350 degrees for 10 minutes.

Mrs. Patricia Booth
Xi Iota Phi
Sidney, Ohio

Parmesan-Fried Mushrooms

1 lb. fresh mushrooms
⅓ c. flour
1 egg
¼ c. milk
¾ c. seasoned bread crumbs
½ c. Parmesan cheese

Wash and trim mushrooms. Coat with flour. Combine egg and milk. Dip mushrooms in egg mixture. Roll in seasoned bread crumbs. Deep fry until golden brown. Drain. Roll in Parmesan cheese. Yield: 4-6 servings.

Diane Lindahl, V.P.
Sigma No. 2093
Northport, Alabama

A friend never forgets someone who remembers.   Edith Savage

Kathy's Baked Mushrooms

2 lb. med. mushrooms
½ c. butter, melted
1 c. soft bread crumbs
1 tsp. onion powder
½ tsp. salt
½ tsp. garlic powder
Pinch of ground pepper
Parsley, chopped

Wash mushrooms; trim. Place in 13 x 9 x 2 inch baking dish. Pour butter over mushrooms; mix well. Bake, uncovered, at 400 degrees for 30 minutes. Mix bread crumbs, onion powder, salt, garlic powder, and pepper. Sprinkle over mushrooms. Bake at 400 degrees for 10 minutes. Sprinkle with chopped parsley. Yield: 6-8 servings.

Kathy O'Connor, Corr. Sec.
Lambda Phi No. 7956
West Palm Beach, Florida

Spinach-Stuffed Mushroom Caps

½ c. scallions, finely chopped
Butter
1 10-oz. package frozen chopped spinach, thawed and
    squeezed dry
3 tbsp. flour
1 c. hot milk
Salt and pepper to taste
¾ c. boiled ham, finely chopped
24 lg. mushroom caps, stems removed

Saute scallions in 3 tablespoons butter until soft. Add spinach; toss for 3 to 4 minutes. Place spinach mixture in a bowl. Combine 2 tablespoons butter, flour, hot milk, salt and pepper. Stir in ham and flour mixture. Season to taste. Brush mushroom caps with additional melted butter. Sprinkle with salt. Spoon spinach mixture into mushroom caps. Place caps on a shallow baking sheet. Bake at 350 degrees for 20 minutes. Yield: 5-6 servings.

Mrs. Gwenn Lyons, Rec. Sec.
Beta Chapter No. 1944
Kirkland, Quebec, Canada

Southern Pepper Grits

½ c. grits
1 tsp. salt
2 rolls garlic cheese, grated
2 rolls jalapeno cheese, grated
4 eggs, beaten

Stir grits into 2½ cups boiling salted water. Cook, covered, 30 minutes. Reserve ½ cup each of the cheeses. Add remaining cheese to hot grits; stir until melted. Add a small amount of grits to beaten eggs.

Stir eggs into remaining grits. Pour into greased 2-quart casserole; sprinkle with remaining cheese. Bake at 350 degrees for 20 minutes. Yield: 8-10 servings.

Jean H. Blocksom, City Coun. Pres.
Preceptor Laureate Delta PL276
Pine Bluff, Arkansas

Cheesy-Potato Bake

4 lg. baking potatoes, peeled and thinly sliced
2 c. shredded mozzarella cheese
1 2 oz. package white sauce mix
1½ c. milk
1 tsp. salt
1 tsp. caraway seed
¼ tsp. pepper
Paprika

Alternate layers of potatoes and cheese in 2-quart buttered baking dish. Prepare white sauce mix according to package directions, using 1½ cups milk. Add salt, caraway seed and pepper. Pour over potatoes; sprinkle with paprika. Bake in a preheated 350 degree oven 50 to 60 minutes or until potatoes are tender. Yield: 6-8 servings.

Photograph for this recipe on page 84.

Oven-Fried Potatoes

8 lg. potatoes
½ c. oil
2 tbsp. Parmesan cheese
1 tsp. salt
½ tsp. garlic powder
½ tsp. paprika
¼ tsp. pepper

Cut unpeeled potatoes into 8 wedges each. Arrange wedges, peel-side down, into 2 shallow pans. Mix remaining ingredients; brush over potatoes. Bake at 375 degrees for 45 minutes, basting occasionally with oil mixture. Yield: 4 servings.

Jan Kelly, Pres.
Xi Alpha Rho
Kitchener, Ontario, Canada

Potatoes Romanoff

6 lg. potatoes
2 10-oz. cartons sour cream
1½ c. shredded sharp Cheddar cheese
1 bunch green onions, chopped
1½ tsp. salt
¼ tsp. pepper
Paprika

Cook potatoes in jackets until tender; peel. Cool; shred into large bowl. Stir in sour cream, 1 cup cheese, onion, salt and pepper. Place in greased 2-quart casserole. Cover with remaining cheese, sprinkle with paprika. Refrigerate, covered overnight. Bake, uncovered, at 350 degrees for 40 minutes. Yield: 8 servings.

Linda Mayberry, Pres.
Xi Mu X4561
Hudson Heights, Quebec, Canada

Potato-Ham Pizza

1½ tsp. margarine
3 or 4 med. potatoes, pared and thinly sliced
Salt and pepper to taste
½ c. diced onion
½ c. diced green pepper
2 c. cubed ham
3 eggs, beaten
½ c. shredded sharp cheese

Melt margarine in 9-inch skillet. Spread half the potatoes over bottom; sprinkle with salt and pepper. Cover with half the onion and half the green pepper. Arrange half the ham over onion and green pepper. Repeat layers. Cover; cook over low heat 30 minutes until tender. Pour eggs over potatoes evenly. Cook, covered, 10 minutes until eggs are set. Sprinkle with

cheese. Cook, covered, 2 minutes or until cheese melts. Cut into wedges to serve. Yield: 6 servings.

Constance D. Darrah, Prog. Chm.
Preceptor Zeta XP1104
Bangor, Maine

Basque Potato Casserole

Instant mashed potatoes for 6
2 tbsp. olive oil
1 green pepper, seeded and sliced
½ c. sliced onion
1 clove of garlic, minced
½ c. coarsely chopped pitted ripe olives
1 8-oz. can whole tomatoes
½ tsp. salt
¼ tsp. dried leaf basil
¼ tsp. dried leaf oregano
2 tbsp. grated Parmesan cheese

Prepare mashed potatoes according to package directions; keep warm. Heat olive oil in small skillet. Add green pepper, onion and garlic; cook until tender. Add olives, tomatoes with liquid, salt, basil and oregano. Simmer uncovered for 5 minutes. Turn into 1½-quart casserole. Spoon mashed potatoes over vegetables. Sprinkle with Parmesan cheese. Place under broiler 2 to 5 minutes or until lightly browned. Yield: 6 servings.

Photograph for this recipe on page 85.

If you tickle the earth with a hoe, she laughs with a harvest.   Eileen M. Blanchet

Party Potatoes

8 to 10 potatoes
1 8-oz. package cream cheese, softened
1 8-oz. package sour cream
Garlic salt to taste

Cook potatoes; mash. Blend cheese and sour cream. Add to potatoes; mix well. Add garlic salt. Place in greased casserole. Bake at 350 degrees until thoroughly heated. Yield: 6-8 servings.

Sally Bickford, Treas.
Xi Chi X730
Cedar Rapids, Iowa

Gourmet Potatoes

6 med. potatoes
Butter
3 c. sharp Cracker Barrel cheese, shredded
1½ c. sour cream
⅓ c. chopped green onion
1 tsp. salt
¼ tsp. pepper
1 tsp. chopped parsley
Paprika

Cook potatoes in jackets until tender; cool. Peel; shred coarsely. Combine ¼ cup butter and cheese in medium saucepan. Cook over low heat. Stir until partially melted. Remove from heat; blend in sour cream, onion, salt and pepper. Fold in potatoes. Season to taste. Place in greased 2-quart casserole. Sprinkle with parsley and paprika. Dot with 2 tablespoons butter. Bake at 350 degrees for 30 minutes. Yield: 8-10 servings.

Thelma Shaw,
International Member
Fairmont, West Virginia

Baked Hashed Browns

2 lb. frozen hashed brown potatoes
2 c. grated Cheddar cheese
½ c. chopped onion
1 tsp. salt
¼ tsp. pepper
1 c. butter, melted
1 can cream of chicken soup
1 c. corn flake crumbs

Combine potatoes, cheese, onion, salt, pepper, ½ cup butter and chicken soup. Place in 2-quart casserole. Combine ½ cup butter and corn flakes. Sprinkle over

potato mixture. Bake at 350 degrees for 1 hour. Yield: 8 servings.

Evelyn Garrett
Xi Zeta Kappa No. 2918
Haskins, Ohio

Sandy's Hashed Brown Casserole

2 lb. frozen hashed brown potatoes
¼ c. chopped onion
1 c. sour cream
1 can cream of chicken soup
1 8-oz. jar Cheez Whiz
2 c. crushed corn flakes
¾ stick margarine

Thaw potatoes. Combine potatoes, onion, sour cream and soup. Melt Cheez Whiz slightly; spread over potato mixture. Mix corn flakes with ½ stick margarine; sprinkle over cheese. Melt remaining butter; pour over mixture. Bake, uncovered, at 350 degrees for 40 minutes. Yield: 8 servings.

Sandy Sunderland, Pres.
Xi Gamma Tau X2882
Mexico, Missouri

Diane's Delicious Potatoes

1 2-lb. package hashed brown potatoes
2 cans cream of potato soup
1 pt. sour cream
Salt and pepper to taste
2 c. grated Cheddar cheese

Combine all ingredients except cheese in large casserole; mix well. Sprinkle with cheese. Bake at 350 degrees for 1 hour.

Diane Williams, Pres.
Delta Kappa
Ellisville, Mississippi

Spinach Gourmet

½ tsp. ground marjoram
¼ tsp. seasoned salt
¼ tsp. garlic salt
1 tbsp. butter
½ lb. sliced fresh mushrooms
12 oz. fresh spinach
¾ c. shredded Cheddar cheese
¼ c. cooked crumbled bacon (opt.)

Combine marjoram, seasoned and garlic salts. Melt butter in a 3-quart saucepan; add mushrooms and half the seasonings. Add spinach and remaining seasonings; cover. Cook for 3 to 5 minutes or until spinach is

To love and honour is okay for those who promise to obey, but what turns most wives slowly gray is what to cook each blessed day.
Margaret Elizabeth Brake

just wilted. Place in serving dish. Sprinkle with cheese and bacon. Yield: 4 servings.

Photograph for this recipe on page 84.

Greek Spinach Pie

1 10-oz. package frozen chopped spinach
½ lb. feta cheese, crumbled
2 c. cottage cheese
4 eggs
6 tbsp. flour
½ tsp. salt
½ tsp. pepper
1 to 2 tbsp. butter

Thaw spinach; drain. Combine all ingredients except butter. Butter an 8 x 8-inch baking pan. Pour mixture into baking pan; spread evenly. Bake at 350 degrees for 1 hour or until knife inserted in center comes out clean. Let cool for a short time. Cut into squares. Sharp Cheddar cheese, grated, may be substituted for feta cheese. Yield: 4-6 servings.

Diane Heacock, Rec. Sec.
Eta Kappa No. 3388
Aurora, Illinois

Kelly's Spinach Bake

3 slices bacon
1 sm. onion
2 c. chopped uncooked spinach
1 c. grated Cheddar cheese
2 eggs
½ tsp. salt
¼ c. milk or sour cream
Dash of pepper
Dash of nutmeg
3 tbsp. bread crumbs

Cut bacon in small pieces. Fry until brown and crisp; remove bacon. Saute onion in bacon drippings. Combine spinach, cheese and onion. Beat eggs with salt, milk, pepper and nutmeg. Add to spinach mixture. Pour into 9 x 12-inch baking pan. Sprinkle with bread crumbs. Bake at 350 degrees for 40 minutes. Yield: 8-10 servings.

Kelly Guffin, Corr. Sec.
Xi Zeta Psi X1888
Vista, California

Herbed Squash Casserole

1 ½ lb. squash, sliced
1 sm. package herb stuffing mix
½ c. butter
1 sm. pimento, chopped
1 can cream of chicken soup
2 sm. onions, chopped

4 sm. carrots, grated
1 c. sour cream

Cook squash; drain. Prepare package of herb stuffing using butter. Line casserole with half the stuffing mixture. Set aside small portion of remaining stuffing mixture for topping. Combine remaining stuffing mixture with all other ingredients. Pour into lined casserole. Top with reserved stuffing mixture. Bake at 350 degrees, uncovered, for 30 minutes. Yield: 8-10 servings.

Sharon Ann Halligan
Xi Eta Omicron X4003
Tampa, Florida
Eileen Foley,
Inter. Hon. Mem.
Portsmouth, New Hampshire

Mary Sue's Squash Casserole

5 sm. yellow squash, cut into sm. pieces
1 onion, chopped
1 tsp. salt
½ tsp. pepper
½ stick margarine
1 c. grated cheese
1 slice bread, torn in small pieces

Cook squash and onion in a small amount of water until tender. Drain and mash. Add salt, pepper, margarine, cheese and bread; mix well. Pour into a greased 1-quart baking dish. Bake at 350 degrees for 30 minutes or until bubbly. Yield: 6 servings.

Mary Sue Armstrong, V.P.
Alpha Pi
Covington, Virginia

Guatemala Squash

1 egg
1 3-oz. package cream cheese, softened
⅔ c. (firmly packed) brown sugar
½ tsp. salt
1 tbsp. bread crumbs
2 c. cooked squash
1 tbsp. butter
½ tsp. cinnamon
⅓ c. raisins
¼ c. slivered almonds

Beat egg, cream cheese, brown sugar, salt, bread crumbs, squash and butter. Add cinnamon, beating again. Stir in raisins and almonds. Pour into greased 1-quart casserole. Bake at 350 degrees for 40 minutes. Yield: 6 servings.

June C. Hackett, Publ. Chm.
Preceptor Upsilon XP883
Sunbury, Pennsylvania

Juanita's Squash Casserole

2 c. canned mashed squash
1 med. onion, finely chopped
1 8-oz. carton sour cream
1 can cream of chicken soup
1 tsp. sugar
1 med. carrot, grated
1 stick margarine, melted
2 c. herb stuffing crumbs

Combine squash, onion, sour cream, chicken soup, sugar and carrot. Mix margarine and herb stuffing crumbs. Place half the crumb mixture in 10-inch casserole. Cover with squash mixture. Sprinkle with remaining crumbs. Bake at 350 degrees for 40 minutes. Yield: 6-8 servings.

Juanita Stamper, Pres.
Xi Omicron X1025
Americus, Georgia

Savory Squash

1½ lb. yellow summer squash or zucchini, sliced
½ c. chopped onions

3 c. cooked rice
2 c. grated Cheddar cheese
1 tsp. seasoned pepper
½ tsp. salt
3 eggs, beaten
½ c. mayonnaise
1 c. soft bread crumbs
½ c. sliced almonds

Cook squash and onions covered, in a small amount of water until squash is tender. Drain well. Combine with rice, cheese and seasonings. Blend eggs and mayonnaise; stir into vegetable mixture. Turn into buttered 2-quart casserole. Top with bread crumbs and almonds. Bake at 350 degrees for 30 minutes. Yield: 6-8 servings.

Photograph for this recipe on page 88.

Sweet Potato Casserole

3 sweet potatoes, cooked or 1 16-oz. can, drained
1 c. sugar
2 eggs, beaten
1 tsp. salt
1 tbsp. vanilla extract

Kindness is becoming at any age. Carolyn Newman

½ c. butter or margarine, melted
1 c. (firmly packed) brown sugar
⅓ c. flour
1 c. chopped pecans
½ c. butter or margarine, softened

Mix first 6 ingredients. Pour into buttered 9-inch square casserole. Mix remaining ingredients to crumble consistency. Sprinkle on top of potato mixture. Bake at 350 degrees for 30 minutes. Yield 8-10 servings.

Dorothea Williamson
Zeta Omega No. 9477
Wilmington, North Carolina

Kristina's Sweet Potato Souffle

3 c. sweet potatoes, mashed
¾ c. sugar
⅓ c. milk
1 tsp. vanilla extract
1 tsp. butter flavoring
Pinch of salt
Margarine or butter, softened
1 c. (firmly packed) brown sugar
⅓ c. flour
1 c. chopped nuts

Mix first 6 ingredients with ⅓ stick margarine. Pour into greased 2-quart casserole. Combine brown sugar, flour and ⅓ cup margarine until crumbly. Add nuts. Sprinkle over casserole. Bake at 350 degrees for 30 minutes. Yield: 12 servings.

Kristina Allen, V.P.
Xi Xi No. 3227
Gautier, Mississippi

Hawaiian Sweet Potatoes

8 med. sweet potatoes or 2 1-lb. cans yams
2 c. flaked coconut
2 tbsp. brown sugar
½ c. light cream
4 tbsp. butter or margarine, melted

Whip sweet potatoes with electric mixer in a large bowl until fluffy. Add 1 cup coconut, brown sugar and cream; beat until light and fluffy. Spoon mixture into 2-quart buttered baking dish. Mix remaining 1 cup coconut and butter. Sprinkle over casserole. Bake, uncovered, at 325 degrees for 20 minutes. Yield: 8 servings.

Jan DeMers, Pres.
Xi Gamma Nu X3736
Burton, Washington

Crunchy-Topped Sweet Potatoes

2 c. mashed sweet potatoes
½ c. sugar
2 eggs, beaten
½ tsp. salt
½ c. milk
1½ tsp. vanilla extract
Melted butter
½ c. (firmly packed) brown sugar
⅓ c. flour
1 c. chopped pecans

Combine first 6 ingredients with ½ cup melted butter. Pour into buttered casserole. Combine brown sugar, flour, 3 tablespoons butter and pecans. Crumble mixture on top of casserole. Bake at 350 degrees, uncovered, for 35 minutes. Yield: 6-8 servings.

Polly A. Patton, Pres.
Eta Chi
Woodstock, Virginia

Vegetables a la Espana

1 can chicken broth
2 tbsp. lemon juice
⅓ c. olive or salad oil
¼ tsp. pepper
1 clove of garlic, crushed
1 tsp. oregano leaves
4 med. carrots, pared and cut in ½-in. slices
1 c. sliced celery
1 lg. green pepper, cut in 1-in. squares
2 10-oz. packages frozen cauliflower
1 lb. zucchini, cut in ¾-in. slices
1 c. sliced large pimento-stuffed olives

Bring chicken broth, lemon juice, oil, pepper, garlic and oregano to a boil in large saucepan. Add carrots, celery, green pepper, cauliflower and zucchini; cover. Simmer for about 10 minutes or until vegetables are tender. Drain cooking liquid. Stir in olives. Serve vegetables hot or cold. Yield: 8-10 servings.

Photograph for this recipe on page 76.

Vera's Vegetable Casserole

1 10-oz. package frozen broccoli
1 10-oz. package frozen cauliflower
1 10-oz. package frozen Brussels sprouts
1 10¾-oz. can cream of mushroom soup
1 8-oz. jar Cheez Whiz

Prepare vegetables according to package directions; drain. Combine soup and Cheez Whiz. Heat until smooth. Place vegetables in 9 x 12-inch baking dish. Cover with soup mixture. Bake at 400 degrees for 15 minutes. Yield: 8-10 servings

Vera G. Hansen, Pres.
Xi Beta Alpha X1725
Davenport, Iowa

We make a living by what we get—We make a life by what we give. Rose Marie Ireland

Meats

For the fullest flavor, heartiest nutrition, and the most appetizing menus, meats are the answer! They are the food with universal appeal, and just as importantly, there's no mysterious secrets to the preparation of meats. The robust flavors are each enhanced by spicy marinades, herbed sauces, as well as fruits, vegetables, and cheeses.

People-pleasing menus are built around high-quality, full-flavored meats. Brunch would just be another breakfast without the addition of glazed Canadian bacon slices or corned beef hash with applesauce to suggest a few. The meat can set the tone for a special-occasion luncheon. Tender lamb kabobs served over rice pilaf or veal flavored delicately with a cream sauce, mushrooms, celery or mild cheeses give the menu a lady-like touch, while men thrive on prime rib au jus, scored pork roast, and marinated venison. For family meals, meats are not only tasty, but go a long way in appeasing the appetites of growing children and the hungry adults. Still, you don't have to buy the most expensive meats to serve the tastiest meats—to family or company. There is very little flavor difference between meat cuts; so, use marinades and meat tenderizers on less expensive cuts for expensive-tasting results. Depend on hearty stews filled with colorful vegetables, casseroles topped with bubbling cheese and glazes of all kinds to enhance any meat cut to stretch the meat supply. But, don't overlook the pleasures, ease, and unbeatable taste that barbecuing brings to all your favorite meats!

You just can't miss! Meat in a meal assures it will be both appetizing and delicious. As these ever-popular Beta Sigma Phi meat recipes show, there is always a new and unexpected way to bring meat to the table.

Corned Beef and Noodle Casserole

1 8-oz. package medium-sized noodles
1 can cream of chicken soup
1½ c. milk
¼ lb. Velveeta cheese, cubed
1 12-oz. can corned beef, flaked
¼ c. finely chopped onions
1½ c. bread crumbs
1 stick butter, melted

Cook noodles according to package directions; drain. Combine soup and milk in saucepan; heat, stirring constantly. Add cheese; stir until melted. Add noodles, flaked beef and onions. Pour into greased 9 × 13-inch pan. Combine bread crumbs with butter. Cover casserole with crumb mixture. Bake for 1 hour at 350 degrees. Yield: 8-10 servings.

Beatrice L. Shrene, Pres. City Coun.
Preceptor Upsilon XP1344
Parkersburg, West Virginia

Ann's Creamed Beef

5 tbsp. milk
1 8-oz. package cream cheese, softened
5 oz. dried beef
1 c. sour cream
¼ c. chopped onion
¼ c. chopped green pepper
1¼ tsp. garlic powder
¼ tsp. pepper
1 tbsp. Worcestershire sauce
1 c. chopped pecans
2 tbsp. butter

Combine milk, cream cheese, dried beef, sour cream, onion, green pepper, ¼ teaspoon garlic powder, pepper and Worchestershire sauce. Place in baking dish. Saute pecans in butter; sprinkle with 1 teaspoon garlic powder. Sprinkle over casserole. Bake at 350 degrees for 30 minutes. Keep warm. Serve spread on party rye bread.

Mrs. Ann Titus, Pres.
Xi Gamma Zeta X1297
Dallas, Texas

Nancy's Barbecued Beef

1 bottle of catsup
1 4 oz. can taco sauce
1 tbsp. brown sugar
1 tbsp. vinegar
1 onion, chopped
2 cloves of garlic
Pinch of oregano
Pinch of dry mustard

2 tbsp. Worcestershire sauce
3 to 4 lbs. boneless stew meat

Combine first 9 ingredients; mix well. Pour over stew meat in Dutch oven. Cover. Bake 5 to 6 hours at 300 degrees. Can also be made in Crock•Pot. Serve on buns.

Nancy Wadley
Rho Tau
Jefferson City, Missouri

Crock•Pot Barbecue

3 lb chuck roast, cubed
1 onion, chopped
¾ c. catsup
1 tbsp. vinegar
1 tbsp. Worcestershire sauce
1 tsp. salt
½ tsp. pepper
1 tsp. paprika
1 tbsp. chili powder
2 tbsp. brown sugar
1 tsp. garlic salt or powder

Combine all ingredients and ¾ cup water in Crock•Pot. Cook on Low for 12 hours. Mash with potato masher. Serve on split buns. Freezes well. Yield: 6 servings.

Mary Ellen Bartlett, Pres.
Preceptor Epsilon XP318
Carlsbad, New Mexico

Working Girl's Barbecued Brisket

4 to 6 lb. beef brisket
1 c. barbecue sauce
Salt and pepper to taste

Brush all sides of brisket with barbecue sauce. Place in roasting pan fat-side up. Add ¾ cup water. Cover tightly. Bake in 350-degree oven for 3 to 4 hours. Remove from oven. Cool; refrigerate overnight. Remove brisket from pan; remove the fat. Slice meat across grain into thin slices. Skim fat from pan drippings. Add ½ cup barbecue sauce, ½ cup water and salt and pepper to broth. Bring to a boil. Place the meat slices in electric skillet basting between slices with the hot broth. Simmer for about 1 hour. Yield: 6-10 servings.

Marian Whiteaker
Preceptor Beta Omega XP1796
Kansas City, Missouri

Beef In Beer

3 lb. chuck steak, cut into 1-inch cubes
3 onions, chopped

Up to your neck in hot water? Do what the kettle does—SING! Jacqueline C. Getthens

1½ cloves of garlic, crushed
¾ c. butter or margarine
½ c. flour
1½ c. beer
1½ c. beer consomme
3 tbsp. brown sugar
2 bay leaves
1½ tsp. thyme
1½ tbsp. minced parsley
Salt and pepper to taste

Brown steak cubes, onions and garlic, a small amount at a time, in butter in a large Dutch oven. Add flour; coat well. Combine beer and beef consomme. Pour over meat. Season with remaining ingredients. Bake in 300-degree oven about 3 hours or until meat is tender. Can be prepared earlier, then reheated on top of stove when ready to serve. Yield: 6 servings.

Elizabeth Holthaus, Treas.
Xi Chi X450
Butler, Pennsylvania

Kay's Beef Burgundy

6 strips of bacon
3 lb. beef cubes
1 med. onion, chopped
1 lg. carrot, cut up
Salt and pepper to taste
3 tbsp. flour
2 cans beef broth
2 c. red Burgundy
1 tbsp. tomato paste
2 cloves of garlic
½ tsp. thyme
1 bay leaf
2 lb. mushrooms
3 tbsp. butter
2 tbsp. salad oil
1 lb. small white onions, chopped

Cook bacon until crisp in Dutch oven; remove. Brown beef in drippings; remove. Brown onion and carrot in drippings. Spoon off dripping; return beef and bacon to pan. Season with salt and pepper. Stir in flour. Reserve ½ cup broth; add remaining broth to stew. Add Burgundy, tomato paste and herbs; cover. Simmer for 3 hours. Quarter large mushrooms. Sauté mushrooms in mixture of butter and salad oil for 5 minutes; remove. Add onions; brown. Add reserved broth. Simmer, covered, for 10 minutes or until tender. Add to beef mixure. Serve with noodles or steamed rice. Yield: 8-10 servings.

Kay Dodge, Pres.
Beta Preceptor
Owls Head, Maine

Beef Goulash

¼ c. butter or margarine
4 c. sliced onions
2 cloves of garlic, minced
3 lb. boned round or chuck, cut in 1-inch cubes
1 8-oz. can whole tomatoes, drained and chopped
2 c. Brown Sauce Base
4 tsp. paprika
½ tsp. salt
½ tsp. dried leaf marjoram
1 bay leaf

Melt butter in large saucepan or Dutch oven. Add onions and garlic; cook until lightly browned. Add beef; brown on all sides. Stir in tomatoes, Brown Sauce Base, paprika, salt, marjoram and bay leaf; cover. Simmer for 1 hour and 30 minutes to 2 hours, stirring occasionally, until meat is tender. Serve over noodles, spaetzle, mashed potatoes or rice. Yield: 6-8 servings.

Brown Sauce Base:
2 tbsp. butter
2 tbsp. flour
1 c. canned beef broth or 1 beef bouillon cube dissolved in 1 c. water
¼ tsp. Tabasco sauce

Melt butter in saucepan; cook until golden brown. Blend in flour; cook over low heat, stirring constantly, until dark brown. Stir in broth; add Tabasco. Cook, stirring constantly, until sauce thickens and comes to a boil. Serve with additional Tabasco sauce. Yield: 1 cup.

Photograph for this recipe on page 94.

India Goulash

1½ lb. round steak, cut in strips
2 tbsp. flour
2 onions, chopped
2 tsp. salt
1 tbsp. curry powder
2 c. rice
1 to 1½ c. each, coconut, peanuts, raisins, sliced bananas, pineapple chunks, chopped tomato, chopped red onion, sweet and dill pickles, crumbled bacon, chopped hard-boiled eggs

Coat meat in flour. Brown with chopped onions. Add salt and curry powder. Cover with water. Simmer for 5 to 6 hours. Add thickening, if necessary, to consistency of thick gravy. Steam rice according to package directions; keep warm until serving time. Place remaining ingredients in individual bowls. Serve buffet-style. Top rice with meat sauce; add a portion of each of the remaining ingredients. Hot rolls and a light dessert complete this "fun" meal! Yield: 6-8 servings.

Barbara Shrode, Pres.
Preceptor Phi XP542
Spokane, Washington

Look for the good in others and they will surely find the good in you. Carol Serur

Chop Suey

1 lb. lean beef, cubed
1 med. onion, chopped fine
2 tbsp. shortening
3 lg. stalks celery, chopped
2 16-oz. cans bean sprouts, drained
2 16-oz. cans fancy mixed chop suey vegetables,
    drained
2 8-oz. cans mushrooms
5 tbsp. soy sauce
2 tbsp. cornstarch

Saute beef and onion in shortening until brown in a Dutch oven. Add celery and 2 cups water. Simmer for 1 hour or until meat is tender. Add bean sprouts, mixed vegetables and mushrooms to meat mixture. Add enough water to almost cover. Simmer for 30 minutes to 1 hour. Combine soy sauce and cornstarch; thin with liquid from meat mixture. Add to chop suey. Heat thoroughly. Serve over rice. Yield: 10 servings.

Jeanette A. Fettig, Pres.
Xi Gamma Xi
Logansport, Indiana

Oriental Beef Chow Mein

1 lb. round steak, cubed
4 stalks celery, chopped
4 lg. onions, chopped
2 cans bean sprouts
1 can bamboo sprouts
1 can mushrooms
4 tbsp. soy sauce
1 tsp. ginger
Salt and pepper to taste
4 tbsp. cornstarch

Cook steak cubes until tender. Add celery and onions. Cook for 15 minutes. Add remaining ingredients, except cornstarch. Cook for 30 minutes longer. Mix cornstarch with enough water to make a paste; add to meat mixture. Cook until thickens; remove from heat. Serve with rice and Chinese noodles and additional soy sauce, if desired. Yield: 4-6 servings.

Mildred H. Sharpe, Treas.
Xi Alpha Nu X1910
Alexandria, Virginia

Ozark Mountain Stew

2 lb. stew meat, browned
½ c. black-eyed peas

Giving your best today is the recipe for a better tomorrow. Patricia Seifert

1 bay leaf
1 sm. onion, chopped
4 tsp. parsley flakes
2 tbsp. instant beef bouillon
1 tsp. coarsely ground pepper
1½ c. 1-in. celery pieces
6 c. carrots, cut into 1 in. slices
1 green pepper, diced
½ med. head cabbage, cut into wedges
1 5-oz. can sliced water chestnuts, drained
Salt to taste
Kitchen Bouquet (opt.)

Place first 7 ingredients in large Dutch oven. Add enough water to cover. Cook until peas are tender-crisp. Add celery and carrots; cook until tender-crisp. Add next 3 ingredients. Cook until meat is tender and vegetables tender-crisp. Season with salt. Add Kitchen Bouquet for color. Yield: 6 servings.

Jane Mielke, Treas.
Xi Alpha Lambda X4925
Sioux Falls, South Dakota

Beef-Rice with a Flair

1 sm. head cauliflower
1 lb. boneless round steak, cubed
2 tbsp. margarine or butter
1 med. green pepper, chopped
½ c. soy sauce
1 clove of garlic
3 tbsp. cornstarch
½ tsp. sugar
1 c. green onions with tops, chopped
3 c. cooked rice

Separate cauliflower into floweretes. Brown meat in margarine about 5 minutes. Add cauliflower, green pepper, soy sauce and garlic. Stir lightly to coat vegetables with soy sauce. Cover. Simmer until vegetables are tender-crisp about 10 minutes. Blend cornstarch, sugar and 1½ cups water. Add to meat mixture; mix well. Add green onions. Cook, stirring constantly, until thoroughly heated and sauce is thickened. Serve over fluffy rice. Especially good for Wok cooking. Yield: 6 servings.

Sandy Shaffer, Acting Sec.
Alpha Epsilon No. 6905
Rock Springs, Wyoming

Super One-Skillet Dinner

1 lb. round steak, cut up
¼ c. flour
1 tbsp. vegetable oil
1 lg. onion, chopped
1 16-oz. can sliced potatoes
¼ c. catsup
1 tbsp. A-1 sauce

2 tsp. bell pepper flakes
1 tsp. salt
¼ tsp. pepper
1 can French green beans
1 sm. can mushrooms
1 2-oz. jar sliced pimento, drained

Coat steak cubes with flour; pound into beef. Brown meat in oil in 10-inch skillet; push beef aside. Cook onion in oil, stirring constantly, until tender; drain. Drain potatoes, reserving liquid. Add enough water to reserved potato liquid to measure 1 cup. Mix potato liquid, catsup, A-1 sauce, pepper flakes, salt and pepper. Pour over beef and onions. Bring to a boil; reduce heat. Cover. Simmer for 1 hour and 30 minutes or until beef is tender. Add potatoes, beans, mushrooms and pimento to skillet. Bring to a boil; reduce heat. Cover. Simmer for 10 minutes longer. Yield: 4 servings.

Phyllis Woods, Ext. Off.
Xi No. 1413
Paducah, Kentucky

Muriel's Beef Stroganoff

2 lb. top round steak
1 tsp. tenderizer
4 tbsp. butter or margarine
1 c. chopped onion
1 clove of garlic, finely chopped
3 tbsp. flour
1 tsp. meat extract paste
1 tbsp. catsup
½ tsp. salt
½ tsp. pepper
1 10½-oz. can beef bouillon
¼ tsp. dried dill
1 10½-oz. can cream of mushroom soup
½ c. sour cream
1 sm. can sliced mushrooms
4½ c. cooked rice
2 tbsp. chopped parsley

Trim fat from beef. Slice beef lengthwise into thirds; sprinkle with tenderizer. Cut each slice across grain into ½-inch strips. Heat large heavy skillet slowly. Melt 1 tablespoon butter. Add beef strips; sear quickly on all sides. Remove beef as it browns. Add 3 tablespoons butter to same skillet. Saute onion and garlic in hot butter about 5 minutes. Remove from heat. Add flour, meat-extract paste, catsup, salt and pepper; stir until smooth. Add bouillon gradually. Bring to a boil, stirring. Simmer for 5 minutes. Reduce temperature. Add dill, soup and sour cream, stirring well. Add mushrooms and beef. Simmer slowly just until sauce and beef are hot. Serve surrounded with rice. Sprinkle with parsley. Yield: 6 servings.

Muriel Hedstrom, Rec. Sec.
Preceptor Iota XP1278
Hettinger, North Dakota

Those who bring sunshine to the lives of others cannot keep it to themselves. Carol Voss

Jan's Beef Stroganoff

1 round steak, cut into strips
Meat tenderizer
Flour
1 or 2 tbsp. fat
1 can beef broth
2 tbsp. catsup
1 to 2 tsp. mustard
Worcestershire sauce to taste
½ pt. sour cream

Season beef with meat tenderizer. Coat well with flour. Brown in fat in large skillet. Add beef broth; mix well. Add catsup and 1 to 2 tsp. mustard. Sprinkle with Worcestershire sauce. Simmer for 45 minutes. Add sour cream; mix well. Simmer for 15 minutes longer. Serve over rice. Yield: 4-6 servings.

Jan Dorsey, W. and M. Chm.
Xi Eta Phi
Kansas City, Missouri

Season roast with salt and pepper. Place roast, fat side up, on rack in open roasting pan. Insert meat thermometer in center of thickest part. Do not add water. Do not cover. Roast in 325-degree oven until meat thermometer registers 140 degrees to 160 degrees. Allow 30 to 35 minutes per pound for roasting one 6 to 8-pound beef tip or 35 to 40 minutes per pound for one 3½ to 4-pound roast. Allow roast to set for 20 minutes for easy carving.

Blue Cheese Sauce:

1 5-oz jar blue cheese spread
2 tbsp. dry Sherry
1 tbsp. Worcestershire sauce
½ c. sour cream
2 tsp. chopped chives

Combine blue cheese spread, dry Sherry and Worcestershire sauce in a saucepan. Heat at low temperature, stirring to blend. Stir in sour cream and chives. Heat to serving temperature. Yield: 1 cup

Photograph for this recipe on page 96.

Beef Tip Roast

1 4 to 8-lb. beef tip roast
Salt and pepper to taste

Chianti Beef Roast

3 tbsp. shortening
5 lb. rolled beef rump roast

A friend is a present you give yourself. Carole Maltrud

1 tsp. salt
½ tsp. pepper
2 c. Chianti

Melt shortening in Dutch oven. Brown roast in shortening over medium heat about 15 minutes. Season with salt and pepper. Pour Chianti over roast; cover. Bake in 325-degree oven for 3 hours to 3 hours and 30 minutes or until roast is tender. Serve hot or chill and slice. Yield: 10 servings.

Becky Ledford
Zeta Lambda No. 8894
College Park, Georgia

Heavenly Pot Roast

1 can mushroom soup
2 1½-oz. packages spaghetti sauce mix
1 c. wine
4 or 5-lb chuck or round bone roast

Combine mushroom soup, spaghetti sauce mix, wine and 1 cup water in large roaster. Add roast; cover. Bake in 325-degree oven for 3 hours. Serve with gravy on rice. Yield: 8 servings.

Nola Larson, Corr. Sec.
Xi Upsilon X3677
Casper, Wyoming

Italian Beef

¼ c. lemon juice
2 tbsp. oregano
1 tsp. pepper
1 tbsp. garlic salt
1 tbsp. salt
2 bay leaves
1 or 2 cans beef consomme
1 lg. rump roast

Combine first 7 ingredients; mix well. Place roast in roasting pan. Pour sauce over roast. Bake at 325 degrees in covered roaster, about 4 hours or to desired doneness. Baste several times during cooking. Remove bay leaves. Slice meat thin. Return to beef broth. Serve hot on buns. This is an old family recipe given to me by my daughter-in-law.

Shirley Sanderson, Life Member
Xi Iota Lambda X4654
Olney, Illinois

Southern-Yankee Pot Roast

1 5-lb. bottom round roast
⅓ c. oil
1 c. diced onions
½ c. diced celery

½ c. flour
2 tsp. Kitchen Bouquet
5 c. beef consomme
3 bay leaves
Salt and pepper to taste

Brown meat in oil on all sides in a heavy covered skillet. Remove meat. Add onions and celery to oil. Saute for 12 minutes. Blend in flour; stir until smooth, adding more oil if necessary. Cook for 8 minutes longer. Add Kitchen Bouquet and consomme. Stir until smooth. Add bay leaves. Season with salt and pepper. Add meat; cover. Cook at 400 degrees for 2 hours or until meat is tender. Remove meat from gravy. Strain; adjust seasoning. Slice and serve with potato pancakes. Yield: 10 servings.

Dorothy Holbrook, Pres
Xi Zeta Epsilon X3360
Orlando, Florida

Stuffed Eye of Round

1 4 to 6 lb. eye of round
Salt and pepper to taste
Prepared mustard
1 ½ c. seasoned bread crumbs
¾ stick butter or margarine, melted
Green pepper, chopped
Onions, chopped
Shallots, chopped
Celery, chopped
Parsley, chopped
1 med. apple, chopped
Butter
1 can mushrooms
½ oz. red wine
1 8-oz. can brown gravy

Season meat with salt and pepper. Rub with mustard to coat well. Cut a 2-inch deep slit in meat 1 inch from each end. Combine bread crumbs with melted butter. Add ½ cup each green pepper, onions, shallots, celery and parsley. Cook until vegetables are tender, stirring often. Add apple; toss well. Stuff dressing into pocket in meat; pack well. Place roast in Brown-and-Serve bag. Add 2 pats of butter and mushrooms. Add additional green pepper, onions and celery to taste. Add wine and a small amount of water. Tie bag loosely. Place in pan; make 2½-inch slit in bag. Bake at 325 degrees for 1 hour and 30 minutes for medium well. Remove roast from bag; add drippings to a saucepan. Add brown gravy. Heat thoroughly. Serve with sliced roast. Yield: 8 servings.

Avis L. Lewis, Sec.
Preceptor Sigma XP1815
Slidell, Louisiana

A good thought today means a better tomorrow. Diana A. Burge

Bulkogi

½ c. chopped onion
4 cloves of garlic, chopped
5 tbsp. soy sauce
5 tbsp. salad oil
1 tbsp. sugar
1 tbsp. pepper
3 tbsp. dry Sherry
2 lb. flank steak

Combine first 7 ingredients; mix well. Add steak. Marinate steak overnight. Fry for 5 minutes on each side. Serve on a platter of rice. Yield: 4 servings.

Linda Rollins, Pres.
Xi Gamma Zeta X5083
Hendersonville, North Carolina

Delicious Grilled Flank Steak

¾ c. oil
¼ c. soy sauce
3 tbsp. honey
2 tbsp. red wine vinegar
1 clove of garlic, crushed
1½ tsp. ground ginger
1 green onion, chopped
1 flank steak

Combine all ingredients except steak. Pour over steak in large plastic bag in shallow pan; tie securely. Let stand in refrigerator about 5 hours, turning several times. Grill about 2 inches above coals to desired doneness on each side. Slice thin diagonally across grain. Yield: 4 servings.

Anita Karl, City Coun. Pres.
Xi Gamma X676
Cheyenne, Wyoming

Florentine-Stuffed Flank Steak

1 10-oz. package frozen chopped spinach
2 1-lb. pieces beef flank steak
1 egg, slightly beaten
½ c. shredded sharp American cheese
½ tsp. ground sage
¼ tsp. salt
Dash of ground pepper
¾ c. soft bread crumbs
2 tbsp. cooking oil
1 8-oz. can tomato sauce
½ c. dry red wine
½ c. chopped onion
1 clove of garlic, minced
2 tbsp. flour

Cook spinach according to package directions; drain. Pound each steak to ¼ inch thickness; set aside. Combine egg, spinach, cheese, sage, salt and pepper.

Stir in bread crumbs. Spread mixture over steaks. Roll up starting at narrow side. Tie with string to hold together. Brown roll-ups in oil. Place in 10 × 6 × 2-inch baking dish. Combine tomato sauce, wine, onion and garlic. Pour over meat; cover with foil. Bake at 350 degrees for 1 hour and 30 minutes. Combine flour with ¼ cup cold water. Stir into drippings until thickened. Serve gravy with roast. Yield: 8 servings.

Mrs. Ann M. Clapper, Pres.
Kappa Omicron No. 8089
Shawnee on Delaware, Pennsylvania

Steak Tournedos

2 lb. beef flank steak
½ lb. bacon
Garlic salt to taste
1 tsp. freshly ground pepper
1 tsp. meat tenderizer
2 tbsp. snipped parsley
¼ tsp. dried tarragon, crushed
1¾-oz. envelope Hollandaise sauce mix

Pound flank steak to even thickness, about ½ inch thick. Cook bacon until almost done but not crisp. Sprinkle flank steak with garlic salt, pepper, and meat tenderizer. Score steak diagonally, making diamond shaped cuts. Place bacon strips lengthwise on flank steak. Sprinkle with parsley. Roll up, jelly roll-fashion, starting at narrow end. Skewer with wooden toothpicks at 1 inch intervals. Cut into 1 inch slices. Grill over medium coals for 15 minutes, turning once for rare. Add tarragon to dry Hollandaise sauce mix in saucepan according to package directions. Serve sauce with flank steak. Yield: 4 servings.

Mary Lou Massie, Sec.
Preceptor Alpha Beta XP1826
Morgantown, West Virginia

The Luck of the Irish

Salad oil
1 egg
½ c. melted butter
½ tsp. parsley flakes
¼ tsp. pepper
½ c. horseradish mustard
1 c. instant potatoes
4 lg. minute steaks

Heat oil in regular skillet to medium temperature. Combine egg, melted butter, parsley, pepper and mustard in bowl. Place instant potatoes in shallow dish. Dip minute steak in egg mixture then into instant potatoes. Set side on foil or waxed paper. Redip steaks in egg and instant potatoes. Fry in skillet until tender and brown. Garnish with red and green pickled apple rings and parsley sprigs. Serve with a tossed salad and corn on cobb. Yield: 4 servings.

Allena M. Brunken, Pres.
Xi Alpha Tau X5127
Hopkinsville, Kentucky

Beef with Oyster Sauce

1½ lb. beef sandwich steaks
1 pkg. Oriental oyster sauce
2 lg. onions, chopped
1 green pepper, chopped
2 tomatoes, chopped
Fresh mushrooms
3 stalks celery, chopped
1 can water chestnuts, sliced
1 bok choy
1 tbsp. cornstarch
1 tsp. rice wine
1 tsp. sesame seed oil
1 tsp. ginger
1 tbsp. Accent
Cooked rice

Sprinkle beef with oyster sauce. Saute until brown in wok. Remove meat. Saute vegetables quickly. Thicken sauce with cornstarch. Add seasonings; mix well. Serve over rice. Yield: 6 servings.

Joan L. Marvin, Pres.
Preceptor Upsilon XP950
Valparaiso, Indiana

Steak Diane

4 6-oz. filet mignons
Salt to taste
Freshly ground pepper to taste
2 tbsp. olive oil
3 tbsp. butter
3 tbsp. chopped chives or shallots
2 tbsp. Cognac
3 tbsp. chopped parsley
1 tsp. imported mustard
½ tsp. Worcestershire sauce
2 tsp. fresh or canned beef stock

Place filets on flat surface; pound with a flat mallet to about ¼ inch thickness. Sprinkle meat on both sides with salt and pepper. Heat oil and 2 tablespoons butter in a large skillet until hot. Add 2 steaks. Cook about 1½ minutes on one side; turn. Cook 30 seconds on second side. Do not overcook. Transfer steaks to hot serving dish. Add remaining steaks to skillet. Repeat process; transfer to serving dish. Remove skillet from heat; add chives. Return skillet to heat. Cook about 10 seconds. Add Cognac; stir. Add parsley, mustard and Worcestershire sauce. Add broth; stir. Swirl in remaining butter. Sprinkle steaks with pepper. Pour sauce over all. Serve at once. Yield: 4 servings.

Ellen Ventress, Pres.
Preceptor Eta Beta XP1530
Malibu, California

Swiss Steak and Mushrooms

1 tsp. onion salt
1 tsp. garlic salt
Pepper to taste
2 lbs. round steak
Flour
Oil
1 pt. tomatoes
1 med. onion, diced
1 lg. can sliced mushrooms

Mix onion and garlic salts together; add pepper. Sprinkle over steak on both sides. Coat with flour. Brown steak in oil. Remove steak from large skillet; reduce temperature. Add tomatoes and onion. Return steak to skillet. Pour mushrooms over steak. Add 1 to 2 cups water. Simmer for 2 hours on medium heat. Reduce temperature to low; simmer 1 hour longer. Yield: 6 servings.

Linda Vannatta, Soc. Chm.
Alpha Theta No. 7195
Nashville, Tennessee

Beef Chaufleur

1 lb. boneless beef round steak, cut ⅓ inch thick
2 tbsp. oil
1 med. head cauliflower, separated into floweretes
1 green pepper, cut in ¾ inch pieces
¼ c. soy sauce
1 clove of garlic, minced
2 tbsp. cornstarch
½ tsp. sugar
1½ c. beef broth or water
1 c. green onions with tops, sliced
½ lb. fresh mushrooms, sliced
3 c. hot cooked rice

Cube meat into ½-inch squares. Brown meat in oil. Add cauliflower, green pepper, soy sauce and garlic. Stir lightly to coat vegetables with soy sauce, cover. Simmer until vegetables are barely tender, about 8 to 10 minutes. Blend cornstarch, sugar and broth until smooth. Add to meat mixture with green onions and mushrooms. Cook, stirring constantly, until thoroughly heated and sauce is thickened. Serve over fluffy rice. Yield: 6 servings.

Lois Sherpitis, Ext. Off.
Xi Eta Beta X3176
Aurora, Illinois

Tart words make no friends; a spoonfull of honey will catch more flies than a gallon of vinegar. Mary Kotter

Skillet Sherried Steak

1 1½-lb tenderized round steak, cut into serving
    pieces
Salt to taste
Shortening
1 16-oz. can tomatoes
1 pkg. spaghetti with mushrooms mix
⅓ c. cooking Sherry
1 16-oz. can peas or peas & carrots, drained

Season steak with salt; roll in flour. Brown in
shortening in large skillet. Pour off fat. Stir in
tomatoes, spaghetti sauce mix and Sherry. Bring to a
boil. Reduce heat; cover. Simmer for 10 minutes,
stirring occasionally. Add mushrooms and peas;
cover. Simmer for 10 minutes longer. Serve with salad
and hot bread. Yield: 6 servings.

Peggy Coffman
Alpha Mu Alpha No. 9285
Wheeler, Texas

Cheesed-Sirloin Steak

¼ c. flour
½ tsp. salt
¼ tsp. garlic salt
⅛ tsp. pepper
1 to 1¼ lb. boneless sirloin steak, about ½-in. thick
3 tbsp. cooking oil
¼ c. chopped onion
¼ c. chopped green pepper
½ c. shredded Cheddar cheese

Combine flour, salt, garlic salt and pepper. Pound into
meat until meat is ¼-inch thick. Cut meat into 4 pieces.
Brown meat slowly in cooking oil in large skillet. Add
1½ cups hot water. Sprinkle remaining seasoned flour
mixture over meat. Add onion and green pepper. Stir
gently; cover. Simmer for 1 hour. Add cheese, cover.
Heat to melt cheese, approximately 5 minutes.
Remove meat with melted cheese from skillet. Pour
remaining gravy into bowl. Serve with rice or mashed
potatoes. Yield: 4 servings.

Cynthia Hanselman
Xi Omicron Lambda X4246
Del Rio, Texas

Sukiyaki

3 tbsp. cooking oil
1½ lb. sirloin steak, sliced into thin strips
2 tbsp. sugar
½ c. soy sauce
1 8-oz. can bamboo shoots or chinese vegetables
1 c. sliced onions
1 c. sliced celery
½ c. mushrooms
⅛ tsp. monosodium glutamate

¾ c. green onions and tops
¾ c. watercress, sliced in 1-in. lengths

Heat oil in large 10-inch frying pan. Add meat strips;
brown lightly. Combine sugar, soy sauce and ⅓ cup
water; stir until sugar dissolves. Add to meat; stir.
Bring mixture to a boil; cover. Cook for 40 minutes at a
low temperature, or until meat is tender. Add
remaining ingredients, except green onions and
watercress. Cook for 10 minutes. Add green onions
and watercress. Cook 5 minutes longer. Serve at once
over hot steamed rice. Yield: 6-8 servings.

Betty Jean Price, V. P.
Epsilon Omega No. 8555
Sylva, North Carolina

Crown Loaf

2 8-oz. cans tomato sauce
1 tsp. prepared mustard
3 lb. ground chuck
1 med. onion, chopped
2 eggs, beaten
1 tbsp. salt
¼ tsp. pepper
⅔ c. bread crumbs
4 slices Cheddar cheese
1 avocado, sliced lengthwise

Mix ½ can tomato sauce with mustard. Refrigerate.
Mix remaining ingredients, except cheese and avocado. Place in 9-inch bundt pan. Bake at 350 degrees for 1
hour. Cut cheese in 2 inch wide strips. Turn meat loaf
from pan onto ovenproof platter. Drain excess fat.
Pour tomato-mustard sauce over ring. Place avocado
slices on. Top with cheese slices. Bake 5 minutes
longer. Yield: 8-10 servings.

Photograph for this recipe on page 90.

Hamburger-Green Bean Casserole

1 to 1½ lbs. hamburger
1 sm. onion, chopped
1 tsp. salt
¼ tsp. pepper
1 can tomato soup
1 can green beans, drained
Instant mashed potatoes
4 slices American cheese

Brown hamburger and onion in large skillet. Add salt
and pepper. Mix hamburger with tomato soup. Place
in 2-quart casserole. Place green beans on top. Prepare
instant mashed potatoes according to package directions for 4 to 6 servings. Spread over green beans. Top
with cheese slices. Bake at 350 degrees for 30 minutes
or until cheese is melted and slightly brown. A
meal-in-one! Yield: 4-6 servings.

Mary Rose Hayes
Nu Upsilon No. 6776
Sandusky, Ohio

Think a good thought each day. Kathy Ellison

Triple-Bean Hot Dish

1 lb. hamburger
½ lb. bacon, chopped
1 c. chopped onions
1 c. catsup
¼ c. (firmly packed) brown sugar
2 tbsp. vinegar
2 tsp. dry mustard
1 can each kidney beans, lima beans, pork and beans

Brown hamburger, bacon and onions in small amount of shortening. Skim off excess fat. Add remaining ingredients, mix well. Place in baking dish; cover. Bake for 1 hour 30 minutes to 2 hours at 350 degrees. Add a small amount of water as needed to prevent becoming dry. Yield: 6-8 servings.

Lorene Hays, Treas.
Laureate Beta PL128
Longview, Washington

Three-Bean Bake

1 lb. hamburger
½ lb. bacon, cut up
¾ c. onion, chopped
1 c. (firmly packed) brown sugar
2 tbsp. prepared mustard
2 tbsp. (or more) vinegar
1 can brown beans
1 can kidney beans, drained
1 can large white butter beans

Brown hamburger; add bacon and onion Cook for 3 to 5 minutes. Add brown sugar, mustard, vinegar and beans. Bake at 350 degrees for 1 hour. Yield: 12 servings.

Ann Gerrick, Pres.
Theta Beta
Peachtree City, Georgia

Mock Filet

2 lb. ground beef
½ potato, shredded
1 egg
1 med. onion
1 tbsp. butter
¼ c. catsup
1 tsp. Worcestershire sauce
1 tsp. salt
1 tsp. pepper
1 2-oz. can mushrooms
8 slices of bacon

Combine all ingredients except for bacon strips; mix well. Shape meat mixture into 8 thick patties. Wrap individually with slice bacon; secure with toothpick.

Place 6 to 7 inches apart on broiler pan. Broil for 10 to 15 minutes on each side. Yield: 8 servings.

RaNae Proffitt, V. P.
Xi Epsilon Phi No. 2729
Pana, Illinois

Homemade Salami

5 lb. hamburger
5 tsp. curing salt
2½ tsp. mustard seed
2½ tsp. coarsely ground pepper
2½ tsp. garlic salt
1 tsp. hickory-smoked salt

Combine all ingredients; mix well. Chill overnight. Mix and chill each day for 3 days. Shape mixture into four 2-inch rolls. Place on baking pan. Bake at 140 degrees for 2 hours. Turn on one side for another 2 hours. Turn 2 additional times. Bake for 2 hours on each side. Increase temperature to 200 degrees for last hour of cooking. Total cooking time, 8 hours. Yield: 7 rolls.

Susan E. Kerrick
Xi Alpha Mu X3140
Flagstaff, Arizona

Quick Manicotti

8 manicotti shells
1 lb ground beef
1 clove of garlic, crushed
1 c. cottage cheese
1 c. shredded mozzarella cheese
½ tsp. salt
¼ c. mayonnaise
1 15½-oz. jar spaghetti sauce
½ tsp. whole oregano
⅓ c. grated Parmesan cheese

Cook manicotti shells according to package directions; drain. Rinse in cold water; drain. Set aside. Saute ground beef and garlic, stirring to crumble beef, until beef is no longer pink. Drain off pan drippings. Add cottage cheese, mozzarella cheese, salt and mayonnaise to skillet; stir well. Stuff manicotta shells with meat mixture. Arrange in a lightly greased 13 × 9 × 2-inch baking dish. Combine spaghetti sauce and oregano; pour over manicotta. Sprinkle with Parmesan cheese; cover. Bake at 350 degrees for 15 minutes. Uncover. Bake for 10 additional minutes. Yield: 8 servings.

Mayme B. Campbell
Xi Alpha Zeta
Birmingham, Alabama

Prepare your food with love and all who partake will be uplifted. Carmen Huff

Betty's Baked Steak

1½ to 2 lb. ground beef
Salt to taste
Seasoned pepper to taste
Garlic salt to taste (opt.)
1 onion, sliced
1 16-oz. can stewed tomatoes

Shape ground beef into six 1 to 1½ inch thick patties. Place in 9 × 13-inch baking dish. Sprinkle each steak with seasonings to taste. Top each with 1 slice sweet onion. Place pieces of stewed tomatoes on top of each onion slice. Pour juice over all. Add ⅓ can water. Bake at 350 degrees for 1 hour or to desired doneness. Drain liquid from baking dish. Serve immediately.

Betty L. Hart, Sec.
Preceptor Epsilon XP384
Coeur d'Alene, Idaho

Joyce's Hamburger Stew

1 lb. ground beef
1 tsp. garlic salt
1 c. thinly sliced cabbage
2 tsp. shortening
1 c. sliced cooked carrots
1 c. cubed cooked potatoes
1 c. (firmly packed) brown sugar
1 bottle of barbecue sauce
2 16-oz. cans pork and beans

Brown beef and garlic salt in skillet. Cook cabbage in 2 cups water and shortening until tender in large saucepan. Add beef and remaining ingredients. Bring to a boil. Reduce temperature. Let simmer for about 30 minutes. Serve with crackers or corn bread.

Joyce Lewis, V. P.
Alpha Pi Mu
Mt. Pleasant, Texas

Cabbage Buns

¼ c. margarine
2 pkg. dry yeast
½ c. sugar
1½ tsp. salt
6½ c. flour
1 egg
Meat filling

Melt margarine; cool. Combine 2 cups warm water and yeast. Sift dry ingredients. Add yeast mixture, egg and margarine. Refrigerate for 4 hours. Roll out onto floured board. Cut into 16 squares. Fill with Meat Filling. Fold corners to center; seal. Place on greased sheets. Bake at 350 degrees for 20 minutes.

Meat filling:

1½ lb. hamburger
½ c. chopped onion
1 clove of garlic, minced
3 c. chopped cabbage

Ability is a wonderful thing, but its value is greatly enhanced by dependability. Carolyn Zoza

1½ tsp. salt
½ tsp. pepper
Dash of Tabasco sauce.

Brown meat, onion and garlic. Drain excess fat. Add remaining ingredients and ½ cup water. Simmer for 4 hours. Cool before filling buns.

Susan Kautzsch
Zeta Eta No. 6221
Hooker, Oklahoma

Best Meat Loaf with Piquant Sauce

2 lb. hamburger
¾ c. cracker crumbs
1 can tomatoes, drained
1 tsp. celery salt
1 tsp. onion salt
½ tbsp. chili powder
½ tsp. sage
3 eggs, well beaten
1 lg. onion, chopped
3 tbsp. brown sugar
¼ c. catsup
¼ tsp. nutmeg
1 tsp. dry mustard

Combine first 9 ingredients; mix well. Shape into a loaf. Place in baking pan. Combine remaining ingredients; mix well. Pour over meat loaf. Bake at 350 degrees for 45 minutes to 1 hour. Yield: 8 servings.

Eleanor Braton, Prog. Chm.
Xi Delta Delta X3630
Olathe, Kansas

Company Meat Loaf

2 lb. ground beef
3 eggs
1½ c. oats
1 env. onion soup mix
8 oz. tomato sauce
2 tsp. Worcestershire sauce
Pie crust for 2-crust pie

Combine ground beef, 2 eggs, oats, soup mix, tomato sauce and Worcestershire sauce. Shape into 2 loaves. Place on rack in baking dish. Roll pie crust to fit over each loaf, covering sides of each loaf well. Beat 1 egg. Brush tops of crusts with beaten egg. Bake for 1 hour at 400 degrees. Let stand for 10 minutes before serving.

Nancy Panger, Pres.
Xi Epsilon X1236
Gulfport, Mississippi

Hickory-Smoked Meat Loaf

1½ c. bread crumbs
½ cup minced onions
1 tbsp. horseradish
2 tsp. celery salt

2 tsp. liquid hickory smoke
1 tsp. garlic salt
¼ tsp. pepper
2 eggs
1½ lb. ground beef
Hickory Sauce

Combine bread crumbs, onions, 2 tablespoons water, horseradish, celery salt, hickory smoke, garlic salt, pepper and eggs. Add beef; mix well. Place in loaf pan. Bake in 350 degree-oven for 30 minutes. Drain off grease. Pour Hickory Sauce over loaf. Continue baking for 30 to 45 minutes, occasionally spooning sauce over meat loaf. Yield: 8 servings.

Hickory Sauce:

⅓ c. grape jelly
1 tsp. lemon juice
½ c. chilli sauce
½ tsp. hickory smoke

Melt jelly in saucepan. Blend all ingredients well.

Jennie Shanks, V. P.
Alpha Theta No. 419
Chariton, Iowa

Dilled-Lasagna Roll-Ups

12 lasagna noodles
1 tbsp. salt
¾ lb. ground beef
2 tbsp. minced onion
White Sauce
¾ c. chopped dill pickles
½ c. grated mozzarella cheese
1 8-oz. can tomatoes
⅓ c. grated carrots

Add lasagna noodles and salt gradually to 3-quarts rapidly boiling water so water continues to boil. Cook uncovered, stirring occasionally, until barely tender. Drain in colander; reserve. Brown beef and onion in medium skillet. Stir ⅔ cup White Sauce and pickles into beef. Mix in cheese; reserve. Add tomatoes and carrots to remaining White Sauce; simmer 10 minutes. Spread ¼ cup beef-pickle mixture on each lasagna noodle; roll up. Place rolls, seam side down, in shallow baking dish. Pour sauce over rolls. Bake at 375 degrees oven for 25 minutes. Garnish with additional pickle slices.

White Sauce:

¼ c. butter or margarine
¼ c. flour
1 tsp. salt
Dash of pepper
1⅓ c. milk

Melt butter in small saucepan. Blend in flour, salt and pepper. Stir in milk until smooth. Cook, stirring constantly, until mixture thickens and boils.

Photograph for this recipe on page 104.

A man should hear a little music, read a little poetry, and see a fine picture every day of his life. Mrs. Sylvia L. Miles

Baked Lasagna

2 lb. Italian sausage or ground beef
2 cloves of garlic, minced
1 tbsp. basil
1 1-lb. can tomatoes
3 6-oz. cans tomato paste
4 tbsp. parsley flakes
3½ tsp. salt
1 10-oz. box lasagna noodles
3 8-oz. packages cream cheese, softened
2 eggs, beaten
½ tsp. pepper
½ c. grated Parmesan cheese
1 lb. sliced mozzarella cheese

Brown meat; remove excess fat. Add next 4 ingredients and 2 tablespoon parsley flakes and 1½ teaspoons salt. Simmer, uncovered, about 30 minutes, stirring occasionally. Cook noodles in boiling salted water until tender. Drain; rinse in cold water. Combine cream cheese with eggs, 2 teaspoons salt, 2 tablespoons parsley flakes, pepper and Parmesan cheese. Place half the noodles in 13 × 9 × 2-inch baking dish; spread half the cheese mixture over noodles. Top with half the mozzarella cheese and half the meat sauce. Repeat layers. Bake at 350 degrees for 30 minutes. Let stand for 10 to 15 minutes. Cut in 12 serving squares. Serve with tossed green salad, garlic bread and red wine. Yield: 12 servings.

Laurie Gindler, Prog. Chm.
Xi Upsilon Epsilon X5214
Hallettsville, Texas

Cheryl's Lasagna

2 16-oz. cans tomato sauce
1 16-oz. can tomato paste
½ c. red wine
2 tsp. oregano
1 tsp. sweet Basil
1 tsp. garlic salt
1 tsp. minced garlic
1 lb. hamburger
1 4-oz. can mushrooms
1 package lasagna noodles, cooked
1 pt. cottage cheese
1 tbsp. parsley
½ lb. mozzarella cheese, grated
1 c. Parmesan cheese, grated
½ lb. Swiss cheese, grated

Combine first 7 ingredients and 1 cup water in large bowl; set aside. Fry hamburger. Add mushrooms. Drain off excess grease. Add sauce. Simmer for 20 minutes. Cook lasagna noodles according to package directions. Drain; let stand in cold water. Combine cottage cheese and parsley. Layer in oblong baking dish, in order listed, half the sauce, noodles, cottage cheese mixture, mozzarella cheese, Parmesan cheese and Swiss cheese. Repeat layers, ending with sauce.

Bake at 350 degrees for 30 minutes. Let stand several minutes before serving. Yield: 8-10 servings.

Cheryl Hinnenkamp, W. and M. Chm.
Alpha Pi No. 5079
Caldwell, Idaho

Lasagna For A Crowd

8 tbsp. salad oil
4½ lb. ground beef
1½ lb. fresh Italian sausage
8 cloves of garlic, crushed
4 8-oz. cans tomato sauce
3 lg. cans Italian-style tomatoes
4½ tsp. salt
1 tsp. pepper
2 tsp. oregano
3½ 8-oz. packages broad lasagna noodles
4½ lb. mozzarella cheese, sliced
4 lb. soft ricotta cheese
1¼ lb. fresh grated Parmesan Cheese

Heat oil in skillet. Add meats; brown. Add next 6 ingredients. Simmer 30 minutes or until slightly thickened. Cook noodles in boiling salted water until tender. Drain and rinse. Arrange in layers in 4 large rectangular baking dishes; layer of noodles, mozzarella cheese, ricotta cheese, meat sauce and Parmesan cheese. Repeat layers, ending with layer of sauce and Parmesan cheese. Bake in 350-degree oven about 30 minutes or until brown on top and cheeses are melted. Let stand for a few minutes before serving. Serve with tossed salad, garlic bread and a good red wine.

Gloria Brooks
Xi Beta X241
Salem, Oregon

Mexican Casserole

2 lb. ground beef
1 lg. onion, chopped finely
1 lg. bell pepper, chopped finely
2 buds garlic, minced
2 cans refried beans
2 cans chili without beans
½ lb. sharp cheese, grated
1 pkg. large corn chips

Cook ground beef, onion, bell pepper and garlic until done. Place refried beans in large casserole. Add chili, meat mixture, cheese and corn chips. Bake at 350 degrees for 30 minutes. Serve hot with green salad and French bread. Yield: 6 servings.

Gustava M. Guthrie, Rec. Sec.
Omega No. 2376
Florence, Alabama

Ole to Mexico

1 lb. lean ground beef
1 c. chopped onions

Be not forgetful to entertain strangers, for thereby some have entertained angels unawares. Blanche C. Doernhoefer

¼ tsp. cumin
¼ tsp. hot sauce
Salt and pepper to taste
Garlic salt to taste
2 pkg. tortillas
1½ c. grated longhorn cheese
1 4-oz. can chopped green chilies
1 13-oz. can cream of mushroom soup

Brown beef with onions and seasonings until onions are tender. Tear tortillas into fourths. Arrange tortillas to cover bottom of 9 × 13-inch baking dish. Alternate layers of cheese, chilies and ground beef. Repeat with tortillas until all ingredients are used. Prepare soup according to can directions. Pour over top slowly. Bake at 350 degrees for 30 minutes. Or cover with waxed paper; bake in microwave oven on high for 15 minutes. Yield: 12 servings.

Lois Anne Ellison, Centennial Coun. Pres.
Preceptor Nu XP1038
Phoenix, Arizona

Taco Bake

2 lb. hamburger
1½ c. onions
1 15-oz. can tomato sauce
2 tsp. chili powder
1½ tsp. salt
½ tsp. pepper
1 15-oz. can kidney beans
1 5-oz. can green chili peppers, chopped
1 5-oz. taco shells
2 c. shredded Cheddar cheese
½ head lettuce, chopped
2 tomatoes, chopped

Cook hamburger and onions until tender. Stir in tomato sauce, chili powder, salt, pepper, kidney beans and green chili peppers. Break each taco shell in half at the fold. Arrange halves on the bottom and sides of 13 × 9-inch baking pan. Spoon meat mixture evenly over tacos. Sprinkle with cheese. Bake in preheated 350-degree oven for 15 to 20 minutes. Remove from oven. Top with lettuce and tomatoes while hot. Serve with your favorite hot sauce. Yield: 8 servings.

Theda Mae Lee, V. P.
Xi Beta Rho X2592
Lakewood, Colorado

Chiles Rellenos

6 green chilies
1 lb. ground beef
1 med. onion, chopped
Comino seed to taste
½ c. flour
3 eggs, separated
1 c. cooking oil

Place chilies on ungreased cookie sheet. Bake in preheated 400-degree oven for 15 minutes. Brown ground beef and onion in skillet; drain grease. Add seasoning; continue to brown well. Remove chilies from oven; peel. Slit chilies from end to end on one side, remove seeds, being careful not to tear chilies. Roll chilies in flour. Fill with meat mixture. Secure closing with small skewers or toothpicks. Beat egg whites until fluffy. Beat egg yolks slightly. Fold into egg whites. Dip chilies into egg mixture. Place in hot oil in skillet. Brown lightly on both sides. Remove from skillet; drain. Serve with fried rice, refried beans and tortillas. Yield: 6 servings. Buen Apetito!

Martha R. Hernandez, Pres.
Xi Lambda Epsilon X3233
Houston, Texas

Gringo Chili

1 to 1½ lb. ground beef
1 30-oz. can red kidney beans
1 28-oz. can peeled whole tomatoes
2 15-oz. cans tomato sauce
1 3½-oz. can diced green chilies
1 12-oz. can whole kernel corn, drained (opt.)
Salt and pepper to taste

Brown ground beef in Dutch oven. Combine beans, tomatoes, tomato sauce, green chilies and corn. Stir into browned meat. Season with salt and pepper. Bring chili to a boil; stir. Simmer for at least 1 hour, stirring occasionally. Yield: 12 servings.

Barbara Ann Fraley
Delta Delta No. 8726
Tucson, Arizona

Kay's Chili

3 lb. hamburger
1 med. onion, chopped
4 cloves of garlic
4 tbsp. cuminseed
1 tsp. oregano
1 tsp. crushed red pepper (or to taste)
6 tbsp. paprika
6 tbsp. chili powder
1 lg. can tomato juice
Salt and pepper to taste
1 can beans (opt.)

Brown meat with onion and garlic in a 3-quart saucepan or roaster. Add remaining ingredients except beans; stir well. Add enough water to cover. Simmer, covered, for 3 hours. Add beans, heat thoroughly. Yield: 6-8 servings.

Kay Witcher, V. P.
Xi Epsilon Theta X1800
Odessa, Texas

Better is a dinner of herbs where love is, than a stalled ox and hatred therewith.   Terri Bourland

Jan's Meatballs

1 10-oz. can pineapple chunks
1 lb. ground beef
½ tsp. salt
1 egg
¼ c. flour
2 tbsp. salad oil
¼ c. (firmly packed) brown sugar
¼ c. vinegar
1 tbsp. soy sauce
2 tbsp. cornstarch
2 green peppers, cut in chunks

Drain pineapple, reserving half the juice. Mix ground beef with salt. Shape into balls. Beat egg with 1 teaspoon water. Dip meatballs into egg mixture, then in flour to coat. Brown in salad oil in frying pan. Remove from pan; set aside. Mix reserved juice, brown sugar, vinegar and soy sauce in frying pan. Add cornstarch. Cook until thickens. Boil for 3 minutes longer. Add meatballs, green peppers and pineapple chunks. Simmer for 10 minutes. Serve with rice and a green salad. Yield: 6 servings.

Jan Moody, Rec. Sec.
Iota No. 2735
Portage la Prairie, Manitoba, Canada

Susan's Sweet and Sour Meatballs

1 lb. ground beef
1 egg
1 tsp. salt
1 tsp. Accent
2 tbsp. flour
Cooking oil
½ c. beef broth
1 lg. green pepper, cut into bite-sized pieces.
1 8-oz. can pineapple chunks, drained
1 8-oz. can tomatoes, drained
3 tbsp. cornstarch
½ c. sugar
½ c. pineapple juice
½ c. white vinegar
1 tbsp. soy sauce

Mix ground beef, egg, salt, Accent, flour and 1 teaspoon water. Shape into 1-inch balls. Brown in hot oil; drain oil. Add beef broth, green pepper, pineapple chunks and tomatoes. Mix cornstarch, sugar, pineapple juice, vinegar, and soy sauce in mixing bowl. Add to meatballs. Cook until thick. Serve over rice. Yield: 6-8 servings.

Susan Altemeier, Pres.
Xi Theta Xi X2224
Torrance, California

Hawaiian Potluck Meatballs

1½ lb. ground beef
¼ c. grated onion
1½ tsp. salt
⅛ tsp. freshly ground pepper
1 egg, slightly beaten
¼ c. cornstarch
1 8-oz. can pineapple chunks
2 tbsp. vegetable oil
1 c. beef broth or bouillon
2 tbsp. lemon juice
1 lemon, thinly sliced
¼ c (firmly packed) brown sugar
½ c. gingersnap bits

Mix ground beef, onion, 1 teaspoon salt, pepper and egg. Form into 1-inch balls. Roll lightly in cornstarch. Drain pineapple, reserving ½ cup juice. Heat oil in skillet. Brown meatballs on all sides. Add broth, reserved pineapple juice, lemon juice, lemon slices, brown sugar and remaining sugar; cover. Cook over low heat for 35 minutes. Stir in gingersnap bits; add pineapple. Cook for 10 minutes longer. Yield: 6 servings.

Eileen Shuttleworth, Pres.
Xi Zeta Delta X1728
Whittier, California

Kendal's Sweet and Sour Meatballs

3 tbsp. lemon juice
¾ c. sugar
1½ c. chopped onions
2 lb. lean ground beef
3 slices water-soaked bread
1 egg, slightly beaten
1 tsp. salt
1 14½-oz. can stewed tomatoes
1 8-oz. can tomato sauce
6 gingersnaps, crumbled
3 tbsp. vinegar

Place lemon juice, sugar, onions and 1½ cups water in 10-inch skillet. Simmer for 30 minutes. Mix ground beef, bread, egg and salt. Shape into 1-inch meatballs. Stir stewed tomatoes, tomato sauce, gingersnaps and vinegar into lemon-sugar mixture. Place meatballs in single layer in simmering sauce. Simmer for 1 hour or until meatballs are cooked. Yield: 10 servings.

Kendal Charlene Gee
Lambda Pi No. 7757
Kansas City, Missouri

Italian Spaghetti Sauce with Meatballs

1 48-oz. can tomato juice
2 19-oz. cans tomatoes, cut up

Cabbage, like a good wife, is often taken for granted.   Carol Cameron

1 sm. can tomato paste
2 or 3 bay leaves
½ tsp. sugar
¼ c. Parmesan cheese
½ tsp. pepper
2 tsp. oregano
2 tsp. sweet basil
2 tsp. garlic salt
1 lb. pork or veal
1 lb. ground beef
½ c. bread crumbs
½ c. milk
Salad oil
1 clove of garlic
1 1-lb. package spaghetti

Combine first 7 ingredients with 1 teaspoon each oregano, sweet basil and garlic salt in a saucepan; mix well. Simmer gently for 5 to 10 minutes. Combine next 3 ingredients with remaining oregano, sweet basil and garlc salt and milk to moisten. Shape into 1-inch meatballs. Heat enough oil in skillet to brown meatballs. Add garlic clove to season oil; remove. Fry meatballs on all sides until brown. Add to simmering sauce. Continue to simmer for 3 to 4 hours, stirring occasionally. Prepare spaghetti according to package directions. Serve meatballs and sauce over spaghetti with Caesar salad, garlic bread and wine. Yield: 10 servings.

Mrs. Diane Cerisano, W. and M. Co-Chm.
Alpha Nu No. 5198
North Bay, Ontario, Canada

Southern Spaghetti and Meatballs

2 lg. cans tomatoes, sieved
2 cans tomato paste
1 can Parmesan cheese
Salt and pepper to taste
2 lb. ground round steak, ground twice
1 lb. ground pork
1 c. raisins
2 or 3 cloves of garlic
1 tsp. chopped parsley
3 slices bread soaked in water and squeezed dry

Combine tomatoes, tomato paste, and half can Parmesan cheese. Season with salt and pepper. Simmer gently for 5 to 10 minutes. Combine remaining ingredients, seasoning to taste with salt and pepper; mix well. Shape into 1-inch meatballs. Fry in small amount of oil until brown on all sides. Place in simmering sauce. Cook for 1 hour. Serve over cooked spaghetti. Yield: 8 servings.

Mary Hensley, L. B. A. C. Past Pres.
Preceptor Gamma Gamma XP757
Westminster, California

Spaghetti Amore

1 lb. ground beef
½ c. chopped onion
¼ c. chopped green pepper
1 garlic clove, minced
2 tbsp. shortening
1 can cream of mushroom soup
1 can tomato soup
1 c. shredded sharp Cheddar cheese
½ lb. cooked, drained spaghetti
¼ tsp. Italian herb seasoning

Brown ground beef, onion, green pepper and garlic in shortening. Add soups and 1 soup can water. Heat thoroughly. Blend with ½ cup cheese and spaghetti. Pour into 3-quart casserole. Sprinkle with remaining cheese and herb seasoning. Bake at 350 degrees for 35 to 40 minutes. Yield: 4-6 servings.

Irene G. Berghoff, Rec. Sec.
Preceptor Omega XP695
Bethalto, Illinois

Michele's Spaghetti

1½ lb. ground beef
⅓ c. chopped onion
1 clove of garlic, minced
½ tsp. oregano leaves
½ tsp. salt
¼ tsp. pepper
1 4-oz. can sliced mushrooms
1 1-lb. jar meatless spaghetti sauce
8 oz. spaghetti, cooked and drained
½ c. sour cream
1 c. cream-style cottage cheese
½ c. Parmesan cheese

Saute ground beef, onion, garlic, oregano, salt and pepper in skillet until meat is browned. Stir in undrained mushrooms, and spaghetti sauce. Simmer, uncovered, for 10 minutes. Place half the spaghetti in bottom of greased 9-inch square baking dish. Spoon on half the meat mixture. Combine sour cream and cottage cheese. Spread over meat mixture. Add remaining spaghetti. Cover with remaining meat mixture. Sprinkle Parmesan cheese over all. Bake at 375 degrees for 35 minutes. Let stand for 5 minutes. Cut in squares. Yield: 6 servings.

Michele D. VanDyke, Pres.
Gamma Kappa No. 7602
Crete, Nebraska

Hospitality consists of a little fire, a little food, and an immense quiet. Betty Carmichael

Dolmades

12 lg. cabbage leaves
2 med. onions, chopped
2 tbsp. oil
½ lb. minced lamb
1 tbsp. minced parsley
½ tsp. sage
½ tsp. salt
½ c. rice
2 tbsp. raisins
1½ c. tomato juice
Juice of ½ lemon
1 c. yogurt

Pour boiling water on cabbage leaves. Let stand for 2 minutes; drain. Saute onions in oil. Add next 5 ingredients; stir until rice is glazed. Add ½ cup water and raisins. Simmer for 10 minutes or until liquid is absorbed. Spoon meat mixture into cabbage leaves. Roll up loosely as rice will swell as it cooks. Place, seam side down, in Dutch oven in layers with additional leaves between layers. Combine tomato juice and lemon juice. Pour over cabbage rolls; cover. Cook over low heat for 1 hour and 30 minutes. Remove cabbage rolls from sauce; strain. Stir in yogurt. Serve sauce with cabbage rolls. Yield: 6 servings.

Martha Ortiz, Soc. Chm.
Alpha Epislon Sigma No. 7853
San Antonio, Texas

Lamb Balls in Lemon Sauce

1 lb. ground lamb
½ c. chopped onions
⅓ c. milk
1 tsp. salt
Dash of pepper
3 eggs
½ c. snipped parsley
1 beef bouillon cube
1 to 1½ tbsp. lemon juice

Combine first 5 ingredients and 1 beaten egg. Form into twenty-five 1-inch balls. Roll in parsley. Dissolve bouillon cube in ¾ cup hot water. Add meatballs; cover. Simmer for 30 minutes, turning occasionally. Beat lemon juice with 2 slightly beaten eggs. Stir a small amount of bouillon into egg mixture. Pour over meatballs. Cook, stirring constantly until mixture thickens. Serve meatballs and sauce over cooked noodles. Yield: 5-6 servings.

Barbara L. Lidden, Pres.
Xi Rho Eta X3994
Ben Lomond, California

Sweet and Sour Riblets

1 tsp. salt
2 lbs. lamb riblets
1 tbsp. vegetable oil
1 bouillon cube
1 clove of garlic, minced
2 tbsp. brown sugar
2 tbsp. soy sauce
¼ c. cider vinegar
1 c. pineapple juice
2 tbsp. cornstarch
¼ c. diced onion
1¼ c. thinly sliced carrots
1 green pepper, diced
6 sm. sweet pickles, sliced
1 c. pineapple chunks

Add salt and lamb to 3 cups boiling water. Simmer for 1 hour or until tender. Brown lamb in oil in large skillet. Dissolve bouillon in ¼ cup boiling water in saucepan. Add next 6 ingredients and ½ cup water. Cook until thick and clear. Add to browned meat. Add vegetables and pineapple. Simmer, covered, until vegetables are tender-crisp. Serve with rice. Yield: 4 servings.

Mary Taylor, Pres.
Preceptor Alpha XP427
St. John's, New Foundland, Canada

Toad-in-the-Hole

2 c. flour
1 egg, beaten well
Milk
2 tbsp. butter
Salt and pepper to taste
8 lamb chops

Combine flour and egg with enough milk to make a batter. Spread in baking dish. Pour ½ cup water over batter. Dot with butter. Season with salt and pepper. Top with lamb chops. Cover with foil. Bake at 350 degrees for 1 hour. Yield: 8 servings.

M. Margaret Roth
Xi Lambda
Deadwood, South Dakota

Sweet and Sour Liver

1 lb. liver, cut into strips
2 tablespoons hot shortening
1 beef bouillon cube
½ tsp. salt
1 13-oz. can pineapple tidbits
3 tbsp. brown sugar
2 tbsp. cornstarch
2 or 3 tbsp. vinegar

The only way to help people be what they want to be is to accept them as they are.   Nancy Panger

1 tbsp. soy sauce
1 med. green pepper, cut into strips

Brown liver in hot shortening in large heavy skillet. Stir in 1 cup water, bouillon cube and ¼ teaspoon salt. Simmer over low heat for 5 minutes. Drain pineapple, reserving juice. Combine the reserved juice with next 4 ingredients and ¼ teaspon salt in a saucepan. Cook until thick. Add sauce to liver. Stir in pineapple and green pepper; heat thoroughly. Serve over rice. Yield: 4 servings.

Juanita McGann, Prog. Chm.
Xi Gamma Pi X3839
Colorado Springs, Colorado

Ponsit

1 pkg. rice sticks
4 chicken breasts
4 pork steaks
¼ lb. shrimp
⅓ c. oil
6 cloves of garlic, chopped
¾ head cabbage, cut into strips
4 celery stalks
2 carrots, chopped
1 lg. onion, chopped
Soy sauce to taste

Soak rice sticks in water to cover until soft; drain. Parboil chicken breasts and pork. Cut in ¼ × 1 inch strips. Saute chicken, pork and shrimp in oil and garlic; set aside. Saute vegetables until tender-crisp. Add vegetables and meat in a large wok, tossing until mixed well. Add soy sauce. Add rice sticks, mix well. Serve with lemon wedges and additional soy sauce. Yield: 6-8 servings.

Pat Klay, Scrapbook Chm.
Xi Beta Epsilon X803
Watsonville, California

Ham and Broccoli Bake

1 10-oz. package frozen chopped broccoli
12 to 14 slices white bread
1 c. shredded Cheddar cheese
2 c. cooked, sliced ham
2 tsp. chopped onion
6 eggs, slightly beaten
3½ c. milk

Thaw broccoli; drain water. Cut each slice of bread with a doughnut cutter. Fit scraps into greased 9 × 13-inch baking dish. Layer cheese, broccoli and ham over bread scraps. Sprinkle with onion. Arrange doughnuts on top. Combine remaining ingredients. Pour over bread; cover. Chill at least 6 hours. Bake, uncovered, at 325 degrees for 1 hour. Let stand a few minutes before cutting. Cut so each piece has doughnut on top. Yield: 12 servings.

Nancy A. Reid, Pres.
Eta Omega
Marion, Iowa

Ham-Broccoli Royale

1 c. rice
2 c. chopped onion
1 stick butter
2 10-oz. packages chopped broccoli
1½ lb. ham, chopped
1 or 2 cans cream of mushroom soup
1 lb. Velveeta pimento cheese, cubed

Cook rice in 3 or 4 cups water in saucepan until tender. Saute onion in butter until transparent. Cook broccoli according to package directions; drain. Combine all ingredients in baking dish. Bake at 350 degrees until bubbly. Yield: 8 servings.

Janice Peterson, Pres.
Alpha Eta XP1433
Afton, Iowa

Curried Ham in Avocados

1 egg
1 c. mayonnaise
⅓ c. grated Parmesan cheese
1 single-serving env. instant onion soup mix
1 tsp. curry powder
⅛ tsp. garlic powder
2 c. chopped fully-cooked ham
1 c. cooked rice
3 med. avocados
Lemon juice
Chopped salted peanuts (opt.)
Chopped tomatoes (opt.)

Combine egg, mayonnaise, cheese, soup mix, curry powder and garlic powder in small mixer bowl. Beat at medium speed of electric mixer for 20 to 30 seconds or until smooth and creamy. Stir in ham and rice. Cover; chill for 1 hour. Cut avocados in half lengthwise; remove pits. Brush cut surfaces with lemon juice. Place each avocado half on a lettuce-lined salad plate. Mound about ½ cup ham mixture in center of each avocado half. Sprinkle with chopped salted peanuts and chopped tomato. Yield: 6 servings.

Linda Vo Moser, Rec. Sec.
Delta Tau No. 5093
Morrison, Colorado

A warm hearth, A pleasant smile, A contented appetite, Makes life worthwhile! Allena M Burnken

Ham Rolls Polonaise

1 12-oz. package curly noodles
9 tbsp. butter
12 slices boiled ham
12 American cheese strips, cut 2½ × 1 × ¾ inch thick
2 10-oz. packages frozen broccoli spears, thawed slightly
3½ tbsp. flour
3 c. milk
Salt to taste
¼ tsp. nutmeg
¼ cup dry, fine bread crumbs

Cook noodles according to package directions; drain well. Spread on bottom of well-buttered 9 × 13-inch baking dish. Dot with 2 tablespoons butter. Roll each ham slice around a cheese stick; place on top of noodles. Arrange broccoli spears around ham. Melt 4 tablespoons butter in saucepan. Stir in flour, mixing until smooth. Cook over medium heat for about 1 minute. Remove pan from heat. Stir in milk slowly. Season to taste with salt. Cook over medium heat, stirring constantly, until thickened. Stir in nutmeg. Pour over casserole. Melt 3 tablespoon butter. Add bread crumbs; toss together well. Sprinkle evenly over casserole. Cover tightly with aluminum foil. Bake at 350 degrees for about 30 minutes. Uncover and bake about 5 minutes longer. Yield: 6 servings.

Muriel M. Hollenbeck, Pres.
Eta Beta No. 8085
Sedalia, Colorado

Ham Loaf Supreme

5 lb. ground ham
3 eggs, beaten
3 c. crushed graham crackers
2 c. milk
1 tbsp. onion
2 cans tomato soup
¾ c. vinegar
2 ¼ c. (firmly packed) brown sugar
2 tsp. dry mustard

Combine first 5 ingredients; mix well. Place in shallow 8 × 12-inch baking pan. Combine soup, vinegar, brown sugar and dry mustard; mix well. Pour sauce over ham mixture. Bake for 1 hour in 350-degree oven. Yield: 12-16 servings.

Herma Colwell, Pres.
Preceptor Epsilon Zeta XP1136
Merced, California

Mary Lou's Ham Loaf

2 lb. ground pork
2 c. crushed graham crackers
3 eggs

2 lb. ground ham
1½ c. milk
1 can tomato soup
½ c. vinegar
1 c. (firmly packed) brown sugar
1 tbsp. mustard

Combine first 5 ingredients; mix well. Pack into a large baking pan. Dilute soup with 1 soup can water. Combine with remaining ingredients; mix well. Pour over ham mixture. Bake at 325 degrees for 2 hours or until done, basting with sauce occasionally. Yield: 20 servings.

Mary Lou Stark, Pres.
Preceptor Delta Alpha XP923
Anaheim, California

Delores' Ham Loaf

2 c. leftover ham, minced
24 saltines, crushed
½ med. onion, minced
2 eggs. slightly beaten
½ c. milk
Dash of pepper
½ c. (firmly packed) brown sugar
3 tsp. vinegar
2 tsp. dry mustard
1 8½-oz. can crushed pineapple

Blend ham, saltines and onion; mix well. Add eggs, milk and pepper. Shape into 5 × 9-inch loaf. Place in loaf pan or small casserole. Combine brown sugar, vinegar, dry mustard and pineapple. Pour over loaf. Bake at 350 degrees for 30 minutes. Yield: 6 servings.

Delores Strohl, Pres.
Xi Eta Upsilon No. 3715
Steubenville, Ohio

Pork Tenderloin

4 pork tenderloins
Salt, pepper, chives, onion powder, parsley to taste
4 slices Swiss cheese
1 can mushroom soup
½ c. dry white wine
4 tbsp. sour cream

Season tenderloins as desired. Place cheese slice on each chop. Roll up; secure with toothpick. brown chops lightly in skillet. Add mushroom soup. Simmer on low to medium heat. Add wine, sour cream and additional seasonings, about 20 minutes before serving. Serve with a dry white or rose wine. Yield: 4 servings. Bon Appetit!

Alyce D. Vanek
International Honorary Member
Laguna Hills, California

"Praise God, from whom all blessings flow." Lois Sherpitis

Barbecued Spareribs

4 to 6 lbs. spareribs
1 med. onion, chopped
½ c. catsup
1½ tsp. salt
¼ tsp. Tobasco sauce
½ tsp. chili powder
½ tsp. dry mustard
2 tbsp. brown sugar

Cut spareribs into serving pieces. Place in roaster. Sprinkle onion over meat. Combine 1 cup water with remaining ingredients. Pour sauce over spareribs. Cover. Bake for 2 hours at 350 degrees. Remove cover the last 30 minutes. Yield: 4-6 servings.

Janet E. Rendall, V. P.
Delta Epsilon No. 5403
Oakville, Ontario, Canada

Cote de Porc Farcie

1 or 2 pork chops per person, butterflied and boned
Sage to taste
Salt and pepper to taste
1 slice ham per chop
1 slice Swiss cheese per chop
1 c. dry white wine

Sprinkle chops with sage, salt and pepper. Arrange 1 slice ham and cheese on each chop; trim to fit. Fold chops in half, tie securely with string. Sear one side over high heat in greased frypan. Transfer to another pan. Cook, uncovered, for 15 minutes. Repeat process for second side. Pour wine over chops just before serving.

Suzanne Andersen, Pres.
Alpha Gamma
Fort Qu'Appelle, Saskatchewan, Canada

Pork Chop-Rice Bake

4 pork chops
Shortening
Salt and pepper to taste
1 c. uncooked rice
1½ c. apple juice
2 10½-oz. cans chicken with rice soup

Brown pork chops in small amount of hot shortening. Season with salt and pepper. Combine rice, apple juice and soup in medium-sized baking dish. Arrange chops on top; cover. Bake at 350 degrees for 1 hour 15 minutes or until chops are tender and liquid is absorbed.

Betty Lockhart, Serv. Chm.
Alpha Upsilon No. 1605
Steamboat Springs, Colorado

Brown-Baked Pork Chops

4 eggs, well beaten
¼ c. milk
Salt and pepper to taste
6 lean pork chops
12 double-sectioned soda crackers, crushed

Combine eggs, milk, salt and pepper in a small bowl; beat well. Dip chops in egg mixture then in cracker crumbs. Be sure each piece is well coated. Fry on medium high heat to form a crispy crust. Place chops on rack in baking pan. Bake at 350 degrees for 20 minutes.

Jane L Mader
Kappa Sigma No.9847
Nortonville, Kansas

Shrimp-Stuffed Pork Chops

1 pkg. herb-flavored bread stuffing
¾ c. chopped onion
1 c. chopped celery
½ c. margarine
1 4½-oz. can sm. shrimp
4 1-inch thick pork chops with pockets

Prepare stuffing according to package directions. Saute onions and celery in ¼ cup margarine. Add to stuffing. Add shrimp with liquid. Fill pork chop pockets with shrimp mixture. Secure with toothpicks. Brown lightly in remaining margarine. Place in buttered casserole. Bake for 2 hours at 350 degrees.

Helen Crawford, Pres.
Xi Delta Tau X3455
Princeton, Missouri

Pork Chops with Sauerkraut

6 pork chops, trimmed
Salt and pepper to taste
1 lg. onion, sliced
1 lg. can sauerkraut
2 or 3 apples, sliced
4 or 5 lg. potatoes, sliced
Butter

Season pork chops with salt and pepper. Brown chops in large heavy skillet. Arrange onion slices on chops. Add sauerkraut and enough water to keep chops moist. Place apples on sauerkraut; add potato slices. Season with salt and pepper. Cook, covered, over medium heat until potatoes are soft. Season with butter.

Norma Jean Lane, Pres.
Xi Alpha X429
Makakilo, Hawaii

Murphy's law states, that the hunger level of your family is inversely proportional to the quantity of food served.   Emily C Sullivan

Seafood

Like treasures from the deep, succulent seafoods are a valuable discovery for those trying to overcome the monotony of a meat-oriented menu. And, thanks to modern packaging and transportation, fresh and saltwater fish and shellfish are available even to people who live miles and miles from an ocean, lake or river. So, if you're a homemaker that takes every opportunity to serve unique and attractive dishes to family and guests alike, serve seafood often.

The menu variety available from the many kinds of seafood is astounding. Both souffles and crepes are an excellent addition to a brunch menu—but all the more excellent when they feature seafood, such as a lobster or tuna souffle, or savory shrimp crepes. With today's interest in casual entertaining, fish and seafood are right at home. A fish-fry, clam bake, or lobster boil is certainly as much fun as a backyard barbecue, and the outdoor grill is as perfect for lobster, shrimp and trout as it is for steak. For formal meals, seafood, such as stuffed crab or curried shrimp, could not be more impressive. And, if you have added stir-frying to your favorite cooking techniques, seafood is a natural in your recipe repertoire.

Don't hesitate—"fish" for complements! You will be rewarded greatly every time you place fish and seafood on the menu. Beta Sigma Phis are glad to share this collection of seafood recipes because they know the variety that Neptune's bounty has to offer.

Cioppino Cinzano

2 tbsp. olive or salad oil
¾ c. chopped onion
½ c. chopped green pepper
2 med. garlic cloves, crushed
1 c. Cinzano Asti Spumante wine
1 28 oz. can tomatoes
1½ tsp. salt
¼ tsp. rosemary, crushed
¼ tsp. thyme, crushed
Dash of cayenne
18 hard-shelled clams
1 lb. striped-bass fillets, cut into serving pieces
1 lb. shelled, deveined fresh shrimp
Chopped parsley

Heat oil in a Dutch oven or large saucepan. Add onion, green pepper and garlic. Saute over medium heat, stirring occasionally, until onion and pepper are tender, about 5 minutes. Add wine, undrained tomatoes, salt, rosemary, thyme and cayenne. Heat to boiling point. Reduce heat to low; cover. Simmer for 15 minutes. Increase heat to medium-high. Add clams. Cook, uncovered, for 5 minutes, stirring occasionally. Add bass and shrimp. Cook, uncovered, about 5 minutes or until shrimp turns pink and bass flakes easily when tested with a fork; stir occasionally. Sprinkle with chopped parsley. Serve immediately in soup bowls. Yield. 6-8 servings.

Photograph for this recipe on page 114.

Clam Sauce with Linguine

2 cans clams
1 lg. onion, chopped
⅓ c. olive oil
4 tbsp. butter
1 tsp. garlic powder
¼ tsp. pepper
1 tsp. oregano
1 tsp. salt
1 or 2 tbsp. parsley flakes
Juice and grated rind or 1 lemon
1 16-oz. package linguine or fettuccine

Drain clams, reserving liquid. Saute onion in olive oil and butter in 10-inch skillet. Add garlic powder, pepper, oregano, salt and reserved clam liquid. Simmer for 5 minutes. Add clams, parsley and lemon juice and rind. Simmer for a few minutes. Prepare linguine according to package directions. Serve clam sauce over linguine. Yield: 4 servings.

Frances K. Sullivan, Pres.
Zeta Chi No. 9504
Douglasville, Georgia

Mary Ann's Crab Quiche

1 9-inch pastry shell
1 egg white, slightly beaten
2 tbsp. chopped onion
1 tbsp. butter or margarine
1 c. crab meat, drained and shredded
1 tbsp. flour
1½ c. shredded Swiss cheese
3 eggs, beaten
1 c. half and half or milk
½ tsp. salt
Dash of hot sauce
Dash of nutmeg

Brush pastry shell with egg white; set aside. Saute onion in butter until tender. Combine crab meat and flour; add onion. Sprinkle half the cheese into pie shell; add crab. Add remaining cheese. Beat eggs, half and half and seasonings until mixed but not frothy. Pour into pie shell. Bake at 350 degrees for 30 to 40 minutes. Yield: 6 servings.

Mary Ann Apland
Xi Gamma Beta X2881
Nevada, Iowa

Carol's Crab Quiche

1 9-inch pie shell, unbaked
1 c. shredded Swiss cheese
⅓ c. minced onion
1 6-oz. package frozen snow crab thawed
4 eggs, beaten
2 c. whipping cream
¾ tsp. salt
¼ tsp. sugar
⅛ tsp. cayenne pepper

Layer pie shell with cheese, onion and crab meat. Combine remaining ingredients. Pour cream mixture over crab mixture. Bake at 425 degrees for 15 minutes. Reduce heat to 350 degrees; bake 30 to 45 minutes longer, or until set. Let stand 15 to 20 minutes before cutting. Yield: 6 servings.

Carol Serur, Pres.
Epsilon Upsilon No. 2314
San Marcos, Texas

Crab Souffle

10 slices white bread, crusts removed
½ lb. butter or margarine, melted
1 lb. crab meat
½ lb. Cheddar cheese, grated
½ lb. mozzarella cheese, grated
6 eggs, beaten
3 c. milk

Dip bread in melted butter. Layer 5 slices of bread in bottom of 9 x 13½-inch baking dish. Spread with half the crab and cheeses. Top with remaining bread. Spread with remaining crab and cheese. Combine eggs and milk; pour over bread mixture. Let stand overnight. Bake at 350 degrees for 1 hour or until knife inserted in center comes out clean. Yield: 10-12 servings.

Gayle Miller, Pres.
Preceptor Alpha XP189
Fairbanks, Alaska

Crab Meat Bel Paese

1 lg. onion, chopped
5 tbsp. butter
15 mushrooms thinly sliced
1 lb. lump crab meat
¾ lb. chicken breasts, cooked, boned, and chopped
2½ cans cream of chicken soup
¾ c. white wine
2 lg. avocados, peeled, seeded, and diced
1¼ c. slivered almonds
1¼ c. grated Gruyere cheese

Saute onion in butter in a large skillet until tender. Add mushrooms. Saute until mushrooms are tender. Stir in crab meat, chicken, chicken soup and white wine. Simmer for 5 minutes. Add avocado. Pour mixture into buttered casserole. Sprinkle top with almonds and cheese. Bake at 375 degrees for 20 minutes. Yield: 12-18 servings.

Barbara Wormser, Rec. Sec., Corr. Sec.
Xi Gamma Beta X3958
Annandale, Virginia

Hot Crab Souffle

8 to 10 slices white bread
6 oz. crab or shrimp
½ to ¾ c. mayonnaise
1 med. onion, diced (opt.)
½ green pepper, diced
1 c. diced celery
4 eggs, beaten
3 c. milk
1 to 2 cans cream of mushroom soup
½ to ¾ c. grated Cheddar cheese
Paprika to taste

Dice ½ of the bread. Place in 3-quart baking dish. Mix crab, mayonnaise, onion, green pepper and celery. Spread over bread. Trim crust from remaining bread slices. Place over crab mixture. Mix eggs and milk. Pour over bread. Refrigerate overnight. Bake at 325 degrees for 15 minutes. Remove from oven. Top with soup and cheese. Sprinkle with paprika. Bake at 325 degrees for 1 hour. Yield: 8-10 servings.

Marti Beall, Pres.
Delta Epsilon No. 8512
McGuire AFB, New Jersey

Crab En Coquille

1 lb. crab meat
½ c. cooked diced carrots
1 can cream of mushroom soup
Dash of pepper
½ c. grated sharp cheese
Paprika to taste

Combine crab meat, carrots, soup and pepper. Place in well-greased baking shells. Sprinkle cheese and paprika over top of mixture. Bake in 350-degree oven for 20 to 25 minutes or until brown. Yield: 4 servings.

Mary Lou Fennimore, Pres.
Xi Beta Phi X4374
Norcross, Georgia

Baked Crab Imperial Casserole

4 tbsp. butter
4 tbsp. flour
2 c. milk
1 tsp. salt
⅛ tsp. pepper
½ tsp. celery salt
Red pepper to taste
1 egg yolk, beaten
2 tbsp. Sherry
1 c. soft bread crumbs
1 lb. crab meat
1 tsp. minced parsley
1 tsp. minced onion
½ c. buttered crumbs
Paprika to taste

Melt butter. Add flour; blend. Add milk and seasonings gradually. Cook over low heat, stirring constantly, until thick. Add egg yolk gradually. Cook 2 minutes longer. Remove from heat. Add Sherry, bread crumbs, crab meat, parsley and onion; mix well. Pour into greased 1½-quart casserole. Top with buttered crumbs. Sprinkle with paprika. Bake in 400-degree oven for 20 to 25 minutes. Yield: 6 servings.

Nancy Whitever
Delta Rho No. 3225
Hayti, Missouri

Today is the first day of the rest of your life. Elizabeth Holthaus

Seafood Enchiladas With Lemon

1 lb. frozen fish fillets, thawed
Lemon slices
1 7½-oz. can crab meat, drained
1 tbsp. grated lemon peel
2 tbsp. fresh lemon juice
2 tbsp. instant minced onion
3 tbsp. butter or margarine
10 tortillas, fresh or frozen Enchilada Sauce

Add fillets with 1 lemon slice to boiling salted water. Cook for 5 minutes or until just done; drain fillets. Combine with crab; flake with fork. Combine lemon peel, lemon juice and onion; set aside. Melt a small amount of butter in skillet. Fry 1 tortilla for a few seconds on each side until limp. Fill with about 1 teaspoon onion mixture and ⅓ cup flaked seafood; roll up. Repeat until all enchiladas are prepared. Pour half the Enchilada Sauce in shallow baking pan. Arrange enchiladas on top; cover with remaining sauce. Top each enchilada with lemon slice. Bake at 350 degrees for about 30 minutes.

Enchilada Sauce:

1 tbsp. butter or margarine
1 6-oz. can tomato paste
½ c. chopped fresh parsley
½ tsp. oregano leaves, crushed
½ tsp. salt
⅛ tsp. pepper
1 clove of garlic, crushed
1 pt. sour cream
1 8-oz. can tomato sauce
1 tbsp. grated lemon peel
2 tbsp. fresh lemon juice

Melt butter in skillet; add tomato paste, parsley, oregano, salt, pepper and garlic. Saute mixture, stirring frequently, about 5 minutes. Remove from heat. Combine with ½ cup water and remaining ingredients; mix thoroughly. Yield: 5-6 servings.

Photograph for this recipe on page 118.

Crawfish Supreme

1½ c. butter
½ c. chopped onion
½ c. chopped celery
¼ c. chopped green pepper
1 tbsp. hot sauce
1 lb. crawfish tails chopped
Juice of 1 lemon
2 pimentos, chopped

Happiness is being a Beta Sigma Phi. Betty Jean Price

1 sm. can mushrooms
½ c. Sherry
2 tsp. salt
½ c. flour
2 c. milk
1 tsp. pepper
½ c. cracker crumbs

Melt 1 cup butter in skillet. Saute onion, celery and green pepper until tender; do not brown. Remove from heat. Add next 6 ingredients and 1 teaspoon salt; stir to blend flavors. Place flour in top of double boiler. Stir in milk gradually. Cook over hot water until smooth, stirring constantly. Season with 1 teaspoon salt and pepper. Remove from heat. Add ½ cup butter; mix well. Add cream sauce to crawfish mixture. Pour into a baking dish. Cover with cracker crumbs. Bake at 325 degrees for 20 to 25 minutes. Serve over rice or egg noodles. Yield: 6-8 servings.

Alice H. Lancon
Theta Eta
Erath, Louisiana

Lobster a la Newburg

6 tbsp. butter
3 c. cooked fresh lobster
½ c. Madeira or Sherry
1½ c. whipping cream
5 egg yolks, beaten
¾ tsp. salt
¼ tsp. cayenne pepper
½ tsp. lemon juice
Patty shells or toast points
Paprika to taste

Melt butter over moderate heat. Add lobster. Cook for 1 minute, stirring constantly. Pour in Madeira and 1 cup cream. Bring to a boil. Reduce heat to simmering; cook for 2 minutes. Beat egg yolks with remaining ½ cup cream in a small bowl. Add ¼ cup simmering lobster sauce; mix well. Pour mixture back into saucepan, stirring constantly. Cook over medium heat until sauce thickens; do not boil. Season with salt, cayenne, pepper and lemon juice. Serve over patty shells or toast points. Sprinkle with paprika. Yield: 6 servings.

Hon. F. Elsie Inman, Senator
Ottawa, Ontario, Canada

Scallops Newburg

½ c. dry white wine or vermouth
½ tsp. seasoned salt
2 lb. scallops
⅓ c. butter
3 tbsp. flour
½ tsp. salt
½ tsp. paprika
Dash of cayenne pepper

1½ c. half and half
3 egg yolks, beaten
2 tbsp. dry Sherry
Toast points or English muffins, toasted

Bring 3 cups water, white wine and seasoned salt to a boil. Add scallops. Return to simmer; cook for 4 to 5 minutes. Drain; set aside. Melt butter; blend in flour and seasonings. Add half and half gradually. Cook until thick, stirring constantly. Stir a small amount of sauce into egg yolks; add to remaining sauce, stirring constantly. Add scallops; heat. Remove from heat. Stir in Sherry slowly. Serve on toast points or toasted English muffins. Yield: 6 servings.

Catherine Bowen, Past Pres.
Xi Alpha Iota X2786
Ocean City, New Jersey

Fruited Shrimp Kabobs

1 c. orange juice
½ c. vinegar
½ c. vegetable oil
½ c. soy sauce
Salt to taste
1 lb. fresh shrimp
2 lemons or limes, cut in wedges
Maraschino cherries to taste
4 lg. bananas, cut into thick slices

Combine orange juice, vinegar, oil, soy sauce and salt; blend well. Add remaining ingredients. Chill for at least 1 hour. Arrange shrimp, lemons and cherries on 6 greased skewers. Reserve bananas and marinade. Broil kabobs 3 to inches from source of heat for 6 minutes per side. Place skewered bananas 3 to 4 inches from source of heat; broil for 6 minutes. Heat remaining marinade; serve as sauce. Yield: 4 servings.

Linda Thorstenson, Pres.
Alpha Theta Zeta No. 8409
Houston, Texas

Shrimp with Wild Rice

1 pkg. long grain wild rice
1 c. chopped green peppers
½ c. chopped onions
2 cans bits and pieces of mushrooms
1 jar pimento, chopped
1 can water chestnuts
2 cans cream of mushroom soup
1½ lb. cooked shrimp

Cook rice according to package directions. Add remaining ingredients; mix well. Place in casserole. Bake for 1 hour at 350 degrees. This freezes nicely. Yield: 6 servings.

Patricia B. Henderson, Rec. Sec.
Alpha Eta No. 2482
Hopewell, Virginia

The only right we have is the right to be useful. Linda Rollins

Shrimp Rockefeller Manicotti

1 egg, slightly beaten
2 c. dry cottage cheese or pot cheese
⅓ c. Parmesan cheese
8 oz. cream cheese
2 tbsp. minced parsley
1 tsp. sugar
1 tsp. sweet basil
2 c. cleaned, deveined shrimp
8 manicotti shells
8 fresh spinach leaves
1 can cream of shrimp soup
1 c. chopped white onions
2 c. buttered bread crumbs
1 c. shredded sharp Cheddar cheese
¼ c. cooking Sherry

Combine egg, cottage cheese, Parmesan cheese, cream cheese, parsley, sugar, sweet basil and shrimp; mix well. Prepare manicotti shells according to package directions. Fill each shell with shrimp mixture. Wrap each shell in spinach leaf. Place side by side in greased 8 x 13-inch casserole. Pour soup over; spread evenly. Layer onions, bread crumbs and cheese over soup. Pour Sherry over all. Bake at 350 degrees for 35 minutes. Serve with tossed greens. One cup shrimp and 1 cup crab meat may be substituted for 2 cups shrimp. Yield: 4 servings.

Pauline Doubrava, Courtesy Chm.
Preceptor Pi XP386
Port Arthur, Texas

Coquille St. Jacques with Shrimp

1 lb. cooked shrimp, deveined
2 dried shallots, finely chopped
¼ c. dry white wine
Salt to taste
Freshly ground white pepper to taste
1 c. hot basic white sauce
Dash of cayenne pepper
2 tbsp. thin cream
¼ c. Gruyere cheese, grated
Parsley

Combine shrimp, shallots, wine, ¼ cup water, salt and pepper in a saucepan; cover with buttered foil. Seal inner ring of pan by pressing around edge. Bring liquid to a boil over high heat. Reduce temperature to medium. Simmer for 2 minutes. Remove shrimp from liquid. Set aside; keep warm on hot platter. Reduce remaining liquid in saucepan by two-thirds over high heat. Reduce temperature to medium. Blend in white sauce. Season with additional salt, pepper and cayenne pepper. Simmer, uncovered for 8 to 10 minutes. Return shrimp to sauce; pour in cream. Transfer mixture to 4 coquille St. Jacques shells or ramekins. Sprinkle each coquille with grated cheese. Bake 6 to 8 inches from source of heat for 6 to 8 minutes. Garnish with parsley; serve immediately. Yield: 4 servings.

N. Erryle George, Pres.
Xi Gamma Xi X3682
Barrie, Ontario, Canada

Savory Shrimp

2 c. sliced fresh mushrooms
¾ c. chopped green onion
7 tbsp. butter
¼ c. flour
10 oz. chicken bouillon
1 19-oz. can pineapple chunks, well drained
2 lb. shrimp, cooked and deveined
¼ c. pale dry Sherry
1 tbsp. lemon juice
1 tsp. salt
1 tsp. (heaping) ground nutmeg
⅛ tsp. white or black pepper

Saute mushrooms and ½ cup green onion in 3 tablespoons butter in medium saucepan. Melt remaining 4 tablespoons butter in same saucepan; stir in flour. Stir in chicken bouillon gradually. Cook until it thickens. Add remaining ingredients except green onion; blend well. Heat through. Serve on bed of white rice. Garnish with remaining green onion. Yield: 5 servings.

Vera P. Wilson
Preceptor Alpha Phi XP1301
Ottawa, Ontario, Canada

Shrimp St. Jacques

3 tbsp. butter
3 green onions, chopped
½ c. fresh mushrooms, sliced
½ clove of garlic, chopped
2 tbsp. all-purpose flour
Salt and pepper to taste
¾ c. milk
2 tbsp. white wine (opt.)
¼ c. grated Swiss cheese
1 4-oz. can med. shrimp

Melt 2 tablespoons butter in medium skillet. Stir in onions, mushrooms and garlic. Cook until lightly brown; remove from pan. Add 1 tablespoon butter to skillet. Blend in flour and seasonings. Stir in milk and wine. Cook, stirring constantly, until thickened. Add cheese; stir until melted. Mix in mushroom mixture and shrimp. Transfer to buttered 1-quart casserole. Bake in 350-degree oven for 10 to 15 minutes or until bubbly. Serve on seafood shells. Yield: 4 servings.

Maxine Prentice, Pres.
Xi Iota X482
Peterborough, Ontario, Canada

If you are dogged tired at night, maybe it's because you growled all day! Martha Bennet

Butterflied Shrimp

1 lb. jumbo shrimp
Bacon, cut into sm. pieces
½ c. flour
4 eggs, lightly beaten
2 tsp. light soy sauce
2 tsp. cooking Sherry
2 green onions, chopped
White pepper to taste
½ c. sugar
½ c. vinegar
¼ c. pineapple juice
¼ tsp. Tabasco
4 tbsp. catsup
Salt to taste
2½ tsp. cornstarch
Peanut oil

Butterfly shrimp. Place bacon strip on each shrimp. Place on paper towel to drain. Mix next 6 ingredients together for batter. Combine next 6 ingredients in saucepan. Bring to a boil. Dissolve cornstarch in ½ cup water. Add cornstarch slowly to sauce stirring constantly until thick and smooth. Keep warm. Dip shrimp and bacon in batter. Place ½ inch peanut oil into skillet. Deep fry shrimp. Serve sauce poured over shrimp. Yield: 6-8 servings.

Mrs. Diane Thrasher, W. and M. Chm.
Xi Upsilon X1173
Thunder Bay, Ontario, Canada

Pantry-shelf Jambalaya

¼ c. butter or margarine
¼ c. chopped onion
½ c. diced green pepper
½ c. chopped celery
1 4½-oz. can deviled ham
2 5-oz. cans shrimp, drained
1 4-oz. can mushrooms
1 1-lb. can tomatoes
1 10½-oz. can bouillon
½ tsp. each sugar and chili powder
½ tsp. hot pepper sauce
1 c. uncooked rice
1 8-oz. can peas, drained

Melt butter in a 12-inch skillet. Add onion, green pepper and celery; cook until onion is tender, but not brown. Add deviled ham and shrimp. Drain mushrooms and tomatoes, reserving liquids. Measure liquids and bouillon; add enough water to measure 2 cups. Add to skillet with seasonings. Add rice; cover. Simmer 15 minutes. Uncover; top with tomatoes, mushrooms and peas. Cover; simmer 15 minutes or until rice is tender. Toss lightly before serving. Yield: 6 servings.

Peggy Stala, Pres.
Preceptor Alpha Kappa XP966
Seminole, Florida

Shrimp Tetrazzini

2 tbsp. margarine
1 med. onion, chopped
8 oz. shrimp
8 oz. mushrooms sliced, drained
¼ c. flour
¼ c. mayonnaise
1 tsp. salt
2 c. milk
¼ c. Sherry (opt.)
1 8-oz. package spaghetti
Parmesan cheese

Melt margarine in skillet. Saute onion until tender. Add shrimp and mushrooms. Cook for 5 minutes, stirring often. Remove from skillet. Mix next 3 ingredients in skillet. Add milk and Sherry slowly. Cook until thickened. Cook spaghetti according to package directions. Combine shrimp, spaghetti and sauce. Pour into 2-quart casserole. Top with cheese. Bake in 350-degree oven for 30 minutes. Yield: 6 servings.

Jackie Hoskins, Pres.
Xi Alpha Xi X2183
Las Cruces, New Mexico

Fruits of the Sea

1 4 lb. sockeye salmon, head and tail removed
1 bay leaf
½ tsp. each thyme, celery salt, onion powder
½ lb. med. shrimp
½ lb. bay scallops
Dry white wine
½ lb. fresh mushrooms, sliced
1 tbsp. butter
1 10-oz. can cream of shrimp soup
1 10-oz. can cream of mushroom soup
½ c. light cream
White pepper to taste
Salt to taste

Poach salmon in water to cover with bay leaf, thyme, celery salt and onion powder. Drain; cool. Remove skin and bones; cut into 6 to 8 pieces. Place in a single layer in 13 x 9-inch baking pan. Cook shrimp and scallops in half white wine and half cold water just to cover. Bring to a boil. Drain, devein and shell shrimp. Place over salmon. Sauté sliced mushrooms in butter. Sprinkle over seafood. Blend soups, cream, white pepper and salt. Pour over seafood. Bake, covered at 350 degrees for 30 minutes or until just hot. Serve with steamed rice and mixed vegetables. Yield: 6 servings.

Linda Faye Falconer, W. and M. Com.
Preceptor Mu XP464
Scarborough, Ontario, Canada

Worry is like a rocking chair—It gives you something to do, but doesn't get you anywhere. Jolene Fransdal

Rhinelander Casserole

1 10-oz. can tomato soup
2 tbsp. (firmly packed) brown sugar
1 tbsp. instant minced onion
1 to 2 tsp. caraway seed
2 cups drained sauerkraut
16 frozen precooked fish sticks
2 slices natural Swiss cheese, cut into 8 strips (opt.)

Grease a shallow, oblong 2-quart baking dish. Combine soup, brown sugar, onion and caraway seed; mix in sauerkraut. Spoon sauerkraut mixture into baking dish. Arrange frozen fish sticks over top. Bake in preheated 400-degree oven for 15 to 20 minutes or until fish flakes easily when tested with a fork. Place 1 cheese strip diagonally over every 2 fish sticks. Bake 5 minutes longer or until cheese melts. Yield: 4 servings.

Photograph for this recipe on page 122.

New Orleans Creole-Style Gumbo

½ lb. ground veal
½ lb. cured ham
1 soupbunch
1 bell pepper, cut up
2 lg. onions, cut up
1 clove of garlic
1 stalk celery, cut up
2 cans tomatoes
2 tbsp. flour (or cornstarch)
1 lb. okra, chopped
1 can chopped shrimp
2 cans fresh crab meat
Salt and pepper to taste
Red pepper and thyme to taste
1 lb. steamed rice
File Gumbo Seasoning

Saute ground veal and cured ham in small amount of fat. Add soupbunch, bell pepper, onions, garlic, celery and tomatoes. Cook until well-done, stirring constantly. Add flour; stir constantly. Cook okra in 2 quarts water. Add to above mixture. Add shrimp and crab meat. Season to taste with salt, pepper and thyme. Serve with steamed rice. Sprinkle File Gumbo on each serving for added flavor.

Barbara J. Sell, Treas.
Xi Epsilon No. 598
Oklahoma City, Oklahoma

Seafood Lasagna

8 lasagna noodles
1 c. chopped onion
2 tbsp. butter or margarine
1 8-oz. package cream cheese, softened
1½ c. cream-style cottage cheese
1 egg, beaten
2 tsp. dried crushed basil
½ tsp. salt
⅛ tsp. pepper
2 cans cream of mushroom soup
⅓ c. milk
⅓ c. dry white wine
1 lb. shelled shrimp, cooked and halved
1 7½-oz. can crab meat, drained, flaked
¼ c. grated Parmesan cheese
½ c. shredded sharp process Amercian or Cheddar cheese

Cook lasagna noodles according to package directions; drain. Arrange half the noddles in bottom of greased 9 x 13-inch baking dish. Cook onion in butter until soft. Blend in cream cheese. Stir in cottage cheese, beaten egg, basil, salt and pepper. Spread half this mixture on top of noodles. Combine soup, milk and wine; add shrimp and crab. Spread half this mixture over cottage cheese layer. Repeat layers. Sprinkle with Parmesan cheese. Bake, uncovered, for 45 minutes in a 350-degree oven. Top with shredded American cheese. Bake 2 or 3 minutes longer. Let stand for 15 minutes before serving.: Yield 12 servings.

Sue Thompson, V.P.
Preceptor Alpha Omega XP1179
Middletown, Ohio

May your happiest yesterdays be your saddest tomorrows. Sandra Bennet

Seafood Quiche

¾ c. crab meat
¾ c. cooked deveined shrimp, chopped
1 c. grated Swiss cheese
⅓ c. sliced cooked celery
⅓ c. chopped green onions
2 9-inch unbaked pie shells
⅔ c. mayonnaise
¼ c. flour
1 c. milk
6 eggs, slightly beaten

Combine crabmeat, shrimp, Swiss cheese, celery and green onions in bowl; mix well. Divide in half. Place in 2 pie shells. Combine mayonnaise, flour, milk and eggs in bowl; mix well. Divide in half. Pour over seafood mixture. Bake for 25 to 30 minutes at 375 degrees. This freezes well. Yield: 12 servings.

Pat Sterling, V.P.
Alpha Theta XP797
Warrensburg, Missouri

Skewered Seafood

1 lb. uncooked shrimp
1 lb. fresh or frozen scallops
⅔ lb. fresh mushroom caps
3 green peppers, cut in 1 in. squares
1 20-oz. can pineapple chunks, well drained
¼ c. melted butter
¼ c. fresh lemon juice
¼ c. soy sauce
1 tbsp. minced parsley
Salt and pepper to taste

Cook shrimp in boiling salted water for 5 minutes. Drain; cool. Wash scallops to remove any shell particles. Place shrimp, scallops, mushrooms, green peppers and pineapple in shallow glass dish. Combine remaining ingredients. Pour over seafood mixture. Cover; let stand for 1 to 2 hours. Drain, reserving marinade. Alternate marinated ingredients on long skewers. Place 4 inches from source of heat over medium-hot coals. Grill for 7 minutes on each side, occasionally brushing with marinade. Yield: 6 servings.

Kathy Webb
Tau Epsilon
Wauconda, Illinois

Stuffed Red Fish

1 15-oz. can tomato sauce
½ lg. white onion, sliced
½ bell pepper, chopped
1 qt. stewed tomatoes
Dash of garlic
Pinch of sugar
Salt and pepper
7 inch long French bread
1 bunch green onions, chopped
2 stalks celery, minced
Butter
¼ tsp. thyme
½ tsp. garlic powder
1 tbsp. Worcestershire sauce
½ lb. crab meat or chopped shrimp
5 lb. red fish, dressed

Saute tomato sauce, onion, bell pepper in oil. Add stewed tomatoes to onion mixture. Add garlic, sugar ½ teaspoon salt and ⅛ teaspoon pepper. Simmer for 1 hour and 30 minutes. Break up bread; soak in water. Press water from bread. Saute green onions and minced celery in butter. Add bread; simmer 30 minutes. Add more butter if necessary. Sprinkle thyme, garlic powder and Worcestershire sauce. Season with salt and pepper. Add crab meat just before stuffing fish. Stuff fish; pack well. Bake at 350 degrees, uncovered, for 45 minutes. Baste fish occasionally with tomato sauce mixture the last 20 minutes of baking time. Remaining basting mixture may be served with the dish. Yield: 4-6 servings.

Patsy M. Lynch, Pres.
Gamma Sigma No. 7277
Tuscaloosa, Alabama

Fish Cyremort

Filet of trout or grouper
Salt and pepper to taste
Red pepper to taste
Celery Salt to taste
Onion Powder to taste
Garlic powder to taste
Paprika
Margarine
1 10-oz. bottle Worcestershire sauce
Fresh lemon juice to taste

Season fish to taste with salt, peppers, celery salt, onion powder and garlic powder; sprinkle with paprika. Arrange fish on aluminum foil tray. Melt margarine enough to cover fish. Add ½ bottle of Worcestershire sauce. Add lemon juice to margarine; mix well. Pour over fish. Place on barbecue grill over hot coals. Cook approximately 15 minutes or until fish flakes when tested with fork. Punch holes in foil evenly to allow margarine to drip on coals. Cover; close vents. Let smoke for 5 minutes.

Debbie W. Mattson
Eta Chi No. 5870
Ft. Pierce, Florida

When life give you lemons, make lemonade! Sandra Bennet

Fish Chowder

¼ lb. salt pork, cubed
3 onions, sliced
4 c. diced raw potatoes
1 tsp. salt
3 lb. fresh skinned haddock with bones
1 13-oz. can evaporated milk
1 tbsp. butter
¼ tsp. pepper

Render salt pork in large saucepan. Remove fried pork. Add onions, potatoes and ½ teaspoon salt to saucepan. Cover with hot water. Cook until potatoes are tender, but not broken. Cut fish into 3 pieces; place in separate saucepan. Add boiling water with remaining ½ teaspoon salt. Simmer until fish flakes. Remove bones, keeping pieces as large as possible. Strain fish stock. Add stock and fish to heated chowder dish. Add milk, butter and pepper. Yield: 5 servings.

Margaret Chase Smith
United States Senate
Washington, D.C.

Fish Court Bouillon

½ c. oil
3 lb. catfish or redfish
Salt and pepper to taste
2 onions, chopped fine
1 clove of garlic, chopped fine
1 sm. lemon, sliced thin
1 15-oz. can tomato sauce
1 sm. bay leaf
Chopped parsley (opt.)
Red pepper to taste

Bring oil to medium heat in iron pot. Add alternate layers of fish sprinkled with salt and pepper then onions and garlic then lemon slices and tomato sauce. Add remaining seasonings. Do not add water; cover. Simmer for 1 hour. Add a small amount of water toward the end of cooking time if needed for more liquid. Serve on rice.

Jenny T. Bono Treas.
Beta Gamma No. 3536
Lake Charles, Louisiana

Salmon Casserole

2 c. hot milk
16 crackers, rolled fine
3 tbsp. butter
1 tsp. salt
1½ c. salmon
4 hard-cooked eggs, sliced

Pour hot milk over cracker crumbs, 2 tablespoons butter and salt; beat until smooth. Butter 1½-quart casserole. Layer salmon and sliced egg in casserole. Pour crackers mixture over top. Dot with remaining butter. Bake in 475-degree oven for 10 to 15 minutes. Yield: 5 servings.

Judy Ann Bespalec, Pres.
Xi Beta Mu X4662
Crete, Nebraska

Jacqueline's Salmon Quiche

1 7¾-oz. can salmon
1 c. shredded Cheddar cheese
2 tbsp. chopped chives
2 eggs, beaten
1 c. milk
¼ tsp. basil
1 unbaked 9-inch pie shell

Drain salmon, reserving liquid. Sprinkle cheese in pie shell. Cover cheese with chives and salmon. Combine eggs, reserved liquid and milk; pour over salmon. Sprinkle with basil. Bake at 375 degrees for 55 minutes. Yield: 3-4 servings.

Mrs. Jacqueline Robinson, City Coun. Rep.
Beta No. 7880
Toronto, Ontario, Canada

Bernice's Salmon Quiche

1 15½-oz. can salmon
3 eggs, beaten
1 c. sour cream
¼ c. mayonnaise
1 tbsp. grated onion
½ c. shredded cheese
Tabasco sauce to taste
1 baked 9-in. pie shell

Drain salmon, reserving liquid. Add enough water to liquid to measure ½ cup. Remove bones and skin; flake salmon. Combine eggs, sour cream, mayonnaise and liquid in a medium bowl. Add salmon, onion, cheese and Tabasco. Spoon filling into crust. Bake at 325 degrees for 45 minutes or until firm in the center. Yield: 6 servings.

Bernice Cogburn, Publ. Chm.
Xi Eta Delta X3830
Jacksonville, Florida

Keatings Easy-Poached Salmon

1 8 to 10-lb. salmon
2 bay leaves
3 to 7 cloves
5 or 6 peppercorns
1 tbsp. celery seed
¼ tsp. thyme

Cooking comes from the heart as well as the hearth. Glora Shaw

¼ tsp. basil
¼ to ½ clove of garlic
1 c. white wine
¼ c. dill pickle juice
4 tbsp. wine vinegar
Juice of 1 lemon
¼ tsp. Tabasco

Place salmon in foil tray with 2 inch sides. Toss dry ingredients together; sprinkle over fish. Combine remaining ingredients; pour over fish. Seal tight. Bake in 350-degree oven for 35 to 45 minutes or until fish flakes evenly. May be refrigerated overnight and served cold in jellied sauce. Yield: 16-20 servings.

Rose Shona Keating
Xi Beta Pi X2700
Auburn, Washington

Seven-Layered Sandwich

1 lg. round Italian-style or Pumpernickel bread
4 hard-cooked eggs, finely chopped
2 tbsp. mayonnaise
3 strips bacon, fried crisp and crumbled
Curry to taste
3 oz. process Cheddar cheese
1 tbsp. caraway seed
Butter

1 8-oz. can smoked salmon
2 tsp. chopped chives

Cut bread into 7 slices crosswise. Combine next 4 ingredients; mix well. Set aside. Blend cheese and caraway seed. Set aside. Spread 1 slice bread with egg mixture. Butter next bread slice. Arrange salmon on butter, sprinkling with chives. Spread cheese filling on next slice bread. Alternate layers. Add top slice bread. Cut into wedges to serve. Yield: 6 servings.

Photograph for this recipe on page 125.

Alma's Casserole

2 cans asparagus tips, drained
2 cans solid white tuna, drained
4 slices brown bread, cubed
2 cans cream of chicken soup
1 pkg. cheese slices

Place all ingredients in 9 x 13-inch pan in order listed. Cover with foil or lid. Bake at 350 degrees for 1 hour. Remove cover; bake for 15 minutes longer. Serve with salad and rolls. Yield: 8 servings.

Janet A. Brooks, Pres.
Xi Gamma Delta X3297
Windsor, Ontario, Canada

It is chance that makes brothers but hearts that make friends. Faye Richardson

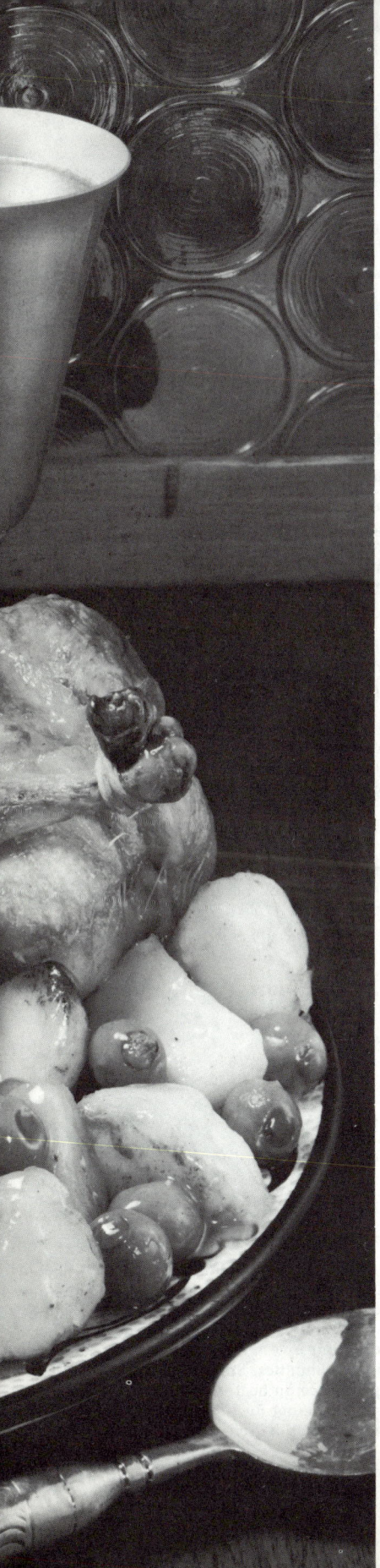

Poultry

For just pennies a serving, poultry offers tender texture, succulent flavor and a personality that pleases the full range of appetites. Its flavor may seem delicate, but in truth it blends just as well with full-flavored herbs and sauces as it does mild, creamy sauces or a quiet lemon-butter baste. Equal to the heartiest cut of beef, poultry as a favorite never fails to satisfy hungry men and children when barbecued on the outdoor grill. With equal ease, poultry caters to the most discriminating tastes as the feature in an elegant menu.

Chicken is the most popular type of poultry, and cooks love it because it can be served over and over again and not get monotonous. It can be fried, served hot or cold for delicious picnic fare—it can be stuffed with a savory dressing and roasted for a memorable Sunday dinner, and it's great for sandwiches, casseroles, salads and dieters—because it's nourishing and low in calories. Turkey is a cornerstone of Thanksgiving, but shouldn't be overlooked as a menu money-saver all through the year. One family-sized turkey costs only pennies per meal when it is used for soups, casseroles, pies and sandwiches—after the Holiday feast.

Moreover, poultry cookery includes more than chicken and turkey. Cornish hens, wild duck, quail and even pheasant are superb entrees for change-of-pace family meals and truly impressive company menus. With all of these you can roast, braise, saute or grill—but be elegant, because each lends itself to a proud display.

Fine feathered friends! You will never tire of preparing meals that feature poultry, especially when you depend on these Beta Sigma Phi recipes to show you the way.

Cornish Game Hens with Rice Stuffing

2 1-lb. Cornish game hens
Salt and pepper
2 tbsp. slivered almonds (opt.)
2 tbsp. finely chopped onion
1/3 c. uncooked long grain rice
3 tbsp. butter or margarine
1 chicken bouillon cube
1 tsp. lemon juice
1 3-oz. can chopped mushrooms, drained
Melted butter

Season game hens inside and out with salt and pepper. Place almonds, onion, and rice in butter in small saucepan. Cook for 5 to 10 minutes, stirring frequently. Add 1 cup water, bouillon cube, lemon juice and 1/2 teaspoon salt. Bring mixture to a boil, stirring to dissolve bouillon cube. Reduce temperature; cover. Cook slowly about 20 to 25 minutes or until liquid is absorbed and rice is fluffy. Stir in mushrooms. Lightly stuff game hens with rice mixture. Place breast-side up on rack in shallow baking dish. Brush with melted butter. Roast, covered, in 400-degree oven for 30 minutes. Uncover. Roast for 1 hour longer or until drumstick can be twisted easily in socket. Brush game hens with additional melted butter during last 15 minutes of roasting time. Yield: 2 servings.

Brenda Bedard, Pres.
Xi Beta X388
Calgary, Alberta, Canada

Cornish Game Hens with Wild Rice Dressing

1 6-oz package long grain and wild rice
1 can water chestnuts, drained and sliced
1 can mushroom pieces, drained
1/2 c. chopped celery
1 tbsp. soy sauce
Salt to taste
2 lg. Cornish game hens
1/2 stick butter, melted
1/2 c. white wine

Cook rice according to package directions. Add next 4 ingredients; mix well. Salt insides of game hens; stuff with dressing. Place game hens in baking dish. Combine butter and wine. Bake at 375 degrees for 2 hours, basting frequently with wine mixture. Yield: 2-4 servings.

Suzanne Bond, Charter Member
Xi Delta Nu X4173
Kansas City, Kansas

Roast Ducklings with Olive Sauce

2 4 to 5-lb. ducklings
8 med. potatoes, pared and quartered
Salt
1/2 c. dry Sauterne
1 quart duckling stock
3 tbsp. olive oil
1 med. onion, chopped
3 tbsp. flour
1 c. small pimento-stuffed olives
1/2 tsp. thyme leaves
1/2 tsp. paprika
1/8 tsp. pepper

Combine duckling necks, giblets and 4 1/2 cups water in saucepan to make stock; cover. Simmer for 1 hour. Prick through skins of breasts and thighs of ducklings with fork for fat to drain during roasting. Place ducklings, breast side down, on rack in large shallow roasting pan. Roast uncovered in 400-degree oven for 30 minutes. Turn ducklings and roast at 350 degrees for 45 minutes longer. Drain off fat. Place potatoes on rack in roasting pan around ducklings; sprinkle lightly with salt. Pour Sauterne and 2 cups stock over ducklings and potatoes. Roast uncovered 30 to 45 minutes or until ducklings and potatoes are tender; baste occasionally. Heat oil in skillet about 20 minutes before potatoes and ducklings are tender. Saute onion in oil until lightly browned; stir in flour. Add remaining 2 cups stock, olives and seasonings. Cook, stirring constantly, until sauce boils for 1 minute. Transfer ducklings and potatoes to platter. Skim fat from drippings in roasting pan. Add drippings to olive sauce. Reheat sauce. Serve over ducklings and potatoes.

Photograph for this recipe on page 126.

Roast Duck a la Monique

1 5 to 6-lb. duck
1 tsp. salt
1 tsp. finely chopped garlic
1 tsp. finely chopped parsley
1 tsp. paprika
3/4 tsp. pepper
1 c. apple jelly
1 c. blackberry jelly, seedless
1 c. orange juice
1 jar Bing cherries, pitted and drained
1/2 c. Cherry Brandy
2 tbsp. Cognac, heated

Rinse duck; pat dry. Place in baking pan. Combine salt, garlic, parsley, paprika and pepper; rub mixture on skin of duck. Roast duck in 350-degree oven for 2 hours and 30 minutes to 3 hours. Turn often to brown evenly; drain off excess fat. Remove from oven; let stand about 15 minutes. Split in half; remove breast from thighs. Place on heatproof platter, keep warm. Heat jellies and orange juice in saucepan until melted. Remove from heat. Stir in cherries and Cherry Brandy.

To have a good friend or neighbor, be one. Betty H. Alderton

Spoon sufficient amount of sauce over duck. Add heated Cognac to remaining sauce. Ignite; baste duck with flaming sauce. Yield: 4 servings.

Barbara Desveaux, Treas.
Xi Alpha Gamma No. 8097
Plymouth, Massachusetts

Roast Duckling with Filbert-Fruit Stuffing

4 c. white bread crumbs
2 c. pared chopped appled
1 c. chopped celery
½ c. chopped onion
2 c. toasted chopped filberts
Juice and grated rind of 1 lemon
Juice and grated rind of 1 orange
2 eggs, lightly beaten
½ c. white wine
2 tsp. salt
½ tsp. each pepper and thyme
¼ tsp. nutmeg
2 4 to 5-lb. ducklings
8 tbsp. melted butter or margarine

Combine all ingredients except duckling and 4 tablespoons melted butter. Toss lightly to mix well. Stuff ducklings; truss. Place on rack in large shallow roasting pan. Brush with remaining melted butter. Roast in 425-degree oven for 30 minutes. Reduce temperature to 375 degrees. Continue roasting 1 hour and 30 minutes or until tender. Yield: 8 servings.

Emerald Sykes, Rec. Sec.
Laureate Zeta No. 211
Brockville, Ontario, Canada

Duckling Glazed with Plum Jam

1 4 to 5-lb. ready-to-cook duckling
2 onions, cut in lg. pieces
1 tsp. garlic salt
2 whole peppercorns
¼ c. shortening
½ c. plum jam or jelly

Stuff duckling with onions, garlic salt and peppercorns; truss. Place duckling on wire rack in shallow pan, breastside up. Cover with shortening. Roast, uncovered in preheated 425-degree oven for 30 minutes. Reduce temperature to 375 degrees. Continue roasting for 40 minutes, basting twice with pan drippings. Turn duckling over. Roast for 20 minutes, basting twice. Turn again, breast side up; roast for 30 minutes, basting twice. Remove from oven. Cut into fourths with shears. Discard onions and peppercorns. Place 4 sections on cookie sheet, breast side up; remove wings. Spread plum jam over skin surface. Return to oven for 10 minutes before serving. Yield: 4 servings.

Alice VanLandingham
Honorary Member
Morgantown, West Virginia

Duck Yummie

2 c. diced green pepper
2 c. diced onions
¼ lb. butter
6 to 8 duck breasts, diced
Salt and pepper to taste
¼ tsp. garlic powder
2 3. oz. cans sliced mushrooms
2 c. sour cream

Saute green pepper and onions in butter for 15 minutes. Add duck cubes. Season with salt, pepper and garlic powder. Cook for 30 minutes. Add mushrooms and sour cream. Continue cooking until duck is tender, about 30 minutes. Serve with mixture of rice and wild rice. Yield: 8 servings.

Marsha Forsberg
Xi Alpha Theta X4608
Watertown, South Dakota

Chicken and Dried Beef

¾ lb. dry chipped beef
6 strips bacon
6 chicken breasts, boned
1 can cream of mushroom soup
½ c. Sherry
½ c. mushrooms

Place dried beef in casserole. Wrap bacon strip around each chicken breast. Arrange over beef. Combine soup with Sherry and mushrooms. Spread soup mixture over chicken. Cover with foil. Bake at 300 degrees for 2 hours, basting frequently. Yield: 6 servings.

Elaine Myers, V. P.
Xi Beta Iota X3705
Chamblee, Georgia

Jessica's Chicken

8 slices bacon, partially cooked
4 whole chicken breasts, halved and deboned
1 jar dried beef, chopped
1 c. sour cream
2 cans cream of mushroom soup

Wrap one bacon slice around each chicken piece. Place side-by-side in 8 × 12-inch baking dish. Sprinkle with dried beef. Mix sour cream and soup; pour over chicken. Bake at 225 degrees for 3 hours and 30 minutes. Garnish with parsley and cooked mushrooms. Serve with rice. Yield: 8 servings.

Jo McMasters, Corr. Sec.
Preceptor Beta Lambda XP919
McAllen, Texas

There's nothing better than a balanced budget, except a surplus. Juacile VanCorbach

Special Baked Chicken

1 3-oz. package dried beef
3 lg. chicken breasts, boned, skinned, halved
6 slices bacon
Rosemary to taste
1 can mushroom soup
1 c. sour cream

Soak dried beef in cold water to cover for 5 minutes; drain. Arrange in 12 × 8-inch casserole. Place chicken breasts over beef. Top each breast with bacon slice. Sprinkle with rosemary. Bake, uncovered, at 350 degrees for 30 minutes. Combine soup and sour cream. Pour over chicken. Bake for 40 to 50 minutes longer. Yield: 6 servings.

Lois Larson, Pres.
Xi Alpha Epsilon X3450
North St. Paul, Minnesota

Chicken in Chablis

2 whole chicken breasts, split, boned and skinned
⅛ tsp. salt
⅛ tsp. nutmeg
2 tbsp. butter
2 tbsp. minced onion
¼ lb. mushrooms, sliced
Chablis
2 tsp. cornstarch

Sprinkle chicken with salt and nutmeg on all sides. Brown in butter. Add minced onion, mushrooms and ⅔ cup Chablis. Bring to a boil; cover. Reduce heat; simmer 15 minutes. Place chicken on warm serving platter. Bring pan juices to a boil; cook, stirring until liquid is slightly reduced. Stir in cornstarch and 1 teaspoon Chablis; cook until thickened. Spoon sauce over chicken. Serve with rice. Yield: 4 servings.

V. Gail Lokey, Pres.
Xi Alpha Nu X2959
Old Hickory, Tennessee

Joy's Chicken Kiev

1 c. butter or margarine, softened
2 tbsp. chopped parsley
1½ tsp. dried tarragon
1 clove of garlic, crushed
6 chicken breasts
¾ c. flour
3 eggs, beaten
1½ c. dry bread crumbs

Combine butter, parsley, tarragon and garlic; mix well. Shape into a butter stick. Freeze. Bone and halve chicken breasts. Pound chicken pieces between 2 pieces waxed paper until flat. Cut frozen butter into 6 pieces. Place 1 piece on each chicken breast; roll up, tucking ends inside to encase butter. Secure with a toothpick. Roll chicken rolls in flour to coat well. Dip into beaten eggs then in bread crumbs. Chill for at least 1 hour. Fry in 3-inch deep fat at 400 degrees until brown on all sides. Drain; keep warm until serving time. Yield: 6 servings.

Joy Whiteman, V. P.
Xi Tau X1663
Boise, Idaho

Joanie's Chicken Kiev

2 lb. boneless chicken breasts, halved
4 tbsp. softened butter
1 tbsp. parsley
⅛ tsp. dried tarragon
Few drops of lemon juice
Dash of garlic powder
1 egg, beaten
¾ c. flour
¾ c. soft bread crumbs

Place each chicken breast between 2 sheets waxed paper; pound each to ⅛ to ¼ inch thick. Combine butter, parsley, tarragon, lemon juice, and garlic powder. Form into four 4-inch long sticks. Chill or freeze until hard. Chill chicken covered. Place 1 stick on each chicken piece. Roll up, folding in edges to encase butter stick. Press seam to seal. Mix egg and 1 tablespoon water in small bowl. Roll each chicken nugget in flour to coat well. Dip into egg then crumbs. Chill about 1 hour. Heat 2 to 3 inches cooking oil in skillet to 375 degrees. Fry nuggets for 5 to 6 minutes or until golden. Remove nuggets; drain well. Serve immediately with hot rice. Yield: 4 servings.

Joanie Clark
Kappa Zeta
Pottsville, Pennsylvania

Chicken and Macaroni Stew

1 chicken, cut up
¼ c. flour
2 tsp. paprika
Salt to taste
½ tsp. pepper
¼ c. oil
1 qt. tomatoes, quartered
1 tbsp. onion flakes
1 tbsp. parsley flakes
1 tbsp. garlic salt
¼ tsp. hot pepper sauce
2 c. macaroni, cooked
1 pkg. frozen peas

Combine flour, paprika, salt and pepper. Coat chicken with flour mixture. Heat oil in electric skillet. Brown

You can hardly make a friend in a year, but you can lose one in an hour. Elizabeth B. Thompson

chicken. Add tomatoes, onion, parsley, garlic salt, hot pepper sauce and 1 cup water. Simmer for 45 minutes. Add macaroni. Add peas. Simmer until peas are tender. Yield: 6 servings.

Polly Davenport, Rec. Sec.
Xi Kappa X770
Corvallis, Oregon

Chicken Marchand de Vin

1 c. flour
Salt
1 tsp. Accent
½ tsp. pepper
1 tsp. paprika
3 chicken breasts, halved
3 c. Mazola oil
1 8-oz. package flat egg noodles

Combine flour, 1 teaspoon salt, Accent, pepper and paprika. Roll chicken breasts in seasoned flour to coat well. Heat oil in skillet over medium heat until hot. Add chicken, skin side down. Fry, covered, for 6 to 8 minutes on each side, turning only once. Cook noodles in 2½-quarts boiling water with 1 tablespoon salt until tender; drain. Place in lightly greased 9 × 13 inch baking dish. Place fried chicken over noodles.

Sauce:

¼ c. Mazola oil
½ c. Mazola margarine
1 4-oz. can mushrooms
1 c. minced ham
⅔ c. chopped green onions
1 c. chopped white onions
4 buds garlic, minced
4 tbsp. flour
¼ tsp. each black and red pepper
1 10½-oz. can beef bouillon
1 c. red cooking wine

Place oil and margarine in 3-quart saucepan. Heat over low heat until margarine melts. Add mushrooms, ham, green onions, white onions and garlic. Cook over low heat until onions are clear. Add flour, black and red pepper. Cook 5 minutes longer, stirring to prevent sticking. Pour in beef bouillon and red wine; stir. Simmer, covered, about 15 minutes, stirring occasionally. Spoon sauce mixture over chicken and noodles. Bake at 350 degrees for 20 minutes or until thoroughly heated. Garnish with parsley and cherry tomatoes. Yield: 6 servings.

Janith C. Frederick, Past Pres.
Xi Beta Pi X4678
Natchitoches, Louisiana

Chicken Saltimbocca

3 lg. chicken breasts, skinned, boned and halved
6 thin slices boiled ham
3 slices mozzarella cheese, halved
1 med. tomato, seeded and chopped
Dash of sage (opt.)
⅓ c. fine dry bread crumbs
2 tbsp. grated Parmesan cheese
2 tbsp. snipped parsley
4 tbsp. melted butter or margarine

Place chicken, boned side up, between 2 pieces waxed paper; pound lightly to 5 × 5 inches. Place one ham slice and ½ slice cheese on each cutlet, cutting to fit. Top each with chopped tomato and dash of sage. Tuck in sides; roll up like jelly roll, pressing to seal well. Combine bread crumbs, Parmesan cheese and parsley. Dip chicken rolls in melted butter; roll in crumb mixture. Place in shallow baking pan. Bake in 350-degree oven for 45 minutes to 1 hour. Yield: 6 servings.

Zola Larke, Rec. Sec.
Xi Iota Gamma X4572
Coral Springs, Florida

Chicken and Shrimp Skillet

1 lb. chicken breasts, boned
2 cloves of garlic, halved
2 tbsp. salad oil
1 lg. onion, sliced thin
1 green pepper, cut in thin strips
1 5-oz. can bamboo shoots, drained
¾ c. chicken broth
1 tsp. salt
¼ c. molasses
¼ c. soy sauce
¼ c. vinegar
3 tbsp. cornstarch
1 lb. shrimp, cooked and peeled
1 can pineapple tidbits, drained

Cut chicken breasts into thin strips. Saute chicken and garlic in salad oil in large skillet over medium heat for 5 minutes. Remove garlic. Add onion, green pepper, bamboo shoots, chicken broth and salt to chicken. Simmer, covered, 10 minutes. Combine molasses, soy sauce, vinegar and cornstarch; mix thoroughly. Stir molasses mixture into chicken mixture. Cook, stirring constantly, until thickened. Add shrimp and pineapple. Heat to serving temperature, stirring occasionally. Serve with Chinese noodles or rice. Yield: 6 servings.

Margaret J. Biados, Pres.
Preceptor Theta Mu XP1811
Santa Rosa, California

If you are taking a beating, cheer up—God is just stirring up the "batter" to bring you a blessing.   Joy Urschel.

Chicken Parisienne

4 lg. chicken breasts
1 can cream of mushroom soup
1 4-oz. can mushroom stems and p eces, drained
1 c. sour cream
½ c. Sherry
Paprika to taste

Arrange chicken breasts, skin side up, in 12 × 8-inch baking dish. Combine soup, mushrooms, sour cream and Sherry in 1-quart bowl; mix well. Pour over chicken breasts. Sprinkle generously with paprika. Bake, covered at 325 degrees for 45 minutes or until chicken is fork-tender. Yield: 4 servings.

Maureen M. Kinley, Pres.
Gamma Tau
El Dorado, Arkansas

Chicken Crepes with Cheese Sauce

7 c. chicken broth
6 eggs
6 tbsp. chicken fat
Salt
Dash of nutmeg
Cayenne pepper to taste
2 c. flour
1 c. butter or margarine
4 onions, chopped
½ lb. mushrooms, sliced
1 10-oz. package frozen chopped spinach, drained
4 c. cooked, chopped chicken
½ c. sour cream
1¼ c. Sherry
2 c. milk
1 c. Parmesan cheese
1 c. grated Swiss cheese

Pour 3 cups chicken broth, eggs, chicken fat, 1½ teaspoons salt, nutmeg, and dash of cayenne pepper in blender container. Blend on Mix until smooth. Add 1½ cups flour gradually until smooth. Refrigerate, covered, for at least 2 hours. Melt ½ cup butter in large skillet. Saute onions until soft and golden. Add mushrooms. Cook, stirring occasionally, for 4 minutes. Stir in spinach, chicken, sour cream, ¼ cup Sherry, 1 teaspoon salt and a dash of cayenne pepper. Remove from heat. Chill until needed. Melt ½ cup butter. Blend in ½ cup flour until smooth. Stir in 4 cups chicken broth and milk gradually. Cook over low heat, stirring constantly, until smooth. Add cheeses and salt to taste. Stir over low heat until cheese is melted. Remove from heat. Stir in 1 cup Sherry. Pour ¼ cup crepe batter onto lightly greased hot griddle. Brown on one side only, removing from griddle when surface is bubbly and dry. Place, brown side down, on towel to cool. Repeat until all batter is used. Divide chilled filling into same number of portions as crepe. Place each portion on uncooked side of crepes. Roll as for jelly roll. Place in baking dish, seamside down. Spoon

1 tablespoon sauce over each crepe. Bake at 375 degrees for 30 minutes or until lightly browned. Heat remaining sauce. Spoon 1 tablespoon sauce over each crepe as served. Garnish with parsley.

Marguerite Dimerling
International Honorary Member
Beaumont, Texas

Chicken Crepes with Almonds

3 eggs, beaten
2½ c. milk
½ c. pancake mix
Butter
1 c. sliced fresh mushrooms
¼ c. all-purpose flour
¼ tsp. pepper
2 chicken bouillon cubes, crumbled
2 c. cooked cubed chicken
Toasted sliced almonds

Combine eggs and ½ cup milk. Add pancake mix; beat with rotary beater until smooth. Place small amount of butter in 8-inch skillet; heat until butter bubbles. Pour in enough batter to coat bottom of skillet with a thin layer. Bake until browned on underside. Turn and bake on other side. Stack on a plate; cover with plastic wrap. Set aside. Saute mushrooms in 2 tablespoons butter in small skillet. Melt 4 tablespoons butter in medium saucepan. Stir in flour and pepper. Cook for 1 minute over low heat, stirring frequently. Add 2 cups milk and chicken bouillon cubes gradually; blend well. Bring to a boil, stirring constantly until mixture is thickened. Stir in mushrooms and chicken; heat thoroughly. Separate crepes carefully. Lay, underside up, on waxed paper. Spread about ⅓ cup filling across center of each crepe. Fold 2 sides to center overlapping slightly. Place on 15 × 10-inch jelly roll pan. Sprinkle with toasted almonds. Bake in preheated 325-degree oven for 8 to 10 minutes or until piping hot. Yield: 4 servings.

Photograph for this recipe on page 133.

Chicken-Tortillas Casserole

4 to 6 chicken breasts
1 med. onion, chopped
1 c. milk
1 can cream of celery soup
1 can chili without beans
1 7-oz. can diced green chilies
12 corn tortillas
1 lb. Jack or Cheddar cheese, grated

Place chicken breasts in baking dish; cover with foil. Bake at 350 degrees for 1 hour. Combine onion, milk, soup, chili and diced chilies; mix well. Tear tortilla into 1-inch squares. Grease 9 × 13-inch baking pan with broth from chicken. Cut chicken into tiny pieces.

You can live on a little if you have a lot to live for, but you can't live on a lot if you have little to live for.   Suzanne Patterson

Reserve enough cheese to top casserole. Alternate layers of tortillas, chicken, sauce and cheese in baking pan. Top with reserved cheese. Bake at 375 degrees for 30 minutes. Yield: 10-12 servings.

Janice Canisso, V. P.
Delta Nu
Livingston, California

Chicken Wings

2 pkg. chicken wings, wing tips removed
Cornstarch
1 egg, beaten
½ c. chicken broth
¼ c. catsup
¾ c. sugar
⅜ c. vinegar
1 tbsp. soy sauce
1 tsp. Accent

Coat chicken with cornstarch. Dip into beaten egg. Brown chicken in oil. Place in 9×13-inch casserole. Combine next 6 ingredients. Pour sauce over casserole. Bake at 325 degrees for 1 hour. Yield: 4 servings.

Betty G. Hopkins, Pres.
Theta Preceptor XP652
Buhl, Idaho

Coq Au Vin

1 tbsp. butter
1 slice lean bacon, chopped into 20 pieces
20 sm. onions, peeled
20 sm. fresh or canned mushrooms, washed and drained
3 pinches of salt
1 sprig thyme
1 bay leaf
1 tbsp. flour
1 chicken, quartered
2 c. red wine

Melt butter in deep saucepan. Add bacon, onions, garlic, mushrooms, salt, thyme and bay leaf. Cook covered for 5 minutes. Sprinkle flour over mixture. Add chicken; blend with wooden spoon. Cook, covered for 10 minutes longer. Add wine; reduce temperature. Simmer for 40 minutes longer, stirring occasionally. Yield: 4 servings.

Leota J. Banks, Parliamentarian
Xi Alpha X104
Albuquerque, New Mexico

Life without friends is like a desert without an oasis. Delores Reeves

Cordon Bleu au Poulet

4 chicken breasts, deboned
4 slices Swiss or Gruyere cheese
4 slices ham
½ c. flour
½ tsp. salt
½ tsp. onion salt
2 eggs, beaten
1 c. fine bread crumbs
2 tbsp. butter

Slit chicken to form deep pocket. Place 1 slice cheese and ham inside each pocket. Seal edges around filling. Mix flour, salt and onion salt. Dip chicken carefully in flour mixture. Dip in beaten eggs; coat with bread crumbs. Saute in butter in large, heavy skillet on medium high heat for 10 to 15 minutes on each side, adding more butter if necessary. Yield: 4 servings.

Trudy Kennedy, Pres.
Sarnia City Coun.
Sarnia, Ontario, Canada

Creamed Chicken a La King

4 tbsp. butter or margarine
2 tbsp. flour
1½ c. hot milk
1 c. sliced mushrooms
¼ c. green pepper, minced
1½ c. cooked diced chicken breasts
2 egg yolks, beaten
2 tbsp. lemon juice
¼ tsp. mustard
1 tsp. salt
1 tsp. paprika

Melt butter in double boiler. Blend in flour. Add hot milk slowly. Cook, stirring constantly, until thickened. Saute mushrooms; add to sauce. Add green pepper and chicken. Combine remaining ingredients. Add to chicken mixture. Heat to boiling point; reduce heat. Simmer 10 minutes. Serve over rice or toast points. Yield: 4 servings.

Phyllis Greeley, Pres.
Xi Beta Delta X2154
Staten Island, New York

Crab-Stuffed Breasts of Chicken

4 12-oz. chicken breasts, halved
½ c. thinly sliced green onions
¼ lb. mushrooms, thinly sliced
¼ c. butter or margarine
3 tbsp. all-purpose flour
½ c. chicken broth
½ c. milk
½ c. dry white wine
Salt and pepper to taste
1 6-oz. can crab meat, drained
1⅓ c. fine bread crumbs
1⅓ c. finely chopped parsley
1 c. shredded Swiss cheese

Pound chicken breasts between 2 pieces plastic wrap until ¼ inch thick. Saute onions and mushrooms in butter until tender. Stir in flour; blend in broth, milk and wine. Cook, stirring constantly, until sauce is thickened. Season with salt and pepper. Mix ¼ cup mushroom-onion sauce, crab, bread crumbs and parsley. Spoon mixture equally onto chicken breasts. Roll breasts around filling, tucking in edges to encase filling. Place rolled chicken breasts, seam side down, in greased 8 × 12-inch baking dish. Pour remaining sauce over all. Sprinkle with cheese. Bake, covered, in 400-degree oven for 40 minutes or until chicken is tender. Yield: 8 servings.

Joan R. McDonald, Treas.
Xi Beta Rho X2701
Bellevue, Washington

Diane's Wiener Schnitzel

3 whole chicken breasts
2 tbsp. flour
1½ tsp. salt
¼ tsp. pepper
2 eggs, beaten
2 c. cracker meal
½ c. butter
½ c. salad oil
½ c. dry white wine
¼ c. dry Vermouth
2 tbsp. chopped parsley
2 tbsp. chopped chives

Bone and halve chicken breasts. Pound between 2 pieces waxed paper until thin. Blend flour, salt and pepper. Add eggs; beat until smooth. Dip chicken breasts into egg mixture, coating evenly. Roll in cracker meal to coat well. Chill in single layer on cookie sheet for 15 minutes. Melt butter and oil in large skillet until hot. Saute chicken breasts until golden brown, about 3 to 4 minutes per side. Drain; keep warm. Drain all but 2 tablespoons pan drippings. Add wine and Vermouth. Heat, stirring to loosen particles. Add parsley and chives. Simmer for 1 minute. Pour over warm chicken breasts. Serve immediately. Yield: 4 servings.

Diane Elizabeth Linden
Delta Nu
Waupaca, Wisconsin

It takes both the rain and the sunshine to make a rainbow. Louise Munday

Easy Chicken Enchiladas

1 3-lb. chicken, cooked and boned
1 can cream of mushroom soup
1 can cream of chicken soup
1 4-oz. can chopped green chilies
2 tbsp. dry onion
1 13-oz. can evaporated milk
1 10-oz. package Doritos
5 oz. Cheddar cheese, grated

Combine first 6 ingredients. Line 9 × 13-inch casserole with Doritos. Pour chicken mixture over casserole. Top with cheese. Bake at 325 degrees for 30 minutes. Yield: 6 servings.

Mary Clark
Delta Theta No. 9953
Perry, Oklahoma

Egyptian Lemon Chicken

2 sm. chickens, cut into serving pieces
4 tbsp. olive oil
1 clove of garlic, minced
Grated rind and juice of 1 lemon
½ tsp. thyme
Salt and freshly ground pepper to taste
Butter
2 tbsp. finely chopped parsley

Place chicken in shallow bowl. Sprinkle with olive oil garlic, lemon rind, lemon juice, thyme, salt and ground pepper. Marinate for at least 2 hours, turning occasionally. Place chicken and marinade in buttered baking dish. Bake at 350 degrees for 1 hour or until tender, basting frequently. Remove from oven. Sprinkle with parsley. Serve immediately. Yield: 6 servings.

Jerri Balsam
Beta
Miles City, Montana

Apricot Chicken

½ 8-oz. bottle of French or Russian dressing
¾ package onion soup mix
1 sm. jar apricot jam
8 chicken pieces
Salt and pepper to taste

Combine first 3 ingredients. Place chicken pieces in 9 × 13-inch casserole. Season with salt and pepper. Pour soup mixture over casserole. Bake at 325 degrees for 2 hours, basting once or twice. Yield: 4 servings.

Diane Small, Pres.
Beta Rho No. 4829
Hobbs, New Mexico

Chicken Breasts with Grape Sauce

4 chicken breasts, boned and halved
Salt and pepper to taste
7 tbsp. butter
8 thin slices of ham
1½ c. wild rice, cooked
3 tbsp. flour
½ tsp. monosodium glutamate
1½ c. chicken stock
2 tbsp. lemon juice
2 tbsp. sugar
1 c. seedless grapes

Line broiler pan with foil. Sprinkle chicken with salt and pepper. Place chicken on foil, skin side down. Brush chicken with a portion of 4 tablespoons melted butter. Broil 3 to 4 inches from heat source for 15 minutes. Turn chicken; brush with remaining portion melted butter. Broil for 10 minutes or until tender. Place wild rice in casserole. Place each breast over ham slice; place over rice. Melt 3 tablespoons butter in saucepan. Blend in flour, monosodium glutamate and ½ teaspoon salt. Add chicken stock slowly; cook, stirring constantly, until thickened. Add lemon juice and sugar. Add grapes. Pour sauce over casserole. Serve warm. Yield: 8 servings.

Ruth Neumann, Pres.
Preceptor Gamma Epsilon XP1865
DeKalb, Illinois

Chicken and Peaches Francisco

1 29-oz. can cling peach halves
3 1½-lb. broiler fryer chickens, halved
4 tbsp. flour
1 tsp. poultry seasoning
½ tsp. salt
¼ c. butter or margarine
1 pint sour cream
1 tbsp. peanut butter
1 4-oz. can sliced mushrooms

Drain peaches, reserving syrup. Combine flour, poultry seasoning and salt. Coat chicken with seasoned flour, reserving leftover flour. Melt butter in flat baking pan. Place chicken in pan, skin side down. Bake in 400-degree oven about 20 minutes. Turn chicken, skin-side up. Place peach halves around chicken; continue roasting about 20 minutes, basting 2 or 3 times with peach syrup. Blend sour cream and peanut butter. Stir in mushroom slices and liquid with ¼ cup peach syrup. Remove chicken and peaches to a warm platter. Stir 1 tablespoon remaining seasoned flour into baking pan drippings. Add sour cream mixture. Cook over low heat, stirring constantly, until sauce comes to a boil. Spoon sauce over chicken. Serve remaining sauce in gravy boat or bowl. Yield: 6 servings.

Photograph for this recipe on page 138.

It's better to wear out than to rust out. Margie Calhoun

Mandarin Chicken

1 3-lb. chicken, cut up
½ tsp. salt
1½ tsp. Accent
½ tsp. garlic salt
3 eggs, beaten
3 c. cornstarch
¾ c. sugar
½ c. vinegar
¼ c. chicken stock or boullion
4 tbsp. catsup
1 tsp. soy sauce
½ tsp. ginger
1 med. can crushed pineapple with juice

Sprinkle chicken with salt, 1 teaspoon Accent and garlic salt. Let stand for 1 hour. Dip chicken in beaten egg. Roll in cornstarch. Saute until brown. Combine remaining ingredients for sauce. Place chicken in casserole; pour sauce over chicken. Bake at 350 degrees for 1 hour. Serve with rice. Yield: 4 servings.

Karen Harris, Ext. Off.
Xi Psi X2129
Emmett, Idaho

Oriental Chicken and Peaches

1 med. can sliced peaches
1 can button mushrooms
Chicken pieces for 6
Seasoned flour
¼ c. oil
1 chopped green pepper
2 tbsp. chopped onions
2 tbsp. soy sauce
2 tbsp. vinegar
1 tbsp. cornstarch
⅓ c. blanched slivered almonds

Drain peaches and mushrooms, reserving liquid. Coat chicken with flour; brown in large skillet with oil. Remove chicken. Set aside. Add mushrooms and green pepper to pan drippings; saute 1 minute. Return chicken to pan. Combine onion, soy sauce, vinegar and ½ c. reserved liquid. Pour over chicken; cover. Simmer for 40 minutes or until tender. Add sliced peaches; cook 5 minutes. Remove chicken from pan. Stir cornstarch and 1 tablespoon water into drippings to make gravy. Place chicken on serving tray. Cover with peach mixture. Sprinkle with almonds.

Carol Ann Robinson, Pres.
Xi Psi X2516
North Vancouver, British Columbia, Canada

Listening to what someone has to say is the nicest compliment you can pay. Judith Roentsch

One-Pot Chicken

1 chicken, cut in pieces
2 chicken bouillon cubes
1 med. onion, cubed
½ c. sliced celery
½ c. sliced carrots
1 tbsp. butter
4 med. potatoes, cubed
Salt and pepper to taste

Place chicken on a foil-covered cookie sheet. Bake at 450 degrees for 20 to 30 minutes until golden brown. Combine bouillon cubes and 2 cups water for broth. Saute onion, celery and carrots in butter until tender. Place chicken, cooked vegetables and potatoes in 5-quart casserole; cover with chicken broth. Add salt and pepper to taste. Bake, covered, at 325 degrees for 1 hour and 15 minutes or until potatoes are cooked. Yield: 4 servings.

Joyce Wenner, Treas.
Xi Kappa X848
Nanaimo, British Columbia, Canada

Best-Ever Chicken and Rice

½ pkg. long grain and wild rice, uncooked
8 chicken breasts, skinned and halved
1 can golden mushroom soup
1 env. dry onion soup mix
1 c. chopped celery (opt.)

Cover greased 9 × 13-inch casserole with rice. Place chicken over rice. Combine soups and 1 soup can water in saucepan. Cook, stirring constantly until smooth. Pour soup mixture over chicken. Add celery. Bake, covered, at 350 degrees for 1 hour and 30 minutes. Yield: 6-8 servings.

Sharon Woodworth, Pres.
Xi Eta Nu X3420
Jacksonville, Illinois

Cheryl's Chicken and Rice Casserole

2 c. rice
1 can cream of chicken soup
1 can cream of mushroom soup
1 pkg. onion soup mix
1 fryer, cut up

Combine first 4 ingredients with 2 cups water. Pour into 9 × 13-inch casserole. Place chicken pieces over soup mixture. Bake at 350 degrees for 40 minutes. Cover; bake 20 minutes longer. Yield: 4 servings.

Cheryl Ann Hug, Treas.
Xi Delta Psi X2883
Sarasota, Florida

New England Poultry Stuffing

3 sm. onions, diced
2 or 3 med. stalks celery, diced
3 tbsp. salad oil
1 lb. fresh country sausage
1 lb. hamburger
¼ c. butter or margarine
1 sm. can mushrooms and liquid
1 sm. loaf bread, diced
4 c. (about) milk
Salt and pepper to taste
½ tsp. poultry seasoning

Combine onions and celery with salad oil in deep skillet. Saute until brown. Add sausage and hamburger, a small amount at a time; brown. Add butter and mushrooms with liquid. Remove from heat. Add bread. Add enough milk to completely moisten mixture, stirring constantly. Add salt, pepper and poultry seasoning. Return to heat; cook, stirring constantly, for 10 to 15 minutes. Correct seasoning to taste. This is enough stuffing for a 10 to 12-pound bird.

Rosalind Seeley, Rec. Sec., Prog. Chm.
Xi Beta Beta X4688
Boise, Idaho

Gourmet Chicken and Rice

2 cans cream of mushroom soup
2 3½-oz. cans sliced mushrooms
12-oz. carton sour cream
1 small onion, minced
1½ c. chopped celery
6 oz. butter, melted
Salt and pepper to taste
2¼ c. cooked wild rice
Juice of ½ lemon
1½ tsp. Worcestershire sauce
2 c. canned milk
8 to 10 chicken or pheasant breasts

Combine soup, mushrooms with liquid, sour cream, onion, celery, 3 ounces butter, salt and pepper. Stir in rice. Place in casserole. Combine 3 ounces butter, lemon juice, Worcestershire sauce, milk, salt and pepper. Coat chicken with sauce. Place chicken pieces over rice. Pour remaining sauce over casserole. Bake, uncovered, at 350 degrees for 1 hour and 15 minutes or until chicken is tender. Yield: 8-10 servings.

Barbara Courter
Alpha Rho No. 1031
Maryville, Missouri

It is better to keep your words nice and sweet because you never know when you will have to eat them. Ruth M. Gillan

Chicken-Rice Squares

8 slices bread, cubed
3 c. chicken broth
3 to 4 c. cooked cubed chicken
½ c. rice, cooked, unsalted
½ c. chopped pimento
2 tbsp. parsley
2 tsp. salt
4 eggs, beaten
1 can cream of chicken, mushroom or celery soup
¼ c. milk

Saturate bread in broth. Add chicken, rice, pimento, parsley and salt. Stir in eggs. Pour mixture into greased 8½ × 12-inch casserole. Bake at 325 degrees for 1 hour or until firm. Combine soup with milk; heat through. Serve casserole with sauce spooned over. Yield: 8 servings.

Florence D. Williams
Xi Chi X2714
Alexandria, Louisiana

Simple-y Delicious Chicken

1 stick margarine
½ c. Sherry
1 3-lb. fryer, cut up
Salt and pepper to taste
3 tsp. oregano
2 c. sour cream

Melt margarine in 10-inch skillet over medium heat. Brown chicken in margarine. Sprinkle with salt, pepper and oregano. Turn; sprinkle with salt, pepper and oregano. Brown. Reduce heat. Combine Sherry and ½ cup water. Pour over chicken; cover. Simmer 35 minutes or until tender. Remove chicken from skillet. Combine drippings with sour cream. Heat; do not boil. Return chicken to skillet; heat through. Serve with rice. Yield: 4-6 servings.

Margaret Cash, Soc. Chm.
Preceptor Eta Psi XP1706
San Diego, California

Thelma's Chicken Casserole

1 pkg. frozen French-style green beans
1 pkg. Pepperidge Farm herb stuffing mix
3 tbsp. blanched slivered almonds
2 c. cooked chopped chicken or turkey
1 can mushroom soup
½ c. milk
2 tbsp. butter or margarine
Grated cheese to taste (opt.)

Partially cook green beans according to package directions; drain. Sprinkle ⅔ cup stuffing mix in greased 8 × 8-inch baking dish. Layer green beans, almonds and chicken in baking dish. Blend soup and milk; pour over chicken. Moisten remaining 1⅓ cups stuffing mix and butter with ¼ cup hot water. Spread over top of casserole. Sprinkle with cheese if desired. Bake at 350 degrees for 30 minutes or until bubbly and brown. Yield: 8 servings.

Thelma Dodd, Ext. Off.
Xi Theta Iota Exemplar X3752
Dongola, Illinois

Yummy Chicken Casserole

6 cooked chopped chicken breasts
2 c. sour cream
2 c. mushroom soup
½ c. Sherry (opt.)
1 tsp. Worcestershire sauce
1 6-oz. can sliced mushrooms, drained
1 pkg. Pepperidge Farm stuffing mix

Place chicken in bottom of buttered casserole. Mix sour cream, soup, Sherry, Worcestershire sauce and mushrooms. Pour over chicken. Prepare stuffing mix according to package directions; cool. Spread over casserole. Bake, uncovered, at 350 degrees for 30 minutes. Yield: 6-8 servings.

Emily F. Miller, Prog. Com. Chm.
Alpha Preceptor Laureate PL108
West Chester, Pennsylvania

Broccoli and Chicken

2 c. cooked, boned chicken
1 8-oz. package frozen broccoli, partially cooked
1 10½-oz. can cream of celery soup
2 oz. sliced mushrooms
1 can onion rings or 1 c. Chinese noodles
½ c. evaporated milk

Place chicken in greased 2-quart casserole. Cover with broccoli. Combine soup, mushrooms and milk; pour over casserole. Bake at 350 degrees for 30 minutes. Cover with onion rings or Chinese noodles; bake for 5 minutes. Yield: 8 servings.

Betty Behrend, Pres.
Xi Alpha Eta Exemplar X1095
Atchison, Kansas

Berniece's Chicken Divan

2 10-oz. packages frozen broccoli spears
3 whole chicken breasts, halved
4 tbsp. margarine
4 tbsp. flour
2 c. milk or broth
1 6-oz. can sliced mushrooms
½ lb. crumbled American cheese

Happiness is found along the way, not at the end of the road. Colleen B. Nelson

Cook broccoli according to package directions; drain. Line 2-quart casserole with broccoli. Boil chicken until tender. Remove bones. Place chicken over broccoli. Melt margarine. Stir in flour. Add milk slowly; cook until thickened. Add mushrooms and cheese. Pour over casserole. Bake at 250 degrees for 1 hour. Yield: 4 servings.

Berniece Kadolph, Sec.
Xi Zeta Delta X4280
Bethany, Missouri

Cleo's Chicken Divan

2 10-oz. packages frozen broccoli
2 c. cooked, sliced chicken
2 cans cream of chicken soup
1 c. mayonnaise or salad dressing
1 tsp. lemon juice
½ c. shredded cheese
½ c. soft bread crumbs
1 tbsp. butter

Cook broccoli according to package directions; drain. Arrange broccoli in greased 11×7-inch casserole. Place chicken over broccoli. Combine soup, mayonnaise and lemon juice; pour over chicken. Sprinkle with cheese. Top with bread crumbs; dot with butter. Bake at 350 degrees for 25 to 30 minutes. Yield: 6-8 servings.

Cleo Overholser, Soc. Chm.
Theta Epsilon No. 10831
Roswell, Georgia

Betty's Chicken Divan

2 c. cookied rice
2 10-oz. packages frozen broccoli, cooked
½ c. melted butter or margarine
½ c. grated Cheddar cheese
2 c. chicken or turkey, cooked, diced
1 can cream of mushroom soup
1 c. chicken broth

Place rice in greased 9×13-inch casserole. Place broccoli over rice. Drizzle butter over broccoli. Sprinkle half the cheese over casserole. Place chicken over broccoli. Combine soup and broth until smooth. Pour over casserole. Sprinkle remaining cheese over top. Bake at 375 degrees for 20 to 25 minutes. Yield: 8-10 servings.

Betty Wilde, Pres.
Preceptor Theta XP565
Eagle Grove, Iowa

Chicken-Mushroom Quiche

1½ c. flour
1¾ tsp. salt
½ c. shortening
4 eggs, beaten
¼ tsp. white pepper
⅛ tsp. tarragon
1½ c. half and half, scalded
½ c. Sauterne
1 c. cooked diced chicken
½ c. sliced mushrooms, sauteed
⅓ c. grated Swiss cheese

Combine flour and ¾ teaspoon salt. Cut in shortening. Sprinkle with enough cold water to make stiff dough. Shape into 10-inch pie pan. Press pastry against edges with tines of fork. Place waxed paper in bottom of pastry shell; cover with uncooked beans to prevent puffing. Bake at 425 degrees for 10 minutes. Remove beans and paper. Bake at 425 degrees for 2 to 3 minutes. Combine eggs, 1 teaspoon salt, white pepper and tarragon. Stir half and half slowly into egg mixture. Add Sauterne, chicken and mushrooms. Place in pastry shell. Sprinkle with cheese. Bake at 375 degrees for 30 minutes. Let stand 10 minutes; cut into wedges. Yield: 6 servings.

Eva S. Hansen, Pres.
Preceptor Gamma XP144
Petaluma, California

Chicken-Zucchini Flips

¼ c. chopped onion
¼ c. sliced celery
2 tbsp. butter
1 10¾-oz. can cream of chicken soup
¼ c. milk
2 c. diced, cooked chicken
2 eggs, beaten
¼ c. flour
2 tbsp. Parmesan cheese
1 tsp. snipped parsley
1 tsp. chives
Salt and pepper to taste
3 med. zucchini, shredded and drained

Saute onion and celery in butter in medium skillet. Add soup and milk. Stir in chicken; heat thoroughly. Keep warm. Combine eggs, flour, Parmesan cheese, parsley, chives, salt and pepper and zucchini in medium bowl; mix well. Drop ¼ cup batter onto hot greased griddle; flatten slightly. Cook until browned. Turn; brown second side. Remove; keep warm. Repeat process. Spoon chicken filling on each crepe. Fold over. Place on serving platter. Top with remaining sauce. Yield: 4-6 servings.

Margaret Newman, Ext. Off.
Xi Alpha Tau X2420
Jal, New Mexico

Man shall not live by bread alone, but by every word that proceedeth out of the mouth of God. Mrs. Gorlon Mobley Webb

Breads

Thank goodness for the tantalizing aroma of bread baking in the oven! It fills every room in the house, putting appetites into action and proving to the cook just how talented she really is. And, in this age of convenience foods, golden-crusted loaves of homemade breads are a happy addition to any table. But, yeast loaves are just the beginning—waffles, biscuits, quick breads, rolls, sweet loaves, and muffins are just a few more of the rewards of baking and bread-making.

Homemade breads, full of health and flavor, are almost mandatory to mealtime. But, with the imaginative use of herbs, spices, cheese, raisins, and other seasonings, you should never have to worry about monotony. A plain waffle mixture takes on new excitement with the addition of blueberries or crushed strawberries for breakfast, brunch or dessert; and for dinner, consider the additions of ham, poultry or cheese. Yeast and sweet or quick breads can also be baked in any variety of uniquely shaped pans for added impression. Glaze and garnish your breads with a creative flair. Remember, too, that homemade breads are excellent holiday and/or hostess gifts. Once you begin making your own homemade breads, your family may never allow "storebought" breads in the house again. And, you may not want to give up the personal satisfaction inevitably derived from bread-making—plus the knowledge that you are giving your family and friends the very best.

The staff of life—wholesome and satisfying. Beta Sigma Phis know the nutrition and creative scope that bread making offers, quite evident in the collection of bread recipes that follow. Use them often!

Butter Dips

⅓ c. butter
2¼ c. flour
1 tbsp. sugar
3½ tsp. baking powder
1½ tsp. salt
1 c. milk

Melt butter in saucepan; set aside. Sift dry ingredients together in mixing bowl. Add milk; mix well. Place on floured board. Knead a few times. Pat dough to about ¾-inch thickness. Cut into 1 x 2-inch pieces. Dip each piece in melted butter. Place on 9 x 13-inch baking pan. Bake at 450 degrees for 15 to 20 minutes.

Mrs. Ellis B. Hatton
Theta Psi
Chillicothe, Ohio

Heavenly Biscuits

2 c. all-purpose flour, sifted
1 tbsp. sugar
4 tsp. baking powder
½ tsp. salt
½ c. shortening
1 egg, beaten
⅔ c. milk

Sift together dry ingredients in mixing bowl. Cut in shortening until crumbly. Combine egg and milk; add to flour mixture. Stir until dough leaves the side of bowl. Turn out onto lightly floured surface. Knead about 20 times. Cut out biscuits with 2-inch floured biscuit cutter; do not twist cutter. Place on ungreased baking sheet. Bake at 450 degrees for 10 to 14 minutes or until browned. Yield: 24 servings.

Barbara A. Gunby
Xi Kappa Omicron X2645
Roseville, California

Kentucky Corn Bread

1½ c. cornmeal
3 tsp. baking powder
1 tsp. salt
2 eggs, beaten
⅔ c. salad oil
1 c. sour cream
1 c. cream-style corn
2 tbsp. minced green pepper (opt.)
½ lb. Cheddar cheese, grated

Combine all ingredients except cheese with a fork. Pour ½ of the mixture in greased iron skillet. Sprinkle ½ of the grated cheese over mixture. Pour remaining mixture carefully on top. Top with remaining cheese. Bake in 350 degree oven for 35 to 40 minutes.

Maratha Benet, Scrapbook/Yardstick Chm.
Xi Gamma Nu X5249
Hendersonville, Tennessee

Stir and Drop Doughnuts

2 c. sifted flour
¼ c. sugar
3 tsp. baking powder
1 tsp. salt
½ tsp. nutmeg
¼ c. oil
¾ c. milk
1 egg, beaten
Cinnamon to taste

Sift first 5 ingredients together. Combine oil, milk and egg; add to dry ingredients. Stir with fork until thoroughly mixed. Drop by teaspoonfuls into deep hot fat. Fry about 3 minutes or until golden brown. Drain on absorbent paper. Shake in a bag in mixture of cinnamon and additional sugar. Yield: about 2½ dozen.

Arlene Haller
Zeta Rho No. 9131
Asheville, North Carolina

Spiced French Toast

2 eggs
1 c. milk
1 c. unsifted flour
1½ tsp. baking powder
½ tsp. salt
1 tsp. ground cinnamon
1 tsp. vanilla extract
8 to 10 bread slices
6 tbsp. butter
3 tbsp. salad oil

Place eggs and milk in blender container; blend well. Add flour, baking powder, salt, cinnamon and vanilla; blend until smooth. Pour mixture into shallow baking dish. Cut bread in half to form triangles. Heat 2 tablespoons butter and 1 tablespoon oil in wide skillet. Soak bread triangles in egg mixture until coated on both sides. Fry until golden brown. Repeat, adding butter and oil as needed. Yield: 4-6 servings.

Della Ramsay, Treas.
Xi Delta Xi X1418
Lakewood, California

How poor are they that have not patience.   Deby Shibley

Marsha's French Toast

4 eggs
2 tbsp. evaporated milk
2 tbsp. margarine
8 slices of bread

Beat eggs. Add milk; continue beating until thoroughly mixed. Melt margarine in large skillet over medium heat. Dip bread slices in egg mixture. Place bread in skillet; cook about 2 minutes or until lightly browned. Turn; continue cooking until lightly browned. Serve plain or with maple syrup. Yield: 4 servings.

Marsha Rose, Sec.
Xi Beta X504
Charlotte, North Carolina

Cold-Oven Popovers

3 eggs
1 c. milk
1 c. flour
½ tsp. salt

Grease 12 muffin cups or 6 custard cups generously. Place in refrigerator to chill. Beat eggs and milk until well blended. Add flour and salt; mix well. Pour into muffin cups until half full. Place in cold oven. Bake at 450 degrees for 30 minutes for muffin cups or 45 minutes for custard cups. Do not peek. Yield: 6 servings.

Anne Handschke, Pres.
Xi Alpha Upsilon X4438
Nikoosa, Wisconsin

Best-Ever Muffins

Sugar
1¾ c. sifted flour
2½ tsp. baking powder
¾ tsp. salt
1 egg, well beaten
¾ c. milk
⅓ c. oil
½ c. melted butter
Cinnamon to taste

Sit 2 tablespoons sugar and next 3 ingredients into bowl; make well in center. Combine egg, milk and oil. Add to dry ingredients. Stir quickly until moistened. Drop into greased muffin cups. Bake at 400 degrees for 25 minutes. Combine ½ cup sugar with cinnamon to taste. Roll hot muffins in melted butter, then in mixture of cinnamon and sugar. Serve hot. Quick and delicious! Yield: 12 servings.

Julie Halligan
Epsilon Eta No. 3703
Hawarden, Iowa

Cheesy Egg Muffins

3 English muffins, split
1 lb. sausage
8 eggs
½ c. milk
½ tsp. sweet basil
Salt and pepper to taste
2 drops of Tabasco
1 can cheese soup
½ soup can milk

Toast muffins. Place muffin halves on bottom of 8 x 10-inch baking pan. Brown sausage. Sprinkle evenly over muffins. Beat eggs, milk, seasonings and Tabasco in bowl. Pour over muffins and sausage. Bake in 350-degree oven about 10 to 15 minutes or until eggs set. Combine cheese soup and milk in a saucepan. Cook until heated through. Serve over Egg Muffins. Yield: 6 servings.

Marilyn Peirce, V. P.
Theta Epsilon No. 7681
Slater, Iowa

Six-Week Bran Muffins

7 c. raisin bran flakes
5 c. unsifted all-purpose flour
2 c. sugar
5 tsp. soda
2 tsp. salt
4 c. milk
2 tbsp. vinegar
1 c. vegetable oil
½ c. molasses
4 eggs, beaten

Combine raisin bran flakes, flour, sugar, soda and salt in large bowl; mix well. Combine milk and vinegar; add to bran flakes mixture. Add vegetable oil, molasses and eggs; mix well. Fill muffin cups ⅔ full. Bake at 400 degrees for 15 to 20 minutes. Refrigerate, covered, until ready for use. Batter will keep in refrigerator for 6 weeks.

Margaret B. Diener, Sec. Chm.
Laureate Mu PL322
Fort Collins, Colorado
Sandra E. Nelson, Corr. Sec.
Epsilon Chi No. 7056
Vancouver, Washington

A child's memory of her grandmother's kitchen and delicious cake with frosting. Patricia Cleland Blinn

June's Beer Bread

3 c. self-rising flour
2 tbsp. sugar
1 12-oz. bottle of beer
Melted butter

Mix flour and sugar. Add beer. Combine only until flour is completely mixed. Pour into well greased 9 x 5-inch loaf pan. Bake at 350 degrees for 1 hour and 15 minutes. Remove from pan; cool on rack. Brush top of loaf with melted butter.

June Sponaugle, Treas.
Preceptor Chi XP1844
Bellevue, Nebraska

Bread-Made-Easy

1 pkg. yeast
Sugar
1 tbsp. salt
3 tbsp. Crisco
6½ c. flour

Dissolve yeast and pinch of sugar in ½ cup warm water; let rise to full cup. Place yeast mixture in large mixing bowl. Add ¼ cup sugar, salt, Crisco and 2 cups warm water. Add flour gradually. Turn out onto lightly floured board; knead until smooth and elastic. Place in greased bowl; turn once to grease surface. Cover; let rise for 2 hours. Punch down. Turn out onto lightly floured board; knead slightly. Cover; let rise for 1 hour. Punch down; turn onto lightly floured board. Divide in half. Shape dough into 2 loaves. Place in greased loaf pans. Cover; let rise 1 hour to 1 hour and 30 minutes or until doubled in bulk. Bake at 350 degrees for 45 minutes or until brown on top. Yield: 2 loaves.

Sandra A. Bennett
Xi Tau X3949
Biloxi, Mississippi

Dutch Onion-Rye Bread

2 pkg. dry yeast
2 c. scalded milk
⅓ c. dark molasses
1 tsp. salt
⅓ c. salad oil
2½ c rye flour
5 c. sifted all-purpose flour
1 env. onion soup mix
1 egg white, slightly beaten

Soften yeast in 1 cup lukewarm water. Combine milk, molasses, salt and oil; cool to lukewarm. Stir in rye flour; beat well. Add yeast mixture and soup mix. Add enough white flour to make moderately stiff dough. Turn dough on lightly floured surface. Knead until smooth and satiny. Place in greased bowl, turning once to grease surface. Let rise in warm place until doubled in bulk. Divide in 3 portions. Let rest for 10 minutes. Shape loaves. Place seam side down on greased baking sheet. Slash tops diagonally every 2½ inches; brush with egg white. Let rise until doubled in bulk. Bake at 375 degrees for 35 to 40 minutes or until golden brown. Remove to rack; cool.

Doris E. Bradley, Pres.
Preceptor Beta Gamma XP1336
Bremerton, Washington

Paska (Easter Bread)

¼ c. sugar
1 stick butter
4 tsp. salt
3 c. scalded milk
1 pkg. yeast
5 eggs
7 c. flour

Add sugar, butter and salt to scalded milk; let cool. Dissolve yeast in about ¼ cup warm water. Beat 4 eggs until foamy; add to cooled milk. Add yeast. Beat in 1 cup flour; continue adding flour until dough is stiff. Knead until elastic, about 10 minutes. Place in greased bowl, turning once to grease surface; cover. Let rise about 1 hour. Punch dough down. Let rise again until doubled in bulk. Cut off enough dough to make braid; set aside. Shape remaining dough into round loaf. Place in greased baking pan. Beat 1 egg with 1 teaspoon water; brush on dough. Divide reserved dough into 3 portions. Roll into strips; braid loosely. Arrange braid on loaf. Brush with egg white. Cover. Let rise until doubled in bulk. Bake at 350 degrees for 50 minutes.

Adelia Derbak
Theta Rho No. 3862
Royalton, Illinois

Wheat Germ Loaves

1 c. toasted unsweetened coconut
1¼ c. wheat germ
1½ c. unsifted all-purpose flour
2 tsp. baking powder
½ tsp. soda
1 tsp. salt
1 tsp. lemon juice
1 tsp. vanilla extract

What is a home without love? Gail E. Frics

½ tsp. almond extract
½ c. milk
⅓ c. butter
⅔ c. sugar
2 eggs
1 c. mashed bananas

Spread coconut on cookie sheet. Toast at 350 degrees for 3 to 4 minutes stirring often. Combine wheat germ, flour, baking powder, soda and salt in bowl; mix well. Add lemon juice, vanilla and almond extract to milk. Cream butter and sugar until blended in mixer. Add eggs; beat on High for 4 minutes or until pale and light. Remove beaters. Stir in dry ingredients alternately with milk mixture in thirds until blended. Mix in coconut and bananas. Pour into well-oiled baking pans. Bake at 350 degrees for 30 minutes.

Doris S. Decker, Corr. Sec.
Preceptor Nu XP458
Kingston, Ontario, Canada

Whole Wheat Bread

2 tsp. sugar
2 pkg. yeast
½ c. molasses
¼ c. (firmly packed) brown sugar
¾ c. instant dry milk
6 c. white flour
2 tbsp. salt
¼ c. soft lard
5 c. whole wheat flour

Combine sugar, ½ cup warm water and yeast; let stand 10 minutes. Combine 4 cups warm water, molasses, brown sugar and instant dry milk. Add white flour gradually, stirring until smooth. Add to yeast mixture; beat vigorously. Add salt, lard and whole wheat flour. Add additional whole wheat flour, if necessary, to form soft dough. Cover; let rise 15 to 20 minutes. Turn out onto lightly floured board. Knead until smooth and elastic. Cover; let rise until doubled in bulk. Punch down. Cover; let rise until doubled in bulk. Turn out onto lightly floured board. Shape into 4 loaves. Place in greased loaf pans. Bake at 400 degrees for 50 minutes. Reduce oven temperature to 350 degrees; bake for 15 minutes longer. Yield: 4 loaves.

Jolene Fransdal, Treas.
Lambda Epsilon
Ankeny, Iowa

Donna's White Bread

3 pkg. dry yeast
4 c. scalded milk

4 tsp. salt
4 tbsp. sugar
2 tbsp. Crisco
11 to 11½ c. sifted flour

Soften yeast in ½ cup warm water. Add milk, salt, sugar and Crisco. Add 4 cups flour; mix well. Add enough remaining flour to make moderately stiff dough. Knead dough for 10 minutes or until smooth. Form into ball. Place in lightly greased bowl, turning once to coat surface. Cover; let rise for 1 hour and 30 minutes in warm draft-free area or until doubled in bulk. Punch down; let rise for 45 minutes or until doubled in bulk. Cut dough into 4 equal parts; shape into balls. Cover; let rest for 10 minutes. Turn onto unfloured surface; roll out to ½-inch thickness. Roll dough as for jelly roll. Place in greased loaf pan seam side down. Let rise for 1 hour or until doubled in bulk. Bake in preheated 400-degree oven for 15 minutes; cover with foil to avoid overbrowning. Bake an additional 20 minutes. Yield: 4 loaves.

Donna G. Oshnock, Pres.
Mu Delta
Latrobe, Pennsylvania

Pita (Middle Eastern Pocket Bread)

1 tbsp. dry yeast
2 tbsp. honey
1 tbsp. salt
5½ c. unbleached white flour

Combine yeast, honey, salt and 2 cups hot water. Allow to stand until yeast is dissolved. Add 4 cups flour, 2 cups at a time. Sprinkle 1 cup flour over kneading board. Knead dough on flour on board; kneading flour into dough. Add enough of the remaining flour as needed to make medium-stiff dough. Knead for 5 minutes. Place dough in greased bowl; cover. Let rise in draft-free place for 1 hour and 15 minutes. Punch down. Turn out onto lightly floured board. Knead out large air bubbles. Divide dough into 12 balls. Cover; let rest for 10 minutes. Preheat oven to 475 degrees. Place one oven rack to lowest position and one to highest. Roll balls into ½ x 5-inch rounds. Roll dough from the center out; one direction only. Rotate dough as you roll. Lay 2 rounds on greased cookie sheet. Bake on bottom rack until bottom is brown and pita puffs. Turn oven setting to broil; place baking pan on top oven rack. Brown tops. Repeat process. Cool. Cut and fill with desired filling. Yield: 6-8 servings.

Lonnie Brajcich, V.P.
Delta Eta No. 9246
Delta, British Columbia, Canada

Live your life with love and you will be eternally happy. Paulette Semmes

Israeli Heroes in Pita

2 c. drained sauerkraut
½ c. sliced pimento-stuffed olives
⅓ c. chopped onion
½ c. diced seeded tomato
2 tbsp. olive or salad oil
3 Pita rolls
1 c. Sesame Seed Sauce
½ lb. corned beef slices
½ lb. salami slices
Falafel

Place sauerkraut, olives, onion and tomato in bowl. Sprinkle with oil. Toss lightly until combined. Set aside. Cut each Pita in half crosswise, then split to make a pocket in each half. Spread interior liberally with Sesame Seed Sauce. Fill each Pita with corned beef and salami slices; add kraut and olive mixture and Falafel. Serve any remaining Sesame Seed Sauce with heroes.

Sesame Seed Sauce:

1⅓ c. sesame seed
⅓ c. salad oil
1¼ tsp. salt
2 cloves of garlic, crushed
Dash of cumin
¼ c. fresh lemon juice

Spread sesame seed in shallow pan. Toast in 350-degree oven for 10 to 15 minutes or until lightly browned; stir occasionally. Place seed in blender container; cover. Blend at high speed until powdery. Stop blender occasionally and redistribute seed with spatula. Add salad oil gradually, while running blender at low speed; blend until smooth. Add salt; mix well. Stir sesame seed paste and garlic together in large bowl. Add 1 teaspoon salt, cumin and lemon juice. Beat in ½ cup water with whisk. Beat in ¼ to ½ cup water, 1 tablespoon at a time, until sauce has consistency of mayonnaise.

Falafel:

1 egg
½ c. coarsely chopped parsley sprigs
2 cloves of garlic
⅓ c. sliced scallions
¼ tsp. salt
⅛ tsp. ground cumin
Dash of pepper
1 c. drained canned garbanzo beans
½ tsp. soda

Place egg, parsley, garlic, scallions and seasonings in electric blender. Blend mixture until puree consistency. Scrape sides of blender occasionally with rubber spatula. Add beans, ¼ cup at a time, blending until smooth. Pour mixture into bowl; stir in soda. Allow batter to stand for 15 minutes. Heat about ½ inch oil in skillet to 370 degrees. Drop mixture from teaspoon into hot oil; fry until browned on both sides. Drain falafel on paper towels. Falafel should be about 1¼ inches wide. Sprinkle falafel with Sesame Seed Sauce before placing in hero if desired.

Photograph for this recipe on page 142.

Beer Rolls

4 cups Bisquick
1 tbsp. sugar
1 tsp. salt
1 can warm beer

Place first 3 ingredients in deep bowl. Pour warm beer over all; stir until well mixed. Drop into greased muffin tins. Bake in 350-degree oven for 20 minutes or until golden brown. Yield: 20 servings.

Evelyn Gladden
Xi Beta Eta X3468
Eunice, New Mexico

Butterfly Rolls

2 pkg. dry yeast
Milk
Sugar
1 tsp. salt
2 eggs, beaten
½ c. Crisco
5⅓ c. all-purpose flour
Melted butter
2½ tsp. cinnamon
2 tbsp. butter
1 c. confectioners'
½ tsp. vanilla extract

Dissolve yeast in ½ cup warm water. Scald ½ cup milk; cool. Stir in ½ cup sugar, salt, eggs, Crisco and 2½ cups flour. Beat until smooth. Add 2½ cups flour; beat until smooth. Turn dough onto lightly floured board. Knead until smooth, about 5 minutes. Place in greased bowl, turning once to grease surface. Let rise for 1 hour and 30 minutes. Punch down. Roll dough out into 9 x 18-inch rectangle. Brush with melted butter. Combine ½ cup sugar and 1 teaspoon cinnamon; sprinkle over dough. Roll up; pinch ends to seal. Shape evenly. Slice into 1-inch rolls. Make indention in center of each slice; press almost through dough. Place on greased cookie sheet; cover. Let rise for 30 minutes. Combine ⅓ cup flour, 2 tablespoons sugar, butter and 1½ teaspoons cinnamon. Sprinkle over "butterfly" slices. Bake at 375 degrees for 12 minutes. Combine confectioners' sugar, 1 tablespoon milk and vanilla. Drizzle over hot butterfly rolls. Yield: 18 servings.

Linda Rae Burk, Pres.
Sigma Mu No. 9900
Golconda, Illinois

Happiness is to be able to go to sleep easily at night, knowing you've done your best. Rebecca Ann Blake

One-Hour Buttermilk Rolls

2 pkg. yeast
1½ c. lukewarm buttermilk
½ c. melted margarine or shortening
3 tbsp. sugar
1 egg, beaten
4½ c. flour
½ tsp. soda
1 tsp. salt
Brown sugar to taste
Cinnamon to taste
Butter

Crumble yeast in ¼ cup warm water. Combine buttermilk, melted margarine and sugar. Stir in beaten egg and yeast. Sift flour with soda and salt. Stir into yeast mixture; beat until smooth. Let rest for 10 minutes. Roll dough on floured surface. Sprinkle with brown sugar and cinnamon; dot with butter. Roll up dough into jelly roll fashion. Slice. Place on buttered baking pans. Let rise for 30 minutes. Bake at 375 degrees for 15 to 20 minutes. Yield: 2 dozen.

Juacile VanCorbach
Xi Alpha Nu X3829
Pierce, Idaho

Potato Refrigerator Rolls

2 pkg. dry yeast
⅔ c. sugar
1½ tsp. salt
⅔ c. soft shortening
2 eggs, beaten
1 c. lukewarm mashed potatoes
7 to 7½ c. all-purpose flour

Dissolve yeast in 1½ cups very warm water in large mixing bowl. Stir in next 5 ingredients; mix well. Mix in flour with spoon or by hand until dough is easy to handle. Turn onto lightly floured surface. Knead until smooth and elastic. Place a small amount of oil in large bowl; place dough in bowl, turning once to grease surface. Cover with waxed paper then damp cloth. Refrigerate for about 2 hours. Shape dough into desired rolls; cover. Let rise for 1 hour and 30 minutes or 2 hours or until doubled in bulk. Place on lightly greased baking sheet or muffin pans. Bake at 400 degrees for 12 to 15 minutes until brown. Yield: 3 dozen.

Suzanne Patterson, Pres.
Preceptor Alpha XP115
South Charleston, West Virginia

Sixty-Minute Yeast Rolls

1 pkg. yeast
Sugar
¾ c. milk, warmed
⅛ tsp. salt
⅛ c. butter or margarine
2¼ c. flour

Dissolve yeast in ⅛ cup water with 2 teaspoons sugar in bowl. Add milk, 3 tablespoons sugar, salt and butter. Stir in flour until smooth. Cover; let rise until doubled in bulk. Do not knead. Turn out on floured board. Roll out to ½-inch thickness. Cut with biscuit cutter. Brush top with additional butter; fold in half. Place in greased 8 x 8-inch pan. Let rise until doubled in bulk. Bake at 450 degrees for 15 to 20 minutes.

Barbara Booth, Pres.
Xi Zeta Lambda X2943
Perrysburg, Ohio

Quick Delicious Rolls

2 c. self-rising flour
4 tbsp. mayonnaise
1 c. milk
1 tsp. sugar

Combine all ingredients in mixing bowl; mix about 2 minutes. Pour into 12-cup ungreased muffin pan. Bake at 450 degrees for 10 minutes or until golden brown. Yield: 12 servings.

Nancy Heriot Richardson, Pres.
Delta Omega No. 6912
Savannah, Georgia

Delicious Crispies

1 pkg. yeast
1 c. margarine
1 c. sour cream
1 tsp. vanilla extract
½ tsp. salt
4 c. flour
Cinnamon to taste
Sugar to taste

Dissolve yeast in ¼ cup warm water. Combine next 4 ingredients in large mixing bowl. Add yeast; mix well. Add 1 to 2 cups flour slowly; mix well. Stir in remaining flour with a spoon. Knead as for bread dough, about 3 minutes. Chill 1 hour. Cut dough in half. Roll out as for thin cinnamon rolls. Prepare mixture of cinnamon and sugar. Spread on dough. Roll up. Repeat process with remaining dough. Cut into ¼ inch thick slices, about 30 for each roll. Mix additional sugar and cinnamon on pastry sheet. Roll each slice, turning continually, in mixture, forming a round ball. Place on baking sheet. Bake at 350 degrees for 5 to 7 minutes.

Ardis J. Gadeken
Epsilon
Lincoln, Nebraska

Food served with a smile is easier to digest. Mary Ann Apland

Pennsylvania Dutch Snecken Rolls

5 to 6 c. unsifted flour
1 c. sugar
1 tsp. salt
2 pkg. dry yeast
1 c. milk
¼ c. margarine
2 eggs, at room temperature
Melted margarine
1 tsp. ground cinnamon
Confectioners' sugar frosting

Mix 1¾ cups flour, ¼ cup sugar, salt and undissolved yeast in large bowl thoroughly. Combine milk, ½ cup water and ¼ cup margarine in saucepan. Heat over low heat until liquids are warm. Add to dry ingredients gradually. Beat for 2 minutes at medium speed of electric mixer, scraping bowl occasionally. Add eggs and ½ cup flour or enough flour to make thick batter. Beat at high speed for 2 minutes, scraping bowl occasionally. Stir in enough additional flour to make a soft dough. Turn onto lightly floured board. Knead until smooth and elastic, about 8 to 10 minutes. Place in greased bowl, turning to grease top; cover let rise in warm place, free from draft, until doubled in bulk, about 30 minutes. Punch dough down. Turn out onto lightly floured board. Divide dough into 3 equal pieces. Roll each piece into 14 x 9-inch rectangle. Brush lightly with melted margarine. Sprinkle with mixture of ¾ cup sugar and cinnamon. Roll each up as for jelly roll, 9 inches long. Seal edges firmly. Cut each roll into 9 equal pieces. Place, cut side up, in greased muffin cups; cover. Let rise in warm place, free from draft, until doubled in bulk, about 30 minutes. Bake at 350 degrees about 20 to 25 minutes or until done. Remove from muffin cups. Place on wire racks to cool. Frost with confectioners' sugar frosting. Yield: 27 rolls.

Photograph for this recipe on page 150.

Peanut Rolls

4 eggs
2 c. sugar
2 c. flour
4 tsp. baking powder
¼ tsp. salt
2 tsp. vanilla extract
1⅛ sticks margarine, softened
1½ boxes, confectioners' sugar
¼ c. milk
1 1-lb. bag raw peanuts, blender-chopped

Beat eggs until light and fluffy. Add sugar gradually, stirring. Sift flour, baking powder and salt together 4 times. Add 1 cup boiling water, 1 teaspoon vanilla and sifted ingredients to egg mixture. Place in greased and floured 13 x 9 x 2-inch baking pan. Bake at 350 degrees for 35 to 40 minutes. Cool; cut into squares. Combine margarine, confectoners' sugar, milk and 1 teaspoon vanilla. Cover each square entirely with icing. Let stand 24 hours. Roll each square in peanuts. Yield: 14 servings.

Mrs. Marilyn Morse, V.P.
Alpha Sigma XP985
Boonville, Missouri

Breakfast Cookies

⅔ c. butter or margarine
1 c. sugar
1 egg
1 tsp. vanilla extract
1 c. flour
½ tsp. soda
½ tsp. salt
3 c. quick oats, uncooked
1 c. shredded sharp Cheddar cheese
6 crisply cooked bacon slices, crumbled
¼ c. wheat germ

Beat together butter sugar, egg and vanilla. Combine flour, soda and salt. Add to butter mixture; mix well. Stir in oats, cheese, bacon and wheat germ. Drop by rounded tablespoonfuls onto greased cookie sheet. Bake in preheated 350-degree oven for 8 to 10 minutes or until lightly browned. Yield: 3 dozen.

Norene M. Fossick, Pres.
Laureate Beta PL410
Nashville, Tennessee

Caramel Rolls

2 pkg. yeast
1½ c. scalded milk
2¼ c. sugar
1 tsp. salt
2 eggs, beaten

And ye shall eat the fat of the land. Rosemary Buchanan

6½ to 7 c. flour
¾ c. butter
1½ tbsp. cinnamon
2 tbsp. dark Karo syrup

Dissolve yeast in ½ cup warm water. Combine milk, ½ cup sugar and salt; cool to lukewarm. Add eggs to yeast mixture. Stir into milk mixture. Add about 4 cups flour; beat until smooth. Melt ½ cup butter; cool. Add butter to dough; beat until smooth. Stir in enough flour to form smooth elastic dough. Place in a lightly greased bowl; turn once to coat surface. Cover let rise in warm place 1 hour or until doubled in bulk. Turn out onto lightly floured surface. Roll dough into 15 x 7 x ½-inch rectangle. Combine ¾ cup sugar and cinnamon. Sprinkle over dough. Roll up as for jelly roll. Seal edge; cut into 1-inch slices. Melt ¼ cup butter in saucepan; add 1 cup sugar, ¼ cup water and syrup. Cook until sugar dissolves. Pour into 9 x 9 x 2-inch baking pans. Arrange dough slices over caramel sauce in baking pans. Let rise 45 minutes or until doubled in bulk. Bake at 350 degrees for 20 minutes. Invert rolls onto plate before caramel hardens. Yield: 15-20 servings.

Juanita Eardley, Corr. Sec.
Gamma Zeta No. 3301
Sand Spring, Oklahoma

Caramel-Nut Biscuit Rounds

⅔ c. (firmly packed) brown sugar
6 tbsp. butter
⅓ c. chopped nuts
1 can refrigerator biscuits

Combine brown sugar, butter and 2 tablespoons water in saucepan. Cook until sugar dissolves. Add nuts. Pour half the mixture into baking dish. Cut biscuits into quarters; place in baking dish. Cover with remaining brown sugar mixture. Bake at 350 degrees for 15 to 20 minutes. 4-6 servings.

Gretchen Maris
Lambda Chi
Protection, Kansas

Cinnamon Rolls

½ c. (firmly packed) brown sugar
1 3¾ oz. package butterscotch pudding mix
3 tsp. cinnamon
1½ c. chopped nuts
2 pkg. frozen bread rolls
1 stick margarine, melted

Combine brown sugar, pudding mix, cinnamon and nuts. Place ½ of the rolls in greased and floured bundt pan. Sprinkle with ½ of the dry ingredients. Repeat layers. Pour margarine over rolls. Let stand, lightly covered, overnight. Invert on plate immediately. Yield: 12-15 servings.

Irene H. Becker, Sec.
Preceptor Laureate Alpha PL147
Laramie, Wyoming

Cinnamon Surprise Buns

Sugar
2 tsp. cinnamon
48 miniature marshmallows
Melted butter
1 pkg. dry yeast
2 tbsp. shortening
2½ c. Bisquick
Nuts, coarsely chopped

Combine ⅔ cups sugar and cinnamon; set aside. Dip each marshmallow in ¼ cup butter; coat with sugar mixture. Set aside. Dissolve yeast in ⅔ cup warm water. Stir in 2 tablespoons sugar, shortening and Bisquick. Beat vigorously. Turn dough onto floured surface; knead 20 times on until smooth. Divide dough into 12 pieces; flatten into 4-inch circles. Wrap each circle around 4 marshmallows and several nut pieces. Pinch edges together tightly. Dip into additional butter; coat with sugar mixture. Place in greased muffin cups. Cover; let rise 30 minutes or until doubled in bulk. Bake in preheated 400-degree oven for 20 minutes. Invert immediately onto serving platter. Yield: 12 servings.

Sue Campbell, Prog. Chm.
Alpha Omicron Preceptor XP921
Festus, Missouri

Friendship Caramel Rolls

1 c. chopped nuts
2 loaves uncooked frozen bread dough, thawed
½ c. butter or margarine
1 c. (firmly packed) brown sugar
1 3¾-oz. package vanilla pudding and pie mix
2 tsp. cinnamon
2 tbsp. milk

Sprinkle nuts evenly in generously buttered 9 x 13-inch pan. Slice each loaf of dough into 18 slices. Arrange slices of one loaf in pan to cover nuts. Combine butter, brown sugar, pudding mix, cinnamon and milk in small saucepan. Bring to a boil, stirring constantly to dissolve sugar. Cool slightly. Pour half the mixture over loaf slices. Arrange slices of second loaf over first loaf. Top with remaining caramel mixture. Let rise for 1 hour and 30 minutes or until doubled in bulk. Bake at 350 degrees for 30 minutes. Turn out immediately on cookie sheet. Yield: 12-16 servings.

Betty H. Alderton, Ser. Chm.
Preceptor Iota XP343
Quincy, Illinois

It is our attitude at the beginning of a task which, more than anything else, will affect it's successful outcome.   Debbra A. Hone

Pecan Rolls

2 pkg. dry yeast
Sugar
⅔ c. lard
2 tsp. salt
2 eggs, beaten
6½ to 7½ c. sifted flour
Butter
1 c. (firmly packed) brown sugar
3 tbsp. corn syrup
1 c. pecans, halves or chopped
2 tsp. cinnamon

Dissolve yeast in ½ cup warm water in large bowl. Add 2 tablespoons sugar, stirring until sugar is dissolved. Melt lard in 1 cup boiling water in small bowl. Add salt, eggs and 1 cup flour. Pour into yeast mixture; mix by hand or slowly by mixer. Add enough flour to handle easily; mix by hand. Turn onto lightly floured board; knead for 5 minutes or until smooth. Place in greased bowl; cover. Let rise in warm place 2 hours or until doubled in bulk. Punch down; let rest. Melt ⅔ cup butter in medium saucepan. Add brown sugar and corn syrup. Bring to a boil. Pour into 9 x 12-inch cake pan. Sprinkle with pecans. Turn dough out on lightly floured surface. Roll out into 9 x 15-inch rectangle. Spread with 4 tablespoons butter. Combine ½ cup sugar and cinnamon; sprinkle over dough. Roll up tightly; seal edges. Cut roll into ½-inch slices. Place 1 inch apart over pecans. Let rise until doubled in bulk. Bake at 375 degrees for 25 to 30 minutes. Let rest 3 minutes. Invert onto platter. Yield: 12 servings.

Gloria Shaw
Preceptor XP237
Sedan, Kansas

Basic Oatmeal Mix

7 c. sifted all-purpose flour
3½ c. sugar
1½ tbsp. salt
¼ c. baking powder
2 c. shortening
2½ c. rolled oats

Sift flour, sugar, salt and baking powder 3 times. Cut in shortening until mixture is crumbly. Add oats; mix well. Store in covered container at room temperature.

Date Muffins:

1 egg, beaten
½ c. milk
3 c. Basic Oatmeal Mix
¾ c. chopped dates or nuts

Combine egg and milk; add to Basic Oatmeal Mix. Stir 30 strokes. Add dates. Stir 10 strokes. Pour into muffin cups, filling ⅔ full. Bake at 425 degrees for 20 minutes.

Olive Aldous Garrett, Soc. Chm.
Preceptor Alpha Beta
North Delta, British Columbia, Canada

Sherron's Date Muffins

2 eggs
3 tbsp. flour
¾ c. sugar
½ c. chopped dates
1 c. chopped pecans
1 to 2 c. confectioners' sugar

Mix all ingredients except confectioners' sugar. Place in small greased and floured muffin pans. Bake at 350 degrees until slightly brown. Roll in confectioners' sugar while hot.

Ella Louise Sherron, Pres.
Xi Zeta Xi X2071
La Porte, Texas

Pumpkin Muffins

1½ c. flour
½ c. sugar
2 tsp. baking powder
¾ tsp. salt
½ tsp. cinnamon
½ tsp. nutmeg
¼ c. shortening
1 egg, beaten
½ c. pumpkin
½ c. milk
½ c. raisins

Sift together dry ingredients. Cut in shortening until fine. Combine egg, pumpkin and milk. Add to dry mixture. Mix until just moistened. Stir in raisins. Fill greased muffin cups ⅔ full. Bake at 400 degrees for 18 to 20 minutes. Yield: 12 servings.

Jane Evasiuk, Corr. Sec.
Alpha Tau
Whitecourt, Alberta, Canada

French Pancakes with Orange Sauce

3 c. flour, sifted
2 tsp. salt
4 tsp. baking powder
2½ c. confectioners' sugar
8 eggs
2⅔ c. milk
2 tsp. vanilla extract
2 tsp. lemon rind

1 c. butter
10 tbsp. orange juice
2 tbsp. lemon juice
4 tsp. orange rind

Sift flour with salt, baking powder and ½ cup confectioners' sugar. Make a well in center of flour mixture. Add eggs, milk, 1⅓ cups water, vanilla and lemon rind. Mix until smooth. Pour desired amount of batter onto hot griddle. Pancakes will be thin and flat. Cook until lightly browned on each side. Combine next 4 ingredients with 2 cups confectioners' sugar in a saucepan. Bring to boiling point. Serve over pancakes.

Andrea L. Rogers, Pres.
Xi Beta Beta X2130
Sedro Woolley, Washington

Blender Sourdough Pancakes

1 pkg. dry yeast
2 c. buttermilk biscuit mix
1 c. milk
1 egg, at room temperature

Place yeast in blender. Add biscuit mix. Heat milk and ⅔ cup water until warm. Pour over dry ingredients. Cover; blend for 1 minute. Scrape down sides. Add egg; cover. Blend 1 minute longer. Pour batter into large bowl. Cover; let stand at room temperature for 30 minutes. Stir batter down. Pour ¼ cup batter per pancake on lightly greased hot griddle. Cook until lightly browned on each side. Stir down batter occasionally as used. Serve with butter and syrup.

Shirley Rockhold
Xi Epsilon Phi X2499
Lima, Ohio

Apple Pie Pancakes

1 c. unbleached white flour
1 c. whole wheat flour
1 tsp. soda
½ tsp. salt
1 tbsp. cinnamon
½ tsp. nutmeg
¼ tsp. cloves
2 eggs, beaten
2 tbsp. oil
1¾ c. milk
¼ c. lemon juice
2 c. peeled, finely chopped apples

Combine first 7 ingredients in large bowl. Combine remaining ingredients, except apples. Add liquid to dry ingredients; mix well. Stir in apples; blend well. Pour desired amount onto hot greased griddle; cook on both sides until brown. Serve with warm maple syrup.

Pamela Bishop
Xi Zeta X3349
Durham, New Hampshire

Rice-Buttermilk Waffles

3 eggs, separated
1 tsp. sugar
2 c. buttermilk
6 tbsp. vegetable oil
2 c. flour
½ tsp. salt
1 tbsp. baking powder
½ tsp. soda
1 c. cooked rice
½ c. soft margarine
½ c. peach or apricot preserves
Dash of nutmeg

Beat egg whites with sugar until stiff but not dry in small mixer bowl. Set aside. Beat egg yolks until thick and lemon color in large mixer bowl. Add buttermilk and oil. Sift together next 4 ingredients. Stir into egg yolk mixture. Beat only until smooth. Stir in rice. Fold egg whites into batter. Bake in a waffle iron. Beat margarine until fluffy. Add peach preserves and nutmeg. Beat again. Spread on hot waffles; serve. Yield: 6 servings.

Photograph for this recipe on page 154.

Maple Coffee Cake

1 pkg. hot roll mix
Sugar
1 tsp. cinnamon
1¼ tsp. maple flavoring
⅓ c. chopped nuts
6 tbsp. butter, softened
1 c. confectioners' sugar
2 to 3 tbsp. milk

Prepare hot roll mix according to package directions. Combine ½ cup sugar, cinnamon, 1 teaspoon maple flavoring and nuts in small bowl. Set aside. Divide dough into 3 portions. Roll each portion into a circle to fit 12-inch round pizza pan. Place one portion dough on greased pan. Spread with 2 tablespoons butter. Sprinkle with ⅓ of the cinnamon mixture. Repeat layers. Place 8-ounce drinking glass in center of top layer; cut 16 wedges, starting at edge of glass to rim of pan. Twist each wedge several times to form rope effect. Let rise for 45 minutes in a warm place or until doubled in bulk. Bake at 375 degrees for 30 minutes or until brown. Combine confectioners' sugar, ¼ teaspoon maple flavoring and milk, mix until smooth. Pour glaze over top. Yield: 16 servings.

Marianne Donato, W. and M. Chm.
Xi Gamma Delta X3683
Schenectady, New York

A friend is to be taken with his faults. Sandra Freeman

Pecan Coffee Cake

2 pkg. dry yeast
½ c. sugar
1 c. milk
1½ tsp. salt
2 eggs, beaten
1¼ c. Wesson oil
5 c. sifted all-purpose flour
2 c. (firmly packed) light brown sugar
2 tbsp. cinnamon
2 c. chopped pecans
¼ c. confectioners' sugar
2 tbsp. butter
½ tsp. vanilla extract

Soften yeast in ½ cup water with 1 teaspoon sugar for 10 minutes. Scald milk. Pour into bowl with remaining sugar and salt. Stir softened yeast into milk mixture. Stir in eggs, ¾ cup oil and flour. Mix well. Turn dough onto floured board; cover. Let rest for 10 minutes. Knead for 10 minutes or until smooth and elastic. Place dough in large greased bowl; turn to grease dough. Cover; let rise in warm place free from drafts for 1 hour or until doubled in bulk. Punch down dough; cover. Let rise again for 45 minutes or until doubled in bulk. Combine brown sugar, ½ cup oil, cinnamon and pecans in small bowl. Turn dough onto floured board; divide in half. Cover; let rest for 10 minutes. Roll dough portion into large rectangle. Sprinkle with ½ of the brown sugar mixture. Roll as for jelly roll; pinch edges to seal. Join ends to form ring. Place in greased 8 or 9-inch cake pan. Cut slits at 1-inch intervals across top with sharp knife. Repeat for second ring. Cover; let rise for 45 minutes or until doubled in bulk. Bake at 375 degrees for 15 minutes; reduce heat to 350 degrees. Bake for 15 minutes. Cool. Combine confectioners' sugar, butter, 1 tablespoon hot water and vanilla. Ice cooled cake rings. Yield: 24 servings.

Kathy Uhlich, Pres.
Xi Pi Eta X4399
Lewisville, Texas

Poppy Seed Coffee Cake

¼ c. poppy seed
1 c. buttermilk
1 tsp. almond extract
1 c. margarine or butter
2 c. sugar
4 eggs, separated
2½ c. all-purpose flour
1 tsp. soda
½ tsp. salt

A day of worry is more exhausting than a week of work. Sandra Freeman

1 tsp. baking powder
1 tbsp. cinnamon

Combine poppy seed, buttermilk and almond extract; set aside. Cream margarine and 1½ cups sugar until smooth. Add egg yolks; beat well. Sift flour, soda, salt and baking powder together. Add to creamed mixture alternately with buttermilk mixture. Beat egg whites until stiff; fold into batter. Pour ½ of the batter in tube pan. Combine ½ cup sugar and cinnamon; sprinkle half the mixture over batter. Add remaining batter; sprinkle with remaining sugar mixture. Cut through batter to make a marble effect. Bake at 350 degrees for 1 hour. Yield: 15 servings.

Velma I. Decker, Pres.
Preceptor Mu XP358
Moundridge, Kansas

Sour Cream Coffee Cake

1 stick margarine
1½ c. sugar
2 eggs, beaten
1 c. sour cream
2 tsp. vanilla extract
1½ c. flour
1 tsp. soda
1 tsp. baking powder
1 tsp. cinnamon
1 c. chopped nuts

Cream margarine and 1 cup sugar until smooth. Add eggs stirring constantly. Add sour cream and vanilla. Sift flour, soda and baking powder; add to creamed mixture. Pour ½ of the mixture into greased and floured 8-inch square baking pan. Combine ½ cup sugar, cinnamon and nuts. Sprinkle topping mixture over batter. Add remaining batter. Bake at 350 degrees for 45 minutes. Yield: 8 servings.

Elizabeth B. Thompson, City Coun. Pres.
Xi Beta Zeta X1817
Bradenton, Florida

Cranberry Coffee Cake

Butter
1 c. sugar
2 eggs, beaten
2 tsp. almond extract
1 tsp. vanilla extract
2 c. flour
½ tsp. salt
1 tsp. baking powder
1 tsp. soda
1 c. sour cream
1 12-oz. can cranberry sauce with whole cranberries
½ c. chopped walnuts
½ c. confectioners' sugar

Cream 1 stick butter and sugar until smooth. Add eggs, 1 teaspoon almond extract and vanilla; beat until smooth. Sift flour, salt, baking powder and soda in large bowl. Add sifted ingredients alternately with sour cream to creamed mixture. Pour half the batter in greased tube pan. Layer with half the cranberries and walnuts. Cover with remaining batter. Layer with remaining cranberries and walnuts. Bake at 375 degrees for 55 minutes. Combine confectioners' sugar, 1 teaspoon almond extract, 2 teaspoons hot water and 1 teaspoon butter. Drizzle topping over warm cake.

Elaine Rodgers, Pres
Preceptor Lambda XP999
Tempe, Arizona

Macadamia Sour Cream Coffee Cake

1 stick butter
1¼ c. sugar
1 c. sour cream
1 tsp. soda
2 eggs, beaten
1½ c. flour
1½ tsp. baking powder
1 tsp. vanilla extract
1 tbsp. cinnamon
¾ c. macadamia nuts, chopped

Cream butter with 1 cup sugar until smooth. Combine sour cream and soda. Add eggs and sour cream to creamed mixture; blend well. Sift flour and baking powder; add to batter. Add vanilla. Pour into 8 x 10-inch baking pan. Combine ¼ cup sugar, cinnamon and macadamia nuts; sprinkle over batter. Cut through the batter to make marble effect. Bake at 350 degrees for 45 minutes. Yield: 14 servings.

Faye Richardson
Preceptor Alpha Upsilon XP1493
Plains, Kansas

Apple-Anna Bread

½ c. Crisco
1½ c. sugar
2 eggs
2 bananas, mashed
2 c. finely chopped apples
1 tsp. vanilla extract
1 c. nuts (opt.)

Cream Crisco and sugar until smooth. Add eggs, one at a time, beating until smooth after each addition. Add bananas, apples, vanilla and nuts. Pour into 1 large or 2 small greased loaf pans. Bake at 350 degrees for 1 hour.

Nancy L. Hunter, Serv. Chm.
Preceptor Epsilon XP904
Cape Elizabeth, Maine

The greatest wealth is contentment with little. Sandra Freeman

Desserts

Dessert is to a good meal what a decorative icing is to a freshly-baked cake. Many of the best chefs in history have gained their fame from the creation of a magnificent confection, and for good reason. Desserts are at the heart of creativity in cooking, and few people can resist a change to satisfy their sweet tooth. So, there is just no substitute for ending the perfect meal with the perfect dessert.

Deciding which dessert to serve—from all the mouth-watering possibilities—is the hard part, because the preparation is fun and the eating delectable. A crisp, sweet meringue shell with semisweet chocolate syrup may be your chosen finish for a brunch, unless it's fruit-filled crepes with whipped cream, or even custard-filled cream puffs. What a choice! And, for the finale of an elegant dinner—will it be a deliciously sweet and airy souffle, a multi-layered chocolate cake, or sherbert and petits fours? Your family members probably can't help in the decision making, either. One will want homemade cookies and ice cream, while another craves strawberry shortcake, apple pie or cheesecake.

If desserts seem unnecessary, remember that they can be an excellent way to use gelatin, dairy foods, fresh fruits, honey, nuts, eggs and other wholesome foods in the menu plan—one answer to the problem of finicky eaters. Moreover, the preparation of desserts, such as cookies, candies, brownies, and homemade ice cream, can be a memorable family activity. These same foods also make very welcome gifts, any time of the year.

How sweet it is! Beta Sigma Phis believe that any collection of recipes should be chock-full of the most irresistable desserts ever tasted. The ones that follow are family-tested and company-perfect—why not try one tonight?

Peggy's Peanut Patties

3 c. peanuts, shelled
3 c. sugar
¾ c. white Karo syrup
½ tsp. red cake coloring, (opt.)

Place peanuts on cookie sheet; roast in 350-degree oven. Combine sugar, Karo syrup and ½ cup water in heavy 2-quart saucepan. Bring to a rolling boil. Boil until spins a thread. Turn off heat; add cake coloring. Pour peanuts into syrup mixture; stir with wooden spoon until mixture begins to cloud. Pour into buttered muffin tins; let cool. Yield: 20-24 servings.

Peggy House Dorsey
Zeta Theta No. 2393
Henderson, Texas

Never-Fail Peanut Butter Fudge

½ c. milk
2 c. sugar
1 18-oz. jar peanut butter
1 7-oz. jar marshmallow creme

Combine milk and sugar in saucepan; cook until mixture begins to boil. Do not stir. Boil for 3 minutes. Remove from heat. Add peanut butter and marshmallow creme. Place in buttered 9 x 13-inch pan. Chill until firm. Cut into 1-inch squares.

Kandee Graham, W. and M. Chm.
Xi Epilson Phi X4353
Campbelltown, Pennsylvania

Easy Pecan Pralines

1 pkg. butterscotch pudding mix
1 c. sugar
½ c. (firmly packed) brown sugar
½ c. evaporated milk
1 tbsp. margarine
1½ c. pecan halves and pieces

Combine all ingredients except pecans; cook slowly until dissolved. Add pecans; cook until candy reaches soft-ball stage. Remove from heat. Beat until thick. Drop from spoonfuls onto waxed paper. Yield: 20-30 servings.

Janis J. Templeton, Pres.
Pi Rho No. 4593
Austin, Texas

Pecan Pralines

1 c. sugar
1 c. (firmly packed) brown sugar
½ c. evaporated milk

½ stick butter or margarine, softened
1½ c. pecans or small can coconut

Combine sugars and evaporated milk in heavy saucepan; cook over medium heat. Stir in butter and pecans; cook until candy reaches soft-ball stage. Cool for 2 minutes. Beat until thick but glossy. Drop by tablespoonfuls onto waxed paper. Cool thoroughly. Yield: 36 servings.

Cathy Stockton, Rec. Sec.
Xi Alpha Sigma
Metairie, Louisiana

Sicilian Crepes

3 eggs, beaten
¼ tsp. salt
2 c. flour
2 c. milk
¼ c. butter, melted

Combine eggs and salt in medium mixing bowl. Add flour gradually alternately with milk; beat until smooth. Beat in butter. Pour small amount of batter into hot buttered small skillet; rotate skillet to cover bottom evenly. Turn; brown remaining side. Repeat with remaining batter.

Sicilian Filling:
1 lb. ricotta
2 tbsp. light cream
⅓ c. sugar
2 tbsp. orange liqueur
⅓ c. mixed candied fruit, chopped
1 1-oz. square semisweet chocolate, coarsely grated
Confectioners sugar

Blend ricotta and cream in medium mixing bowl. Add sugar and orange liqueur; beat until smooth. Stir in fruit and chocolate. Place small amount of filling into each crepe; roll up as for jelly roll. Refrigerate several hours. Sprinkle with confectioners' sugar. Yield: 12-15 servings.

Ginny Troyan, V.P.
Preceptor Gamma Beta XP1838
Cincinnati, Ohio

Apple-Filled Crepes

⅓ c. flour
¼ tsp. salt
2 tbsp. sugar
3 eggs, beaten
¾ c. milk
1 tsp. butter

Combine flour, salt and sugar in mixing bowl. Add eggs, milk and butter; beat with rotary beater until smooth. Pour ¼ cup batter into lightly buttered hot small skillet; rotate skillet to allow batter to evenly

---

We all travel in the wilderness of this world—and the best that we can find in our travels, is an honest friend.   Delores Strohl

cover bottom of skillet. Heat until bubbly. Turn; brown remaining side. Repeat with remaining batter.

Apple Filling:

> 1 1-lb can sliced apples, drained and chopped
> ¼ c. sugar
> 1 tbsp. flour
> ¼ tsp. cinnamon
> ¼ tsp. nutmeg
> Confectioners sugar

Combine all ingredients except confectioners sugar; spread thin layer on each crepe. Roll up as for jelly roll. Place crepes in buttered baking pan. Bake at 350 degrees for 10 minutes. Sprinkle with confectioners sugar. Yield: 12 servings.

Lorraine Belk, City Coun. Rep.
Xi Eta Tau X5067
Joplin, Missouri

Caramel Dumplings

> 3 c. sugar
> 6 tbsp. butter
> 2 c. flour
> ½ c. milk
> Pinch of salt
> 1 tbsp. baking powder
> 1 tsp. vanilla extract

Heat ½ cup sugar in large heavy skillet over low heat; shake pan as sugar melts. Heat until melted to golden brown syrup. Add 2¼ cups hot water, 2 cups sugar and 3 tablespoons butter. Simmer. Melt 3 tablespoons butter in small saucepan. Stir in flour, milk, ½ cup sugar, salt, baking powder and vanilla; mix well. Drop batter into caramelized liquid, one teaspoon at a time. Bake at 400 degrees until brown. Yield: 6 servings.

Nellontean Jameson, Treas.
Beta Rho No. 6520
Bowling Green, Kentucky

Chocolate-Glazed Eclairs

> 10 tbsp. butter or margarine
> ¼ tsp. salt
> 1 c. all-purpose flour
> 4 eggs
> 1 sm. package chocolate pudding mix
> ¼ tsp. almond extract
> 2 squares semisweet chocolate
> 1 c. confectioners sugar
> 3 tbsp. milk

Combine 8 tablespoons butter, 1 cup water and salt in large saucepan. Cook over high heat until butter melts. Bring to a boil. Reduce heat to low; stir in flour vigorously until mixture forms a ball. Remove from heat; cool for 2 minutes. Beat eggs into mixture until well blended. Drop mixture by ¼ cup onto greased cookie sheet. Shape each mound into ¾ x 5-inch rectangle; round up the edges. Bake at 375 degrees for 40 minutes or until lightly browned. Slit each shell lengthwise on the side; bake an additional 10 minutes. Cool. Prepare pudding according to package directions adding almond extract. Cover to avoid film forming; chill. Combine chocolate and 2 tablespoons butter in small saucepan over low heat; stir constantly until melted and blended. Add confectioners sugar and milk; blend until smooth. Slice ⅓ from top of each shell; fill with pudding. Replace top; spread each shell with chocolate glaze. Yield: 10-12 servings.

Laura June Catoire, Treas.
Xi Beta Epsilon X4162
Harahan, Louisiana

Chocolate Angel Pie

> 3 egg whites
> ¼ tsp. cream of tartar
> Sugar
> 1 3-oz. package chocolate pudding mix
> 2 sq. unsweetened chocolate
> 1 c. heavy cream
> 1 tsp. vanilla extract

Beat egg whites until frothy. Add cream of tartar; beat until soft peaks form. Beat in ¾ cup sugar gradually. Spread in well-buttered 9-inch pie pan. Bake at 275 degrees for 20 minutes. Increase oven temperature to 300 degrees; bake for 40 minutes. Cool. Prepare pudding as directed on package. Remove from heat; stir in chocolate. Stir until melted. Cover pudding to avoid film forming; chill. Combine cream, 1 tablespoon sugar and vanilla; blend until cream is whipped stiff. Spread half the mixture over meringue shell. Layer with pudding; top with remaining whipped cream. Garnish with chocolate curls. Chill 24 hours before serving. Yield: 6-8 servings.

Linda Davis, Corr. Sec.
Gamma Nu No. 4218
Richland, Washington

Daddy's Rice Pudding

> 5 c. milk
> 1 c. rice
> ½ c. sugar
> 1 c. raisins
> 1 tsp. cinnamon

Combine all ingredients in 3-quart double boiler. Bring to a boil. Simmer, stirring occasionally, for about 1 hour or until rice absorbs milk. Yield: 6-8 servings.

Barbara Pohl
Sigma Zeta No. 9525
Bolingbrook, Illinois

"There is no love sincerer than the love of food." George Bernard Shaw Linda Faye Falconer

Best-Ever Apple Pudding

¾ c. butter
2 c. sugar
1 egg, beaten
2 lg. apples, peeled and grated
1 c. sifted flour
1 tsp. soda
1 tsp. cinnamon
Nutmeg
¼ tsp. salt
½ c. chopped nuts
½ c. half and half
1½ tsp. vanilla extract

Cream ¼ cup butter and 1 cup sugar until smoth. Add egg, apples, flour, soda, cinnamon, ½ teaspoon nutmeg, salt and nuts; blend well. Pour into greased 8-inch square baking dish. Bake at 350 degrees for 35 to 45 minutes. Combine ½ cup butter, 1 cup sugar, half and half and dash of nutmeg in saucepan. Cook slowly for 10 to 15 minutes. Stir in vanilla. Pour warm sauce over pudding. Yield: 8 servings.

Evelyn Willis, Treas.
Preceptor Delta Rho XP1535
Longview, Texas

Country-Style Banana Pudding

2 c. milk
½ stick butter or margarine
1½ c. sugar
3 tbsp. flour or cornstarch
3 eggs, separated
¾ tsp. vanilla extract
2 lg. bananas
2 c. vanilla wafers, crushed

Combine milk and butter in medium saucepan over low heat. Combine 1 cup sugar, flour and egg yolks; add to milk mixture. Cook over medium heat, stirring constantly until thickened. Remove from heat; stir in ½ teaspoon vanilla. Pour into 10-inch baking dish. Layer with bananas and vanilla wafers. Beat egg whites until fluffy. Add ½ cup sugar, beating until peaks form. Add ¼ tsp. vanilla; blend well. Bake at 350 degrees until light brown. Yield: 6 servings.

Nadine Powell, Pres.
Gamma Eta No. 7193
Carrollton, Kentucky

Nannie's Cabinet Pudding

24 almond macaroon cookies
1 c. pecans, chopped
1 6-oz. jar red maraschino cherries
6 tbsp. sugar
6 egg yolks
2 tbsp. unflavored gelatin
1 c. white wine
6 egg whites, stiffly beaten
Whipped cream

Crumble almond macaroon cookies into a 13 x 9 x 2-inch glass dish. Sprinkle pecans over cookies. Cut cherries in half; distribute evenly over cookies and pecans. Combine sugar and egg yolks, beating well. Dissolve gelatin in 1 cup cold water. Add gelatin and white wine to egg mixture. Cook over low heat, stirring constantly until mixture is smooth; cool. Fold in egg whites. Pour over cookies; chill. Serve with whipped cream. Yield: 16-20 servings.

Rickie S. Walker
Epsilon Lambda No. 2218
Greenville, Texas

Aggression Cookies

3 c. (firmly packed) light brown sugar
3 c. butter or margarine, softened
6 c. instant oats
1 tbsp. soda
3 c. flour
Sugar

Combine all ingredients in large bowl. Mash it! Knead it! Squeeze it! Just beat the general bejunior out of it! The better you begin to feel, the closer your cookies are to being finished. When you feel just super, your cookies will be just right to bake. Shape into small balls. Place on ungreased cookie sheet. Butter bottom of small glass; dip into sugar. Press each cookie halfway. You may only need to butter bottom of glass once or twice, but sugar each time. Bake at 350 degrees for 10 to 12 minutes. Yield: 15 dozen.

Shirley Quinn, Soc. Comm.
Xi Epsilon Kappa X4597
Ligonier, Indiana

Almond Kringler

2 c. flour
1 c. butter or margarine
1 tbsp. sugar
3 eggs
½ tsp. almond extract

Combine 1 cup flour, ½ cup butter, 1 tablespoon water and sugar as for pie crust. Pat on cookie sheet in 2 long strips, 3 inches wide. Place 1 cup water in saucepan with remaining butter. Bring to a boil. Remove from

---

Happiness is not given it is exchanged. Catherine Bowen

Smooth evenly in 2 well-greased jelly roll pans. Bake in preheated 350-degree oven for 20 minutes. Allow to cool in pans. Sprinkle with light topping of confectioners sugar. Cut into bars. Store in an airtight cookie jar. Yield: 5 dozen.

Photograph for this recipe on page 161.

Cheesecake Cookies

⅓ c. (firmly packed) brown sugar
½ c. chopped walnuts
1 c. flour
⅓ c. butter, melted
¼ c. sugar
1 8-oz. package cream cheese
1 egg, beaten
1 tbsp. lemon juice
2 tbsp. cream or milk
1 tsp. vanilla extract

Combine brown sugar, walnuts and flour in large bowl. Stir in butter; mix until crumbly. Reserve 1 cup of mixture for topping. Place remaining mixture in 8-inch square baking pan; press firmly. Bake at 350 degrees for 12 to 15 minutes. Cream sugar and cream cheese until smooth. Beat in egg, lemon juice, cream and vanilla. Pour into crust. Top with reserved mixture. Bake at 350 degrees for 25 minutes. Cool thoroughly. Cut into 2-inch squares. Cover with plastic wrap. Keep refrigerated. Yield: 16 cookies.

Shirley Kuhlmann, Treas.
Gamma Phi No. 4252
Everett, Washington

heat. Add 1 cup flour; mix until smooth. Beat in eggs, one at a time, beating well after each addition. Add almond extract. Spread on strips. Bake at 350 degrees for 50 minutes or until golden brown. Cool. Prepare your favorite confectioners sugar icing recipe; flavor with almond extract. Spread on baked mixture. Cut into ½ x 3 inch strips. Yield: 12 servings.

Carolyn Ryan, V.P.
Preceptor Beta Iota XP1772
Colorado Springs, Colorado

Apricot-Nut Bars

4 eggs, well beaten
2½ c. (firmly packed) light brown sugar
1 tall can evaporated milk
2 tbsp. lemon juice
2½ c. sifted flour
1½ tsp. soda
1 tsp. cinnamon
½ tsp. salt
1 c. chopped dried apricots
1 c. chopped walnuts
1 c. flaked coconut
Confectioners sugar

Combine eggs, brown sugar, evaporated milk and lemon juice in a large mixing bowl. Sift together flour, soda, cinnamon and salt. Add all at once to egg mixture. Stir just until blended. Fold in apricots, walnuts and coconut. Do not overmix. Divide batter.

Easy Cherry Squares

1½ c. sugar
1 c. margarine
4 eggs
2 c. flour
1 tbsp. lemon juice
1 c. canned cherry pie filling
Confectioners sugar

Cream sugar and margarine until smooth. Add eggs, one at a time, beating well after each addition. Add flour and lemon juice; blend well. Place in greased and floured jelly roll pan. Mark off 24 squares in batter. Put 1 tablespoon cherry filling in each square. Bake at 350 degrees for 45 to 50 minutes. Cool. Sprinkle with confectioners sugar. Cut into 24 squares.

Kathleen S. Mayer, Serv. Chm.
Xi Alpha Omega X4886
Oconomowoc, Wisconsin

The best gift one can ever give or receive is that of friendship. Kathy Webb

German Chocolate Brownies

1 c. margarine
1 8-oz. package German chocolate
2 oz. semisweet chocolate
2 c. sugar
4 eggs, beaten
4 tsp. vanilla extract
½ tsp. salt
½ tsp. baking powder
2 c. chopped nuts

Place margarine, German chocolate and semisweet chocolate into 9 x 12-inch baking pan. Place baking pan in unheated oven. Turn oven setting to 325 degrees to melt chocolates. Combine remaining ingredients; do not stir. Pour ingredients into melted chocolates, stirring only to mix well. Bake at 325 degrees for 45 to 60 minutes or until toothpick inserted into center comes out clean. Cool. Cut into squares. Yield: 12 servings.

Susie Willyard, Pres.
Alpha Gamma Omega No. 8700
San Angelo, Texas

Cinnamon Squares

1 c. butter
1 c. sugar
1 egg, separated
2 c. flour, sifted
2 tsp. cinnamon
1 tsp. vanilla extract
Chopped nuts

Cream butter, sugar and egg yolk until smooth. Add flour and cinnamon. Add vanilla; mix well. Spread on greased 11 x 17-inch cookie sheet. Beat egg white slightly; spread on mixture. Sprinkle with chopped nuts. Bake at 350 degrees for 30 minutes. Cut in squares while warm.

Lynn E. Visbeck, Soc. Chm.
Preceptor Eta Theta XP1597
Livermore, California

Marilyn's Icebox Cookies

Graham crackers
Margarine
1 c. sugar
1 egg
1 egg yolk
Milk
1 c. coconut
1 c. chopped pecans
2 c. confectioners' sugar

Arrange 12 whole graham crackers on cookie sheet, turning all the same directions. Melt 2 sticks margarine

in top of double boiler. Combine sugar, egg and egg yolk and ½ cup milk. Add to margarine; cook for 10 minutes. Remove from heat. Combine coconut, pecans and 1 cup crushed graham crackers. Pour egg mixture into pecan mixture. Cool for 1 minute. Spread over graham crackers. Layer 12 whole graham crackers over mixture in the arrangement as first layer. Melt ¾ cup margarine. Add confectioners' sugar and 4 teaspoons milk. Blend until smooth. Spread on second layer. Chill briefly. Slice along graham cracker creases. Yield: 48 servings.

Marilyn Tatum, Pres.
Xi Gamma Alpha X4652
Lenoir, Tennessee

Jubilee Jumbles

½ c. shortening, softened
1 c. (firmly packed) brown sugar
½ c. sugar
2¾ c. flour
1 c. evaporated milk
1 c. chopped walnuts
2 eggs, beaten
1 tsp. salt
½ tsp. soda
1 tsp. vanilla extract

Combine all ingredients. Mix until moist. Place by teaspoonfuls on greased cookie sheet. Bake at 375 degrees for 10 minutes. Yield: 6 dozen.

Carolyn Betz, Membership Comm.
Theta No. 225
Greeley, Colorado

Lemon Bars

2¼ c. sifted flour
½ c. confectioners' sugar
1 c. butter, softened
4 eggs, beaten
2 c. sugar
⅓ c. lemon juice
½ tsp. baking powder

Combine 2 cups sifted flour and confectioners' sugar; cut in butter. Pat into 13 x 9 x 2-inch baking pan. Bake at 350 degrees for 20 minutes or until brown. Combine eggs, sugar, lemon juice, baking powder and ¼ cup flour; beat well. Pour over crust. Bake at 350 degrees for 25 minutes or until lightly browned. Sprinkle with additional confectioners' sugar. Cut into squares.

Kathy Ellison
Beta Iota No. 7117
McCall, Idaho

What joy to share with good friends some good food and good conversation; it makes for good memories. Mrs. Gwenn Lyons

M and M Party Cookies

1 c. shortening
1 c. (firmly packed) brown sugar
2 tsp. vanilla extract
2 eggs, beaten
2¼ c. all-purpose flour
1 tsp. soda
1 tsp. salt
1½ c. M and M's

Cream shortening and brown sugar in large bowl until smooth. Add vanilla and eggs; beat well. Sift together flour, soda and salt. Add dry ingredients to egg mixture; blend well. Stir in M and M's. Bake at 375 degrees for 10 minutes.

Betty Cornutt, Pres.
Epsilon Theta
Boaz, Alabama

Forget-Me Meringues

2 egg whites
1 tsp. vanilla extract
Pinch of salt
⅛ tsp. cream of tartar
¾ c. sugar
1 6-oz. package chocolate chips
½ c. chopped walnuts

Preheat oven to 350 degrees. Beat egg whites until frothy. Add vanilla, salt and cream of tartar. Beat until soft peaks form. Add sugar gradually. Fold in chocolate chips and walnuts. Drop by teaspoonfuls onto brown paper-lined cookie sheet. Turn off oven. Place cookies in oven for 1 hour and 30 minutes. Yield: 40 cookies.

Mrs. James Wymer
Xi Alpha Omega X4185
Yuma, Arizona

Mother Holston's Energy Drops

½ c. butter, softened
½ c. oil
1 c. (firmly packed) brown sugar
2 eggs, beaten
1 tsp. vanilla extract
1¼ c. flour
1 tsp. soda
½ tsp. salt
½ c. whole wheat flour
2 c. Granola
6-oz. semisweet chocolate chips
1½ c. raisins
¼ c. hulled sunflower seeds

Combine butter, oil and brown sugar in large bowl; beat until fluffy. Add eggs and vanilla, beating well. Sift flour, soda and salt together; add to butter mixture. Add whole wheat flour; stir until just blended. Stir in Granola, chocolate chips, raisins and sunflower seeds. Drop by teaspoonfuls onto greased cookie sheet. Bake at 350 degrees for 12 to 15 minutes. Cool.

Susan Holston, Pres.
Xi Delta Delta X5040
Suffolk, Virginia

Orange Bars

2 11-oz. cans mandarin oranges
2 c. sugar
2 c. flour
2 tsp. soda
2 eggs, beaten
1 tsp. salt
⅓ stick margarine
4 oz. cream cheese
Dash of lemon juice
Confectioners' sugar

Drain mandarin oranges, reserving half the juice. Combine mandarin oranges and reserved juice with sugar, flour, soda, eggs and salt in blender container; blend well. Pour into 8 x 11-inch baking pan. Bake at 350 degrees for 30 minutes. Cool thoroughly. Cream margarine, lemon juice and cream cheese. Add enough confectioners' sugar for easy spreading consistency. Yield: 10-12 servings.

Shirley Slaymaker
Xi Alpha Gamma X3385
Beloit, Wisconsin

Orange Marmalade Bars

Margarine
1 c. sugar
4 egg yolks
1½ tsp. almond extract
2 tsp. baking powder
2¼ c. flour
Orange marmalade
1 c. chopped nuts
1 c. coconut
1 c. powdered sugar

Cream 1 cup margarine, sugar and 1 egg yolk until smooth. Add ½ teaspoon almond extract. Stir in 1 teaspoon baking powder and 2 cups flour. Spread on large greased cookie sheet. Bake at 350 degrees for 15 minutes. Beat 3 egg yolks until thick. Add 1 teaspoon baking powder and ¼ cup flour. Fold in 1 cup marmalade, nuts and coconut. Spoon carefully over pastry. Bake at 350 degrees for 20 minutes. Cool. Combine powdered sugar, 4 tablespoons orange marmalade, 2 tablespoons margarine and 1 teaspoon almond extract; mix well. Spread over filling. Cut into bars. Yield: 25-30 servings.

Rose Ann Hopkins, Rec. Sec.
Xi Mu X355
Muskegon, Michigan

We have the mission of living together in our separate ways, as we love.   Polly A Patton

Rolled Oats Shortbread

1¾ c. all-purpose flour
1 tsp. baking powder
¼ tsp. salt
1 c. margarine, softened
½ c. (firmly packed) brown sugar
¼ c. sugar
½ tsp. vanilla extract
1½ c. rolled oats

Sift flour with baking powder and salt. Cream margarine in mixer bowl; add sugars and vanilla gradually. Add rolled oats, blending carefully. Add flour mixture gradually to make a stiff dough. Turn out onto floured surface; knead lightly. Roll into 9 x 12-inch rectangle. Cut into 1½-inch squares. Place on greased cookie sheet. Bake at 325 degrees for 20 minutes or until golden brown. Yield: 48 cookies.

Carmen Lawrence, Rec. Sec.
Gamma No. 9493
Laval, Quebec, Canada

Peanut Butter Squares

½ lb. butter or margarine
1 c. peanut butter
1¾ c. graham cracker crumbs
1 lb. confectioners' sugar
1 c. chocolate chips

Combine butter and peanut butter in saucepan. Cook, stirring until well blended. Cool to lukewarm. Stir in crumbs and confectioners' sugar. Press into 13 x 19-inch baking pan. Melt chocolate chips in double boiler. Spread over crumb mixture. Cool. Cut into squares. Yield: 24 servings.

Sally Bilsky
Xi Sigma X447
Anderson, Indiana

Peanut Butter-Oatmeal Cookies

2 c. sugar
¼ c. cocoa
½ c. milk
1 stick margarine, softened
½ c. crunchy peanut butter
2 tsp. vanilla extract
3 c. 3-minute oatmeal

Combine sugar, cocoa, milk and margarine in saucepan. Bring to a boil. Cool slightly. Add remaining ingredients; blend well. Drop by spoonfuls onto waxed paper. Yield: 24 cookies.

Janet Marie Epley, Serv. Com.
Beta Beta No. 3600
Eureka Springs, Arkansas

Pecan Curls

½ c. sifted all-purpose flour
¼ tsp. soda
1 c. (firmly-packed) brown sugar
¾ c. butter or margarine, softened
2 eggs
1 tsp. vanilla extract
¾ c. finely-chopped pecans
¾ c. rolled oats
2 tbsp. confectioners' sugar

Sift flour and soda into mixing bowl. Add brown sugar, butter, eggs and vanilla. Beat until smooth, about 2 minutes. Blend in pecans and oats. Drop by teaspoonfuls onto well-greased cookie sheets, allowing about 3 inches between cookies. Bake in preheated 350-degree oven for 8 to 10 minutes or until cookies are brown around edges. Cool about 1 minute. Remove cookies carefully from cookie sheets with wide spatula. Turn upside down over rolling pin or several straight-sided glasses, wrapped in paper towels or napkins. Allow to cool completely before removing from rolling pin. Sift confectioners' sugar into small flat bowl. Dip edge of each cooled cookie carefully into sugar. Yield: 4 dozen.

Photograph for this recipe on page 165.

Banana Split Dessert

1 stick butter, melted
2 c. graham cracker crumbs
2 eggs
2 sticks butter, softened
2 c. confectioners' sugar
3 or 4 sliced bananas
1 can crushed pineapple, drained
1 lg. carton Cool Whip
¾ c. (or more) chopped pecans
½ c. chopped cherries

Combine melted butter and graham cracker crumbs. Pat into 13 × 9 × 2 inch pan. Set aside. Combine eggs, 2 sticks butter, confectioners' sugar; beat at least 15 minutes. Spread over crust. Layer with bananas, pineapple and Cool Whip in order listed. Sprinkle with pecans and cherries. Refrigerate overnight. Cut into squares to serve. Yield: 12 servings.

Debbie Meins
Alpha Epsilon No. 8613
Stuttgart, Arkansas
Berta Starr
Preceptor Alpha Tau XP1099
Lakeland, Florida

Colleen's Blueberry Treat

2 c. packaged graham cracker crumbs
½ c. softened butter

A friend is a fellow who knows all about you, but still likes you. Betsy Porter

1 c. confectioners' sugar
2 eggs, beaten
1 1-lb. 5-oz. can blueberry pie filling
1 c. chopped pecans
1 c. heavy cream, whipped and sweetened

Spread 1½ cups graham cracker crumbs evenly in well-buttered 9 × 9-inch pan. Beat butter until fluffy in small bowl of electric mixer. Add sugar gradually; beat until light and fluffy. Add eggs; blend well. Pour mixture over crumb layer. Spread pie filling over butter mixture. Sprinkle pecans evenly over pie filling. Spread whipped cream evenly over pecans. Top with remaining ½ cup graham cracker crumbs; cover. Chill overnight. Cut into squares to serve. Yield: 9 servings.

Colleen B. Nelson, Soc. Chm.
Beta Beta No. 6760
Cumberland, Maryland

Cherry Dessert

2 3-oz. packages black cherry flavored gelatin
1 No. 2 can crushed pineapple
1 1-lb. 5-oz. can cherry pie filling
1 8-oz. package cream cheese, softened
1 c. sour cream
1 tsp. vanilla extract
½ c. sugar
½ c. chopped pecans

Dissolve gelatin in 2 cups boiling water. Pour into 9 × 13-inch pan. Let set until firm. Combine cream cheese, sour cream, vanilla, sugar and chopped pecans. Spread over gelatin. Chill. Yield: 12 servings.

Karen B. Smith, W. and M. Chm.
Kappa Theta No. 9586
Osborne, Kansas

Bon Bon Delight

1 c. mandarin oranges, drained
2 c. fruit cocktail, drained
1 c. pineapple chunks, drained
1 c. sliced strawberries
2 bananas, sliced
1 c. coconut
1 c. chopped pecans
1 lg. carton Cool Whip
1 lg. carton cottage cheese
1 lg. package strawberry-flavored gelatin

Combine first 5 ingredients in large serving bowl. Fold in coconut and pecans. Stir in Cool Whip and cottage cheese; blend well. Pour dry gelatin directly into mixture; blend. Refrigerate until serving time. Yield: 25-30 servings.

Bonnie M. Hatfield, Yearbook Comm.
Preceptor Beta Theta XP1312
Blue Springs, Missouri

One pound of learning requires ten pounds of common sense to apply it. Mrs. Ann M. Clapper

Fudge Meltaways

¾ c. butter or margarine
3 squares unsweetened chocolate
¼ c. sugar
2 tsp. vanilla extract
1 egg, beaten
2 c. graham cracker crumbs
1 c. coconut
½ c. chopped nuts
1 tbsp. milk
2 c. sifted confectioners' sugar

Melt ½ cup butter and 1 square chocolate in saucepan. Blend sugar, 1 teaspoon vanilla, egg, graham cracker crumbs, coconut and nuts. Fold into chocolate mixture; mix well. Press into 11 × 7-inch or 9 × 9-inch ungreased baking dish. Combine ¼ cup butter, milk, confectioners' sugar and 1 teaspoon vanilla. Spread over crumb mixture; chill. Melt 2 squares chocolate; spread evenly over chilled filling. Chill for 2 minutes. Cut into squares before chocolate hardens: Yield: 20-24 servings.

Mrs. Judie Lopez
Delta Delta No. 2593
Buffalo, New York

Cranberry Fluff Supreme

2 c. chopped fresh cranberries
3 c. miniature marshmallows
1 c. sugar
2 c. diced unpared apples
1 c. seedless green grapes
½ c. English walnuts or pecans
¼ tsp. salt
1 c. whipping cream, whipped

Combine cranberries, marshmallows and sugar. Chill, covered, overnight. Add apples, grapes, walnuts and salt. Fold in whipped cream. Chill until serving time. Yield: 8-10 servings.

Patricia S. Lehman, Pres.
Zeta Lambda No. 4500
Elwood, Indiana

English Trifle

1 16-oz. day-old angel food cake
2 tbsp. Sherry
1 10-oz. jar raspberry preserves
2 3-oz. packages raspberry Jell-O
1 4-oz. custard pudding mix
Whipped cream to taste
½ c. chopped nuts
10 to 12 maraschino cherries

Slice cake; sprinkle with Sherry. Spread with preserves. Arrange in 3-quart glass dish. Prepare Jell-O according to package directions. Cool slightly. Pour over cake. Chill until set. Prepare pudding mix according to package directions. Pour over trifle. Chill until set. Cover with whipped cream. Sprinkle on nuts. Chill for several hours. Garnish with cherries.

Pamela M. Langston, Bi-City Council President
Xi Zeta Omicron
Rock Island, Illinois

Green Mint Desserts

1 pkg. miniature marshmallows
1 c. milk
2 c. whipping cream
1 to 2 drops of peppermint extract
Green food coloring
1 box chocolate wafers, crushed

Combine marshmallows and milk in saucepan. Stir until melted; set aside. Whip cream; add peppermint extract and green food coloring: Add to marshmallow mixture. Cover 9 × 12-inch pan with half the cookie crumbs. Pour peppermint mixture over crumbs. Top with remaining crumbs. Chill at least 1 hour or until serving time. Yield: 10-12 servings.

Barbara Kelley, Prog. and Yearbook Com.
XI Alpha Alpha
Bakersfield, California

Prune Souffle

1½ c. pitted stewed prunes
½ c. sugar
4 egg whites

Cut prunes into small pieces. Sprinkle with ¼ cup sugar. Beat egg whites until stiff; fold in remaining sugar. Blend in prunes. Pour into ungreased baking dish. Bake at 350 degrees for 25 minutes. Chill. Serve with whipped cream or soft custard, if desired. Yield: 6 servings.

Mrs. Garlon Mobley Webb
Omicron Theta No. 8846
Macclenny, Florida

Russian Cream

¾ c. sugar
1 env. unflavored gelatin
1 c. sour cream
1½ tsp. vanilla extract
1 c. thawed Cool Whip
Strawberries or other fruit

Combine sugar and gelatin in saucepan; add 1½ cups water. Stir over low heat to dissolve sugar and gelatin. Remove from heat. Stir in sour cream and vanilla. Chill until slightly thickened. Fold in Cool Whip. Chill in

1-quart mold for 3 hours. Serve garnished with strawberries. Yield: 10-12 servings.

Cindy Lowe
Theta Iota
Pineville, Louisiana

Chocolate-Peanut Souffle

4 squares semisweet chocolate
8 tbsp. sugar
1 env. unflavored gelatin
¼ tsp. salt
1 c. milk
5 eggs, separated
¼ c. rum
1 tsp. vanilla extract
¼ c. coarsely chopped peanuts
2 c. heavy cream
Finely chopped peanuts

Melt chocolate over very low heat. Remove from heat. Stir in 6 tablespoons sugar, gelatin and salt. Add milk gradually stirring to keep mixture smooth. Beat egg yolks slightly. Add small amount of hot mixture to egg yolks; stir well. Add to chocolate mixture. Cook over low heat, stirring constantly, until mixture begins to boil. Remove from heat. Stir in rum, vanilla and coarsely chopped peanuts. Chill until slightly thick-ened, stirring occasionally. Beat egg whites until stiff but not dry. Whip 1 cup heavy cream until stiff. Fold each into chocolate mixture carefully. Pour into 3-cup souffle dish with a 2-inch aluminum foil collar around top of dish. Chill until firm. Whip remaining 1 cup cream with remaining 2 tablespoons sugar. Garnish souffle with whipped cream. Sprinkle on finely chopped peanuts. Yield: 6-8 servings.

Photograph for this recipe on page 167.

Strawberry Cake Dessert

1 lg. package strawberry Jell-O
1 package frozen strawberries
1 loaf angel food cake
1 lg. package vanilla pudding mix
1 carton Cool Whip

Dissolve Jell-O in 2 cups hot water. Add frozen strawberries. Pour ½ of the Jell-O mixture into pan. Let stand until partially congealed. Cut angel food cake into squares. Place squares over Jell-O. Prepare pudding according to package directions. Pour pudding over cake. Cover with remaining Jell-O mixture. Top with Cool Whip. Chill until serving time. Cut into squares. Yield: 12 servings.

Karen Ruskin, City Coun. Pres.
Alpha No. 352
Wheeling, West Virginia

Who practices hospitality entertains God himself. Linda Jo Moser

Apple Crisp

1 c. (firmly packed) brown sugar
1 c. flour
¼ tsp. cinnamon
⅛ tsp. nutmeg
½ cup butter or margarine, melted
2½ c. sliced apples
Whipped Cream

Combine sugar, flour, cinnamon and nutmeg; add butter. Place apples in greased 8 × 8-inch pan. Pour sugar mixture over apples. Bake at 350 degrees for 30 minutes. Cover top with whipped cream. Yield: 4-6 servings.

Nancy Gillis
Xi Beta Tau
Aurora, Colorado

Apple Crunch

2 No. 3-cans pie-sliced apples
1 c. chopped pecans
1 butter cake mix
1 c. (lightly packed) light brown sugar
½ tsp. cinnamon
1 stick butter, melted
Vanilla ice cream

Pour apples into 13 × 9 × 2-inch baking pans. Sprinkle with pecans. Combine cake mix, brown sugar and cinnamon in large bowl. Mix ingredients thoroughly with hands; break up large lumps. Sprinkle mixture evenly over apples and pecans. Smooth dry mixture to corners; pat lightly to seal. Drizzle butter over dry mixture; moisten evenly. Bake at 375 degrees for 45 minutes or until browned. Serve with vanilla ice cream.

Claudette Hill Laurie, V.P.
Alpha Alpha No. 9705
Baton Rouge, Louisiana

Banana Split

2 c. graham cracker crumbs
Margarine
2 c. confectioners' sugar
2 eggs, beaten
1 tsp. vanilla extract
3 to 5 bananas
1 lg. can crushed pineapple
1 lg. carton Cool Whip
Chopped cherries

Place crumbs in 9 × 13-inch baking pan. Add ½ cup melted margarine; mix well. Press on bottom only to form crust. Combine ½ pound softened margarine, confectioners' sugar, eggs and vanilla; beat well. Spread over crust. Layer with bananas, pineapple and

Cool Whip. Garnish with cherries. Yield: 12-14 servings.

Mary Addington
Xi Phi X3695
Gillette, Wyoming

Cherry Pizza

1 recipe for crust pie
1½ 8-oz. packages cream cheese, softened
½ c. sugar
½ c. chopped pecans
1 tsp. vanilla extract
2 eggs, beaten
1 can cherry pie filling
1 carton Cool Whip

Roll pie crust to cover pizza pan. Combine next 5 ingredients; mix well. Pour cream cheese mixture on crust; spread evenly. Bake at 350 degrees for 10 minutes. Cool. Cover with cherry pie filling. Top with Cool Whip. Refrigerate for 2 hours or until firm. Yield: 8-10 servings.

Georgeann Holland
Xi Theta Zeta X2107
San Marcos, California

Fruit Pizza

1 18-oz. package refrigerator sugar dough
1 8-oz. package cream cheese, softened
⅓ c. sugar
½ tsp. vanilla extract
Strawberries
2 bananas
1 sm. can mandarin oranges, drained
1 sm. can pineapple chunks, drained
½ c. peach preserves

Slice cookie dough as for cookies; arrange on pizza pan. Pat dough into crust with ridge around edge. Bake at 350 degrees for 10 to 12 minutes or until golden brown. Combine cream cheese, sugar and vanilla; beat until fluffy. Spread on crust. Chill. Arrange fruit in decorative patterns over cream cheese mixture. Combine preserves and 1 tablespoon water in saucepan. Heat only to form glaze. Do not boil. Drizzle warm mixture over fruit. Chill. Yield: 10-12 servings.

Carol H. Bingle, V.P.
Xi Delta Psi X4591
St. Paul, Kansas

Frosty Fruit Soup

1 stick cinnamon
2½ c. sugar
2 16-oz. cans pitted sour cherries

Those who bring sunshine into the lives of others cannot keep it from themselves. Linda Jo Moser

2 tbsp. cornstarch
2 c. plain yogurt
½ c. dry white wine
Sour cream

Combine cinnamon stick, 3 cups water and sugar in a saucepan. Bring to a boil. Simmer for 15 minutes. Drain cherries; reserve liquid. Combine cornstarch and cherry liquid; stir to dissolve. Remove cinnamon stick from syrup. Add cherry liquid to syrup; remove from heat. Stir with a wire whisk. Return to heat; stir over low heat for 5 minutes or until thickened. Remove from heat. Add yogurt, wine and cherries. Stir until yogurt dissolves. Pour into large stem glasses or bowl. Refrigerate until chilled. Serve garnished with sour cream. Yield: 8 servings.

Carolyn Zaza
Beta Nu
Waterbury, Connecticut

Fruits Glaces

5 lb. watermelon
½ lg. honeydew melon
1 pt. fresh strawberries
1 pt. fresh blueberries
½ lb. grapes
1 grapefruit, peeled and sectioned
2 oranges, peeled and sectioned
1 peach, peeled and sliced
1 apple, cored and thinly sliced
1 banana, sliced
1 c. Sauterne

Scoop balls from melons with melon scoop. Combine next 7 ingredients; add melon balls. Add banana slices. Stir in Sauterne, coating fruit. Refrigerate for 2 hours.

Eileen M Blanchet
Laureate Epsilon PL382
Kamloops, British Columbia, Canada

Omelette Cake Supreme

2 qt. strawberries
Sugar
4 lg. eggs, separated
⅓ c. flour
1 pt. whipped cream

Cut strawberries, cover with sugar. Beat egg whites until stiff but not dry. Add 3 tablespoons sugar, one tablespoon at a time, beating after each addition. Beat egg yolks with 3 tablespoons sugar until thick and light in color. Fold egg whites into egg yolks; blend gently. Fold in flour gradually; blend gently. Pour ½ of the mixture into slightly greased electric skillet; spread evenly. Cook at 250 degrees for 15 to 20 minutes or until cake tests done. Cool on towel. Repeat process

with remaining mixture. Spread ½ of the whipped cream over one layer. Place ½ of the strawberries on whipped cream. Fold in half. Repeat with remaining cake. Wrap in plastic wrap; chill. Decorate with additional whipped cream and strawberries, if desired. Yield: 4 servings.

Terri Bourland, Pres.
Preceptor Eta Omega XP1716
Oakland, California

Peach Dessert

1 29-oz. can sliced peach sauce and juice
1 pkg. butter brickle cake mix
1 stick butter or margarine, melted
1 c. chopped nuts

Pour peach sauce and juice into 9 × 13-inch cake pan. Sprinkle cake mix over peach sauce; do not mix. Drizzle butter over cake mix. Cover with nuts. Bake at 350 degrees for 45 minutes. Serve with ice cream or whipped cream, if desired. Yield: 12-15 servings.

Blanche Geier
Preceptor Zeta XP508
Great Falls, Montana

Raspberry Dessert

1¼ c. graham crackers, crushed
¼ c. butter
¼ c. chopped nuts
50 lg. marshmallows
1 c. milk
2 c. heavy cream, whipped or 1 lg. Cool Whip,
    thawed
½ c. sugar
1 tsp. lemon juice
2 10-oz. cans frozen raspberries
4 tbsp. cornstarch

Combine graham cracker crumbs, butter and nuts. Press into 12 × 9 × 2-inch pan. Melt marshmallows in milk over low heat. Cool. Fold whipped cream into cooled marshmallow mixture. Pour marshmallow mixture into graham cracker crust. Combine 1 cup water, sugar, lemon juice and raspberries in saucepan; heat through. Dissolve cornstarch in ¼ cup cold water. Stir cornstarch mixture into raspberry mixture. Cook until thickened. Cool. Spread cooled raspberry mixture over marshmallow mixture. Refrigerate until firm.

Leslie L. Province
Alpha Chi
Orofino, Idaho

The most valuable antiques are old friends.   Ruth E Strong

Pineapple Surprise

1 pineapple
½ pt. whipping cream, whipped
Sugar
1 1-oz. bottle Kirsch
Fresh fruit salad

Remove top of pineapple. Scoop out pulp. Set pineapple shell and top aside. Press pulp through sieve, reserving liquid. Add sugar to taste to whipped cream. Add pulp and Kirsch. Place whipped cream mixture inside pineapple shell. Place top on pineapple. Arrange your favorite fruit salad in salad bowl. Cover with reserved pineapple liquid. Remove top of pineapple when serving. Spoon whipped cream mixture over fruit salad. Yield: 6-8 servings.

Doreen Hume
Honorary Life Member
Willowdale, Ontario, Canada

Rhubarb Pudding Cake

2 c. sugar
3 tbsp. butter, softened
½ c. milk
2 tsp. baking powder
1 egg
1 c. flour
1 tsp. vanilla extract
Pinch of salt
2 c. diced rhubarb

Combine 1 cup sugar, 2 tablespoons butter, milk, baking powder, egg, flour, vanilla and salt; mix well. Pour into greased 9 × 13-inch baking dish. Pour rhubarb over batter. Sprinkle with 1 cup sugar and 1 tablespoon butter. Cover with 2 cups boiling water. Bake 350 degrees until cake tests done. Yield: 12-15 servings.

Ruth M. Gillan, Pres.
Gamma Psi No. 9203
Central City, Nebraska

Frozen Apricot Delight

2 env. unflavored gelatin
1 env. nonfat milk powder
½ c. honey
Diced canned apricots
½ tsp. peppermint extract

Dissolve gelatin in ½ cup cold water. Add 1 cup hot water. Stir until clear; cool. Combine milk powder and 2 cups cold water in serving bowl. Beat until peaks form. Add honey in a fine stream, beating vigorously. Add gelatin. Fold in apricots and peppermint extract. Place in freezer for 40 minutes. Remove from freezer. Stir for 5 minutes or until slushy. Frozen strawberries

or peaches may be substituted for apricots. Yield: 6 servings.

Florence B. Seibert
International Honorary Mem.
Preceptor Eta
St. Petersburg, Florida

Apricot Spumoni

2½ c. crushed vanilla wafers
½ c. butter, melted
1 tbsp. almond extract
Vanilla ice cream
Apricot preserves
½ c. slivered almonds, toasted

Combine vanilla wafers, butter and almond extract. Place ½ of the crumb mixture in casserole. Cover with a layer of ice cream. Spread with preserves. Sprinkle with almonds. Cover with a layer of ice cream and remaining crumb mixture. Place, covered, in freezer. Freeze until firm. Slice as needed. Yield: 12 servings.

Mary Finley, W. and M. Chm.
Preceptor Xi XP491
Farmington, New Mexico

Bananas Flambe

½ c. butter
⅔ c. (firmly packed) brown sugar
1 tsp. cinnamon
4 bananas, sliced
⅓ c. rum
Vanilla ice cream

Combine butter, brown sugar and cinnamon in saucepan. Cook until golden brown. Stir bananas into brown sugar mixture until heated. Ignite rum; add flaming to bananas. Serve immediately over ice cream. Yield: 6 servings.

Carla Beethe
Delta Nu No. 10016
Beatrice, Nebraska

Banana Foster

2 tbsp. butter
1 banana
2 tbsp. sugar
2 tbsp. Cognac or Brandy
2 scoops vanilla ice cream

Melt butter in small skillet over medium heat. Cut banana into ⅜-inch slices; add to butter. Sprinkle with sugar, stirring until sugar has caramelized slightly and slices are golden. Add Cognac; let warm for 1 to 2

A woman can fail many times, but she isn't a failure until she begins to blame somebody else.   N Erryle George minutes. Ignite; stir until flame subsides. Spoon over ice cream. Serve immediately. Yield: 2 servings.

Beverly A. Luebke
Xi Alpha Upsilon X4438
Wisconsin Rapids, Wisconsin

Chocolate Frozen Dessert

1 lb. Oreo cookies, crushed
2 sticks margarine
½ gal. butter brickle or peppermint ice cream, softened
⅔ c. semisweet chocolate chips
1½ c. evaporated milk
2 c. confectioners' sugar
1 tsp. vanilla extract

Blend cookies with 1 stick melted margarine. Press in 9 x 13-inch glass pan. Chill for 1 hour. Thaw ice cream to spreadable consistency. Cover cookies with ice cream. Melt chocolate chips and 1 stick margarine. Add evaporated milk and sugar. Bring to a boil. Cook, stirring constantly, for 6 minutes. Remove from heat; add vanilla. Pour hot mixture over ice cream; freeze. Yield: 12-15 servings.

Chari Sowers, Pres.
Xi Epsilon Omicron X4943
Valley Center, Kansas

Chocolate Mousse

1 12-oz. package chocolate chips
8 eggs, separated
½ tsp. almond extract

Place chocolate chips in blender container; grind. Combine ¾ cup boiling water, egg yolks and almond extract. Add to chocolate chips in blender container; mix well. Pour into serving bowl. Beat egg whites until stiff. Fold into chocolate mixture. Place waxed paper on surface to prevent film formation. Freeze. Remove waxed paper before serving. Yield: 5 servings.

Carol Cameron, Soc. Com.
Xi Beta Pi X909
Eureka, Canada

Santa's Chocolate Pie

1 6-oz. package semisweet chocolate pieces
1 tbsp. instant coffee
Pinch of salt
2 egg yolks, beaten
1 c. marshmallow creme
1 tsp. vanilla extract
⅛ tsp. almond extract
2 egg whites, stiffly beaten

1 c. heavy cream, whipped
1 9-in. baked pastry shell

Combine chocolate pieces, ¼ cup water, coffee and salt in top of double boiler. Heat over hot water until chocolate melts, stirring occasionally. Pour small amount of chocolate mixture into egg yolks; add egg mixture to chocolate mixture. Cook for 3 minutes, stirring constantly. Remove from heat. Stir in marshmallow creme, vanilla and almond extract. Chill. Fold in egg whites and whipped cream. Pour into pastry shell. Freeze for 10 hours or overnight. Garnish with candy canes or additional whipped cream. Yield: 6 servings.

Marvella Plapp, Sec.
Preceptor Beta Iota XP1687
Leawood, Kansas

Banana Ice Cream

6 eggs, beaten
1 14-oz. can sweetened condensed milk
1½ c. sugar
⅛ tsp. salt
2 tbsp. vanilla extract
4 c. half and half
3 ripe bananas, chopped
Milk

Combine eggs, condensed milk, sugar, salt, vanilla, half and half and bananas in large mixer bowl, in order listed, beating well after each addition. Pour into freezer container. Add enough milk to fill according to freezer instructions. Freeze according to freezer directions. Yield: 5 quarts.

Charlene Jones, V.P.
Rho Chi No. 4945
Pomona, California

Brooks Threes Ice Cream

Juice of 3 oranges
Juice of 3 lemons
3 bananas, mashed
3 c. sugar
3 c. half and half
3 c. milk

Combine all ingredients in freezer container; blend well. Refrigerate overnight. Freeze according to freezer directions. Yield: 1 gallon.

Gayle W. Brooks, Pres.
Xi Kappa Nu X5169
Brooksville, Florida

When you help someone up a hill, you're that much nearer the top yourself. Linda Thorstenson

Homemade Chocolate Ice Cream

3 13-oz. cans evaporated milk
4 c. sugar
1 lg. box chocolate instant pudding mix
4 tbsp. vanilla extract
6 c. milk
1 can Hershey's chocolate syrup

Pour evaporated milk into freezer container. Add sugar and pudding mix; stir until blended. Add vanilla, milk and chocolate syrup. Fill container to about 2 inches from top. Freezing will expand contents. Freeze according to freezer directions. Yield: 6 quarts.

Dorothy M. Lamey, W. and M. Chm.
Xi Alpha Pi X1116
Newburgh, Indiana

Mint Crunch Dessert

1 c. all-purpose flour
¼ c. rolled oats
¼ c. (firmly packed) brown sugar
½ c. butter
½ c. walnuts or pecans, chopped
1 12-oz. jar chocolate fudge ice cream topping
1 qt. mint ice cream, softened

Combine flour, oats and brown sugar; cut in butter until mixture resembles coarse crumbs. Stir in walnuts. Press mixture into 9 x 13-inch baking pan. Bake at 400 degrees for 12 minutes. Stir while still warm to crumble; cool. Spread half the crumbs in a 9 x 9-inch baking pan or 9-inch pie pan. Spoon ice cream carefully into pan. Drizzle with half the fudge topping; sprinkle with remaining crumbs. Freeze. Yield: 9 servings.

Helen Kolka, Serv. Com.
Beta Eta No. 3397
Merrill, Wisconsin

Peachy-Berry Cooler

1 c. milk
1 c. sour cream
¼ c. (firmly packed) brown sugar
2 fresh peaches, peeled and halved
Strawberries, hulled

Combine first 3 ingredients in blender container; blend until smooth. Add peaches and strawberries. Blend for 1 or 2 seconds; fruit should be chunky. Pour into 4 glasses. Freeze until slushy, about 2 hours. Garnish with additional strawberries and fresh peach slices, if desired. Yield: 4 servings.

Photograph for this recipe on page 172.

Peach-Grape Cooler

1 pt. vanilla ice cream
1 c. buttermilk
½ c. grape juice
2 fresh peaches, peeled and halved

Combine first 3 ingredients in blender container; blend until smooth. Add peaches. Blend for 1 or 2 seconds; peaches should be chunky. Pour into 3 glasses. Freeze until slushy, about 2 hours. Garnish with clusters of seedless grapes or fresh peach slices, if desired. Yield: 3 servings.

Photograph for this recipe on page 172.

Peach-Vanilla Cooler

1 8-oz. carton yogurt
1 c. vanilla ice cream
1 tsp. vanilla extract
3 tbsp. honey
3 fresh peaches, peeled and halved

Combine first 4 ingredients in blender container; blend until smooth. Add peaches. Blend for 1 or 2 seconds; peaches should be chunky. Pour into 3 glasses. Freeze until slushy, about 2 hours. Garnish with additional dollop of yogurt and fresh peach slices, if desired. Yield: 3 servings.

Photograph for this recipe on page 172.

French Proverb: To speak kindly does not hurt the tongue. Kitty Lawson

Tangy Peach Cooler

1 6-oz. can lemonade concentrate, thawed
1 pt. vanilla ice cream
1 tsp. crushed fresh mint or ¼ tsp. dried mint
4 drops of yellow food coloring
2 fresh peaches, peeled and halved

Combine first 4 ingredients in blender container. Blend until smooth. Add peach halves. Blend again for 1 or 2 seconds; peaches should remain in small chunks. Pour into 3 large glasses. Freeze for about 2 hours or until slushy. Garnish with mint sprigs, if desired. Yield: 3 servings.

Photograph for this recipe on page 172.

Pineapple Flambé

1 pineapple
½ c. sugar
4 tbsp. dark rum
1 qt. vanilla ice cream

Cut top from pineapple; reserve. Scoop out pineapple; do not puncture shell. Dice pineapple pulp. Combine sugar and 1 tablespoon rum with diced pineapple. Return to pineapple shell. Cover with foil. Place in baking pan. Bake for 30 minutes in 350 degree oven. Place pineapple on attractive serving dish. Replace top of pineapple. Pour 3 tablespoons rum over pineapple. Ignite. Serve flaming with ice cream.

Clarinda Mary Dawc, Pres.
Xi Iota X5038
Conception Bay, Newfoundland, Canada

Frozen Raspberry Pie

1½ c. flour
Sugar
1 tsp. salt
2 tbsp. milk
½ c. salad oil
2 egg whites
1 10-oz. package frozen raspberries, thawed
1 tbsp. lemon juice
1 c. whipping cream

Combine flour, 1½ teaspoons sugar and salt in bowl. Add milk and oil; mix to form pastry. Press into large pie pan. Bake at 425 degrees for 15 minutes. Cool. Beat egg whites until fluffy. Add raspberries, lemon juice and 1 cup sugar. Beat 15 minutes at high speed. Whip cream until stiff; fold into raspberry mixture. Place in pie shell; freeze. Yield: 8 servings.

Vicki Hendrickson, Sec.
Alpha Mu No. 7031
Hastings, Nevada

Frosty Strawberry Squares

1 c. flour
¼ c. (firmly packed) brown sugar
½ c. chopped walnuts
½ c. butter or margarine, melted
2 egg whites
¾ c. sugar
2 c. sliced strawberries
2 tbsp. lemon juice
1 c. whipping cream, whipped

Combine flour, brown sugar, walnuts and butter; stir until blended. Spread evenly in 13 x 9 x 2-inch baking pan. Bake at 350 degrees for 20 minutes, stirring occasionally. Remove from oven; cool. Sprinkle ⅔ of the baked mixture in bottom of same pan; reserve remaining mixture. Combine egg whites, sugar, strawberries and lemon juice in large mixer bowl. Beat on Low for 2 minutes or until mixture begins to thicken. Beat on High for 10 to 12 minutes or until stiff peaks form. Fold in whipped cream; spoon over mixture. Top with reserved crumbs. Freeze overnight. Cut in squares. Garnish with additional fresh strawberries. Yield: 12-15 servings.

Jane Pierce, Pres.
Eta Delta No. 6201
Topeka, Kansas

Aunt Norma's Cheesecake

1⅓ c. graham cracker crumbs
⅓ c. melted butter
Sugar
12 oz. cream cheese, softened
2 eggs
2 tsp. vanilla extract
1 c. sour cream

Combine cracker crumbs, butter and 3 tablespoons sugar; mix well, using a fork. Press into 9-inch pie plate. Combine cream cheese, eggs, ¾ cup sugar and 1 teaspoon vanilla in mixer bowl. Beat until smooth. Pour filling mixture into crumb crust. Bake at 350 degrees for 22 minutes. Remove from oven; cool. Combine sour cream, 3 tablespoons sugar and 1 teaspoon vanilla; mix well. Spread over cake. Bake at 350 degrees for 10 minutes. Chill to serve. May be garnished with fruit topping. Yield: 8-10 servings.

Judith Neher, Scrapbook Chm.
Eta Delta No. 5687
Homestead, Florida

A handful of patience is worth more than a bushel of brains.   Dorothy C Wiederich

Chocolate Swirl Cheesecake

1 6-oz. package semisweet morsels
Sugar
1½ c. graham cracker crumbs
¼ c. melted butter
2 8-oz. packages cream cheese, softened
¾ c. sour cream
4 eggs
1 tsp. vanilla extract

Combine chocolate chips and ½ cup sugar in double boiler over hot water. Heat until smooth. Set aside. Combine graham cracker crumbs, 2 tablespoons sugar and melted butter in small bowl; mix well. Pat into 9-inch springform pan covering bottom and 1½ inches up the side. Set aside. Beat cream cheese until light and creamy in large bowl. Beat in ¾ cup sugar gradually. Add sour cream and vanilla; mix well. Add eggs, one at a time, beating well after each addition. Divide batter in half. Add chocolate mixture to half the batter; mix well. Pour chocolate batter over graham cracker crust. Cover with remaining batter. Stir to marbleize. Bake at 325 degrees for 50 minutes. Refrigerate. Yield: 10 servings.

Vicki Boucher
Beta Chi No. 5011
Albuquerque, New Mexico

Creamy Cheesecake

1 6-oz. package pineapple Jell-O
½ c. sugar
1 8-oz. package cream cheese
½ box graham crackers, crushed
½ c. butter or margarine, softened
½ pt. whipping cream, whipped
½ can crushed pineapple, drained
10 maraschino cherries

Dissolve Jell-O in ½ cup boiling water; let stand. Cream sugar and cream cheese until smooth. Combine graham cracker crumbs with butter. Pat ½ of the mixture in 9 x 9-inch pan. Combine whipped cream and cream cheese mixture. Add Jell-O. Fold in pineapple and cherries. Refrigerate for 2 hours. Top with remaining crumbs. Yield: 8 servings.

Rose Thrower, W. and M. Chm.
Xi Lambda X3625
Thompson, Manitoba, Canada

Lemon Cheesecake

1¾ c. graham crackers, crushed
Sugar
6 tbsp. butter, melted
3 8-oz. packages cream cheese, softened
3 eggs

Lemon juice
2 tsp. vanilla extract
1 tsp. grated lemon rind
1 pt. sour cream
1 lemon
Cornstarch

Combine graham cracker crumbs, ¼ cup sugar and butter. Press onto sides and bottom of lightly greased 10-inch springform pan. Bake at 350 degrees for 5 minutes. Cool. Blend cream cheese until smooth. Add eggs, one at a time, beating after each addition. Add 1⅓ cups sugar, 3 tablespoons lemon juice and 1 teaspoon vanilla gradually; beat well. Stir in lemon rind. Pour into cooled crust. Bake at 350 degrees for 35 minutes. Combine sour cream, 3 tablespoons sugar and 1 teaspoon vanilla. Spread over top of cake. Bake at 350 degrees for 12 minutes. Cool on rack for 30 minutes. Refrigerate until cool. Slice lemon paper thin, removing seeds. Reserve 1 slice for garnish. Chop remaining slices coarsely. Place in saucepan with 1 cup water; bring to a boil. Simmer, uncovered, for 15 minutes. Drain. Combine ½ cup sugar and 1 heaping tablespoon cornstarch; add ½ cup water to form smooth paste. Add hot lemon juice mixture and ¼ cup lemon juice; bring to a boil. Cook for 3 minutes, stirring constantly. Chill until cool but not set. Spread on cheesecake. Garnish with lemon slice. Chill overnight. Yield: 16 servings.

Jane Schwarzkopt; Rec. Sec.
Alpha Psi
St. Albert, Alberta, Canada

Lemon Cheese Tarts

1 pkg. Royal No-Bake Cheesecake Filling mix
¾ c. unsifted flour
⅓ c. sugar
¼ tsp. salt
½ c. margarine
1 egg yolk
1½ c. cold milk
1 c. sour cream
2 tsp. grated lemon peel
Candied fruit

Combine graham cracker crumbs from cheesecake filling mix, flour, sugar and salt. Cut in margarine until mixture resembles coarse meal. Mix in 3 tablespoons cold water and egg yolk thoroughly. Refrigerate for 1 hour. Roll pastry ⅛-inch thick on well-floured board. Cut into 4½-inch circles. Fit into 3½-inch tart pans. Prick sides and bottom. Bake in 425-degree oven about 15 to 20 minutes or until done. Cool. Combine cold milk, sour cream and grated lemon peel in small mixing bowl. Add filling mix. Beat at low speed with electric mixer until blended. Beat at medium speed 3 minutes longer. Pour into tart shells. Chill at least 1 hour before serving. Garnish with candied fruit. Yield: 10 tarts.

Photograph for the recipe on page 175.

Happiness adds and multiplies as we divide it with others.   Naomi Golden

foil; press foil around sides of pan. Press ¾ cup of crumb mixture into bottom and sides of pan. Chill. Blend cream cheese in mixer bowl until smooth. Add 1¼ cups sugar gradually, beating until light and fluffy. Add egg yolks, one at a time, beating after each addition. Stir in sour cream, flour, vanilla, lemon rind and lemon juice; mix until smooth. Beat egg whites until stiff peaks form; fold into cream cheese mixture. Pour into chilled crust. Bake at 350 degrees for 1 hour and 15 minutes or until golden brown. Turn off heat; let cake cool in oven for 1 hour. Remove from oven; cool on wire rack. Sprinkle with remaining crumb mixture. Chill overnight. Sprinkle with confectioners' sugar.

Sharon Evander, Pres.
Xi Epsilon Alpha X4044
Lafayette, Indiana

Jean's Strawberry Cheesecake

1 c. sugar
11 oz. cream cheese, softened
1 lg. carton Cool Whip
¾ tsp. vanilla extract
3 sm. packages ladyfingers
1 can strawberry pie filling

Cream sugar and cream cheese until smooth. Fold in Cool Whip and vanilla. Line bottom and sides of springform pan with ladyfingers. Pour half the cream cheese mixture into pan. Cover with ladyfingers. Add remaining cream cheese mixture. Top with pie filling. Refrigerate at least 2 hours before serving.

Patricia A. Lyon
Preceptor Iota XP1270
Bel Air, Maryland

Sharon's Best Cheesecake

1½ c. graham cracker crumbs
Sugar
½ tsp. ground cinnamon
¼ c. butter, melted
3 8-oz. packages cream cheese, softened
6 eggs, separated
1 pt. sour cream
⅓ c. all-purpose flour
2 tsp. vanilla extract
Grated rind of 1 lemon
Juice of ½ lemon
Confectioners' sugar

Combine crumbs, 3 tablespoons sugar, cinnamon and butter in small bowl; mix well. Place greased 9 x 13-inch springform pan in center of 12-inch square of

Strawberry-Nut Torte

2 pkg. no-bake cheesecake filling mix
1 c. chopped pecans
6 tbsp. sugar
½ c. margarine, melted
3 c. cold milk
Fresh strawberries, sliced

Combine graham cracker crumbs from cheesecake filling mix, pecans, sugar and margarine. Press ⅓ of the crumb mixture into bottom of 8-inch springform pan. Reserve remaining crumb mixture. Pour cold milk into large mixing bowl. Add filling mix. Beat at low speed with electric mixer until blended. Beat at medium speed for 3 minutes longer. Pour ½ of the filling into prepared pan. Top with ⅓ of the reserved crumb mixture. Pour on remaining filling. Sprinkle with remaining crumbs. Chill at least 1 hour before serving. Garnish with fresh sliced strawberries.

Photograph for this recipe on page 175.

Amish Raisin Pie

1 c. milk
3 eggs, separated
1 3-oz. package vanilla pudding and pie mix
1 tsp. vanilla extract
½ tsp. allspice
1½ c. golden seedless raisins
1 9-inch baked pie shell
6 tbsp. sugar

Combine milk and egg yolks in a small saucepan. Stir in pudding mix. Cook, stirring until mixture comes to a boil. Remove from heat; stir in vanilla and allspice. Fold in raisins; cool. Pour into pie shell; chill thoroughly. Beat egg whites until peaks form, gradually adding sugar. Spoon over pie. Bake at 450 degrees for 5 minutes or until meringue is slightly browned. Yield: 6 servings.

Marge Gross, Pres.
Xi Sigma Alpha X4240
Orosi, California

Use the talents you have. The woods would be very silent if only the best birds sang. Suzanne Bond

De Luxe Pineapple-Chocolate Torte

2 c. sifted all-purpose flour
2½ tsp. baking powder
½ tsp. salt
1 c. sugar
½ c. vegetable shortening
5 eggs
1 20-oz. can crushed pineapple
1 tbsp. unflavored gelatin
1 c. heavy whipping cream
Confectioner's sugar
6 oz. semisweet chocolate, melted
1 tbsp. light rum
½ c. butter, softened
1 c. sliced almonds

Resift flour with baking powder and salt. Cream sugar and shortening until light and fluffy. Add 3 eggs, one at a time, beating after each addition. Spread into 2 waxed paper-lined and floured 8-inch round cake pans. Bake at 375 degrees for 25 minutes. Cool for 5 minutes in pans; remove to cooling rack. Drain pineapple, reserving liquid. Dissolve gelatin in ¼ cup reserved pineapple juice in saucepan over low heat. Stir pineapple mixture into crushed pineapple. Chill until slightly thickened. Whip heavy cream with 3 tablespoons confectioners' sugar; fold into pineapple. Chill until firm. Combine chocolate, 2 cups confectioners' sugar, rum and 1 tablespoon reserved pineapple liquid; beat until smooth. Beat in 2 eggs, one at a time, beating after each addition until smooth. Beat in butter. Chill to spreading consistency. Cut each cake layer in half horizonally. Place 1 layer, cut side up, on serving plate. Spread with ⅓ of the pineapple filling. Repeat with 2 more layers. Top with remaining layer, top side up. Spread top and sides with chocolate frosting. Press almonds to sides of cake. Refrigerate 2 hours before serving. Store refrigerated. Yield: 14-16 servings.

Lucille Bredy, W. and M. Chm.
Iota Preceptor XP770
Homedale, Idaho

Delicate Apricot Pie

3 tbsp. butter, melted
Sugar
¾ c. corn flake crumbs
1 tbsp. unflavored gelatin
1½ c. apricot juice
3 tbsp. lemon juice
1 egg white, unbeaten
½ c. heavy cream, whipped

Combine butter, 2 tablespoons sugar and crumbs. Press into 8-inch pie pan. Chill. Combine ½ cup sugar, gelatin and apricot juice in top of double boiler. Cook, stirring constantly, until gelatin is dissolved. Stir in lemon juice. Cool to lukewarm. Stir egg white into apricot mixture. Chill until mixture begins to set. Whip until light and fluffy. Fold cream into apricot mixture. Pour into pie shell. Chill until set. Yield: 8 servings.

Edith Savage, Pres.
Laureate Delta PL194
Sudbury, Ontario, Canada

Blueberry Cheesecake Pie

1 8-oz. package cream cheese, softened
1 c. confectioners' sugar, sifted
1 tsp. vanilla extract
2 c. Cool Whip
1 9-in. baked pastry shell
1 1-lb. 5-oz. can blueberry pie filling

Combine cream cheese, sugar and vanilla until smooth. Fold in Cool Whip. Spoon into pie shell. Spoon pie filling over topping. Chill 2 to 3 hours or until set. Yield: 8 servings.

Becky Gulley
Zeta Rho No. 2959
Springfield, Illinois

Buttermilk Pie a la Lutie

¼ c. flour
1½ c. sugar
½ tsp. salt
½ c. butter
3 eggs, beaten
½ c. buttermilk
½ tbsp. vanilla extract
1 9-in. unbaked pie shell

Combine flour, sugar and salt in bowl. Melt butter; add with eggs to dry ingredients. Mix well. Add buttermilk; stir to combine all ingredients. Add vanilla; blend. Pour into pie shell. Bake at 350 degrees for 30 to 40 minutes or until filling is firm and golden brown. Yield: 8 servings.

Martha L. Fiegel, City Coun. Rep.
Preceptor Xi
North Little Rock, Arkansas

Buttermilk-Pecan Pie

2½ c. sugar
¾ c. butter
1 c. buttermilk
6 eggs, beaten
1 c. chopped pecans
1 c. coconut
2 tbsp. flour
1 tbsp. vanilla extract
2 unbaked 9-in. pie shells

In this day of fast paces—Take time to care. Mrs. Paula Star

Combine sugar and butter in bowl. Combine buttermilk and eggs; add to sugar mixture. Combine pecans, coconut and flour. Add to sugar mixture. Stir in vanilla; mix well. Pour into pie shells. Bake at 325 degrees for 45 minutes. Yield: 6 servings.

Mary Anne Etheridge, City Coun. Rep.
Xi Beta Eta X3587
Albany, Georgia

Cherry-Cream Pie With Almond Crust

½ c. finely chopped almonds
1 unbaked pie shell
1 can sweetened condensed milk
⅓ c. lemon juice
1 tsp. vanilla extract
½ tsp. almond extract
½ c. whipping cream, whipped or Cool Whip
1 can cherry pie filling

Press almonds in unbaked pie shell. Bake at 450 degrees for 12 to 15 minutes. Cool. Combine milk, lemon juice, vanilla and almond extract. Stir until mixture thickens. Fold in whipped cream. Spoon into cooled shell. Top with cherry pie filling. Chill. Top with additional chopped almonds, if desired. Yield: 6-8 servings.

Diana Amon, W. and M. Chm.
Iota Gamma No. 8279
Lewis, Kansas

Chocolate Chip Pie

½ c. sugar
⅓ c. (firmly packed) brown sugar
1 stick butter, melted
2 eggs, slightly beaten
1 c. chopped nuts
1 c. chocolate chips
1 tsp. vanilla extract
1 unbaked 9-in. pie shell

Combine sugars and melted butter in bowl. Add eggs, nuts, chocolate chips and vanilla; mix well. Pour into pie shell. Bake at 350 degrees for 50 to 60 minutes. Cool before cutting. Yield: 8 servings.

Kathy Hamff
Alpha Omega No. 4770
Tupelo, Mississippi

Three-Layer Pie

1 c. flour
1 stick margarine, softened
1 c. chopped pecans
1 8-oz. package cream cheese, softened
1 c. confectioners' sugar
Cool Whip
1 sm. package instant vanilla pudding mix
1 sm. package instant chocolate pudding mix
3 c. milk
1 sm. Hershey bar, grated

Combine flour, margarine and pecans. Press into 9 x 13-inch pan. Bake at 350 degrees for 15 minutes. Cool. Combine cream cheese, confectioners' sugar and 1½ cups Cool Whip; mix well. Spread cream cheese mixture in cooled crust. Combine pudding mixes and milk until slightly thickened. Spread over cream cheese mixture. Top with additional Cool Whip. Garnish with grated Hershey bar. Chill. Yield: 12 servings.

Sharon K. Smith
Xi Pi X622
Girard, Kansas

Speedy Coconut Pie

¾ c. sugar
½ c. biscuit mix
2 c. milk
¼ c. melted butter
4 eggs, beaten
1½ tsp. vanilla extract
1½ c. flaked coconut

Combine sugar, biscuit mix, milk, butter, eggs, vanilla and ½ cup coconut in blender. Blend on low speed for 3 minutes. Pour into buttered 9-inch pie pan. Let stand for 5 minutes. Sprinkle remaining coconut on top. Bake at 350 degrees for 40 minutes, or until knife inserted in center comes out clean. Yield: 6 servings.

Edith Wicker, Treas.
Preceptor Delta Nu XP1000
Newport Beach, California

Yukon Wild Cranberry Pie

1½ c. fresh cranberries, chopped
1 recipe pastry for 2-crust pie
1 c. sugar
Pinch of salt
1 tbsp. flour
½ tsp. vanilla extract

Place cranberries in pie shell. Combine sugar, salt and flour; sprinkle over cranberries. Combine vanilla and almond extract; pour over pie. Cover with top crust. Bake at 425 degrees for 15 minutes. Reduce heat to 350 degrees; bake for 30 minutes. Yield: 6 servings.

Anne McKillican, Pres.
Xi Alpha X4750
Whitehorse, Yukon, Canada

The only time you must not fail is the final time you try.   Sharon Woodworth

Grasshopper Chiffon Pie

1 3-oz. package lime gelatin
3 tbsp. sugar
Dash of salt
3 tbsp. green Creme de Menthe liqueur
3 tbsp. Creme de Cacao liqueur
½ tsp. vanilla extract
1 egg white
1 env. whipped topping mix
1 baked 9-in. cookie crumb pie shell, cooled

Dissolve gelatin, 1 tablespoon sugar and salt in 1 cup boiling water. Add ½ cup cold water, liqueurs and vanilla. Chill about 1 hour and 30 minutes or until thick. Beat egg white until foamy. Add 2 tablespoons sugar, 1 tablespoon at a time, beating well after each addition. Continue beating mixture until stiff peaks form. Prepare topping mix according to package directions, omitting vanilla. Measure ½ cup gelatin mixture; set aside. Blend beaten egg whites, and 1 cup prepared topping into remaining gelatin mixture. Let stand for 5 minutes. Pour half the mixture into cooled pie shell. Drizzle with reserved liqueur-gelatin mixture. Pour remaining creamy mixture into pie shell. Drizzle remaining gelatin over top. Draw knife through mixtures several times to create marbleized effect. Chill until firm, about 3 hours. Garnish with remaining prepared topping and gumdrops cut into shamrock shapes, if desired.

Photograph for this recipe on page 179.

Grandmother's Green Tomato Pie

1 qt. green tomatoes, thinly sliced
1 recipe for 9-inch 2-crust pie
1¾ c. sugar
¼ c. flour
1 tbsp. lemon rind or orange rind
¼ tsp. salt
¼ tsp. cinnamon
⅛ tsp. ginger
¾ c. raisins
2 tbsp. butter
3 tbsp. lemon juice

Cut tomato slices into quarters. Drain for 30 minutes. Fit pastry into pie pan. Combine sugar, flour, lemon rind, salt, cinnamon and ginger. Sprinkle ¼ of the mixture into pastry. Layer tomatoes in pie pan, packing firmly. Sprinkle each layer with sugar mixture and part of raisins. Repeat layers, ending with sugar mixture. Dot with butter. Sprinkle with lemon juice. Cut top crust in design for steam vents. Place on top of pie; seal edges. Let rest 10 minutes; flute edge. Bake at 450 degrees for 15 minutes. Reduce heat to 325 degrees; bake for 40 to 50 minutes or until tomatoes

test tender. Cool on rack for 3 to 4 hours before serving. Yield: 8 servings.

Sylvia L. Miles, Corr. Sec.
Preceptor Beta Kappa XP1862
Rifle, Colorado

Lemon Lite Pie

2 pkg. Dream Whip
1 c. skim milk
1 3-oz. package lemon-flavored gelatin
1 9-in. graham cracker crust
Grated lemon rind (opt.)

Combine Dream Whip with milk; beat until very stiff. Set aside. Prepare gelatin, according to package directions using 1 cup boiling water. Stir in 10 to 12 ice cubes until gelatin is thick. Fold Dream Whip into gelatin. Pour into prepared crust. Sprinkle grated lemon rind on top. Refrigerate until serving time. Yield: 8-10 servings.

Gwendolyn Melton, Pres.
Delta Beta Omicron No. 7040
Arroyo Grande, California

Lemon Pie

Sugar
8 tbsp. cornstarch
3 eggs, separated
Juice of 2 lemons
1 tbsp. grated lemon rind
Pinch of salt
1 9-in. baked pie shell

Combine 1½ cups sugar, 7 tablespoons cornstarch and egg yolks in saucepan; mix well. Stir in lemon juice, lemon rind and salt. Add 1½ cup boiling water. Cook slowly until thick. Cool slightly; pour into pie shell. Beat egg whites until soft peaks form. Add 6 tablespoons sugar and 1 tablespoon cornstarch. Beat until very stiff. Spoon onto filling. Bake at 400 degrees until meringue browns. Yield: 8 servings.

Ina Constance Best, Ser. Comm.
Xi Delta Exemplar X4573
Starke, Florida

Candy's Millionaire Pie

1 8-oz. package cream cheese, softened
1 c. sugar
1 sm. can crushed pineapple, drained
1 c. nuts
1 lg. carton Cool Whip
2 graham cracker pie crusts

If you see someone without a smile, give him one of yours. Lois Larson

Combine cream cheese and sugar until smooth. Add pineapple and nuts. Fold in Cool Whip. Pour into pie shells. Garnish with cherries. Chill until serving time. Yield: 12 servings.

Candy Winningham
Lambda Nu
Markleville, Indiana

Kathy's Millionaire Pie

4 oz. cream cheese, softened
1¼ c. confectioners' sugar
1 sm. can crushed pineapple, drained
½ c. chopped nuts
1 envelope Dream Whip
1 baked pie shell or 1 graham cracker crust

Blend cream cheese and confectioners' sugar; mix well. Add pineapple and nuts. Prepare Dream Whip according to package directions. Fold in Dream Whip.

Pour into pie shell. Refrigerate for 1 hour before serving. Yield: 6-8 servings.

Kathy Willis, V. P.
Iota Tau
Pryor, Oklahoma

Angel Food Pie

2½ c. crushed pineapple with juice
3 tbsp. flour
¾ c. sugar
4 egg whites
2 baked pie shells
Cool Whip

Combine pineapple, flour and ½ cup sugar in small saucepan. Cook until clear. Cool. Beat egg whites with ¼ cup sugar until very stiff. Fold in cooled pineapple mixture. Spoon into pie shells. Top with Cool Whip before serving. Yield: 16 servings.

Margaret Fitzpatrick, Pres.
Preceptor Beta Beta XP1263
Jacksonville, Illinois

If you have knowledge, let others light their candles at it.   Cleo Overholser

Pineapple Chiffon Pies

1 pkg. unflavored gelatin
4 eggs, separated
1 c. sugar
3 tbsp. cornstarch
2 tbsp. flour
½ tsp. salt
2 c. crushed pineapple with juice
2 9-in. baked pie shells

Combine gelatin and ¼ cup water. Set aside to dissolve. Beat egg yolks until creamy. Add ½ cup sugar, cornstarch, flour and salt, beating after each addition. Combine egg mixture with pineapple and ½ cup water in heavy saucepan. Cook over medium heat, stirring frequently. Bring to a boil; remove from heat. Add gelatin to warm mixture; set aside to cool. Beat egg whites with ½ cup sugar until stiff. Fold into cooled pineapple mixture. Pour into pie shells. Refrigerate for 3 hours. Garnish with whipped cream. Yield: 12 servings.

Mary Lee Janiak
Zeta Lambda No. 4500
Elwood, Indiana

Jim's Pineapple Pie

3 eggs, beaten
1 c. light corn syrup
1 c. crushed pineapple with juice
1 c. coconut, flaked or grated
1 c. sugar
2 tsp. flour
½ stick margarine, melted
1 tsp. vanilla extract
1 10-inch baked pie shell

Combine eggs and corn syrup in medium bowl; mix until well blended. Stir in next 6 ingredients; mix well. Spoon into pie shell. Bake at 350 degrees for 30 minutes, or until pastry is brown and filling is firm. Yield: 8-10 servings.

Jeannie Wheeler James, Pres.
Preceptor Kappa XP981
Tulsa, Oklahoma

Million Dollar Pie

1 can sweetened condensed milk
2 tbsp. lemon juice
1 lg. can crushed pineapple, well drained
½ c. chopped cherries, well drained
1 9-oz. carton Cool Whip
1 c. chopped nuts
2 graham cracker pie shells

Combine first 6 ingredients in large bowl; pour into pie shells. Chill for 3 hours before serving. Yield: 16 servings.

Debra Murdock, Pres.
Phi Theta Beta P2802
Nacogdoches, Texas

Rum Cream Pie

Chocolate wafer crumbs
½ c. melted butter
6 egg yolks
1 c. sugar
1 tbsp. gelatin
2 c. whipping cream, whipped
⅓ c. dark rum

Combine 2 cups chocolate wafer crumbs and butter. Press into 9-inch springform pan. Bake at 375 degrees for 8 minutes. Cool. Beat egg yolks until light. Add sugar, gradually, until blended. Dissolve gelatin in ½ cup cold water. Bring to a boil in a small saucepan. Pour over sugar mixture, stirring briskly. Cool; do not let set. Fold in whipped cream; add rum. Pour into pie shell; sprinkle with additional chocolate wafer crumbs or shaved chocolate. Refrigerate for 4 to 5 hours or until set. Yield: 8 servings.

Patti Gaetan
Xi Beta Gamma
Woodstock, Ontario, Canada

Tiny Tarts

2 lg. packages cream cheese, softened
2 eggs, beaten
2 tbsp. milk
½ c. sugar
2 tsp. vanilla extract
2 tbsp. lemon juice
1 pkg. vanilla wafers
1 can cherry pie filling

Beat cream cheese until light and fluffy. Add eggs, milk, sugar, vanilla and lemon juice gradually. Line medium muffin-sized pans with baking cups. Place 1 vanilla wafer in each baking cup. Fill ¾ full with cream cheese mixture. Bake at 400 degrees for 10 to 15 minutes. Remove from muffin pan. Cool. Top each pastry with 1 teaspoon cherry pie filling.

Janice Palagruti, Pres.
Xi Gamma Omicron No. 5082
Augusta, Georgia

Remember: That through God, all Horizons are possible.   U Gail Lokey

Pecan Tarts

1 3-oz. package cream cheese, softened
Butter
1 c. flour
¾ c. (firmly packed) light brown sugar
1 tsp. vanilla extract
1 egg, beaten
Pinch of salt
⅔ c. chopped pecans

Combine cream cheese, ½ cup softened butter and flour; blend well. Chill for 1 hour. Shape into 24 balls. Shape each ball in muffin pan to form small tart. Combine brown sugar, 1 tablespoon softened butter, vanilla, egg, salt and pecans. Fill muffin cups half full with pecan mixture. Bake at 350 degrees until golden brown. Cool. Sprinkle with confectioners' sugar. Yield: 24 servings.

Jacqueline C. Gitthens, Pres.
Zeta Lambda No. 8997
Havelock, North Carolina

Betty's Pie Crust

5 c. sifted flour
1 tsp. baking powder
2 tsp. salt
1 tsp. brown sugar
1 lb. shortening
1 egg
1½ tsp. white vinegar

Combine first 4 ingredients. Cut in shortening until crumbly. Set aside. Break egg into measuring cup; add enough cold water to measure ¾ cup. Beat until foamy; add vinegar. Mix well. Add flour mixture; mix until dough forms. Form dough into 6 balls; each ball will make one crust. Chill for at least 1 hour before using. Yield: 6 crusts.

Betty Reinaking
Kappa Phi No. 3825
Dunsmuir, California

Applesauce Cake

1½ c. unsweetened stewed apples
2 c. sugar
1 c. butter or margarine
1 tbsp. soda
1 tbsp. vanilla extract
1 tbsp. cinnamon
3 c. flour
1 c. raisins
½ c. chopped walnuts (or pecans)

Combine apples and sugar. Add butter; mix well. Combine soda and ¼ cup hot water. Add to apple mixture; stir well. Add vanilla, cinnamon and flour; mix well. Dredge raisins in small amount of flour. Add raisins and walnuts to batter; mix well. Pour into greased and floured 9 × 13-inch baking pan. Bake at 350 degrees for 45 to 50 minutes. Frost with favorite caramel icing recipe.

Nancy E. Hollis, Pres.
Xi Epsilon Pi X2539
Paris, Illinois

Easy Apple Cake

4 c. diced apples
1 c. chopped nuts
2 c. sugar
2 c. flour
2 tsp. baking powder
¼ tsp. salt
2 tsp. cinnamon
2 eggs, beaten
1 c. cooking oil

Combine all ingredients; mix well. Pour into 9 × 13-inch baking pan. Bake at 350 degrees for 35 to 40 minutes. Cool. Serve with ice cream, if desired.

Diane K. Gilbert, 1st. V.P.
Kappa Delta No. 9501
Emporia, Kansas

Grandmother's Apple Cake

2 eggs
6 or 8 green apples, peeled and sliced
2 c. sugar
½ tsp. (or more) cinnamon
½ c. oil
1 c. chopped walnuts
2 c. flour
1 tsp. salt
2 tsp. soda
½ c. butter or margarine
4 oz. cream cheese, softened
½ tsp. vanilla extract
½ lb. confectioners sugar

Break eggs over apples. Add sugar, cinnamon, oil and walnuts; mix with fork. Sift flour, salt and soda together. Add to apple mixture; mix with fork. Place in greased and floured 9 × 12-inch pan. Bake at 400 degrees for 35 minutes or until toothpick inserted into center comes out clean. Cool. Combine butter, cream cheese, vanilla and confectioners' sugar; beat until smooth. Spread on cake. This is an old-fashioned German recipe. Yield: 12 servings.

Kitty Lint, Rec. Sec.
Preceptor Gamma Zeta XP787
San Diego, California

Do something nice for somebody today. Emily F. Miller

Jewish Apple Cake

5 or 6 med. apples
2 tbsp. cinnamon
Sugar
3 c. flour
½ tsp. salt
2½ tsp. baking powder
4 eggs, beaten
1 c. oil
½ c. orange juice or milk
2½ tsp. vanilla extract

Peel, core and slice apples. Combine cinnamon and 5 tablespoons sugar. Coat apple slices with cinnamon mixture; set aside. Sift flour, salt and baking powder together. Add 2 cups sugar and remaining ingredients. Layer greased and floured tube pan with batter and apple slices. Bake at 325 degrees for 1 hour and 30 minutes. Yield: 12-16 servings.

Margie Calhoun, Soc. Chm.
Xi Alpha Nu X833
San Angelo, Texas

Country Blueberry Cake

1 c. shortening
2 c. sugar
2 tsp. vanilla extract
4 eggs, separated
Flour
2 tsp. baking powder
½ tsp. salt
⅔ c. milk
3 c. blueberries
Confectioners' sugar

Cream shortening and 1½ cups sugar until smooth. Add vanilla and eggs yolks; beat until light and fluffy. Sift together 3 cups flour, baking powder and salt. Add to creamed mixture alternately with milk; mix well. Beat egg whites until stiff; add ½ cup sugar gradually. Fold into batter. Dredge blueberries in 1 tablespoon flour; add to batter. Pour into greased 9 × 3-inch cake pan. Bake at 350 degrees for 50 minutes. Cool. Sprinkle with confectioners' sugar. Yield: 8-10 servings.

Judith Roentsch, Pres.
Nu No. 5860
Keene, New Hampshire

The Cake That Won't Last

3 eggs, beaten
3 c. flour
3 c. sugar
1 tsp. salt
1 tsp. soda

1 tsp. cinnamon
1½ tsp. vanilla extract
1 c. Wesson oil
2 c. chopped bananas
1 8-oz. can crushed pineapple
½ c. chopped black walnuts

Combine all ingredients, stirring until just blended. Pour into bundt pan. Bake at 350 degrees for 40 minutes.

Faye McRae, Pres.
Xi Sigma X184
Quincy, Illinois

Carrot Cake

2 c. sugar
2 c. flour
2 tsp. soda
2 tbsp. baking powder
2 tbsp. cinnamon
1 tbsp. salt
1½ c. Wesson oil
4 eggs, beaten
1 c. chopped nuts
2 tbsp. vanilla extract
3 c. finely grated carrots
8 oz. cream cheese, softened
1 stick margarine, softened
1 pkg. confectioners' sugar

Sift first 6 ingredients together. Combine Wesson oil and eggs; beat well. Add to dry ingredients. Add nuts, 1 tablespoon vanilla and carrots. Pour into three 9-inch cake pans. Bake at 300 degrees for 40 to 45 minutes. Blend cream cheese and margarine; add confectioners' sugar, beating until smooth. Add 1 tablespoon vanilla; stir. Spread over cake.

Pam Clay, V.P.
Phi Omicron P2739
Columbus, Mississippi

Chocolate-Applesauce Cake

½ c. shortening
1½ c. sugar
2 eggs, beaten
2 c. applesauce
2 c. flour
1½ tsp. soda
1 tsp. salt
1 tsp. cinnamon
3 tbsp. cocoa
2 tbsp. brown sugar
1 c. chocolate chips
1 c. chopped nuts

Combine shortening, sugar, eggs, and applesauce; beat well. Sift flour, soda, salt, cinnamon and cocoa together. Add to applesauce mixture. Pour into greased and floured 8-inch square pan. Combine brown sugar, chocolate chips, and nuts; sprinkle over batter. Bake at 350 degrees for 30 minutes. Yield: 6-8 servings.

Patti G. Shifflett, Pres. City Coun.
Sigma No. 1503
Ruckersville, Virginia

Devil's Food Cake

1½ c. flour
1 c. sugar
1 tsp. soda
3 tbsp. cocoa
½ tsp. salt
1 tbsp. vinegar
⅓ c. oil
1 tsp. vanilla extract

Sift together flour, sugar, soda, cocoa and salt in 8×8-inch baking pan. Make three wells in dry ingredients. Put vinegar, oil and vanilla into wells separately. Pour 1 cup cold water over all; mix well with fork. Bake in 350-degree oven for 30 minutes.

Patricia Jones
Xi Beta Eta X3005
Chesapeake, Virginia

Fudge Cake

1 c. sugar
2 sticks margarine
5 eggs
1 lg. can chocolate syrup
1 c. flour
1 tsp. baking powder
2 oz. bittersweet chocolate chips
1½ c. confectioners' sugar
1 tsp. vanilla extract
1 sm. package miniature marshmallows
1 c. chopped pecans

Cream sugar and 1 stick margarine until smooth. Add 4 eggs, one at a time, beating after each addition. Add chocolate syrup. Add flour and baking powder; mix well. Pour into 9½×13½-inch pan. Bake at 350 degrees for 30 minutes. Melt 1 stick margarine and chocolate chips. Pour margarine and chocolate over confectioners' sugar. Add 1 egg and vanilla; mix well. Cover top of cake with marshmallows; pour thin stream of chocolate mixture on top of marshmallows. Do not spread. Sprinkle with pecans.

Libby Branton, Pres.
Xi Alpha Phi X3742
Bossier City, Louisiana

Mississippi Mud Cake

2 sticks margarine
4 eggs, beaten
2 tsp. vanilla extract
Cocoa
2 c. sugar
1½ c. flour
Pinch of salt
2½ c. chopped pecans
1 pkg. miniature marshmallows
1 stick butter
6 tbsp. milk
1 1-lb. package confectioners' sugar

Combine margarine, eggs and 1 teaspoon vanilla. Add ⅓ cup cocoa, sugar, flour and salt; mix well. Add 1½ cups pecans. Pour into greased 9×13-inch baking pan. Bake at 350 degrees for 30 minutes. Remove from oven. Cover with marshmallows. Return to oven for 10 to 15 minutes or until browned. Cool. Combine butter, 4 tablespoons cocoa and milk in saucepan. Bring to a boil. Beat in confectioners' sugar, and 1 teaspoon vanilla, mixing well. Add 1 cup pecans. Pour over cooled cake. Yield: 20 servings.

Charlene J. Wilbanks, Pres.
Xi Beta Kappa X4825
Wrightstown, New Jersey

Italian Cream Cake

½ c. shortening
2 c. sugar
¾ c. margarine
1 tsp. soda
2 c. cake flour or sifted flour
5 eggs, separated
1 c. buttermilk
2 tsp. vanilla
1¾ c. chopped nuts
1¾ c. coconut
1 8-oz. package cream cheese, softened
1 box confectioners' sugar

Cream shortening, sugar and ½ cup margarine in mixer bowl until smooth. Combine soda and flour. Beat egg yolks slightly. Add egg yolks, buttermilk and flour alternately to the creamed mixture. Add 1 teaspoon vanilla, 1 cup nuts and 1 cup coconut. Beat egg whites until stiff; fold into cake mixture. Pour batter in two 9-inch pans. Bake at 350 degrees for 25 to 30 minutes or until cake tests done. Cool. Cream ¼ cup margarine and cream cheese until smooth. Add confectioners' sugar and 1 teaspoon vanilla. Fold in ¾ cup nuts and ¾ cup cocunut. Fill and frost cake. Yield: 12 servings.

M. Louise Cahill, Rec. Sec.
Laureate Zeta PL413
Tempe, Arizona
Shirley St. George
Xi Alpha Zeta X1855
Decatur, Georgia

All things bright and beautiful, all creatures great and small, all things wise and wonderful, the Lord God made them all. . . . Marjorie J. Strohl

Brown Sugar Pound Cake

1½ c. shortening
1 lb. (firmly packed) dark brown sugar
½ c. sugar
5 egg yolks, (beaten)
3 c. flour
½ tsp. baking powder
1 c. milk
1 c. chopped nuts
1 tsp. vanilla extract
5 egg whites, stiffly beaten

Cream shortening and sugars until smooth in large bowl. Stir in egg yolks. Sift flour and baking powder together; add alternately with milk to creamed mixture. Add nuts and vanilla. Fold in egg whites. Pour into 2 greased and floured loaf pans. Bake at 325 degrees for 1 hour and 30 minutes.

Joy Y. Jackson, Pres.
Rho Beta
Trenton, Missouri

Orange Blossom Tea Cakes

½ c. butter or margarine
1½ c. sugar
2 c. cake flour
1½ tsp. baking powder
¾ c. milk
3 eggs, beaten
½ tsp. lemon extract
½ tsp. vanilla extract
¼ tsp. almond extract
Juice of 2 lemons
Juice of 2 oranges
Rind of lemon, grated
Rind of 2 oranges, grated
1½ lb. sifted confectioners' sugar

Cream butter and sugar until smooth. Combine flour and baking powder; add to creamed mixture. Add milk, eggs and flour mixture alternately, to creamed mixture. Add extracts. Pour into greased and floured miniature cupcake pans. Bake at 350 degrees for 10 minutes. Combine last 5 ingredients to form thin icing. Dip hot tea cakes in icing to coat. Yield: 6 dozen.

Susan D. Anderson
Zeta Nu No. 9268
Fredericksburg, Virginia

Orange Cake

3 c. sifted flour
½ tsp. soda
½ tsp. baking powder
¾ tsp. salt
2 c. sugar
Shortening

4 eggs
1 c. buttermilk
Rind of 2 oranges, grated
Orange juice
2 tbsp. butter
1 c. (packed) confectioners' sugar

Combine flour, soda, baking powder, salt, sugar, 1 cup shortening, eggs, buttermilk, juice and rind of orange; mix well. Pour into greased and floured tube pan. Bake at 350 degrees for 1 hour. Cream 2 tablespoons shortening, butter and confectioners' sugar until smooth. Add rind of 1 orange and ½ cup orange juice; mix well to form thin icing. Pour icing over cake.

Carolyn Newman
Alpha Xi Mu
Daingerfield, Texas

Old-Fashioned Pound Cake

2 c. butter, softened
4 c. flour, sifted
10 eggs, separated
Pinch of salt
2 c. sugar
1 tsp. vanilla extract
½ tsp almond extract

Cream butter lightly; add flour gradually, stirring until mixture is mealy. Beat egg whites with salt until stiff. Combine egg yolks, sugar, vanilla and almond extract; beat with hand mixer until thick and fluffy. Fold in butter mixture gradually; beat well. Fold in egg whites. Beat for 5 minutes. Pour batter into two waxed paper-lined 4×8-inch loaf pans. Bake at 325 degrees for 1 hour and 15 minues or until cake tests done. Cool before removing from pans. Yield: 36 servings.

Mildred Weld Philbin, Rec. Sec.
Xi Beta Omicron X4779
Green Valley, Arizona

Coconut Cake

1 pkg. butter cake mix
30 oz. frozen coconut
1 lg. carton sour cream
1¼ c. sugar
1¼ c. confectioners' sugar

Prepare cake according to package directions, using 9-inch round pans. Let stand overnight. Combine 24 ounces coconut, sour cream, sugar and confectioners' sugar. Refrigerate overnight. Split layers in half. Fill and frost all 4 layers. Pat remaining coconut on cake. Store refrigerated.

Sharon L. Bradley, Corr. Sec.
Xi Alpha Omega No. 3545
Murfreesboro, Tennessee

"Nature has given men one tongue but two ears, that we may hear from others twice as much as we speak." Linda Sankpill

Turkey and Ham Casino

1 c. chopped onions
1 c. chopped green peppers
¼ c. butter or margarine
½ c. flour
2 c. milk
2 c. chicken broth
¼ c. dry Sherry
1 4-oz. can sliced mushrooms, drained
2 c. coarsely chopped cooked turkey
2 c. coarsely chopped cooked ham
½ c. diced pimentos
1 8-oz. can water chestnuts, drained and sliced
Salt and pepper to taste
1½ to 2 qts. hot cooked rice

Saute onions and green peppers in butter until tender. Blend in flour. Add milk, broth and Sherry. Cook, stirring constantly, until thickened. Add mushrooms, turkey, ham, pimentos and water chestnuts. Add salt and pepper. Heat thoroughly. Serve over beds of rice. Yield: 12 servings.

Photograph for this recipe on page 136.

Orange Scones

2⅔ c. all-purpose flour
1 tsp. soda
1 tsp. baking powder
½ tsp. salt
2 tbsp. sugar
½ c. butter or margarine, softened
1 tbsp. grated orange rind
½ c. currants
3 tbsp. vinegar
¾ c. orange juice
1 egg, beaten
Milk
Sugar

Mix flour with soda, baking powder, salt and sugar. Cut in butter with two knives or pastry blender until mixture resembles coarse corn meal. Stir in orange rind and currants. Combine vinegar and orange juice. Make well in center of flour mixture; add liquid and egg all at once. Stir mixture with fork until dry ingredients are moistened. Turn onto floured board; knead gently 8 to 10 times, adding more flour if necessary. Roll into 12 × 6-inch rectangle. Cut into eight 3-inch squares; cut each square in half diagonally to make two triangles. Brush tops with milk; sprinkle with sugar. Place on greased baking sheets. Bake at 425 degrees for 15 minutes or until golden brown. Yield: 16 scones.

Photograph for this recipe on page 102.

Violets in the Snow

2 env. unflavored gelatin
¾ c. sugar
1 c. Chablis or other light white wine, heated to
    boiling
2 c. orange juice
2 c. heavy cream, whipped
1 c. orange sections
Candied or fresh violets

Combine gelatin with sugar in large mixing bowl. Add boiling wine; stir until gelatin is dissolved. Stir in orange juice. Chill, stirring occasionally, until mixture is consistency of unbeaten egg whites. Fold in whipped cream and orange sections. Turn into 2-quart serving bowl. Garnish with violets and additional whipped cream, if desired. Yield: 10-12 servings.

Photograph for this recipe on page 102.

Garden Green Salad

3 env. unflavored gelatin
¾ c. sugar
1½ tsp. salt
¾ c. tarragon or wine vinegar
3 tbsp. lemon juice
1½ c. shredded cabbage
1 c. chopped green pepper
1 c. sliced green onion

Combine gelatin, sugar and salt in large mixing bowl. Add 3¾ cups boiling water; stir until gelatin is dissolved. Stir in vinegar and lemon juice. Chill, stirring occasionally, until mixture is consistency of unbeaten egg whites. Fold in remaining ingredients. Turn into 6-cup mold or 12 individual molds; chill until firm. Unmold to serve. Yield: 12 servings.

Photograph for this recipe on page 102.

Fresh Lemon Dressing

1⅓ c. salad oil
¼ c. lemon juice
¼ c. tarragon vinegar
2 tsp. salt
1 tsp. dry mustard
¼ tsp. pepper

Combine all ingredients in jar with tight lid. Shake until well mixed. Yield: 2 cups.

Photograph for this recipe on page 101

The way to a man's heart is through his stomach. Sandra Freeman

Grapefruit Glazed Ham

1 5 to 7 lb. canned ham
1 6-oz. can frozen grapefruit juice concentrate,
    thawed
Whole cloves
2 tbsp. prepared mustard
½ c. honey
½ tsp. liquid hot pepper sauce

Remove ham from can; place on rack in shallow roasting pan. Prepare ham according to directions on can. Remove from oven, about 15 minutes before end of cooking time. Make diagonal cuts ⅛-inch deep, about 1 inch apart. Repeat, crossing these lines. Place whole clove at point of each diamond. Combine grapefruit juice concentrate, prepared mustard, honey and pepper sauce for glaze. Brush over ham. Return ham to oven; continue baking 15 minutes longer, brushing occasionally with glaze. Yield: 12 servings.

Photograph for this recipe on page 102.

Vegetable Medley

2 med. eggplant, unpared and cubed
½ c. olive oil
1½ c. sliced onion
3 tomatoes, cubed
1 c. diced celery
3 tbsp. capers
¼ c. wine vinegar
1 tbsp. sugar
1 tsp. salt
¼ tsp. pepper
Chopped parsley
Party bread slices

Saute eggplant in hot oil in skillet until soft and lightly browned. Remove; set aside. Saute onion in oil remaining in skillet until golden. Add tomatoes and celery; simmer for 15 minutes. Add capers, eggplant, vinegar, sugar, salt and pepper. Simmer, covered, for 20 minutes over low heat, stirring occasionally. Chill. Sprinkle with parsley. Serve with party bread slices. Yield: 4-5 cups.

Photograph for this recipe on page 101.

Fresh Cranberry Ice

1 16-oz. package fresh cranberries
1 env. unflavored gelatin
1 c. sugar
1 c. fresh orange juice
2 egg whites

Combine cranberries and 2 cups water in medium saucepan. Bring to a boil; cover. Simmer, covered, for 3 to 5 minutes or until cranberries pop. Press through sieve or a food mill; set aside. Combine gelatin and ¾ cup sugar in large saucepan. Add orange juice; let stand 1 minute. Stir over medium heat for 3 minutes or until gelatin is dissolved. Stir in fresh cranberry puree. Pour into shallow pan or freezer tray; freeze until mixture is partly congealed. Pour cranberry mixture in large bowl; beat until smooth. Set aside. Beat egg whites until soft peaks form. Add ¼ cup sugar; beat until stiff peaks form. Fold into cranberry mixture. Spoon into 8-cup mold. Freeze until firm. Unmold; let stand approximately 20 minutes before serving. Garnish with frosted grapes, if desired. Yield: 10-12 servings.

Photograph for this recipe on page 101.

Julienne Vegetables

6 stalks celery
6 carrots, pared
3 parsnips, pared
2 potatoes, pared
Melted butter or margarine
Salt and pepper to taste

Cut each vegetable into 2½-inch by ¼-inch julienne strips. Drop strips into saucepan of lightly salted boiling water. Reduce heat; simmer, covered, 7 to 10 minutes or until vegetables are crisp-tender. Drain. Toss with melted butter and salt and pepper to taste. Makes: 10-12 servings.

Photograph for this recipe on page 101.

Fresh Mushroom Sauce

¼ c. butter or margarine
3 c. sliced, fresh mushrooms
¼ c. flour
2½ c. beef broth
½ c. reserved drippings from meat loaf
Dash pepper

Melt butter in medium saucepan. Add mushrooms; cook until crisp-tender. Stir in flour; cook 1 minute. Add beef broth gradually. Add meat dippings and pepper. Cook over medium heat, stirring constantly, until mixture thickens and boils. Serve with Meat Loaf Wellington.

Photograph for this recipe on page 101.

Meat Loaf Wellington

2 lb. lean ground beef
1 lb. lean ground veal
1 c. chopped onion
¼ c. chopped fresh parsley
1 clove of garlic, minced
¾ c. soft bread crumbs

Always laugh when you can, it is cheap medicine. Sandra Freeman

¾ *c. dry red wine*
4 eggs
½ *tsp. dried leaf basil, crumbled*
2½ *tsp. salt*
½ *tsp. pepper*
2 10-oz. packages frozen pastry shells, thawed

Combine beef, veal, onion, parsley, garlic, bread crumbs, wine, 3 eggs, basil, salt and pepper in large mixing bowl; mix well. Turn into lightly greased 9 × 5 × 2¾-inch loaf pan. Bake at 350 degrees for 1 hour and 10 minutes or until loaf pulls away from sides of pan. Let cool. Drain meat drippings from loaf; reserve for Fresh Mushroom Sauce. Place thawed pastry shells on lightly floured board; roll out approximately ¼-inch thick to form 18 × 13-inch rectangle. Place cooled meat loaf, top side down, in center of pastry. Fold pastry around loaf. Trim pastry; moisten edges with water. Seal by pressing together. Place on baking sheet with folded sides under. Prick crust to allow steam to escape. Combine 1 egg with 1 teaspoon water; beat well. Brush crust with egg mixture. Decorate loaf with cut-outs from trimmed pastry, moistened slightly with egg mixture, if desired. Bake at 425 degrees for 20 to 25 minutes or until pastry is golden brown. Serve with Fresh Mushroom Sauce. Yield: 10-12 servings.

Photograph for this recipe on page 101.

Winter Holiday Salad

9 c. iceberg lettuce, torn into bite-sized pieces
2 ripe avocados
1 tbsp. lemon juice
4 oranges, peeled and sectioned
1 red onion, peeled and thinly sliced
1 c. seasoned croutons with herbs and cheese

Cut avocado in half lengthwise. Twist halves in opposite direction; remove seed. Peel and slice avocado; sprinkle with lemon juice. Combine lettuce, avocado slices, orange sections, onion and croutons in large bowl. Add Fresh Lemon Dressing, toss to mix well. Serve immediately. Makes: 10-12 servings.

Photograph for this recipe on page 101.

Salmon Pie

1½ *c. flour*
Salt
Fleischmann's Corn Oil Margarine
2 7-oz. cans salmon
Milk
¾ *c. Egg Beaters*
1 c. fresh bread crumbs
1 c. chopped celery
⅓ *c. chopped onion*
2 tbsp. chopped parsley

2 tbsp. lemon juice
⅛ *tsp. pepper*

Combine flour and ½ teaspoon salt in mixing bowl. Cut in ½ cup corn oil margarine with pastry blender until mealy. Stir in 4 to 5 tablespoons cold water; mix well. Shape into ball. Turn out on lightly floured board; roll dough to fit 9-inch pie plate. Place dough on plate; trim and shape edge. Bake a 400 degrees for 8 to 10 minutes. Drain salmon; reserve liquid. Add milk to reserved liquid to equal 1 cup. Combine Egg Beaters and milk mixture; beat slightly. Mix in bread crumbs; set aside. Melt 3 tablespoons corn oil margarine in skillet. Saute celery and onion until tender. Add salmon, celery mixture, parsley, lemon juice, ½ teaspoon salt and pepper to Egg Beaters mixture; mix well. Pour into pastry shell. Bake at 400 degrees for 30 to 35 minutes or until set. Let stand 5 to 10 minutes before cutting. Yield: 6 servings.

Photograph for this recipe on page 67.

Bagel French Toast

4 frozen bagels, pre-sliced
2 eggs
¾ *c. mik*
½ *tsp. vanilla extract*
Dash of salt
Butter or margarine

Thaw bagels. Cut thin slice from top and bottom of bagels. Combine eggs, milk, vanilla and salt; pour into large shallow pan. Dip both side of bagel halves in egg mixture; let stand to absorb all liquid. Saute bagels in butter until browned on both sides. Serve with syrup if desired. Yield: 4 servings.

Photograph for this recipe on page 68.

Breaded Breast of Chicken

2 chicken breasts, boned, skinned and split
1 c. fine dry bread crumbs
1 tbsp. chopped parsley
½ *c. Egg Beaters*
½ *c. Fleischmann's Corn Oil Margarine*
1 clove of garlic, crushed
Lemon slices
Parlsey

Pound chicken with mallet to flatten. Combine bread crumbs and parsley. Dip chicken into Egg Beaters. Coat with bread crumb mixture. Set aside. Melt corn oil margarine in large skillet over medium heat. Saute garlic until golden brown; discard clove. Place chicken in skillet; brown on both sides. Cook 3 to 4 minutes or until chicken is fork-tender. Remove from skillet onto platter. Garnish with lemon slices and parsley. Yield: 4 servings.

Photograph for this recipe on page 67.

Remember that time is money. Sandra Freeman

Frosted Tuna Party Loaf

Savory Tuna Sandwich Filling
Egg Salad Sandwich Filling
1 cucumber, sliced paper thin
1 loaf white bread, unsliced
2 tbsp. butter or margarine, softened
2 8-oz. packages cream cheese, softened
⅓ c. chopped parsley

Prepare fillings. Place cucumber slices on paper towel to absorb excess moisture. Cut all crusts from bread with sharp knife. Lay loaf on its side; cut into 5 even slices. Spread first slice with butter; overlap cucumber slices. Spread second slice with half the Savory Tuna Sandwich Filling. Spread third slice with Egg Salad Sandwich Filling. Spread fourth slice with remaining tuna filling. Stack slices; top with fifth slice of bread. Beat cream cheese until smooth; spread on top and sides of loaf. Gently press chopped parsley on sides of loaf. To make flower garnish on top, use strips of green pepper or cucumber skin for flower stems and circles of carrots, radishes, black or green olives for flowers. Yield: 8-10 servings.

Photograph for this recipe on page 135.

Egg Salad Sandwich Filling

2 hard-cooked eggs, chopped
¼ c. chopped celery
2 tbsp. mayonnaise
⅛ tsp. salt
Dash of pepper

Combine all ingredients in small mixing bowl; mix well.

Photograph for this recipe on page 135.

Savory Tuna Sandwich Filling

1 6½-oz. can tuna, flaked
¼ c. chopped celery
¼ c. mayonnaise
2 tbsp. pickle relish
2 tbsp. capers, chopped

Combine all ingredients in medium mixing bowl; mix well.

Photograph for this recipe on page 135.

"Eggs" Florentine

3 tsp. Fleischmann's Corn Oil Margarine
1½ c. Egg Beaters
1½ tsp. flour
⅛ tsp. salt
Pinch of pepper

1 c. skim milk
2 10-oz. packages chopped spinach, cooked and
   drained

Fill electric skillet with boiling water to depth of 1 inch. Coat six 6-ounce custard cups with 1½ teaspoons corn oil margarine. Pour ¼ cup Egg Beaters into each cup. Set cups in skillet; simmer, covered, for 5 to 6 minutes or until center is softly firm. Melt 1½ teaspoons corn oil margarine in saucepan. Blend in flour, salt and pepper. Cook over low heat, stirring until smooth and bubbly. Gradually add milk, stirring constantly. Bring to a boil; stir until mixture thickens. Arrange spinach on individual dishes. Invert custard cups onto spinach. Cover with sauce to serve. Yield: 6 servings.

Photograph for this recipe on page 67.

Tuna Lemon Butter

1 6½-oz. can tuna in vegetable oil, drained
6 tbsp. butter, softened
¼ c. chopped celery
2 tbsp. chopped ripe olives
1 tbsp. dried or fresh chopped chives
2 tsp. lemon juice
½ tsp. grated lemon rind

Break tuna into fine flakes in medium mixing bowl. Add remaining ingredients; mix well. Use as spread for party sandwiches. Yield: 1½ cups.

Photograph for this recipe on page 135.

Tuna-Apple-Cheese Spread

1 6½-oz. can tuna in vegetable oil, drained
1 3-oz. package cream cheese, softened
1 sm. apple, chopped
¼ c. chopped walnuts
2 tbsp. chopped parsley
2 tbsp. milk
½ tsp. lemon juice
¼ tsp. ground nutmeg

Break tuna into fine flakes in medium mixing bowl. Add remaining ingredients; mix well. Use as spread for party sandwiches. Yield: 2 cups.

Photograph for this recipe on page 135.

No one knows what he can do till he tries.   Sandra Freeman

CAN SIZE CHART

8 oz. can or jar . . . . .1 c.	1 lb. 13 oz. can or jar
10 1/2 oz. can (picnic can) . . . . .1 1/4 c.	or No. 2 1/2 can or jar . . . . .3 1/2 c.
12 oz. can (vacuum) . . . . .1 1/2 c.	1 qt. 14 fl. oz. or 3 lb. 3 oz.
14-16 oz. or No. 300 can . . . . .1 1/4 c.	or 46 oz. can . . . . .5 3/4 c.
16-17 oz. can or jar	6 1/2 to 7 1/2 lb.
or No. 303 can or jar . . . . .2 c.	or No. 10 can . . . . 12-13 c.
1 lb. 4 oz. or 1 pt. 2 fl. oz.	
or No. 2 can or jar . . . . .2 1/2 c.	

EQUIVALENT CHART

3 tsp. . . . . 1 tbsp.	2 pt. . . . . .1 qt.
2 tbsp. . . . . .1/8 c.	1 qt. . . . . .4 c.
4 tbsp. . . . . .1/4 c.	5/8 c. .1/2 c. + 2 tbsp.
8 tbsp. . . . . .1/2 c.	7/8 c. .3/4 c. + 2 tbsp.
16 tbsp. . . . . .1 c.	1 jigger . . . . .1 1/2 fl. oz.(3 tbsp.)
5 tbsp. + 1 tsp. . . . . .1/3 c.	2 c. fat . . . . .1 lb.
12 tbsp. . . . . .3/4 c.	1 lb. butter . . . . 2 c. or 4 sticks
4 oz. . . . . .1/2 c.	2 c. sugar . . . . .1 lb.
8 oz. . . . . .1 c.	2 2/3 c. powdered sugar . . . . .1 lb.
16 oz. . . . . .1 lb.	2 2/3 c. brown sugar . . . . .1 lb.
1 oz. . . . . 2 tbsp. fat or liquid	4 c. sifted flour . . . . .1 lb.
2 c. . . . . .1 pt.	4 1/2 c. cake flour . . . . .1 lb.

3 1/2 c. unsifted whole wheat flour .1 lb.	
8 to 10 egg whites . . . . .1 c.	
12 to 14 egg yolks . . . . .1 c.	
1 c. unwhipped cream . . . . .2 c. whipped	
1 lb. shredded American cheese . . . . .4 c.	
1/4 lb. crumbled blue cheese . . . . .1 c.	
1 chopped med. onion . . . . .1/2 c. pieces	
1 lemon . . . . 3 tbsp. juice	
1 lemon . . . . 1 tsp. grated peel	
1 orange . . . . .1/3 c. juice	
1 orange . . . . about 2 tsp. grated peel	
1 lb. unshelled walnuts . . . . 1 1/2 to 1 3/4 c. shelled	
1 lb. unshelled almonds . . . . .3/4 to 1 c. shelled	
4 oz. (1 to 1 1/4 c.) uncooked macaroni . . . . 2 1/4 c. cooked	
7 oz. spaghetti . . . . .4 c. cooked	
4 oz. (1 1/2 to 2 c.) uncooked noodles . . . . .2 c. cooked	
28 saltine crackers . . . . .1 c. crumbs	
4 slices bread . . . . .1 c. crumbs	
14 square graham crackers . . . . .1 c. crumbs	
22 vanilla wafers . . . . .1 c. crumbs	

SUBSTITUTIONS FOR A MISSING INGREDIENT

1 square *chocolate* (1 ounce) = 3 or 4 tablespoons cocoa plus 1/2 tablespoon fat.

1 tablespoon *cornstarch* (for thickening) = 2 tablespoons flour.

1 cup sifted *all-purpose flour* = 1 cup plus 2 tablespoons sifted cake flour.

1 cup sifted *cake flour* = 1 cup minus 2 tablespoons sifted all-purpose flour.

1 teaspoon *baking powder* = 1/4 teaspoon baking soda plus 1/2 teaspoon cream of tartar.

1 cup *sour milk* — 1 cup sweet milk into which 1 tablespoon vinegar or lemon juice has been stirred; or
    1 cup buttermilk (let stand for 5 minutes).

SUBSTITUTIONS FOR A MISSING INGREDIENT

1 cup *sweet milk* = 1 cup sour milk or buttermilk plus 1/2 teaspoon baking soda.

1 cup *canned tomatoes* = about 1 1/3 cups cut-up fresh tomatoes, simmered 10 minutes.

3/4 cup *cracker crumbs* = 1 cup bread crumbs.

1 cup *cream, sour, heavy* = 1/3 cup butter and 2/3 cups milk in any sour milk recipe.

1 cup *cream, sour, thin* = 3 tablespoons butter and 3/4 cup milk in sour milk recipe.

1 cup *molasses* = 1 cup honey.

1 teaspoon *dried herbs* = 1 tablespoon fresh herbs.

1 *whole egg* = 2 egg yolks for custards.

1/2 cup *evaporated milk* and 1/2 cup *water* or 1 cup *reconstituted nonfat dry milk* and 1 tablespoon *butter* = 1 cup whole milk.

1 package *active dry yeast* = 1 cake compressed yeast.

1 tablespoon *instant minced onion, rehydrated* = 1 small fresh onion.

1 tablespoon *prepared mustard* = 1 teaspoon dry mustard.

1/8 teaspoon *garlic powder* = 1 small pressed clove of garlic

METRIC CONVERSION CHARTS FOR THE KITCHEN

VOLUME

1 tsp.	4.9 cc	2 c.	473.4 cc
1 tbsp.	14.7 cc	1 fl. oz.	29.5 cc
1/3 c.	28.9 cc	4 oz.	118.3 cc
1/8 c.	29.5 cc	8 oz.	236.7 cc
1/4 c.	59.1 cc	1 pt.	473.4 cc
1/2 c.	118.3 cc	1 qt.	.946 liters
3/4 c.	177.5 cc	1 gal.	3.7 liters
1 c.	236.7 cc		

CONVERSION FACTORS:

Liters	X	1.056	=	Liquid Quarts
Quarts	X	0.946	=	Liters
Liters	X	0.264	=	Gallons
Gallons	X	3.785	=	Liters
Fluid Ounces	X	29.563	=	Cubic Centimeters
Cubic Centimeters	X	0.034	=	Fluid Ounces
Cups	X	236.575	=	Cubic Centimeters
Tablespoons	X	14.797	=	Cubic Centimeters
Teaspoons	X	4.932	=	Cubic Centimeters
Bushels	X	0.352	=	Hectoliters
Hectoliters	X	2.837	=	Bushels
Ounces (Avoir.)	X	28.349	=	Grams
Grams	X	0.035	=	Ounces
Pounds	X	0.454	=	Kilograms
Kilograms	X	2.205	=	Pounds

WEIGHT

1 dry oz.	28.3 Grams
1 lb.	454 Kilograms

LIQUID MEASURE AND METRIC EQUIVALENT

(NEAREST CONVENIENT EQUIVALENTS)

CUPS SPOONS	QUARTS OUNCES	METRIC EQUIVALENTS
1 teaspoon	1/6 ounce	.5 milliliters / 5 grams
2 teaspoons	1/3 ounce	.10 milliliters / 10 grams
1 tablespoon	1/2 ounce	.15 milliliters / 15 grams
3 1/3 tablespoons	1 3/4 ounces	.50 milliliters
1/4 cup (4 tablespoons)	2 ounces	.60 milliliters
1/3 cup (5 1/3 tablespoons)	2 2/3 ounces	.79 milliliters
1/3 cup plus 1 tablespoon	3 1/2 ounces	100 milliliters
1/2 cup (8 tablespoons)	4 ounces	118 milliliters
1 cup (16 tablespoons)	8 ounces	1/4 liter / 236 milliliters
2 cups	1 pint / 16 ounces	1/2 liter less 1 1/2 tablespoons / 473 milliliters
2 cups plus 2 1/2 tablespoons	17 ounces	1/2 liter
4 cups	1 quart / 32 ounces	.946 milliliters
4 1/3 cups	1 quart, 2 ounces	1 liter / 1000 milliliters

CONVERSION FORMULAS:

To convert Centigrade to Fahrenheit: multiply by 9, divide by 5, add 32.

To convert Fahrenheit to Centigrade: subtract 32, multiply by 5, divide by 9.

DRY MEASURE AND METRIC EQUIVALENT

(MOST CONVENIENT APPROXIMATION)

POUNDS AND OUNCES	METRIC	POUNDS AND OUNCES	METRIC
1/6 ounce	.5 grams	1/4 pound (4 ounces)	114 grams
1/3 ounce	10 grams	4 1/8 ounces	125 grams
1/2 ounce	15 grams	1/2 pound (8 ounces)	227 grams
1 ounce	30 grams (28.35)	3/4 pound (12 ounces)	250 grams
		1 pound (16 ounces)	454 grams
1 3/4 ounces	50 grams	1.1 pounds	500 grams
2 2/3 ounces	75 grams	2.2 pounds	1 kilogram / 1000 grams
3 1/2 ounces	100 grams		

Index

APPETIZERS
cheese
  balls
    cheesy, 20
    French, 21
    pineapple-nut, 21
  danties, 20
  petit fours, 20
  pineapple, party, 22
  spread
    Marilyn's cream, 20
    two-tone pickle, 21
  wafers, 20
chicken
  and chestnut spread, 22
  livers
    in wine sauce, 22
    pate, 22
  roll-cups, crisp, 22
  sweet-sour, 23
dips
  anchovy, 35
  beef
    chipped, 36
    hot, 36
  capers, 36
  cheese
    Mexican, 38
    onion, 38
      cottage, 38
    pineapple, 38
  chili con queso, 36
  clam
    hot, 36
    tomato, 36
  crab, hot, 36
  cucumber, 37
  daffodil, 37
  guacamole, 37
    Betty's 38
  shrimp, 38
  spinach, 39
  tuna
    curried, 39
  tabouli, 39
  vegetable, dillweed, 38
meat
  bacon, roll-ups, 27
  braunschweiger ball, 20
  ground beef
    Chinese roll-up with mastard sauce, 23
    elegant, 24
    meatballs
      party, 24

tamale, 24
party deluxe, 24
pizza
  deep-dish, 22
  mini, 24
the Dallas monster, 23
ham
  and cheese mousse, 25
  balls
    deluxe, 26
    peanut, 26
  deviled loaf, 25
  kabobs, pineapple, 27
hot dogs
  fancy, 26
  hot, l'bourbon, 26
  spicy, 26
sausage
  balls
    Shirley's, 27
    Yolanda's, 27
  barbecued, 28
  cheese puffs, 27
  party rye pizzas, 27
  sweet-sour bites, 28
peanut butter pips, 26
seafood
  antipasto, 28
    Tosetti's 28
  crab, 29
    loaf, 30
    puffs, 30
    spread, 29
  salmon spread, 30
  shrimp
    cocktail Brasilienne supreme, 28
    easy fresh, 29
    marinated, 29
    mold
      creamy, 28
      double, 28
    olive, 30
vegetable
  artichoke
    cheese, 32
    flaky, 32
    Jackie's, 32
    nibbles, 31
  asparagus rolls, 30
  mushroom
    cups, 32
    stuffed, 35
      sausage, 32
  onion snack, 35

sauerkraut balls, 35
water chestnuts
  bacon-wrapped, 30
zucchini, 35

BEVERAGES
border buttermilk, 40
Bourbon slush, 41
citrus starter, 41
hot
  buttered rum, 41
  cinnamon mocha, 41
  cranberry punch, 41
mock pink champagne, 40
punch
  candlelight, 41
  Champagne, 41
  fruit, 40

BREADS
biscuits
  heavenly, 144
butter dips, 144
corn bread
  Kentucky, 144
crispies, delicious, 149
doughnuts
  stir and drop, 144
loaves
  beer, 146
  made-easy, 146
  onion-rye, Dutch, 146
  paska, 146
  wheat germ, 146
  white, Donna's, 147
  whole wheat, 147
muffins
  best-ever, 145
  cheesy-egg, 145
  six-week bran, 145
pita, 147
popovers
    cold-oven, 145
rolls
  beer, 148
  butterfly, 148
  one-hour buttermilk, 149
  peanut, 150
  Pennsylvania Dutch snecker, 150
  pita, Israeli heroes, 148
  potato, refrigerator, 149
  quick delicious, 149
  sixty-minute yeast, 149
sweet
  apple-anna, 155
  breakfast cookies, 150
  buns, cinnamon surprise, 151
  coffee cake

cranberry, 155
maple, 153
pecan, 154
poppy seed, 154
sour cream, 155
  macadamia, 155
muffins
  date
    basic oatmeal, mix, 152
    Sherron's, 152
  pumpkin, 152
pancakes
  apple pie, 153
  blender sourdough, 153
  French, with orange sauce, 152
rolls
  caramel, 150
    friendship, 151
    nut, rounds, 151
  cinnamon, 151
  pecan, 152
scones
  orange, 185
toast
  French
    bagel, 187
    Marsha's, 145
    spiced, 144
waffles
  rice-buttermilk, 153

DESSERTS
cakes
  apple
    easy, 181
    Grandmother's, 181
    Jewish, 182
  applesauce, 181
  blueberry country, 182
  carrot, 182
  chocolate
    applesauce, 182
    devil's food, 183
    fudge, 183
    Mississippi mud, 183
    that won't last, 182
  coconut, 184
  Italian cream, 184
  orange
    blossom tea, 184
  pound
    brown sugar, 184
    old-fashioned, 184
  violets in the snow, 185
candies
  fudge
    never-fail peanut butter, 158
  peanut patties, 158

pralines
  pecan, 158
    easy, 158
cheesecake
  Aunt Norma's, 178
  chocolate swirl, 174
  creamy, 174
  lemon, 174
    cheese tarts, 174
  Sharon's best, 175
  strawberry, Jean's, 175
chilled
  banana split, 164
  blueberry treat, 164
  bon bon delight, 165
  cherry, 165
  cranberry fluff supreme, 166
  fudge meltaways, 166
  green mint, 166
  Russian cream, 166
  souffle
    chocolate-peanut, 167
    prune, 166
  strawberry, 167
  trifle, English, 166
cookies
  aggression, 160
  almond kringler, 160
  bars
    apricot-nut, 161
    cherry, easy, 161
    cinnamon, 162
    lemon, 162
    orange, 163
      marmalade, 163
    peanut butter, 164
  brownies
    chocolate-
      caramel, 162
  cheesecake, 161
  energy drops
    Mother
      Holstan's, 163
  jubilee jumbles, 162
  Marilyn's icebox, 162
  meringues, forget-
    me, 163
  M & M party, 163
  oatmeal
    peanut butter, 164
    pecan curls, 164
    rolled short-
      bread, 164
crepes
  apple-filled, 158
  Sicilian, 158
dumplings
  caramel, 159

eclairs
  chocolate-glazed, 159
frozen
  apricot
    delight, 170
    spumoni, 170
  banana
    flambe, 170
    Foster, 170
  chocolate, 171
    mousse, 171
    pie, Santa's, 171
  cooler
    peach
      berry, 172
      grape, 172
      tangy, 173
      vanilla, 172
  cramberry, fresh, 186
  ice cream
    banana, 171
    Brook's threes, 171
    homemade
      chocolate, 172
    mint crunch, 172
    pineapple flambe, 173
    raspberry, 173
    strawberry, 173
fruit
  apple
    crisp, 168
    crunch, 168
  banana split, 168
  frosty soup, 168
  glaces, 169
  omelet cake
    supreme, 169
  peach, 169
  pineapple
    supreme, 170
  pizza
    cherry, 168
  raspberry, 169
  rhubarb pudding, 170
pies
  Ammish raisin, 175
  angel food, 179
  apricot, 176
  blueberry cheese-
    cake, 176
  buttermilk
    a la Lutie, 176
    pecan, 176
  cherry-cream with al-
    mond crust, 177
  chocolate
    angel, 159
    chip, 177

coconut, speedy, 177
cranberry, Yukon
  wild, 177
crust, Betty's, 181
grasshopper
  chiffon, 178
green tomato, grand-
  mother's, 178
lemon
  lite, 178
millionaire
  Candy's, 178
  Kathy's, 179
pineapple
  chiffon, 180
  Jim's, 180
rum cream, 180
tarts
  pecan, 181
  tiny, 180
three-layer, 177
puddings
  apple, best-ever, 160
  banana, country-
    style, 160
  Nannie's cabinet, 160
  rice, Daddy's, 159
tortes
  pineapple-chocolate
    deluxe, 176
  strawberry-nut, 175

EGG AND CHEESE

a.m. leftovers, 58
breakfast
  before, 58
  buffet, 59
  casserole, 59
  dish supreme, 59
  do-ahead, 60
  dressing, 60
  in one, 59
  make-ahead, 60
  pizza, 59
  puff, 60
cheese
  chili puff, 74
  continental bake, 74
  fluff, Joan's, 74
  fondue
    Barbara's, 72
    Julie's, 72
    Virginia's, 74
  green chili, 71
  ham bake, 71
  shrimp pie, 72
  souffle, 72
  strata

    Karen's, 71
    Pauline's, 72
    Sally's ham, 74
  Swiss brunch, 74
  tartlets, custard, 73
  Welsh rarebit with oysters, 71
eggs
  baked, 62
  cheese
    delight, 64
    Marion's, 66
    Mornay, 65
    with bacon, 63
    with chili peppers, 63
  Benedict, 62
    easy, 62
  brunch, 62
    Donna's, 64
    Sandra's, 65
  capered, 64
  chipped beef puff, 70
  Eisenhower, 66
  festive, 70
  Florentine, 188
  fondue, 66
    Sandra's, 69
  goldenrod, 64
  ham, 70
    Sally's, 70
  Italian, 64
    Pauline's, 65
  Kentucky governor's, 66
  Letelle's, superb, 69
  Linda's, 71
  omelet, Spanish vegetable, 66
  overnight, 64
  sandwich filling, 188
  sausage, 69
    casserole, 69
    souffle, 70
  scrambled
    creamy, 62
    salmon, 69
  souffle
    Connie's, 65
    Yvonne's, 64
  the temptress, 62
  tuna, a la king, 69
  with shrimp sauce, 63
pancake, easy one-dish, 60
pinwheels, 61
quiche
  Darnell's, 73
  ham, Sandy's, 73
  Ina's, Lorraine, 73
  Patricia's, 73
  spinach, 73
rice

butter-baked, 75
Hawaiian with shrimp, 75
oriental, 75
wild, with almonds, 75
sandwich
baked, 58
Denver, ring, 60
ribbon tea, 61
supreme, 61
souffle, Beta, 58
sunny morn, 61

MEATS
beef
barbecue
brisket, working girl's, 92
crock-pot, 92
Nancy's, 92
bulkogi, 98
burgundy, 93
chaufleur, 99
chop suey, 94
chow mein, oriental, 94
corned, and noodle, 92
creamed, Ann's, 92
goulash, 93
India, 93
in beer, 92
Italian, 97
pot
heavenly, 97
southern-yankee, 97
rice, with a flair, 95
roast
Chianti, 96
tip, 96
steak
Diane, 99
flank
grilled, delicious, 98
Florentine-stuffed, 98
sherried skillet, 100
sirloin, cheesed, 100
Swiss and mushroom, 99
tournedos, 98
stew, Ozark mountain, 94
stroganoff
Jan's, 96
Muriel's, 95
stuffed eye of round, 97
sukiyaki, 100
super one-skillet, 95
the luck of the Irish, 98
with oyster sauce, 99
ground beef
bean
green, 100
three, 103

triple, hot dish, 103
cabbage buns, 104
chiles rellenos, 107
chili
gringo, 107
Kay's, 107
homemade salami, 103
lasagna
baked, 106
Cheryl's, 106
dilled, roll-ups, 105
for a crowd, 106
loaves
company, 105
crown, 100
hickory-smoked, 105
Wellington, 186
with piquant sauce, 105
manicotti
quick, 103
meatballs
Hawaiian potluck, 108
Jan's, 108
sweet and sour
Kendal's, 108
Susan's, 108
Mexican, 106
mock filet, 103
ole to Mexico, 106
spaghetti
amore, 109
Michele's, 109
with meatballs
Italian, 108
southern, 109
steak, Betty's baked, 104
stew, Joyce's, 104
taco bake, 107
ham
broccoli
bake, 111
royale, 111
curried, and avocados, 111
grapefruit glazed, 186
loaves
Deloris', 112
Mary Lou's, 112
supreme, 112
rolls, Polanaise, 112
lamb
balls in lemon sauce, 110
dolmades, 110
sweet and sour riblets, 110
toad-in-a-hole, 110
liver
sweet and sour, 110
ponsit, 111
pork

chops
  brown-baked, 113
  rice bake, 113
  with sauer-kraut, 113
cote de porc farcie, 113
spareribs
  barbecued, 113
  tenderloin, 112

PICKLES
bread and butter, 40
pineapple chunks, 40

POULTRY
chicken
  and dried beef, 129
  and macaroni stew, 130
  and shrimp skillet, 131
  apricot, 137
  baked, special, 130
  breaded, 181
  broccoli, 140
  coq au vin, 133
  cordon bleu au poulet, 134
  crab-stuffed breasts, 134
  creamed, a la king, 134
  crepes
    with almonds, 132
    with cheese sauce, 132
  Diane's wiener schnitzel, 134
  divan
    Berniece's, 140
    Betty's, 141
    Cleo's, 141
  Egyptian lemon, 137
  enchiladas, easy, 137
  in Chablis, 130
  Jessica's, 129
  kiev
    Jeanne's, 130
    Joy's, 130
  mandarin, 138
  marchand de vin, 131
  New England stuffing, 139
  one-pot, 139
  Parisienne, 132
  peaches
    Francisco, 137
    oriental, 138
  quiche
    mushroom, 141
  rice
    best-ever, 139
    Cheryl's, 139
    gourmet, 139
    saltembocca, 131
    simple-y delicious, 140
    squares, 140

Thelma's, 140
tortillas, 132
wings, 133
with grape sauce, 137
yummy, 140
zucchini flips, 141
Cornish game hens
  with rice stuffing, 128
  with wild rice dressing, 128
duck
  a la Monique, 128
  glazed with plum jam, 129
  with filbert-fruit stuffing, 129
  with olive sauce, 128
  yummie, 129
turkey
  and ham casino, 185

QUICHES
chicken and mushroom, 141
crab
  Carol's, 116
  Mary Ann's, 116
Darnell's, 73
ham, Sandy's, 73
Ina's, 73
Patricia's, 73
salmon
  Bernice's, 124
  Jacqueline's, 124
seafood, 123
spinach, 73

SALADS
dressings
  fruit, special, 48
  lemon, fresh, 185
  Marion's, 48
fruit
  apricot, 45
  Champagne cocktail, 44
  citrus cup with lime dressing, 44
  cranberry
    creamy, 46
    frozen, 45
    Grandma's, 46
    Nancy's, 46
  frog eye, 44
  frozen
    Catherine's, 45
    Linda's, 46
  grapefruit and cucumber mold, 46
  Jewel's, 45
  lemon, 47
  molded Waldorf, 47
  orange and onion, 44
    mandarin sherbet, 46
  pistachio, 45

Seven-Up, 47
sweetheart, 47
yummy holiday, 47
main dish
  beef
    sukiyaki, 54
  chicken
    cherry, sweet, 55
    hot, 55
    supreme, 54
    with yeast-riz crust, 55
  ham, hot, 55
vegetable
  bean, 48
  carrot, 54
  cauliflower
    and broccoli, 48
    bowl, 48
  Chinese, 48, 53
  Deloris', 53
  garden, 53
    green, 185
    medley, 53
  hot with herbed walnuts, 49
  layered
    eight, 52
    nine, 52
    peanut, Pattie's, 52
  lime perfection, 54
  marinated, 52
  Michelle's award-winning, 53
  mushroom, fresh, 49
  pea and peanut, 49
  potato
    hot German, 50
      Marge's, 50
    mardi gras, 50
    sour cream, 50
  slaw
    Frances', 50
    JoAnn's, 50
    peanut crunch, 51
  spinach
    fresh, 51
    Kitty's, 52
    Naomi's, 51
    oriental, 51
  supreme, 54
  Windsor, 54
  winter holiday, 187

SEAFOOD
fish
  Alna's, 125
  chowder, 124
  court bouillon, 124
  cyremort, 123
  salmon
    casserole, 124
    pie, 187
    poached, Keatings' easy, 124
    quiche
      Bernice's, 124
      Jacqueline's, 124
  sandwich
    seven-layer, 125
  stuffed red fish, 123
  tuna
    apple-cheese spread, 188
    lemon butter, 188
    loaf, frosted party, 188
    sandwich filling, 188
shellfish
  cioppino Cinzano, 116
  clam sauce with linguine, 116
  crab
    baked, imperial, 117
    Bell Paese, 117
    en coquille, 117
    quiche
      Carol's, 116
      Mary Ann's, 116
    souffle, 116
      hot, 117
  crawfish supreme, 118
  enchiladas with lemon, 118
  fruits of the sea, 121
  gumbo, New Orleans creole-style, 122
  jambalaya
    pantry-shelf, 121
  lasagna, 122
  lobster a la Newburg, 119
  quiche, 123
  Rhinelander, 122
  scallops Newburg, 119
  shrimp
    butterflied, 121
    coquille St. Jacques, 120
    kabobs, fruited, 119
    Rockefeller manicotti, 120
    savory, 120
    tetrazzini, 121
    with wild rice, 119
  skewered, 123

SOUPS
chowder
  chicken-corn, 39
  clam, 39
  fish, 124
court bouillon, 124
gumbo, New Orleans creole-style, 122
onion
  Carolyn's French, 40

VEGETABLES
a la Espana, 89
artichokes and cheese, 78
asparagus
  elegant, baked, 78
  pea, 78
bean
  casserole, 78
  Spanish-style, 78
  supreme, 78
broccoli
  cauliflower au gratin, 79
  rice
    Janet's, 79
    Kay's, 79
  special, 80
  sunshine, 79
Brussels sprouts marinated, 80
cabbage
  bundles in paprika cream sauce, 80
  fried, with noodles, 80
carrots
  heavenly, 81
  ring, 80
  sweet and sour, 81
cauliflower
  con queso, 81
  with shrimp sauce, 81
corn
  chili, 82
  pie, Xi Iota Pi's, 82
  pudding, Pennie's, 82
  scalloped, 82
eggplant
  casserole, 82
  moussaka, 83
  stuffed, 82
julienne, 186

medley, 186
mushrooms
  baked, Kathy's, 84
  Parmesan-fried, 83
  sauce, fresh, 186
  stuffed
    Kay's, 83
    Patricia's, 83
    spinach, caps, 84
pepper
  southern grits, 84
potato
  Basque, 85
  cheesy, bake, 84
  Diane's delicious, 86
  gourmet, 86
  ham-pizza, 85
  hashed browns baked, 86
    Sandy's, 86
  oven-fried, 85
  party, 86
  Romanoff, 85
spinach
  gourmet, 86
  Greek pie, 87
  Kelly's, bake, 87
squash
  Guatemala, 87
  herbed, 87
  Juanita's, 88
  Mary Sue's, 87
  savory, 88
sweet potato
  casserole, 88
  crunchy-topped, 89
  Hawaiian, 89
  Kristina's souffle, 89
Vera's casserole, 89

Photography Credits

Cover: Designer-Lee Hamblen; Best Foods, A Unit of CPC North America; United Fresh Fruit and Vegetable Association; Tuna Research Foundation; Florida Department of Citrus; Rice Council; Lender's Bagel Bakery, Inc.; Fleischmanns Margarine, Egg Beaters; Fostoria Glass Company; Knox Gelatine; Pickle Packers International, Inc.; Olive Advisory Board; National Live Stock and Meat Board; Diamond Walnut Kitchen; Spanish Green Olive Commission; McIlhenny Company; American Dairy Association; Idaho Potatoes; California Avocado Advisory Board; Schieffelin and Company; Sunkist Growers; National Fisheries Institute; Quaker Oats; Cling Peach Advisory Board; Campbell Soup Company; Advisory Council for Jams and Jellies; Evaporated Milk Association; Planters Cocktail Peanuts; California Peach Advisory Board; Standard Brands: Royal Pudding and Gelatin; and General Foods Kitchens.

FAVORITE RECIPES®OF
BETA SIGMA PHI INTERNATIONAL
COOKBOOKS

Add to
Your Cookbook Collection
Select from These ALL-TIME
Favorites

BOOK TITLE	ITEM NUMBER
Recipes From The World Of Beta Sigma Phi (1978) 200 Pages	01341
Dining Room (1979) 200 Pages	10006
Dieting To Stay Healthy (1977) 200 Pages	00949
Bicentennial Heritage Recipes (1976) 200 Pages	70262
Save and "Win" (1975) 200 Pages	70017
Money-Saving Casseroles (1974) 200 Pages	70009
Party Book (1973) 192 Pages	70378
Gourmet (1973) 200 Pages	70025
Fondue & Buffet (1972) 192 Pages	70033
Holiday (1971) 288 Pages	70041
Meats (1968) 384 Pages	70076

FOR ORDERING INFORMATION
Write to:
Favorite Recipes Press
P. O. Box 77
Nashville, Tennessee 37202

BOOKS OFFERED DURING 1978 SUBJECT TO AVAILABILITY.